THE COST OF MORAL LEADERSHIP

THE COST OF MORAL LEADERSHIP

The Spirituality of Dietrich Bonhoeffer

Geffrey B. Kelly

&

F. Burton Nelson

WILLIAM B. EERDMANS PUBLISHING COMPANY
GRAND RAPIDS, MICHIGAN / CAMBRIDGE, U.K.

Wm. B. Eerdmans Publishing Co.
255 Jefferson Ave. S.E., Grand Rapids, Michigan 49503 /
P.O. Box 163, Cambridge CB3 9PU U.K.
www.eerdmans.com

Printed in the United States of America

07 06 05 04 03   7 6 5 4 3 2

Library of Congress Cataloging-in-Publication Data
Kelly, Geffrey B.
The cost of moral leadership : the spirituality of Dietrich Bonhoeffer /
Geffrey B. Kelly & F. Burton Nelson
p.   cm.
Includes bibliographical references and index.
ISBN 0-8028-0511-6 (pbk. : alk. paper)
1. Bonhoeffer, Dietrich, 1906-1945. I. Nelson, F. Burton. II. Title.
BX4827.B57 K43 2003
230'.044'092 — dc21

2002033898

The authors acknowledge with gratitude the permissions to quote and adapt
material from the following copyrighted texts:

A Testament to Freedom: The Essential Writings of Dietrich Bonhoeffer, ed. Geffrey B. Kelly
and F. Burton Nelson. Copyright © 1991 by Geffrey B. Kelly and F. Burton Nelson,
used here by permission of HarperCollins Publishers.
Life Together, by Dietrich Bonhoeffer, published in a new translation and critical edition by Fortress Press, 1995, used here by permission of HarperCollins Publishers.
The Cambridge Companion to Dietrich Bonhoeffer, ed. John de Gruchy, published in 1999
by Cambridge University Press, used here with permission of Cambridge Univer-
sity Press.
Discipleship, by Dietrich Bonhoeffer, translated from the German edition edited by
Martin Kuske and Ilse Tödt; English edition edited by Geffrey B. Kelly and John D.
Godsey; translated by Barbara Green and Reinhard Krauss (Minneapolis: Fortress
Press, 1997). Reprinted with the permission of SCM-Canterbury Press and
Scribner, an imprint of Simon & Schuster Adult Publishing Group. Copyright ©
1949, 1959, 2001 by Simon & Schuster, Inc. and SCM-Canterbury Press Ltd.
The Winter 1995 issue of Dialog: A Journal of Theology.
Various articles that have appeared in Weavings: A Journal of the Christian Spiritual Life.

Contents

CONTENTS

Foreword

When I was a young war bride in Berlin, I buried the letters Dietrich Bonhoeffer had written to my husband, Eberhard, who was then serving in the German army on the Italian front. These letters had been smuggled out of a Nazi prison by a friendly guard. I had no idea back then how those letters and papers would affect my life in such a dramatic way. Eberhard Bethge, Dietrich's best friend, and I were married in May 1943. We had planned that Dietrich would marry us. Six weeks before our marriage he was taken to prison, though, so he wrote a sermon for the occasion from there that was like his blessing on our marriage. A year later, he would send a baptismal letter to our son, Dietrich. Both these texts are part of the now famous *Letters and Papers from Prison.*

Unlike my father, Rüdiger Schleicher, married to Bonhoeffer's sister Ursula, my mother, and my uncles, Dietrich, his brother Klaus, and his brother-in-law, Hans von Dohnanyi, my husband survived because the Russians conquered Berlin before his case was dealt with. The Gestapo, in a good example of their narrow-minded vision, could link him only with my father.

After the war years I helped Eberhard in writing the biography of Dietrich. Eberhard needed me and other family members for information on Dietrich's upbringing, on the influence of his family on his theology and spirituality, and for insights into his personality. Also I went over his style. Many Americans soon knew that I was a niece of Dietrich Bonhoeffer and grew up near him. So I was asked now and then to tell something about him at conferences that I visited together with Eberhard. Sometimes in joint discussions we gave explanations for some of Dietrich's thought, which showed their roots in the family background and German history, especially that of Hitler's time.

And so, for the Oxford Congress in 1980, I was invited to speak on "'Elite' and 'Silence' in Bonhoeffer's Person and Thought." I could make the family connections that explained why these concepts, related to Dietrich's personal sense of ethical responsibility, were ingrained in the Bonhoeffer children from the very beginning. Later I wrote an article on "Bonhoeffer's Family and Its Meaning for His Theology" and was asked to talk about it in different places. This talk in essay form became a chapter in Larry Rasmussen's important study of Bonhoeffer's significance for North Americans. In more recent years, I have given expanded presentations on the role of women among the Bonhoeffers and in the German resistance in which my father, husband, and Dietrich took part.

Now I find myself immersed in the mainstream of Bonhoeffer studies, often asked to be interviewed and filmed, and to give my opinion on the latest books and articles on Bonhoeffer, and of course to contribute my recollections to the living history of the Bonhoeffer family. Fifty-five years ago I never imagined that I, then a young wife and mother with little knowledge of English, would one day be involved in writing and lecturing in both Germany and the United States on the moral legacy of Dietrich Bonhoeffer. This legacy has continued well into the twenty-first century.

It was with distinct pleasure, therefore, that I received the invitation from Burton Nelson and Geffrey Kelly to write the Foreword to this book. I have known both these scholars for a long time, ever since they visited Eberhard and me during the years of their research. Later our relationship was deepened when Burton was the Vice-President of the English Language Section of the International Bonhoeffer Society and Geffrey was the Secretary of the Society and later President. They were responsible for several of the invitations we received to participate in their annual meetings, to respond to papers at those meetings, or simply to enjoy the pleasant exchanges and humorous after-dinner speeches that always characterized their convivial gatherings. That blend of serious scholarship, a dedication to make the world a better place, and a great sense of humor was also the way I remember my uncle Dietrich and my husband Eberhard. The English Language Section always seems to join excellent scholarship with a sense of brotherhood and sisterhood that is rarely seen elsewhere. The English Language Section has, in a real sense, brought Eberhard and me into their family of scholars, pastors, students, and ordinary parishioners who come to the annual meetings or who work to face up to the demands of the gospel in their various ministries in which Bonhoeffer's life and thought are relevant.

The book that Burton and Geffrey have written encapsulates several excellent qualities that make it a significant contribution to the Bonhoeffer legacy. Hardly any book to date has developed to such an extent both Bonhoeffer's qualities as a moral leader and the essence of his spirituality. Their work is based on painstaking research that has spanned their entire academic careers. *The Cost of Moral Leadership* appears at an opportune moment in our history. We have seen how easily people are misled by the evil ideologies that are still floating about and the immoral leadership that causes continuing anguish among vulnerable people everywhere and against which Dietrich and Eberhard fought. In successive chapters, Burton and Geffrey extend the challenge of Bonhoeffer in the many directions that, in sum, constitute his spirituality. They write about Bonhoeffer's Christocentrism, his theology of liberation, the cause of peace that he espoused, the call of Jesus to be his followers through living the Sermon on the Mount, the need for a total revamping of church life through principles enunciated in both *Discipleship* and *Life Together.* They examine how these demands of the gospel are illustrated in Bonhoeffer's prayers and sermons. More pointedly than ever before they show the depth of Bonhoeffer's spirituality in how he coped with suffering, sustained by God, who becomes vulnerable in our own sins and sorrows. Finally, this book contains in Chapter Three the most detailed and extensive analysis of Bonhoeffer's theology of the Holy Spirit, who bestows faith, grace, and strength in the struggles that marked both the Hitler era and our own time.

This is a book that depicts Bonhoeffer's spirituality in the context of how personal faith is expressed in personal and public morality. This is a book that makes available the challenges of Bonhoeffer's theological reflections and his ethical demands on individual Christians, their churches, and would-be moral leaders, both ecclesiastical and political. The world of today needs to be confronted by the insights of Bonhoeffer on all the issues developed in the various chapters of this book.

What is more, although this book incorporates the best research into Bonhoeffer's thought, it is written in clear language that the average layperson can understand. Burton and Geffrey have added questions at the end of the book to facilitate the use of this book in parish adult education forums, in university settings, and in retreats focused on the theology and spirituality of Dietrich Bonhoeffer. For years now we have been exploring the Bonhoeffer legacy and its importance to our future. This book goes a long way toward helping us cope with that future in a spirit of faith. It shows the lessons we can learn from the troubled history in which Bonhoeffer's example and insights offer helpful criticism, a challenge to be courageous followers of Jesus Christ, and a source of inspiration and hope for the world in which we live.

RENATE BETHGE
Wachtberg (Bonn), Germany

Preface

Years ago we were asked by some readers of our lengthy anthology, *A Testament to Freedom: The Essential Writings of Dietrich Bonhoeffer,* if we could take the detailed introductions to the various sections and weave them into a separate book on Bonhoeffer. The texts we included in that book comprised several of the most inspiring writings of Bonhoeffer structured under categories that covered his entire life and astounding literary output. One critic had written that our introductions, which set Bonhoeffer's writings in their proper context amplified by our own analyses, constituted a book in themselves. Could we lift such a book from our introductions? The idea was intriguing.

However much we reflected on the possibility, though, the more we wanted to do an entirely different book and thereby address not only a gap in Bonhoeffer studies but also the many pastoral interests that had surfaced during several of our joint workshops, retreats, and conferences, both national and international, over the past ten years. The groups to whom we spoke ranged from candidates for the ministry studying in clusters of theological schools, clergy and laypersons gathered at retreat centers, scholarly university teachers and their students, directors of campus ministries as well as adults involved in parish education forums and Elderhostels. Everywhere we went we detected a hunger for the kind of inspiration that Bonhoeffer's spiritual journey seemed to spark and an eagerness to discuss the creative force behind his life's decisions, his exemplary moral leadership, and his courageous struggle against Nazism. For our part, we wanted to explore further the many dimensions of Bonhoeffer's faith in all its diverse expressions, searching for the inner core of how God had touched him and directed his life to his final destiny as a Christian martyr.

The general public has had at its disposal multiple analyses of Bonhoeffer's theology in its varying aspects that have appeared on a nearly annual basis for the past several years. The latest books on Bonhoeffer have contributed to a deepened appreciation of the philosophical and theological matrices of his formation and development as a creative thinker and writer of the kind of theology needed to counteract Nazism and the criminal government of Adolf Hitler. Reading these studies leads one to conclude that Bonhoeffer certainly belongs in the inner circle of outstanding theologians of the twentieth century, many of whom had exerted an influence on him. For our part, however, we have intended this book to go beyond the admirable erudition of the vast philosophical, theological probing into his literary legacy. Our audiences at every level seemed less interested in tracing Bonhoeffer's philosophical roots or parsing his theology than in exploring his spirituality and drawing inspiration from his moral leadership. There was also a fascination with the way his writings had folded so well into the adventurous life he was forced to live. We were convinced that the events of his life had shaped the kind of theology Bonhoeffer developed as he sought to understand where God was leading him. His embrace of the gospel, particularly of the Sermon on the Mount, elicited from him a steadfast willingness to take the risks God was demanding of him.

We set out, therefore, to write what we hoped would be a breakthrough book on Bonhoeffer, one that would develop what has been called over the centuries of Christianity his "spirituality" and to do this in the context of his inspirational moral leadership. We have been convinced that an in-depth examination of Bonhoeffer's spirituality can only help readers to pinpoint and appreciate just what has made him such an attractive figure among pastors, Christian church communities, liberation theologians, peace and justice activists, and young and old students everywhere. It is our hope that, through Bonhoeffer's spirituality and writings on moral leadership, our readers may be led to a deeper awareness of their own spiritual life and thereby nourish both their personal faith and help their faith communities become, as Bonhoeffer once described the church, "Christ existing as the church community."

Once having decided to invest our energies and resources in this area, we needed to answer for ourselves the question: what is meant by the term "spirituality" as applied to Bonhoeffer? From our own research we had several definitions of "spirituality" at hand and several divergent viewpoints. It seemed that the word "spirituality" was slippery enough to mean many things within the discipline of ascetical and mystical theology; it was difficult to define with any universalizing precision. When we brainstormed about its meaning among several colleagues, we felt like paraphrasing St. Augustine's statement about time: If no one asks us, we know its meaning; if we wish to define spirituality to those who ask, we don't know how. We just didn't know how to agree on any one definition or description.

Despite our inability to *define* it, we attempt in this book to *explain* the spirituality of this leading figure of the twentieth century, and to show how his spiritual life formed him to be an exceptional moral leader in a century known for its wars, violence, and systemic immorality. The challenges in doing so are many. Bonhoeffer left no theological legacy dealing with "spirituality" designated as such. Despite the several students he inspired during his career as a teacher and seminary director and his many admirers long after his death, he gathered no followers able or eager to continue a "Bonhoeffer spirituality." There is no "Bonhoeffer school of spirituality" and undoubtedly there never will be. How would we then situate him in the long tradition of inspirational people who have been studied and taught as representing a particular way of living out faith, increasing spiritual depth, and exemplifying moral leadership? Bonhoeffer's life is certainly an example of faith lived out amidst the dangers and crises provoked by an ideology that threatened the very existence of Christianity and Christian civilization.

This book is about the spiritual life of a modern martyr, Dietrich Bonhoeffer, about his faith, and about the qualities that made him a moral leader in immoral times. It is also about his relationship with God, with his church, and with the people who became Christ for him, including the Jews he rescued from their would-be murderers. It is about how his theology became the expression of his faith. It is about the experiences in which he had to cope with the Word of God and the Spirit of God directing him in all the twists and turns of the road back to the God whom he loved and revered. It is about his sufferings, his joys, and his accomplishments as a teacher, catechist, preacher, seminary director, theologian, conspirator against a criminal government, prisoner, and eventually a martyr. For all this, it is a book that in its own way offers Bonhoeffer's challenges to those serving in positions where moral leadership is needed in today's world.

Seen in their common lines, most books that deal with particular spiritualities, such as those of Ignatius, Teresa of Avila, Augustine, Aquinas, Catherine of Siena, and Francis of Assisi, speak of spirituality as a particular way of responding to God or a manner of living in obedience to the Word of God and the promptings of God's Holy Spirit. While there is no "Bonhoeffer School," it is equally true that there are many Christians who derive encouragement and hope from his moral leadership and the stirring expressions of faith and courage in his self-sacrificing witness to Jesus Christ. Drawing on that inspiration for our readers and helping people to nourish their hopes, even in the midst of whatever sufferings they may endure, is a central aim of our book.

While this is the first full-length book dealing with Bonhoeffer's spirituality in the context of his moral leadership, the groundwork has been laid by several studies dealing with Bonhoeffer as a person of prayer and deep spiritual convictions.[1] One description that captivated us in our initial probing into the question of Bonhoeffer's spirituality is that of John Godsey, who, in his splendid article on "Dietrich Bonhoeffer and Christian Spirituality," offers this insightful observation: "Christian spirituality has to do with the formation of the self by the Spirit of God into the likeness of Jesus Christ, who in his own person is the true and real human being. It is God's Spirit encountering and transforming our sinful selves into the selves we were meant to be *Coram Deo,* before God."[2] Godsey's timely article examines how Bonhoeffer's spiritual life was formed by God's Spirit into the likeness of Jesus Christ and how in that process he became an intractable foe of the systems that denied freedom and even life itself to countless people.

In a way our own book is a detailed development of Godsey's seminal insights. We will see that Bonhoeffer's spirituality was in essence his life in Jesus Christ shaped through the power and presence of the Holy Spirit. It is, as he wrote in both his *Discipleship* and his *Ethics,* being conformed to the person and teachings of Jesus Christ. Bonhoeffer permitted himself to be led by God's Spirit into a unique communion with the triune God and with those given him by God to be cared for in community as his brothers and sisters in Jesus Christ. Bonhoeffer's spirituality and moral leadership are not merely singular aspects of his Christian faith. They emanate from his Christian life in its totality.

The story of Dietrich Bonhoeffer in the context of his most pastoral, spiritually nurturing texts constitutes the core of how his spirituality and moral leadership have been expressed. We will be telling this story with a view toward exploring all the facets of his moral relevance and spiritual meaning for the people of today who may themselves be searching to understand God's relationship with them in their personal lives or who may be searching for someone who can model Christian faith, discipleship, and community for them. Bonhoeffer's life and faith were animated by his love for Jesus Christ, his discovery of the self-sacrificing demands of the Sermon on the Mount, and his determination that, for Christians, genuine faith needs to be lived in Christian communities whose life together derives from the Gospel mandates. His brash outspokenness was reminiscent of the prophets of old; and, like those prophets, his sense of justice for the oppressed and his outrage at injustice dictated the way he served his church, often with scathing criticism that managed to infuriate several church leaders.

What is more, Bonhoeffer's dedication to daily prayer and meditation on the Scripture was his sustaining force during the crises he had to face, culminating in his martyrdom. His was an activist spirituality ever attuned to the Word of God both in his preaching and in his compassion for the downtrodden of German society. His was a spirituality that took seriously the cross of Jesus Christ standing astride the path he was called to enter upon. His was a moral leadership that embraced the gospel of peace, forgiveness, and reconciliation even as he confronted injustice and indifference in high places. In short, Bonhoeffer was a man of prayer, action, and courage, a moral leader who lived the relationship with God that he described in the closing lines of "Who Am I?" one of his most autobiographical poems from prison: "Whoever I am, you know me, O God, you know I am yours."[3]

We have never lost our desire for moral leaders who can exemplify for us on the practical level what it means to live as Christ did and to risk everything society values in order to be persons of genuine faith, conformed to Jesus Christ. In this book we will be engaged in a process of discerning the heartbeat and the rhythms of Bonhoeffer's spiritual strength. We will return time and again to the intrinsic connection between his prayer and his actions. We will dwell on his willingness to be led by God's Spirit to take Christ-like risks in hope of retrieving freedom and justice for a people living under a cruel dictatorship. In all our explorations into Bonhoeffer's spirituality and moral leadership, our thoughts will remain focused on his relationship with Jesus Christ, whose Spirit moved Bonhoeffer ineluctably toward his own personal Calvary. Bonhoeffer's spirituality reached the moment of death-resurrection on a Nazi gallows as he experienced in his own life what he had written in *Discipleship:* "Whenever Christ calls us, his call leads us to death."[4]

In the chapters that follow we will examine the various dimensions of Bonhoeffer's spirituality and moral leadership under the following aspects: his life story, his compassion and action for justice, the rhythms of his Christocentric spirituality, the Spirit and discipleship, the prophetic dimension of his spirituality, his solidarity with the oppressed, his efforts to achieve peace, his spiritual classics, his theology of Christian vulnerability, his preaching on moral leadership and the spiritual life, and his prayers and poems. The title of our book, *The Cost of Moral Leadership: The Spirituality of Dietrich Bonhoeffer,* reflects the major dynamics of Bonhoeffer's spiritual life: following Jesus Christ and embracing the cross in his efforts to liberate his nation and oppressed peoples from the yoke of Nazism.

This book is a collaborative effort in which we are indebted to many people. We are grateful primarily to the groundwork-laying help in our research provided by the late Eberhard Bethge, Bonhoeffer's closest friend, guide, biographer, and editor of his posthumous writings, and his wife, Dr. Renate Bethge. Renate is a specialist in Bonhoeffer's theology in her own right; over the years she has worked with Eberhard to explore and apply the spiritual legacy of Bonhoeffer through her lectures and writings, particularly in the familial background and influence on Bonhoeffer and his contemporary relevance. We have treasured the friendship of the Bethges over the many years during which we have drawn on their expertise in our own research and writing. We are thankful to Renate for her agreeing to write the Foreword to this book. Among our colleagues in the International Bonhoeffer Society — English Language Section, we acknowledge especially the help and encouragement provided us by John Godsey, John de Gruchy, William J. Peck, Paul Bischoff, Stanley Hauerwas, Martin Marty, and Charles Sensel for their critical reading of the rough drafts of this book. We are grateful also to Pat Kelley, John Matthews, Mary Glazener, Stephen Wise, and Martin Doblmeier for sharing their insights on Bonhoeffer's moral leadership. We appreciate likewise the endless hours of provocative conversation on Christian spirituality with John Weborg. A special note of gratitude is owed to two Bonhoeffer scholars, Clifford Green and Wayne Floyd, the Executive Director and the General Editor of the Dietrich Bonhoeffer Works English Edition, who have sparked a renewed interest in Bonhoeffer through their own writings and through their untiring efforts to bring out the seventeen volumes of the collected writings of Bonhoeffer in new critical editions and translations more faithful to Bonhoeffer's original German. In citing Bonhoeffer in this book we have been fortunate to have several of these translations at our disposal. Our book is in many ways a commentary on selections from these critical editions.

Preface

We owe much to Bill and Sam Eerdmans for their helpful suggestions on improving the text, and especially to David Bratt at Eerdmans Publishing Company for his meticulous reading of and corrections to the penultimate version of our text. We are thankful also to our respective institutions, La Salle University and North Park University and Theological Seminary, for their helping us to pursue the additional avenues of research necessitated by this book.

Finally, and most of all, we are grateful to our wives and children for their never-failing love and familial encouragement throughout all the time it took us to compose our thoughts, argue out and resolve our differences, put our ideas into writing, engage in seemingly endless revisions, and at last to see this book through to completion. To Grace Johnson Nelson, Rebecca, Ingrid, Emily, Sonia, Timothy, and Martha; to Joan Wingert Kelly, Susan, Brendan, and Michael, our undying love and gratitude. Without you, this book would never have gotten beyond the "wouldn't this make a good book?" stage. It is with our deepest affection and appreciation for your presence in our lives that we dedicate this book to you.

GEFFREY B. KELLY
F. BURTON NELSON

CHAPTER ONE

The Life and Martyrdom of Dietrich Bonhoeffer

A Chapter from the Modern Acts of the Apostles

I remember a conversation that I had in America thirteen years ago with a young French pastor. We were asking ourselves quite simply what we wanted to do with our lives. He said he would like to become a saint (and I think it's quite likely that he did become one). At the time I was very impressed, but I disagreed with him, and said, in effect, that I should like to learn to have faith. For a long time I didn't realize the depth of the contrast. I thought I could acquire faith by trying to live a holy life, or something like that. . . . I discovered later, and I'm still discovering right up to this moment, that it is only by living completely in this world that one learns to have faith.[1]

When the life of Dietrich Bonhoeffer came to its abrupt and tragic ending on April 9, 1945, one of his longstanding friends, Reinhold Niebuhr, paid him the ultimate tribute. Two months later, in the journal, *Christianity and Crisis,* he entitled his tribute, "The Death of a Martyr." "The story of Bonhoeffer," he wrote, "is worth recording. It belongs to the modern acts of the apostles."[2]

In that moving essay, Niebuhr predicted that "Bonhoeffer, less known than Martin Niemöller, will become better known. Not only his martyr's death, but also his actions and precepts contain within them the hope of a revitalized Protestant faith in Germany. It will be a faith, religiously more profound than that of many of its critics; but it will have learned to overcome the one fateful error of German Protestantism, the complete dichotomy between faith and political life."[3]

In the past half-century this prediction has come true not only within the boundaries of Dietrich Bonhoeffer's native Germany; it has been amply demonstrated around the world as well. Wherever the Bonhoeffer legacy has penetrated over the years, the dichotomy between faith and political life has been challenged. From our own vantage point, now living in the twenty-first century, a strong case can be made for enlarging the scope of Niebuhr's early judgment. Bonhoeffer's legacy addresses not only the widespread dichotomy between faith and political life; it also challenges the dichotomy between faith and daily life in all its complexities: between faith and discipleship, between faith and lifestyle, between faith and our human relationships, between faith and social action.

Bonhoeffer's life story, Niebuhr said, "belongs to the modern acts of the apostles." Unquestionably it does. Like the apostles, Bonhoeffer was led by God's Spirit along the many twisted paths of his life's journey. His is a story of family solidarity, faith and fidelity, courage, compassion, wisdom, true patriotism, and conviction. More than that, however, Bonhoeffer's life is a necessary key to understanding his theology and his ethics. The numerous writings that flowed from his pen can most effectively be interpreted when seen in the unfolding context of his life and times. In sum, his biography inevitably sheds light on Bonhoeffer's grappling with the foundational themes of theology — God, Christology, the Church, discipleship, ethics, human sociality, Christian community, and the problem of evil. His books *Discipleship* and *Life Together* are prime examples of how, uniquely among contemporary theologians, Bonhoeffer lived what he wrote. What he wrote reveals his personality and inner spirituality.[4]

The Bonhoeffer Family

It is nearly impossible to imagine what Dietrich Bonhoeffer's life might have been like if his family context had not been what it was. His growing-up years in the midst of a cultured, privileged, and prestigious family shaped his value and belief system beyond measure. The capsule judgment by his friend and biographer Eberhard Bethge puts it succinctly: "He grew up in a family that believed that the essence of learning lay not in a formal education but in the deeply rooted obligation to be guardians of a great historical heritage and intellectual tradition. To Dietrich Bonhoeffer, this meant learning to understand and respect the ideas and experiences of earlier generations."[5]

The family trees on both sides of the parental families speak of this "great historical heritage." The father's line, that of Karl Bonhoeffer, is readily traced back to the early sixteenth century (1513) when his ancestors moved to Schwäbisch-Hall in Germany from Holland. An evolving procession of goldsmiths, doctors, clergy, lawyers, and burgomasters evidence the solid middle-class character of the seventeenth- and eighteenth-century generations.[6] Dietrich's paternal grandfather, Friedrich von Bonhoeffer (1828-1907), served as president of the provincial court in Ulm. His grandmother, Julie Tafel Bonhoeffer, died in 1936. From Dietrich's sermon at the funeral one can surmise her great impact and indelible impression on Dietrich and all his brothers and sisters.

Dietrich's mother's family heritage is likewise notable. His maternal great-grandfather was Karl August von Hase (1800-1890), who earned a widespread reputation as a church historian at the University of Jena. His grandfather was Karl-Alfred von Hase (1842-1914), who for several years served as Court Preacher to Wilhelm II, the last of the Hohenzollern emperors in Germany. He was also a distinguished professor of practical theology in Breslau. He was married to Countess Clara von Kalckreuth (1851-1903). Their daughter, Paula von Hase, was to become Dietrich's mother.[7] Paula's Court Preacher father was removed from his position at the court and banished for having reproved the emperor after he had referred to the common people of his kingdom as "rabble." His grandson, Dietrich, was destined to make common cause with Nazi Germany's "rabble," the Jewish community.

Dietrich Bonhoeffer was born in Breslau on February 4, 1906, and a few moments later, his twin sister Sabine entered the world.[8] Prior to their birth, three brothers had been born: Karl-Friedrich (1899), Walter (1899), and Klaus (1901). Two sisters also preceded the twins: Ursula (1902) and Christel (1903). The birth of Susanne (1909) completed the family circle of eight siblings and their parents, Karl and Paula.[9]

The father, Dr. Karl Bonhoeffer, was a distinguished university professor, psychiatrist, and neurologist in Breslau. Moving to Berlin with his young family in 1912, he received an appointment as Professor of Psychiatry and Nervous Diseases at the University of Berlin; he was also the director of the psychiatric and neurological clinic at the Charité Hospital Complex. In the family home Dr. Bonhoeffer parented with authority and discipline, characterized by "empiricism, rationality, and liberalism."[10] Dietrich's twin sister, Sabine Leibholz-Bonhoeffer, offers a more complete portrait: "He was rather distant and reserved, yet his eyes regarded the person in front of him with intense understanding. He would stress a point by preciseness, not loudness, of speech. He educated us by his example, by the way he lived his life. He spoke little, and we felt his judgment in a look of surprise, a teasing word and sometimes a slightly ironical smile. . . . His great tolerance excluded narrowmindedness from our lives and widened our horizons."[11] The father held high expectations for each child of the family, almost as if it were his inherent duty to help them fulfill the potential they had been given. The picture that emerges out of the Bonhoeffer family life evokes a number of descriptive terms: privilege, discipline, security, respect, morality, music, reason, character, closeness, humor, culture, and caring.

The mother, Paula von Hase Bonhoeffer, was completely devoted to her large family. Earlier she had taken the teacher's examination, but once she married in 1898, and especially as the family circle began to enlarge, she shouldered her responsibilities with abandon. As the years passed, it was clear that she "was the soul and spirit of the house."[12] After the family had moved to their new home in the Wangenheimstrasse of Berlin-Grunewald in 1912, she presided over a servant staff of seven: teacher, governess, housemaid, parlor maid, cook, receptionist, and chauffeur. She also home-schooled the older children, at the same time teaching a "large repertoire of poems, songs, and games."[13]

It was also the mother who provided the motivation and encouragement for a foundational religious climate. Like many German families, the Bonhoeffers did not attend weekly worship in the neighborhood church. Nevertheless, one could not grow up in such a household without being exposed to the basic rudiments of the Christian faith. Paula Bonhoeffer in her youthful years had resided several months at Herrnhut, the "life center" of the Moravian Church. In subsequent years she was consistently concerned that her children encounter stories of the Bible, learn the great hymns of the Christian tradition, offer table grace before meals, participate in evening prayers, and be baptized and confirmed in the faith. Grandfather von Hase often served as a kind of family pastor, and following his death in 1914, the maternal uncle, Hans von Hase, was often the spiritual leader. To a more limited extent, the children, especially the three youngest — Dietrich, Sabine, and Susanne — were also influenced by their nannies, Maria and Käthe Horn, who had come to the Bonhoeffer household from the Moravian Brethren.

In later years, once the Confessing Church was born in 1934, the mother, whose piety was by no means ostentatious, resumed her participation in church worship. She became a card-carrying member of the Berlin-Dahlem parish of Martin Niemöller, finding there her "church home."

Familial life was substantially shaped, moreover, by spending holiday time at a second home in Friedrichsbrunn in the eastern Harz Mountains. This habitat provided ample occasions for experiencing the joys of climbing hills and trekking through forests, of swimming, hiking, and gathering mushrooms and berries, of playing ball in the evenings, singing folk songs, and reading. In these serene surroundings, Dietrich first read such classics as *Pinnochio, Heroes of Everyday,* and *Uncle Tom's Cabin,* as well as the works of many poets.[14]

That this segment of family life made its indelible impression on Dietrich's own life is evidenced by the fact that no less than six times in his prison letters he took solace in memories of Friedrichsbrunn. Speaking of the power of church bells to trigger pleasant thoughts that hover "like gracious spirits," he declared that he always thought "first of those quiet summer evenings in Friedrichsbrunn, then of all the different parishes" in which he had ministered.[15]

The serenity of the family was, however, tragically shaken in the closing weeks of World War I. Dietrich's brother Walter, serving in the German army, was wounded on April 23, 1918, and died five days later. The parents were utterly devastated. Paula Bonhoeffer withdrew from family life for weeks on end, and Karl Bonhoeffer discontinued his practice of writing entries in his New Year notebook.[16] Dietrich, only twelve years old at the time, was distraught. His biographer conveys the impact: "The death of his brother Walter and his mother's desperate grief left an indelible mark on the child Dietrich Bonhoeffer. . . . [T]he figure of his brother and the way in which he died were in Dietrich's mind years later, when he talked to his students about the problem of preaching reverently on Memorial Day"[17] and the evils of war. The parents then gave Walter's confirmation Bible to Dietrich, and it accompanied him the rest of his life. It was to be his own personal study Bible for several years, as well as the Bible from which he preached and lectured. The pages were often heavily underlined, along with numerous notes in the margins.

Two years later, at the age of fourteen, Dietrich resolved the question of his vocational future. Much to the disappointment of his father and his older brothers, Karl Friedrich and Klaus, he announced his decision to become a minister and a theologian. They sought to deter him from following this intention, claiming that the church was not really worthy of his commitment. It was, they insisted, "a poor, feeble, boring, petty bourgeois institution." Dietrich's reply — "In that case I shall reform it!"[18] — would prove strangely prophetic.

It was in the context of the family that Dietrich Bonhoeffer encountered a climate of opposition to and continuing critique of the Nazi program and ideology. Practically the entire family was in agreement that Hitler's coming to power in January 1933 was a bad omen for things to come. Grandmother Julie Bonhoeffer exemplified this unflinching opposition. Renate Bethge depicts the scenario: "With the rest of the family, from the very beginning, she was an out-spoken enemy of the Nazis. On April 1, 1933, Hitler ordered that nobody was to buy anything in a Jewish shop, and storm troopers stood guard before such shops and stores. She just walked through the row of these SS troopers, did her shopping, and came out through the row of the perplexed men, saying, 'I do my shopping where I always do my shopping.'"[19]

Three years later she died at the age of ninety-three, and Dietrich gave the funeral sermon. In his well-crafted words, one can sense the impact that she had had on his own evolving views about the plight of Jews in Germany: "She could not bear to see the rights of a person violated. . . . Thus her last years were darkened by the grief that she bore about the fate of the Jews in our country, which she suffered with them. She came out of a different time, out of a different spiritual world, and this world will not sink into the grave with her. This heritage, for which we are grateful to her, puts us under obligation."[20]

The resounding impact and shaping influence of the Bonhoeffer family as a whole persisted all through the years, even in the gloom of Dietrich's lonely, confining months in Tegel Prison. His letters and papers from prison are permeated by references to his own family life; even his prison writings of drama and fiction pictured what life was like growing up in the Berlin of the early twentieth century. Ruth Zerner's observation is surely on target that "in his prison play and novel, Bonhoeffer . . . recreated this family setting from which he drew strength and confidence."[21] One commentator even extends the ideational link between Dietrich's family experience and his views of the church: "The picture he draws in his doctoral dissertation of the structure of the church is in some ways a functional description of this family."[22] In recent years, new glimpses have appeared into the impact of Dietrich's family on his life and spirituality, enriching our understanding and insight into how his family helped shape his thinking and writings.[23]

Dietrich's niece, Renate Bethge, explores this connection at great length. Her essay "Bonhoeffer's Family and Its Significance for His Theology"[24] charts the connecting links between life in the family circle and key theological/ethical motifs: correspondence with reality, telling the truth, persecution for the sake of justice, cheap and costly grace, Who is Christ for us today?, non-religious interpretation, Jesus — the man for others, the church for others. This essay, together with others by both Renate and Eberhard Bethge, and still others by family members and those close to the family, point us to new, engaging vistas of Bonhoeffer studies.

Although his older brothers were oriented toward the sciences, following the model of their empirically minded father, Dietrich leaned toward the realms of reading and music. During his adolescent years, Dietrich read philosophy and religion, including such notables as Euripides, Schleiermacher, Goethe, Schiller, Tönnies, and Max Weber. At the same time, he was cultivating his musical talents; by age ten, he was playing Mozart sonatas. Bethge reports that "on Saturday evenings he skillfully accompanied *Lieder* (songs) by Schubert, Schumann, Brahms, and Hugo Wolf sung by his mother and his sister, Ursula, who had a good voice. After this, no amount of irregularity by any singer could dismay him. He got used at an early age to playing in company without shyness or embarrassment. . . . Thus in his boyhood and youth it was music that gave him a special position at school and among his fellow-students."[25]

Student Years

At the age of seventeen, Dietrich entered his university studies in Tübingen, where his father and older brothers had matriculated. While studying there for a year, he made his home with Grandmother Bonhoeffer. Inflation during the 1920s had begun its skyrocketing climb, rendering the day-to-day economic life of a student unsettling and precarious. He wrote home to his parents in June 1923: "Müller's *History of the Church* now costs 70,000 marks instead of 55,000." In October he reported that "every meal costs 1,000 million marks." To save money, students at that time had contracted for fifty meals in advance for 2,500 million marks.[26]

While at Tübingen, Dietrich joined the students' association called the *Igel* (Hedgehog), which was a Swabian fraternity; his father had been a member earlier. Because the fraternity was excessively nationalistic, it was vulnerable to the rise of Nazism, compelling Dietrich to resign his membership in 1936.

Dietrich's more informal education continued with a three-month visit to Rome in 1924, accompanied by his brother Klaus. The impact of this experience on his mind and spirit can scarcely be exaggerated. Eberhard Bethge's summary comment is indicative of this impact: "Bonhoeffer's attention was soon completely absorbed by the phenomenon of the Church. . . . He based his core theological principles upon this ambiguous but concrete structure. His journey to Rome essentially helped him to articulate the theme of 'the church.' The motive of concreteness — of not getting lost in metaphysical speculation — was a genuine root of this approach."[27]

The daily diary that Dietrich kept during his weeks in Rome offers a kind of kaleidoscope of the city's unique sites, such as St. Peter's, the Colosseum, the Pantheon, the Roman Forum, the Pincio, Trinità dei Monte, the Trevi Fountain, Santa Maria Maggiore, the Catacombs, the Vatican Museum, and St. John Lateran.[28] Dietrich's diary assesses the magnitude of the impact that Holy Week 1924 in St. Peter's made on him: "Palm Sunday . . . the first day on which something of the reality of Catholicism began to dawn on me: nothing romantic or the like. I think I'm beginning to understand the concept of the Church."[29] Following the sojourn in Rome, Dietrich and his brother Klaus continued their travels across the Mediterranean, spending several days in Sicily, Tripoli, and in the Libyan desert.

That same year brought Dietrich's return to his formal education at the University of Berlin, where he was to concentrate on studies in theology for the next three years. His encounter there with such renowned scholars as church historian Adolf von Harnack, Luther interpreter Karl Holl, church historian Hans Lietzmann, and systematic theologian Reinhold Seeberg was strategic in shaping his own theological journey. Under Seeberg's tutelage, he wrote his doctoral dissertation, *The Communion of Saints*, which was published in 1927 and subsequently praised by Karl Barth as a "theological miracle." It was never made clear whether Barth was referring to Dietrich's being able to produce such quality work at his young age or whether the dissertation itself was a miracle of insight. Dietrich, only twenty-one at this time, had begun to read Barth's early writings, particularly *The Word of God and Theology, Epistle to the Romans*, and most likely essays in the new journal *Zwischen den Zeiten (Between the Times)*. The dissertation stands out as the first of Bonhoeffer's published books and as a strong theological beginning of Bonhoeffer's lifelong interest in exploring the nature and vocation of the church within the wider context of human sociality and historical concreteness.[30] His description of the church, "Christ existing as the church community," would prove to be a standard of judgment for his own subsequent ecclesiological perspectives on whether churches truly reflected the spirit of Jesus Christ. His convictions about the nature of the church led to his well-known pungent criticism of the falsifications to which so many church leaders were susceptible.

In 1928 Dietrich turned his attention to a concrete church setting in Barcelona, where in his initial pastoral ministry he interned as a curate in a German-speaking Lutheran congregation composed mainly of businessmen and their families living abroad. Here in the seamier side of the city he encountered his first experiences of poverty. In his sermons he tried to sensitize his congregants to those less fortunate than they through reminders of those other sections of the city where the poor lived in less than humane conditions.

Returning to Berlin in 1929, he continued his formal educational journey by composing a second dissertation, entitled *Act and Being,* a requirement to pave the way for an appointment as a university lecturer. In this substantial volume, Bonhoeffer insisted that God's revelation cannot fit into any preset categorized system. The church community, he argued, not some philosophical or theological system of thought, "is God's final revelation of the divine self as Christ existing as the church community." The profundity of this volume written by the twenty-three-year-old Bonhoeffer still challenges readers in the new millennium. *Act and Being* provides an intricate interplay of philosophies and theologies contending that revelation is either an *act* interrupting our daily routine or a *being* set in community in continuity with its past. But at a deeper level, this second dissertation was a bold effort on Bonhoeffer's part to cope with philosophy's longstanding attempts to speak systematically about the problematic of God's "otherness." Bonhoeffer's concern in this second dissertation was soteriological; in this case, to offer serious reflection on the way individuals and communities "can become locked into self-deceiving, idolatrous substitutes for God's own gift of God's self."[31] It too would be published, though the publishers were dismayed at Bonhoeffer's seeming unwillingness to promote this book, believing as he did that it was too self-serving.

In the meantime, Bonhoeffer continued to discover more of Karl Barth through Barth's *Epistle to the Romans* and his early essays on the Word of God and "crisis theology" that had aroused the antipathy of the liberal elements at Berlin University. Barth had indicted the liberal theology then in vogue for being too euphoric about human progress in the wake of the modern technology trumpeted by the media as the harbinger of another golden age in Germany. The bloodshed in World War I had convinced Barth that liberal theology's myopic optimism had softened Christianity into ill-taken moral compromises and had encouraged the excessive nationalism and uncritical patriotism on which fed national hatreds, desire for vengeance, and wars. The feud between the liberal von Harnack and the Reformed theologian Karl Barth was well known at the time. Von Harnack had even cautioned Bonhoeffer about the dangers of Barth's "contempt for scientific theology." Yet, despite his admiration for von Harnack, Bonhoeffer became a protagonist for Barth's collected lectures, published as *The Word of God and the Word of Man.* Bonhoeffer had been won over by Barth's "crisis theology" but, as was the case with all his influences, not uncritically. He absorbed the best of Barth's theology, though always with his own critical reservations. Barth reminded Bonhoeffer of the need to maintain God's judgment against all human pretentiousness, especially in the awareness of the human potential for sin and the arrogant thought that wars waged by human sinfulness could ever be sanctioned by God. In turn, Bonhoeffer criticized Barth for his seeming disdain of the concreteness, the earthliness of the human condition, to ground both faith and revelation. God is free, not *from* us, as Barth's emphasis on the divine majesty would seem to indicate, but free *for* us, Bonhoeffer would write in his second dissertation.

In the autumn of 1930 Dietrich decided to attend New York's Union Theological Seminary for a year of postdoctoral studies as a Sloane Fellow. It was to be a pivotal year for the young theologian, which he later would associate with the experience of "a great liberation."[32] He found the state of theology in the prestigious Manhattan seminary to be disappointingly shallow. In fact, he wrote in his report that "the theological atmosphere of the Union Theological Seminary is accelerating the process of the secularization of Christianity in America.... A seminary in which it can come about that a large number of students laugh out loud in a public lecture at the quoting of a passage from Luther's *De Servo Arbitrio* on sin and forgiveness because it seems to them to be comic has evidently completely forgotten what Christian theology by its very nature stands for."[33] American students appeared to him to lack the seriousness and depth of their German counterparts.

In spite of these negative notes, however, Dietrich found much to appreciate during his Union days. Reinhold Niebuhr, one of his mentors in "Christian Ethics," challenged him to think deeply about the church's involvement in the frequent spasms of injustice and the scandalous poverty of American society. Niebuhr remained a friend for the following decade, as they exchanged frequent correspondence.[34] Eugene Lyman, too, professor of the philosophy of religion, was instrumental in introducing him to the philosophical treatises of William James, John Dewey, and several others.

Beyond the classroom, Dietrich's circle of friends made powerful impacts on his personal life and his developing spirituality. Erwin Sutz, a Swiss Sloane Fellow, joined him in fulfilling a role as an interpreter of European theology in the seminary community. Having studied under both Karl Barth and Emil Brunner, he significantly deepened and enlarged Bonhoeffer's own appreciation for the emerging "crisis theology." Moreover, he played a key role in enabling Bonhoeffer to spend two weeks with Barth, taking part in Barth's lectures in Bonn later in 1931.[35] This was the beginning of the lifelong personal friendship between Barth and Bonhoeffer, two of the most influential theologians of the twentieth century.

Another European who became a close companion was a Frenchman, Jean Lasserre. The two friends did not speak each other's language, so they practiced their English on each other, sharing hour after hour of theological conversation. It was Lasserre who challenged his German colleague to a new and more profound encounter with the Sermon on the Mount, especially grappling with the claims of Jesus' peace commands. On a trip to Victoria, Mexico, in June 1931, both Bonhoeffer and Lasserre were invited by a Quaker friend of Lasserre to speak together at a public meeting. Lasserre recalled that Bonhoeffer spoke passionately about their peace concerns in a way that marked Bonhoeffer as having turned a corner in his attitude toward the evils of war and the need to embrace Christ's peace on a troubled earth. It was evident that Lasserre's friendship and influence had moved Bonhoeffer to become a pacifist and to be a consistent opponent of Germany's rearmament and its madcap march toward war throughout the 1930s.[36]

Two American students were also among the coterie of Bonhoeffer's best friends in that year abroad. One was Paul Lehmann; Paul and his wife Marian became his "American family." Their apartment at Union was perennially available for conversation, sometimes into the late-night hours. Lehmann helped Bonhoeffer deepen his understanding of the need for church involvement in civil rights and the cause of economic justice.[37] It was through his profound relationship with Lehmann that Bonhoeffer was able to appreciate more fully the insights into social ethics that were being taught by Reinhold Niebuhr. A second friend was a black student from Alabama, Frank Fisher, who was assigned to the Abyssinian Baptist Church in Harlem for his field education. Bonhoeffer accompanied him to church, and during the spring of 1931 assisted in teaching a Sunday School class and being fully engaged in a youth ministry with the children of that parish. Eberhard Bethge concludes that through his friendship with Fisher, Dietrich gained an intimate knowledge of the realities of poverty in the black community in Harlem and the problems of racism in the United States.[38]

Later when back in Berlin at the university, Bonhoeffer shared his Harlem-based experiences with his students, playing records of black spirituals, especially those sung by Paul Robeson. One of his students, Wolf-Dieter Zimmermann, reported him saying at the conclusion of an evening gathering: "When I took leave of my black friend, he said to me: 'Make our sufferings known in Germany, tell them what is happening to us and show them what we are like.' I wanted to fulfill this obligation tonight."[39]

Dietrich Bonhoeffer was now admirably prepared to pursue the next phase of his life journey — undertaking a university teaching career in addition to fulfilling his pastoral calling.

Bonhoeffer the University Teacher

Dietrich Bonhoeffer seemed born to be a teacher; whether we see him in a university setting or in a seminary community, in church ministry, or even in prison and in concentration camps, he was perennially and persistently the teacher. This teaching could be formal classroom lecturing, informal discussion, preaching, or modeling Christianity: it was a part of his persona wherever his adult years took him.

During that same time frame, from 1920-1945, he also embodied a continuing pastoral ministry. Teaching, preaching, and pastoral care were constantly intertwined in his spiritual life, often with no clear-cut demarcation. They are only separated in his life story here for purposes of biographical attention and concentration.[40]

At the age of twenty-four, Bonhoeffer was invited to join the faculty of the University of Berlin as a lecturer in systematic theology. For the following two years he offered such challenging courses as "The History of Systematic Theology in the Twentieth Century," "The Idea of Philosophy in Protestant Theology," "The Nature of the Church," "Creation and Fall," and "Christology." One of his students, Wolf-Dieter Zimmermann, has given us a word picture from that era: "When I entered the lecture room (Bonhoeffer's course on "The Nature of the Church"), there were about ten to fifteen students, a disheartening sight. For a moment I wondered whether I should retreat, but I stayed out of curiosity. A young lecturer stepped to the rostrum with a light, quick step, a man with very fair, rather thin hair, a broad face, rimless glasses with a golden bridge. After a few words of welcome, he explained the meaning and structure of the lecture, in a firm, slightly throaty way of speaking."[41] Zimmermann has recalled that "in the lecture-room Bonhoeffer was very concentrated, quite unsentimental, almost dispassionate, clear as crystal, with a certain rational coldness, like a reporter."[42]

Bonhoeffer's lectures and seminars began to gather student interest, and beyond that, loyalty. It was a time that many of the thousand students of theology at the university were being attracted to National Socialism. Eberhard Bethge even describes the young lecturer as "a minor sensation," as "news about him began to spread. . . . The number of students who became the solid core of his following was determined spontaneously by the intellectual and personal standards he required. There were hardly any German Christians among them, although there were several students who initially believed they could politically align themselves with the Nazi Party."[43]

As a teacher, Bonhoeffer seemed to be aware that effective teaching goes beyond classroom walls. A number of his theological students, and even a class of impoverished teenagers Bonhoeffer was preparing for Confirmation, frequently spent evenings and weekends with him. A hut in the picturesque countryside of Biesenthal on the outskirts of Berlin served as a gathering point. Because of the time and interest he invested in them, it is not surprising that several eventually formed part of the core opposition to Hitler and the Nazi dictatorship. Their names after the war became familiar to a generation of those who have been impacted by the Bonhoeffer legacy: Joachim Kanitz, Albrecht Schönherr, Winfried Maechler, Otto Dudzus, Wolf-Dieter Zimmermann, Herbert Jehle, Christoph Harhausen, Rudolf Kühn, Reinhard Rutenik, Inge Karding, Helga Zimmermann, Klaus Block, and Hans-Herbert Kramm, to name a few.[44] Now in their 80s and 90s, only a few are still alive and accounted for. They provide wellsprings of insights through their observations about the personality, theology, and example of their beloved teacher.

The last lectures that Bonhoeffer gave at the university were offered in the summer of 1933. Adolf Hitler's grip on Germany had formally begun in January when President von Hindenberg, in a surprise move, appointed him chancellor at the urging of industrial leaders eager to control the unionists then leaning toward Bolshevism. It was in this life context that the Christology theme gathered renewed potency. Eberhard Bethge refers to these lectures as "the high point of Bonhoeffer's academic career." In formulating his Christology, Bonhoeffer "was finally trying to bring together all the disparate threads of his new understanding of both himself and of his commitment to Jesus Christ. In these lectures his spiritual life and his theology appeared to converge."[45]

Bonhoeffer the Pastor

In 1928 Bonhoeffer had departed from the demands of the academic life to enter the new world of a pastoral intern in a Barcelona parish. This was the beginning of those pastoral ministries that were to accompany his life story all the way to his untimely death in the concentration camp at Flossenbürg.

During the year away from his native land, Bonhoeffer served as a curate under the supervision of Pastor Fritz Olbricht. The German-speaking congregation was peopled largely by expatriate businessmen. Soon his energies were poured into the lifeblood of that congregation — starting a children's worship service, teaching a group of boys, becoming active in a society related to problems of unemployment and vagrancy, preaching, and even lecturing. Over the course of the year he delivered nineteen sermons. In the middle of the year he wrote to his good friend Helmut Rössler: "I'm getting to know new people every day. . . . here one meets people as they are, away from the masquerade of the 'Christian world,' people with passions, criminal types, little people with little ambitions, little desires, and little sins, all in all people who feel homeless in both senses of the word, who loosen up if one talks to them in a friendly way, real people."[46]

It is clear that Bonhoeffer's pastoral relationships with the people were marked by caring and concern. As his biographer puts it, "Although most of the sermons Bonhoeffer preached so passionately to the Barcelona parishioners went far over their heads, he still addressed them as someone who met them during the week with unaccustomed warmth and pastoral concern."[47]

Bonhoeffer's world was expanding in this new geographical zone. Beyond the boundaries of the congregation he witnessed the plight of the poor and the dispossessed. The devastation of the Great Depression had penetrated the community, moving Bonhoeffer to stir the conscience and the concern of his parishioners. His sermons and his teaching in these early pastoral months were marked with a deepened compassion for the poor.

The report of Pastor Olbricht to the responsible church authorities in Germany bespeaks the sensitivities Bonhoeffer appeared to possess for ministry: "He has proved most capable in every respect and has been a great help in my many-sided work. He has been able in particular to attract children who are very fond of him. Recently an average of forty children have been coming to his Sunday School. He has been very popular throughout the colony."[48] His supervisor concluded the report "by asking to have someone just as good as a replacement, very soon." Consequently, Bonhoeffer was invited to stay for a second year in Barcelona, but he made the decision to continue his studies at the University of Berlin. First, however, he chose to study the following year at Union Theological Seminary in New York.

In America's largest metropolis, it was important to Dietrich that he establish a vital link with a local, thriving congregation. Not satisfied with the preaching and ministry at the adjacent Riverside Church, he found a spiritual home at the large Abyssinian Baptist Church in Harlem, largely through the impact of his close friendship with Frank Fisher. In this congregation Bonhoeffer taught a Sunday School class of junior boys, took part in their sport activities, occasionally helped in a weekday religious school, and led a group of women in Bible studies. Paul Lehmann would later recall how Bonhoeffer became welcome in the homes of the poor blacks with whom he worked: "What was so impressive was the way in which he pursued the understanding of the problem [of racial antagonism in America] to its minutest detail through books and countless visits to Harlem, through participation in Negro youth work, but even more through a remarkable kind of identity with the Negro community, so that he was received there as though he had never been an outsider at all."[49] For Bonhoeffer, it was in that black church that he heard the most authentic preaching of the gospel.[50] Thanks to Frank Fisher, this parish became his personal "social gospel."

Back in Berlin in 1931, Bonhoeffer's pastoral ministries were multiple. Newly ordained, he served for a time as chaplain to the Technical University at Charlottenburg, and then became the teacher of a Confirmation class of fifty teenage boys in the Zion parish of Prenzlauer Berg, Berlin. An insight into his pastoral relationships in this setting is given us in a letter he wrote to his friend, Erwin Sutz: "It's the Confirmation class which I hold for fifty young people in north Berlin. It is about the most hectic part of Berlin, with the most difficult social and political conditions. At the beginning the young lads behaved crazily, so that for the first time I had real problems of discipline. . . . Now there is absolute quiet, the young men see to that themselves, so I need no longer fear the fate of my predecessor, whom they literally worried to death. Recently I was out with some of them for two days; another group is coming tomorrow. We've all enjoyed this being together. As I am keeping them until Confirmation, I have to visit the parents of all fifty of them and will be living in the neighborhood for two months in order to get it done."[51] In his teaching of the Confirmation class, Bonhoeffer was quite flexible in departing from the catechism that was then in vogue in German Protestant parishes. His constant concern was to make Christian community come alive in the lives of his students.

This profound experience in the rhythms of his pastoral ministry forced Bonhoeffer to encounter living conditions marked by squalor and unrelenting poverty. A number of his young friends experienced a significantly different environment when they traveled with him to his parents' summer home in Friedrichsbrunn.

Preaching also frequently served as a conduit for Bonhoeffer's pastoral orientation. On a number of occasions he preached at the prestigious Kaiser Wilhelm Memorial Church in Berlin and in other Protestant congregations. For him the preparation of a sermon and its subsequent delivery in a sanctuary setting was unique in its importance and responsibility. His biographer notes that "Preaching was the great event for him . . . , nothing in his calling competed in importance with preaching."[52]

With Hitler's advent to power in early 1933, Bonhoeffer was immediately aware that a new page in German history was about to be written. This would be a page that could possibly undermine the whole sweep of Christian tradition that was interwoven with Germany's national story. In a radio address delivered only two days after Hitler had become chancellor, he warned against the possibility of Germany slipping into an idolatrous cult of the *Führer* (leader), who could very well turn out to be a *Verführer* (misleader) and one who mocks God himself. His broadcast was cut off while he was still speaking in what may have been the first governmental action against free speech. Bonhoeffer was so fearful that the talk might be distorted into an endorsement of the *Führer* that he privately circulated the entire script and presented a lecture incorporating the segments that were missing from the radio broadcast.

The year 1933 will forever be a milestone year not only in Germany, but also throughout the global community. On January 30 Adolf Hitler be-

came the chancellor of Germany, inaugurating the period that has sometimes been called "the twelve years that shook the world." In a rapid-fire
succession of events over the following months, the new direction of the
nation began to take shape. The burning of the Reichstag building by the
Nazis was followed less than a month later by the establishment of the
first concentration camp in Dachau. Eight days later, on April 1, the SS organized a national boycott of Jewish-owned businesses. This was followed
on April 7 by the dismissal from civil service and the legal profession of
persons of Jewish ancestry. On April 23, Ludwig Müller, a known Nazi
sympathizer, was appointed as Hitler's personal representative to the
Protestant churches and invested with the title of "Bishop." Three days
later the Gestapo was formed. On May 2 the free trade unions were dis-
solved. On May 10 the Nazis organized a public burning of books by Jewish authors and early opponents of Nazism. Soon after these events, on
June 25, Karl Barth sent a strong manifesto to Hitler decrying the deterio-
ration of human rights under these measures. Barth, together with
Bonhoeffer, Martin Niemöller, and Gerhard Jacobi, met to form the Pastors Emergency League. This was the beginning of the Confessing
Church, founded in open opposition to the nazified Reich Church then
under "Hitler's churchman," Bishop Ludwig Müller.

Bonhoeffer was involved in the early stages of this church struggle
against Nazism, notably in drafting the Bethel Confession. Together with
Professor Hermann Sasse of Erlangen, he was commissioned by the Pastors Emergency League to draft this faith statement, which unmistakably
repudiated Aryanism and the Nazi attempt to rid the nation and church
of any Jewish presence. Submitted to a circle of some twenty theologians,
the document became so watered down that Bonhoeffer refused to sign it.
He became increasingly disenchanted with the lack of decisiveness among
so many church leaders that he decided to leave Germany in October 1933.
His outspokenness had made it impossible for him to obtain a pastoral
appointment in Berlin. Congregations simply did not want a pastor so
young, so radical, and so antagonistic toward the ideology of National Socialism.

In the context of the rising momentum of National Socialism and the
weak resistance offered by the churches, Dietrich Bonhoeffer departed for
England in October 1933 to assume the pastorates of two small German-
speaking congregations in London, one in Sydenham, the other in the
East End. For this decision he was roundly chided in a letter from Karl
Barth: "You are a German . . . the house of your church is on fire . . . you
must return to your post by the next ship. As things are, shall we say the

ship after next?"[53] These two congregations to which Bonhoeffer committed himself for the next eighteen months were different. The Sydenham church had thirty to forty congregants gathered in worship on Sundays, mostly businessmen and their families, flanked by a few members of the German diplomatic community. The other church was St. Paul's, a Reformed parish, with about fifty gathering for worship, comprised mostly of tradesmen — butchers, tailors, bakers — and their families.[54]

During his London pastorate, Bonhoeffer's ministry was multifaceted. He preached regularly. He visited the sick and cared for the elderly. He introduced children's services and youth clubs. He encouraged Nativity and Passion plays. He assisted in the revising of a church hymnal. He spearheaded financial subsidies for German refugees. He helped to mobilize the German pastors in London. He sought to interpret the societal changes in Germany to gatherings of pastors from several countries. Eberhard Bethge's judgment is revealing: "It was undoubtedly due to Bonhoeffer's presence in London that, of all the German congregations abroad, only those in England made any attempt to intervene in the church struggle at home."[55]

A most significant result of Bonhoeffer's pastoral months in London was his developing friendship with the Bishop of Chichester, George K. A. Bell. The two had met in 1932 at an ecumenical conference in Geneva; even though they were separated from each other in age by over twenty years, they were readily united in their discernment of the ominous happenings in Bonhoeffer's Germany. The role that Bell was to play in the saga of Bonhoeffer's life was to continue even beyond the day of Bonhoeffer's martyrdom on April 9, 1945.

The call from the Confessing Church to serve as director of a newly formed illegal seminary in his homeland brought the curtain down on Bonhoeffer's pastoral ministry in London. It did not, however, conclude his continuing role as pastor. He was a pastor to the very end.[56]

The Ecumenical Movement and the Church Struggle

The decade of the 1930s was the context for the unfolding of several key components of Dietrich Bonhoeffer's life story. Not only did it prove to be the scenario for his pastoral ministry and his university lecturing; the events in Germany during this time also brought him into considerable ecumenical involvement, catapulted him into a key role in the church struggle and resistance movement against Nazism, and cast him as the director of one of the Confessing Church's illegal seminaries, and as a staunch defender of the Jews against the escalation of their repression in Germany. Likewise, it established his reputation as a prolific writer in the twentieth-century interpretation of the Christian faith. All of these components were intertwined as the decade ran its course.

Through his connection with the ecumenical movement, Bonhoeffer participated in numerous conferences in his capacity as a regional secretary of the joint Youth Commission of two bodies — the World Alliance for Promoting International Friendship through the Churches and the Universal Christian Council for Life and Work. His overwhelming zeal was that the churches of the world would be able to discern their God-given mandate to be in the vanguard for peace. Along with this urgent concern was his incessant demand that the ecumenical movement develop a solidarity with the Confessing Church that had been brought into being at the Barmen Synod in May 1934. In his letters to George Bell, he articulated his belief that the churches were engaged in a life-and-death struggle in his native Germany. He wrote to his friend, "The question at stake in the German Church is no longer an internal issue but is the question of existence of Christianity in Europe; therefore a definite attitude of the ecumenic movement has nothing to do with 'intervention,' but it is just a demonstration to the whole world that Church and Christianity as such are at stake."[57]

Subsequently, Bonhoeffer assisted Bishop Bell in drafting a pastoral Ascentiontide letter that conveyed the seriousness of the church struggle in Germany: "The situation is, beyond doubt, full of anxiety. To estimate it aright we have to remember the fact that a revolution has taken place in the German state, and that as a necessary result the German Evangelical Church was bound to be faced with new tasks and many new problems requiring time for their full solution. . . . The chief cause of anxiety is the assumption by the Reichbishop in the name of the principle of autocratic powers unqualified by constitutional or traditional restraints which are without precedent in the history of the Church."[58]

Fanø, a small island off the western coast of Denmark, was the scene in August 1934 for the meetings of three ecumenical bodies in which Bonhoeffer was involved: the Management Committee of the World Alliance, the Universal Christian Council for Life and Work, and the international Youth Conference (planned and executed by the joint Youth Commission of the World Alliance and the Universal Christian Council).

By his public presentations at this Fanø Conference, by his personal linkage with Bishop Bell, who presided over the sessions, and by his daily dialogue with many of the delegates, Bonhoeffer managed to impart an indelible impact on the development of the fledgling ecumenical church.[59] Especially notable was his sermon "The Church and the Peoples of the World," in which he exhorted the churches to accept their responsibility as peacemakers. "The hour is late," he declared. "The world is choked with weapons, and dreadful is the distrust which looks out of every human being's eyes. The trumpets of war may blow tomorrow. For what are we waiting? Do we want to become involved in this guilt as never before? . . . We want to give the world a whole word, not a half word — a courageous word, a Christian word. We want to pray that this word may be given us today. Who knows if we shall see each other again another year?"[60] One eyewitness, Otto Dudzus, described the sermon as "possibly the most decisive, certainly the most exciting moment of the Conference."[61] He wondered if the hearers could have a good conscience about not following Bonhoeffer's lead in taking radical steps to promote peace and stop war. Another eyewitness reported that Bonhoeffer's word had the "effect of a bomb at Fanø."[62]

As the decade of the 1930s moved on, Bonhoeffer grew disenchanted with the failure of the ecumenical bodies to live in solidarity with the Confessing Church of Germany. He steadfastly refused to participate in any meeting at all to which both the Reich Church and the Confessing Church were invited. In 1935 he had written an essay that was published in *Evangelische Theologie* entitled "The Confessing Church and the Ecumenical Movement." The church struggle, he insisted, "puts demands both on the ecumenical movement, to live up to the spirit of Fanø and so live up to its promise to be the Church of Jesus Christ, and on the Confessing Church, to see the struggle as one for the very life of Christianity."[63] In short, the struggle that was being waged for justice and truth by the Confessing Church was a vicarious struggle for the whole Church of Jesus Christ. When Bonhoeffer realized by 1937 that the ecumenical leaders were not about to follow the clear counsel of the Fanø Conference, he requested that he be relieved of his task as a regional youth secretary. After the war his ongoing impact on the developing ecumenical movement all the way through the twentieth century was widely acclaimed.[64]

As Dietrich Bonhoeffer saw it, the church struggle in Germany, and throughout many other countries, in the decade of the 1930s and early 1940s was not an exercise in a debating society. Neither was it a church meeting to pass resolutions. It was not business as usual, comprised of worship services, sermons, Bible studies, youth meetings, baptisms, Eucharists, and drinking tea and coffee in the church parlors. All these activities may have played their weekly roles in the fabric of church life, but the church struggle was freighted with serious intent and total commitment. It was in essence a struggle to be obedient and faithful to the Lord of the church. It was a struggle that sought to preserve the integrity of the believing community.

At the heart of this church struggle was the challenge to Christians to identify with the plight of the Jews in German society, especially after Hitler's accession to power as chancellor in January 1933. Only a few weeks after that event, following the passing of anti-Jewish legislation in April, Bonhoeffer gave his controversial address on "The Church and the Jewish Question." Originally presented to a group of clergy who were meeting in the home of Pastor Gerhard Jacobi in Berlin, it was shortly afterward published in a journal. From the vantage point of the twenty-first century, a contemporary reader can identify objectionable language here and there in the essay, reflecting centuries of misshapen anti-Jewish theology. The primary thrust of the essay, however, was to help sort out Christian responses to the evolving anti-Semitic policies of the Nazi government, including its insistence that pastors of Jewish ancestry must immediately be dismissed from their posts. Bonhoeffer challenged this immoral legislation, called the churches to come to the aid of the victims of injustice — whether they were baptized or not — and, further, "not just to bandage the victims under the wheel, but to jam a spoke in the wheel itself."[65] In other words, there may be times when it becomes necessary for the church, in the advance of justice, to resort to direct action. The late German theologian Heinz Eduard Tödt gives Bonhoeffer his due importance in the early stages of the church struggle: "In 1933 Bonhoeffer was almost alone in his opinions; he was the only one who considered solidarity with the Jews, especially with the non-Christian Jews, to be a matter of such importance as to obligate the Christian churches to risk a massive conflict with that state — a risk which could threaten their very existence."[66]

In the ensuing decade, 1933-1943, Bonhoeffer's spiritual story constantly intersected with the tragic unfolding of the Nazis' persecution of the Jews: his insistence at the ecumenical conferences that serious attention be given to their plight; his assistance to refugee Jews in England; his unforgettable exclamation in 1935 after the propagation of the infamous Nuremberg Laws ("Only he who cries out for the Jews is permitted to sing Gregorian chants!"); his calling on the students at the Finkenwalde Seminary, 1935-37, to intercede for the Jews; his insistence that there could be no compromise with the "German Christians" or the Reich Church; his participation in rescue efforts on behalf of Jews, notably "Operation 7";

and his eventual entry into the resistance movement. All of these facets of Bonhoeffer's own personal involvement in the church struggle exemplify his conviction that Christianity and Nazism were absolutely and perennially incompatible. His closest friend, Eberhard Bethge, who perhaps knew his mind and spirit better than anyone, insisted that "there is no doubt that Bonhoeffer's primary motivation for entering active political conspiracy was the treatment of the Jews by the Third Reich."[67]

Bonhoeffer's unequivocal stand in support of baptized Jews is likewise attested by his closest friend of the time, Franz Hildebrandt, who recalled that for Bonhoeffer, "The course for the church was clear . . . from the beginning and remained clear to the end; there would be no compromise with the brown hordes of Nazism and no patience with ecclesiastical diplomacy. . . . He reasoned, in view of the so-called 'Aryanization' of the clergy under the Nazi laws, that he could not be in a ministry which had become a racial privilege. I cannot recall or imagine any other man to have taken this line of solidarity with those of us who had to resign their pastorates under that legislation."[68]

Bonhoeffer the Seminary Director

The church struggle in the middle years of the decade of the '30s gave shape to the course of Bonhoeffer's life. It had become apparent that only a sharp break with the Reich Church would salvage some semblance of integrity and faithfulness to the holy gospel.[69] To assist in the preparation of parish pastors, the Confessing Church established five seminaries in Germany, to be supported by freewill offerings and to maintain independence insofar as possible from state government. To the Nazi government, the Confessing Church represented an oppositional, disruptive force in Germany; consequently, Confessing congregations were officially banned. Dietrich Bonhoeffer was invited to return to Germany from England in the spring of 1935 to direct one of these illegal seminaries.

To prepare his own spirit and mind for this challenging assignment, before leaving England he visited several Anglican monasteries and a Quaker center. Bethge reports that "the closer this new task approached, the more it became a focal point for everything that had preoccupied Bonhoeffer in recent years: a theology of the Sermon on the Mount, a community in service and spiritual exercises, a witness to passive resistance and ecumenical openness."[70] Bonhoeffer was strongly attracted at the same time to the philosophy and nonviolent practice of Mohandas

Gandhi in India. He even procured letters of introduction that could have been used if he had indeed journeyed to India.[71]

Over the following three years, 1935-37, all of these motifs were amply taught and unforgettably demonstrated. Twenty-three pastoral candidates convened at Zingst on the coast of the Baltic Sea. A few weeks later in June they moved to an old manor house near a small rural town, Finkenwalde, just east of the Oder River and about 250 kilometers from Berlin.

The men who undertook the communal life in the new seminary community were already well on the way to ordination, most having received a university education that included a rigorous training in theology. The library consisted mostly of Bonhoeffer's own theological books. He also contributed his grand piano and his records of black spirituals that he had acquired in America.

During the extended time that the Finkenwaldians shared a life together under the tutelage of "Brother Bonhoeffer," as most referred to him, their lives were changed forever. The day began with a half hour of common prayer usually adopted from the Psalter, a hymn, Scripture readings, and prayer. Every Sunday a full liturgical service was scheduled, including a sermon.

There may be a tendency to idealize or romanticize these communal experiences from the vantage point of the twenty-first century. The school substantially depended on congregations in western Pomerania for the barest necessities of life — food, furniture, and other household items. Moreover, the seminary was always illegal, never receiving official approval from the National Church or the political authorities.

Bonhoeffer's classic book, *Life Together,* reflects the spiritual corporate atmosphere of the Finkenwalde Community. Written in 1938 at his sister Sabine's home in Göttingen in just four weeks, it brings together the basic rudiments that were embedded in the seminarians' experience — personal and corporate meditation, prayer, solitude, Bible study, fellowship, singing, recreation, ministry, worship, the eucharist, confession, and spiritual care.[72] When the first course was completed, a "Brothers' House" was approved by the Council of Brethren of the Old Prussian Union. This permitted Bonhoeffer to ask six of the seminarians to stay on to form a core community that would serve as a leaven for the new students expected to arrive for the fall semester.[73]

The Finkenwalde years further provided the opportunity for Bonhoeffer and the seminarians to intermingle with a number of Confessing congregations and families of the Pomeranian nobility. Very significantly among these were the von Kleist estates in Kieckow and Klein-Krossin. Ruth von Kleist-Retzow of Klein-Krossin began to attend the Sunday services in Finkenwalde with several of her school-age grandchildren. One of these granddaughters was Maria von Wedemeyer, eighteen years younger than the director of the seminary, but eventually to become engaged to him just prior to his imprisonment.

The Finkenwalde seminary became the context for Bonhoeffer's lectures, the highlight being those on discipleship and his exposition of the Sermon on the Mount. One of his students described Bonhoeffer as being a teacher "without equal." Bonhoeffer's style was intense, drawing students into thinking deeply about and even openly disputing the point in question. He had developed the knack of communicating well, a trait enhanced by his ability to maintain eye contact, to listen attentively, and to debate an issue with energy but also with respect. He was, as his assistant Wilhelm Rott remembered, one "who always had time for his brethren."[74]

The book that came out of these lectures, *Discipleship*, sought to address the penetrating question "of how we are to live as Christians today."[75] This was not only a general question for the followers of Christ in every age. It was a very autobiographical question for Bonhoeffer himself, addressed to the depths of his own soul in the gathering momentum of the church struggle. In the same period that he was writing this foundational work, his brother-in-law Hans von Dohnanyi was assembling his "Chronicle of Shame," a day-by-day account of outrageous Nazi policies and actions then beclouding the honor of Germany. As a member of the Ministry of Justice staff under Franz Gürtner, he was privy to knowledge of widespread injustices and persecutions perpetrated by the Nazi regime — ill treatment of pastors, priests, church leaders, Jehovah's Witnesses; restrictions imposed upon the Catholic Church; the tortures and mistreatment of individuals in prisons and concentration camps, sterilization of the physically and mentally disabled, and the crimes against the Jews.[76] Bonhoeffer consequently knew far more than the average German citizen about the dastardly character of the Nazi rulers of Germany. The following of Jesus in these apocalyptic times could indeed be costly, even to the point of martyrdom. Bonhoeffer's awareness of Nazi atrocities and his decision to become involved in the conspiracy to overthrow the Nazi government would make the cost of following Jesus that he emphasized to his seminarians even more costly to him. It would lead directly to his execution. The net of the Gestapo was tightening around those church leaders who took seriously the words of the 1934 Barmen Declaration: "We repudiate the false teaching that there are areas of our life in which we belong not to Jesus Christ but another Lord, areas in which we do not need justification and sanctification through him." In September 1937, the seminary was closed by order of the Gestapo. By the end of that year, twenty-seven of the students had been arrested and imprisoned.

The church struggle was in high gear. The seminary was shuttered, but the teaching and the learning continued, albeit in a new form. For the next three years, 1938-40, the backwoods of Pomerania housed "the collective pastorate." Co-operating superintendents in two districts, Schlawe and Gross-Schlönwitz, appointed the seminarians as assistant clergy. In 1939 the site of the Schlawe group was moved to Sigurdshof, taking over an empty farmhouse. Bonhoeffer divided his time between the two sites. "Work and meditation, worship, homiletics and examining the underlying concepts of the New Testament — all this was carried on in the small undistracted circle of the collective pastorates, almost more intensively than in the spacious house at Finkenwalde."[77]

The Gestapo continued their relentless pursuit of the illegal seminaries and their participants. Eventually, they moved to close down the Schlawe-Sigurdshof collective pastorate. When they arrived to carry out the deed, they found only an empty farmstead. By March 1940, all of the seminarians had been summoned to military service. There was no exemption for "servants of the Church," nor was there any provision for conscientious objection.[78]

Meanwhile, family matters were also of concern. Bonhoeffer's twin sister and her husband, Gerhard Leibholz, and their two daughters, Marianne and Christiane, were compelled to leave their home in Göttingen. Professor Leibholz's Jewish ancestry placed their existence in jeopardy, and so the painful decision was made to leave Germany. In their dramatic departure from their homeland, they were driven to the Swiss border by Bonhoeffer and Eberhard Bethge. Before the frontier was closed for the night (September 9, 1938), they waved farewell to their two drivers, and clandestinely crossed into Switzerland. Ultimately they made their home in England (primarily Oxford) until their return to Germany in 1947, following the end of the war.[79]

Bonhoeffer's Second Visit to America

With the decade of the 1930s drawing to a close, Dietrich Bonhoeffer had become increasingly disillusioned with the Confessing Church's lack of forthrightness and assertiveness in the enveloping struggle against Nazi domination. Eberhard Bethge refers to 1938 as "the low point of the Church Struggle."[80] This coincided with the infamous "Crystal Night" on November 9, when storm troopers destroyed more than 7,500 Jewish shops and burned many synagogues to the ground. In that orgy of depravity, 20,000 men were sent to concentration camps, 92 Jews were murdered, and hundreds of Torah scrolls were desecrated. In Bonhoeffer's Bible, Psalm 74:8 was deeply underlined: "they say to themselves: Let us plunder them! They burn all the houses of God in the land." In the margin Bonhoeffer wrote "9 Nov. 1938." Scarcely any pastors or church leaders spoke out against these acts of blatant anti-Semitism. Bonhoeffer himself was outraged.

His mood of disillusionment was deepened on the national occasion of Hitler's fiftieth birthday. The Minister for Church Affairs, Friedrich Werner, called on all pastors of the Reich to swear an oath of loyalty to Hitler: "I swear that I will be loyal and obedient to Adolf Hitler, the Leader of the German Reich, and people." Neither from the leadership of the Confessing Church nor from any other church in Germany was there a peep of objection or resistance. Sadly, most of the Confessing Church pastors, after long and exhausting debates and indecision, complied.

Bonhoeffer had become sharply critical of the Confessing Church leadership, writing passionate letters even to the church synods themselves. In one such letter, he pleaded for the church to accept fully its call to be the church of Jesus Christ and to stand with the weak and defenseless — in this case the dissenting pastors of the Confessing Church. His questions were razor-sharp: "Will the Confessing Church be willing openly to confess its guilt and disunity? . . . Will Confessing Synods learn that it is important to counsel in the peace and patience commanded and to decide in defiance of all dangers and difficulties? Will they ever learn that majority decision in matters of conscience kills the spirit?"[81]

Bonhoeffer's distress was sharpened by the possibility of being drafted for military service in Hitler's army. He needed to take action for his own conscience's sake and peace of mind. He therefore accepted an invitation to come to America for a second time. He traveled by way of England, visiting the Leibholz family, then crossing the Atlantic by boat with his brother, Karl-Friedrich, who had been offered a professorship at the University of Chicago. Dietrich was to travel on a lecture tour himself, the plans having been enthusiastically laid by Reinhold Niebuhr, his friend and teacher from Union Seminary days almost a decade earlier, and his closest American friend, Paul Lehmann. He was also to teach a summer course at Union, and it was likewise proposed that he undertake pastoral services to German refugees. The intention of Lehmann and Niebuhr was to save him from the upcoming military draft. All these plans were not to be fulfilled. Bonhoeffer was discomforted, aware not only of the continuing fight against Hitler and his cohorts but also of the possibility of war breaking out in Europe and preventing a return to his country. After wrestling for several days about his situation, he came to his decision to immediately reverse his course and re-enter the fray. In a deeply moving farewell letter to Reinhold Niebuhr, he etched his thoughts:

> I have made a mistake in coming to America. I must live through this difficult period of our national history with the Christian people of Germany. I will have no right to participate in the reconstruction of Christian life in Germany after the war if I do not share the trials of this time with my people. . . . Christians in Germany will face the terrible alternative of either willing the defeat of their nation in order that Christian civilization may survive, or willing the victory of their nation and thereby destroying our civilization. I know which of these alternatives I must choose; but I cannot make that choice in security.[82]

We know now what this decision meant in the life story of Dietrich Bonhoeffer. If he had chosen to remain in the United States he might have survived the years of World War II — indeed, he might even still be alive today. But he chose to return to Germany in July 1939, once again stopping off in London to see the Leibholz family. His sister's later comment attests to the prime motive of his return to Germany. She recalled that in America, "he could perfectly well be replaced, whereas he was needed in Germany. He could not leave his young theologians, his brethren, in the lurch in this difficult crisis of conscience to which the war would now expose them. He must return."[83]

Further words from Dietrich's sister reveal the emotional wrenching caused by his taking leave of his twin sister's family: "We all accompanied Dietrich to the station. It was a grave parting. In his own way, optimistic and self-controlled as ever, Dietrich helped us through it. But we had all seen the storm signals ahead, and we had not much hope of seeing each other again very soon. I never saw Dietrich again."[84] He would later write from prison that he harbored no regret about making his decision to return to Germany.

Bonhoeffer the Double Agent

Dietrich Bonhoeffer's life thus had turned a corner that has intrigued and challenged all those who have followed his biography. Just before leaving for America on his second visit, his disillusionment about the churches of Germany, including his own Confessing Church, had plumbed the depths. His beloved country was completely in thrall to a political regime that clearly ranked with the most tyrannical and despotic governments in all of human history. Its crimes and atrocities seemed to be without parallel. The clergy and their church leaders, the rank and file of the parishioners in the congregations, the universities, the press, the doctors, the lawyers, industries, and the military all seemed helpless in the face of this juggernaut of power and abuse of authority.

When Bonhoeffer returned to Germany after the aborted visit to America, the door opened for him to place his intelligence and experience in the service of the resistance movement. One way or the other, Hitler's design for world conquest had to be stopped. Dietrich's brother-in-law, Hans von Dohnanyi, had joined the staff of the *Abwehr*, the counter-intelligence agency of the armed forces in Nazi Germany. It also happened to be one of the primary centers of the resistance movement against the Nazi government. This agency, headed by Admiral Wilhelm Canaris, with General Hans Oster as chief of staff, was responsible for providing cover-ups for the wartime activities of the military resistance, including various assassination attempts on Hitler's life. Convinced that "true patriotism"[85] called for a concerted attempt to remove Hitler and his entourage from national leadership, Bonhoeffer became a civilian member of the *Abwehr* for four years until his own arrest on April 5, 1943.

Dohnanyi and Oster fronted for Bonhoeffer in securing an exemption from the military draft, insisting that his efforts were indispensable for espionage activities. Their well-crafted argument to the powers-that-be was that Bonhoeffer's ecumenical contacts could be exceedingly useful for gathering intelligence information. Ostensibly, he could provide background for assessing the political situations in such countries as the U.S., Britain, Switzerland, and Scandinavian lands such as Sweden, Norway, and Denmark. In short, the ecumenical friendships that he had established in the years 1931-37 could be manipulated to Nazi Germany's advantage.

In fact, Bonhoeffer did receive approval to travel, but he did so in his guise as a "double agent." He was certified as a member of the *Abwehr* staff, enabling him to receive visas and documentary permission to leave

Germany on a number of occasions. He was also a trusted member of the resistance, using his travels abroad as occasions to cultivate a closer communication between the resistance itself and the Allied forces.

Bonhoeffer was also instrumental in the implementation of a top-secret plan to assist in the smuggling of Jews out of Germany, referred to as "Operation 7." Three times he crossed the border himself to Switzerland, connecting with key ecumenical figures such as Karl Barth, W. A. Visser 't Hooft, and others. He was able to make several important contacts for the resistance. Together with Helmut Count von Moltke, he also traveled to Norway under the auspices of the *Abwehr*. Their mission was to encourage and strengthen the Norwegian Lutheran Church through its clergy and its leaders in their struggle against the Nazi occupiers of their country.

The capstone of Bonhoeffer's dangerous journeys came in the spring of 1942, when he met with his British ecumenical friend, Bishop George Bell, in Sigtuna, Sweden. The crucial importance of this mission can scarcely be exaggerated. In this secret rendezvous, Bonhoeffer relayed to the bishop precise information, including names of key resisters in the German underground. The hope was that Bell would transmit this important message to the British Foreign Secretary Anthony Eden, thence to Prime Minister Winston Churchill, and further to Franklin Roosevelt. It was hoped that the Allies would initiate a contact with the resistance, negotiating a compromise peace after Hitler had been overthrown in a coup. There was no return message by the Allied leaders.[86] The "unconditional surrender" policy of the Allied leaders seemed set in stone, much to the consternation of the resistance movement and also at great cost of life during the final two years of the war.

For several months Bonhoeffer's base of operation as an *Abwehr* agent was the Benedictine Monastery of Ettal, near Munich in southern Germany. It was in this picturesque and serene refuge that he began to write the manuscript that would eventually be known as *Ethics* and that he hoped would truly be his major life's work. As is the case with Bonhoeffer's writings since 1933, this fragmentary collection of his ethical reflections needs to be seen against the telling background of his life story, especially from 1939-43. The themes of Christ and reality, concreteness, the natural, the penultimate and the ultimate, the four mandates, deputyship, responsibility, the state and church, and telling the truth all profoundly reflect the endeavor by Bonhoeffer "to address the great moral dilemmas posed by the war and the need to resist a blatantly evil government."[87]

Bonhoeffer's Engagement to Maria

As the decade of the 1930s came to its close and moved on into the decade of the 1940s, not only was Dietrich Bonhoeffer a full participant in the underground resistance movement, a double agent whose life was full of risks and dangers; he also unexpectedly fell in love. Bonhoeffer had been in love before, with a woman described simply in Bethge's biography as "a girl-friend," but later identified as Elizabeth Zinn. Years later, sitting in his Tegel prison cell, he wrote about this relationship: "I was once in love with a girl; she became a theologian, and our paths ran parallel for many years; she was almost my age. I was twenty-one when it began. We didn't realize we loved each other. More than eight years went by. . . . I sensed at the time that if I ever did get married, it could only be to a much younger girl, but I thought that impossible, both then and thereafter. Being totally committed to my work for the Church in the ensuing years, I thought it not only inevitable but right that I should forgo marriage altogether."[88]

An important side-benefit of Dietrich's relationship with Elizabeth is the survival of several of his sermon manuscripts from the months of his London pastorate, 1933-35. He sent copies to her, and, fortunately for posterity, she kept them. He also sent a number of letters to her, almost all of which she eventually discarded. One, however, from Finkenwalde, dated 1 January 1936, she did retain. It offers us a window into a significant milestone in Bonhoeffer's life story: "I plunged into work in a very unchristian way. An . . . ambition that many noticed in me made my life difficult. . . . Then something happened, something that has changed and transformed my life to the present day. For the first time I discovered the Bible. . . . I had often preached, I had seen a great deal of the Church, and talked and preached about it — but I had not yet become a Christian. . . . The Sermon on the Mount freed me from that."[89]

It was in Finkenwalde that Dietrich first met Maria von Wedemeyer, a granddaughter of Ruth von Kleist-Retzow. The grandmother identified with the Confessing Church, was a supporter of the seminary, often brought her grandchildren to worship services, was an informed conversation partner of Dietrich's, and, in attempting to play matchmaker between Maria and Dietrich, has been described as a "matriarch of conspiracy."[90]

On numerous occasions in the late 1930s Dietrich visited in the von Kleist home, primarily at holiday times. It was there that he completed his manuscript of *Discipleship* in 1937, and later worked on what he had thought would be his most important theological contribution to the postwar religious literature, his *Ethics*. It was there, too, that he filled a pastoral role, particularly after Maria's father had been killed at Stalingrad, and a few months later at services for her brother, Max von Wedemeyer. As late as 1942, Maria continued to address Dietrich as "Pastor Bonhoeffer."

Their love blossomed that same year, despite the fact that Maria was then just eighteen and Dietrich was thirty-six, and despite the fact that Maria's mother had firm reservations about the wisdom of their moving further on the road to matrimony. January 13, 1943 became the red-letter day of their engagement, as Maria's warmhearted letter carried her answer: "With all my happy heart, I can now say yes."[91] The reserved salutation of this monumental letter was still "Dear Pastor Bonhoeffer."

Just a few weeks later on April 5, Dietrich was arrested and incarcerated at Tegel Prison in Berlin. Maria and he were never to consummate their life together in marriage, but in spite of that, their mutual correspondence and the several visits Maria made to the prison deepened and matured their relationship. Bonhoeffer's own letters from prison disclose more clearly than ever before his tender, caring, and loving side. His March 11, 1944 letter from Tegel is illustrative:

> My dear, dear Maria,
>
> It's no use, I have to write to you at last and talk to you with no one else listening. I have to let you see into my heart without someone else, whom it doesn't concern, looking on. I have to talk to you about that which belongs to no one else in the world but us, and which becomes desecrated when exposed to the hearing of an outsider. I refuse to let anyone else share what belongs to you alone; I think that would be impermissible, unwholesome, uninhibited, and devoid of dignity, from your point of view. The thing that draws and binds me to you in my unspoken thoughts and dreams cannot be revealed, dearest Maria, until I'm able to fold you in my arms. That time will come, and it will be all the more blissful and genuine the less we seek to anticipate it and the more faithfully and genuinely we wait for each other.[92]

His unshakable commitment to her is encapsulated in the heartfelt words, "Our marriage shall be a yes to God's earth; it shall strengthen our courage to act and accomplish something on the earth."[93]

In considering the spiritual life of Bonhoeffer, we need this touching portrait of a man in love alongside those of the scholar who wrote *Act and Being*, the seminary director who impacted over one hundred-fifty students, the double agent who sought to stay one step ahead of the Gestapo, and the prisoner who beckoned the contemporary church to ponder the meaning of "nonreligious Christianity" and "The World Come of Age."

In October 1944 Dietrich was transferred to the Gestapo prison in Prinz-Albrecht-Strasse, Berlin, and in February 1945 to the Buchenwald concentration camp. In spite of Maria's desperate, determined efforts to locate his whereabouts, they were not able to have further contact with each other. She did not hear of his execution until several months afterward, in the summer of 1945.

Bonhoeffer the Prisoner and the Martyr

For the final two years of his life, Dietrich Bonhoeffer was a prisoner of the Third Reich, confined for the first eighteen months at Berlin's Tegel military prison. His "home" during this time of incarceration was a cell room, six by nine feet, characterized by the simplest and humblest of accommodations — a hard narrow bed, a shelf, a stool, a bucket, and a skylight window. This scarcely held promise as a setting in which some of the most creative theological thinking of the twentieth century might be born. It did, however, become precisely that as the months of confinement passed.

From April 1943 to August 1944, correspondence from cell ninety-two managed to reach the hands of Dietrich's parents, Maria, and Eberhard Bethge. The greater number of these were addressed to Eberhard Bethge and are among the most inspiring writings in Bonhoeffer's theological legacy and personal spirituality.[94] It is only recently that the dramatic story of how the prison letters, especially those written to Bethge, survived the maniacal Nazi era. Fortunately, one of the guards, Corporal Knobloch, proved to be willing to smuggle letters out of Tegel Prison. When Bethge, then in the German army, was able to return to Berlin, he took them with him, and most of them were buried by Bethge's young wife, Bonhoeffer's niece, Renate, in gas mask containers in the Schleichers' garden. Bethge reports, "We actually found them again after the war — not something to be taken for granted, for many similar caches were not found again, or if they were found, they had already been plundered by others."[95]

Bonhoeffer's own intellectual and spiritual life while in prison was steadily nourished by books that were brought by his parents, many upon his request.[96] Not only were the daylight hours opportunities for reading diversely. They were also the occasions for continuing reading of the Bible; for writing poems, a novel, and a play; and for profound self-searching, deep reflection, and productive theologizing.

In many respects, Bonhoeffer's 1944 letters to his friend, Eberhard Bethge, once published, radically affected the theological landscape of the twentieth century. The enigmatic themes of these letters will profoundly challenge contemporary Christianity in the twenty-first century: "religionless Christianity," "who Christ really is for us today," "world come of age," the "discipline of the secret," "God as the beyond in the midst of our life," "acting as one should even if there were no God," "the profound this-worldliness of Christianity," "Christ, the Man for others," "the Church for others," the "suffering God." These themes from the letters, the essays, ten poems, the novel, and the play written in the six-by-nine-foot Tegel cell are all indicators of how he looked at life amid the ruinous and shattering months of 1944.

After eighteen months in Tegel Prison, Dietrich was transferred in October 1944 to the Gestapo prison at Prinz-Albrecht-Strasse in Berlin. Just the month previously, the relentless pursuits of the Gestapo had discovered secret papers and documents of the *Abwehr* in Zossen; this evidence was damning enough to incriminate key figures in the resistance conspiracy, including Bonhoeffer and Hans von Dohnanyi. Other members of the Bonhoeffer family circle were imminently to be arrested and imprisoned, including Klaus Bonhoeffer, Rüdiger Schleicher, and eventually Eberhard Bethge.

The next stop on the imprisonment trail was the concentration camp at Buchenwald, Bonhoeffer's place of confinement from February until April 3, 1945. From that hellhole of Nazi brutality and cruelty, the major resource of information is *The Venlo Incident*, written subsequently by Captain Payne Best, an officer of the British Secret Service who had been captured by the Gestapo in 1939. His thumbnail sketch of Prisoner Bonhoeffer was laudatory: He "always seemed to diffuse an atmosphere of happiness, of joy in every smallest event in life, and a deep gratitude for the mere fact that he was alive. . . . He was one of the very few men I have ever met to whom his God was real and ever close to him."[97]

Payne Best and Dietrich Bonhoeffer, as "special prisoners," were among those loaded into a prison van on April 3, 1945, heading for still another destination, the extermination camp at Flossenbürg. Just outside the city of Regensburg the van broke down, and the prisoners were transferred to a bus, which stopped at the little Bavarian village of Schönberg. In the little schoolhouse there where the small coterie of prisoners were detained, Bonhoeffer was asked to conduct a prayer service on their behalf. It was Low Sunday in the church calendar, April 8, 1945, and Bonhoeffer, pastor to the end, meditated briefly on two of the pericope texts for the day, Isaiah 53:5 ("By his wounds we are healed") and 1 Peter 1:3ff. ("Blessed be the God and Father of our Lord Jesus Christ! By his great mercy he has given us a new birth into a living hope through the resurrection of Jesus Christ from the dead. . . .") Payne Best would recall that Bonhoeffer "reached the hearts of all, finding just the right words to express the spirit of our imprisonment, and the thoughts and resolutions which it had brought."[98] The calm that ensued was interrupted by the arrival of two "evil-looking" Gestapo agents to take Bonhoeffer away to the court martial and execution.

Before the Gestapo took him away he had time to whisper to his fellow prisoner, Payne Best, his final recorded words, to be relayed eventually to his British friend from the church struggle and the ecumenical movement, Bishop Bell of Chichester: "This is the end — for me, the beginning of life. Tell him . . . with him I believe in the principle of our universal Christian brotherhood which rises above all national interests, and that our victory is certain — tell him, too, that I have never forgotten his words at our last meeting."[99]

The final destination on the road to martyrdom was indeed another of the Nazis' infamous concentration camps, Flossenbürg. That night there was a brief trial in the camp laundry house by the SS summary court. A verdict of high treason was pronounced on these members of the resistance: Wilhelm Canaris, Hans Oster, Karl Sack, Ludwig Gehre, Theodor Strunck, Friedrich von Rabenau, and Dietrich Bonhoeffer.

A stark, single sentence in Eberhard Bethge's classic biography of Bonhoeffer encapsulates the final moment in the martyr's life: "In Flossenbürg the executions took place in the gray dawn that Monday" (April 9, 1945).[100] The summary description of the significance of Bonhoeffer's martyrdom can be seen by all visitors to Flossenbürg on the exterior wall of the camp church: "To Dietrich Bonhoeffer: A Witness to Jesus Christ among his Brothers and Sisters."

The only account of Bonhoeffer's death was given by the prison doctor, who wrote that, after the sentences had been read out to the condemned men, he saw "Pastor Bonhoeffer, before taking off his prison garb, kneeling on the floor praying fervently to his God. I was most deeply moved by the way this lovable man prayed, so devout and so certain that God heard his prayer." He added: "at the place of execution he again said a short prayer and then climbed the steps to the gallows, brave and composed. . . . In the almost fifty years that I worked as a doctor, I have hardly ever seen a man die so entirely submissive to the will of God."[101]

Nearly thirteen years before this ignominious end to Bonhoeffer's life, he had said in a sermon preached at the Kaiser Wilhelm Memorial Church in Berlin, June 19, 1932, "We must not be surprised if once again times return for our Church when the blood of martyrs will be required. But even if we have the courage and faith to spill it, this blood will not be as innocent or as clear as that of the first martyrs. Much of our own guilt will lie in our blood. The guilt of the useless servant who is thrown into the darkness."[102]

The debate about whether or not Dietrich Bonhoeffer stands in the long procession of Christian martyrs since the Age of the Apostles or if he should be primarily counted among the political conspirators against tyranny will unquestionably continue in this new century. Pertinent in consideration of this issue are the words of Bonhoeffer's brother-in-law, Gerhard Leibholz, whose impact on his wife's twin brother is still being studied:

> Bonhoeffer's life and death belong to the annals of Christian martyrdom. . . . His life and death have given us great hope for the future. He has set a model for a new type of true leadership inspired by the gospel, daily ready for martyrdom and death and imbued by a new spirit of Christian humanism and a creative sense of civic duty. The victory which he has won was a victory for us all, a conquest never to be undone, of love, light, and liberty.[103]

Dietrich Bonhoeffer's life on earth ended over a half-century ago at the young age of thirty-nine. The legacy of that life, however, will indisputably affect the course of Christianity for decades to come.

CHAPTER TWO

Compassion and Action for Justice

Bonhoeffer's Christocentric Spirituality

To be conformed to the image of Jesus Christ is not an ideal of realizing some kind of similarity with Christ which we are asked to attain. It is not we who change ourselves into the image of God. Rather, it is the very image of God, the form of Christ, which seeks to take shape within us (Gal. 4:19). It is Christ's own form which seeks to manifest itself in us. Christ does not cease working in us until he has changed us into Christ's own image. Our goal is to be shaped into the entire form of the incarnate, the crucified, and the risen one. Christ has taken on this human form. He became a human being like us. In his humanity and lowliness we recognize our own form. He became like human beings, so that we would be like him.[1]

Dietrich Bonhoeffer's writings, like his life, were remarkably Christocentric. Whether he was speaking from the pulpit, addressing ecumenical gatherings, or teaching at levels that ranged from university to seminary to catechism for teenagers, his constant referent was Jesus Christ, the embodiment of what it means to live as a dedicated Christian. For him, following Christ demanded the unstinting contribution of one's energies to the well-being of the church community and, through that community and one's personal faith, to the betterment of society itself. His ideas on moral leadership emanate from his conviction that Christians must rekindle in their hearts and in their parish life the relationship with Jesus Christ they professed at their baptism or confirmation. His question from prison, "Who really is Jesus Christ for us today?"[2] expresses his lifelong concern to seek out the incarnate presence of Christ, not only in the people who would enter his life or who would evoke his compassion, but also in the historical events that had led to his imprisonment as a willing conspirator against a morally corrupt government. Somehow amid the loneliness and frustration Bonhoeffer experienced in the risky actions of his resistance to Nazism, there remained with him an intimacy with Jesus Christ, whom he described in prison as "the man for others."[3] The compassionate, prophetic figure of Jesus Christ had filled Bonhoeffer's world with meaning and liberated him to the extent that he, a pacifist pastor, could take part in the plot to kill Adolf Hitler and bring Nazi Germany's war of aggression and genocidal murder to an end.

Encounters with Christ Who
Reveals the God of Compassion

Bonhoeffer's relationship with Jesus Christ was intense. His response to Jesus was nurtured through his prayerful reading of the Gospels, in which Jesus' life and teachings are centered upon serving people and freeing them from the poverty, deceptions, and oppressions that contradicted his Father's promise to always care for the weakest of God's children. As early as his 1928 pastoral internship in Barcelona, Bonhoeffer had insisted to his German-speaking congregation that, like Jesus, their lives were bound up with the poorest of the poor, whose worth in the eyes of God far exceeded the monetary goals on which they had set their hearts. In a memorable Advent sermon he told his people, businessmen for the most part, that they were all "faced with the shocking reality: Jesus stands at the door and knocks, in complete reality. He asks you for help in the form of a beggar, in the form of a ruined human being in torn clothing. He confronts you in every person that you meet. Christ walks on the earth as your neighbor as long as there are people."[4] The image of Jesus Christ as the beggar in rags and the neighbor in need was deeply embedded in Bonhoeffer's attitude toward society's outcasts. In his Christology lectures, with which he closed out his teaching career at Berlin University in the summer of 1933, he returned to the same theme. This was his final course before he departed to assume a pastorate in London. The high point of what he wanted Jesus Christ to be for them came as he challenged them to search out the contemporary presence of Jesus and not get bogged down in the heavy theological analyses of how the incarnation of the Word of God was possible or how they could master the intricate formulae of early church councils and possibly think they had come to know Jesus Christ. No, the task of Christology was not to ask the "how" question — probing with all the tools of philosophical investigation the possible explanations of the miraculous incarnation of God's Word at that sacred moment in time — but the more disturbing, existential question: *who* is this Jesus who confronts us today? This is the perennial question before Christ's followers in all places and at all times.

In Bonhoeffer's spirituality, this Jesus can never be the kingly, divine being appearing in triumphant regal splendor. This Jesus comes into people's lives in a way that "must provoke contradiction and hostility." Bonhoeffer goes on in his Christology lectures to declare that Jesus comes to us "incognito, as a beggar among beggars, as an outcast among outcasts, as despairing among the despairing, as dying among the dying."[5] This "incognito" was for Bonhoeffer not only the point of God's humility in becoming human but also the central problem of Christology: Jesus telling his followers to look for him not primarily among the privileged of this earth but among the lowly, who were the object of his Father's special predilection. In his sensitivity to Christ's incarnate nearness in the beggar, the outcast, those caught in the pathos of suffering, those languishing in despair and oppression — in a word, the least of Jesus' brothers and sisters — Bonhoeffer revealed the Christocentric heart of his spirituality and set out what should be the preoccupation of genuine moral leadership.

Bonhoeffer's spiritual life was focused so intensely on Jesus Christ that, as he became more involved in the ecclesiastical and political turmoil of the Hitler years, he was able to question many of the un-Christlike assumptions on which the "smooth" operations of church and state seemed to depend.[6] He spurned the misleading "religious trappings" of Christianity that provided a cover for the political malfeasance he criticized in the Nazi government. The God of extramundane solutions to life's problems, the so-called "stopgap God" or the medieval "deus ex machina," he exposed as unreal escapism, given that Christians were called to assume personal responsibility for extricating their nation from the overwhelming horrors of the war and the murderous concentration camps. God as encountered in Jesus Christ had to be more than a last-ditch solver of seemingly insoluble problems. According to Bonhoeffer, it was one thing to pray for deliverance; it was quite another to act with Christian courage and compassion in order to deliver people from their oppression. As he wrote in his Christmas 1942 letter to his family and fellow conspirators, "mere waiting and looking on is not Christian behavior."[7] Yet waiting to see how the war and the killings would end and watching in silence while the evil of the war and the death camps went on unquestioned by any church directive seemed to be what the Christian churches preferred. In Bonhoeffer's opinion, theirs was not Christian behavior. Nor was it the moral leadership that Christians had the right to expect.

Jesus Christ and a Critique of the False Images of God

Bonhoeffer's dissatisfaction with the false images of God that seemed to be hawked by the mainstream churches extended also to the aloof, unattainable, self-satisfied God, secure in the heavenly realm, a creation of an ideologically distorted theology that desired a God beyond the human pathos of God's creatures. This was a God who dazzled with power and sat on a divine throne, like an oriental potentate, as the final answer to the unanswered (and often unasked) human questions about the meaning of life. This, he said, was the "God of religion" but hardly the God who had become flesh in Jesus Christ and with whom Christians were called to conform. Nor could Bonhoeffer bring himself to believe any longer in a God who inspired the clergy to engage in "religious blackmail" through manipulation of a reinforced sense of sin and guilt among their people. God as the merciless hunter and judge of wretched sinners did not exist for him.

Bonhoeffer also could not accept a God with all the uncomplicated, theologically certified answers to human suffering. God would not rescue God's people from the evils of war, atrocities, and death. That would come only when Christians realized their responsibility before God to save their brothers and sisters the Jews from the horrible fate they would otherwise suffer. God in Jesus Christ had, in fact, come among God's people to live, suffer, and die, fully sharing in their human condition. For this reason Bonhoeffer constantly urged his church to rediscover for itself the freedom of Christ to act with courage, even as it was being constricted in the vise of Nazism. He called on the church to reaffirm its vocation to solidarity in its sufferings with Jesus Christ. Later, at the height of the barbarisms of the war years, he would accuse the church of complicity in the murder of "the weakest and most defenseless brothers and sisters of Jesus Christ."[8] Bonhoeffer's spirituality went so far as to accept even his own death for Christ, not as the end of all his hopes, but as the "last station" in his efforts to free his nation from the pit of Nazism and his fullest experience of true freedom.[9]

Freedom in the Following of Christ

Bonhoeffer saw his life's purpose as one of helping his church and fellow conspirators realize the freedom that had characterized the mission and ministry of Jesus Christ. Jesus invited people to be free again in a new kind of relationship with his Father and with each other, not cramped by scrupulous attention to the minutiae of laws but moved by their love for one another and for the lowliest and most distressed of their brothers and sisters, those targeted for persecution by the ruthless Nazi state. Bonhoeffer believed strongly that only those liberated by deep, interior conviction of their acceptance by God, though they be sinners confronted with choices repulsive to their conscience, would be able to venture the brave deeds of responsibility needed to deliver millions of people from the overwhelming evil of a world at war.

Bonhoeffer understood that Jesus could set his word even above that of the religious leaders of his day. He forgave sins and exercised compassion at the sight of human need, though this meant "violating" the Sabbath and maintaining a warm fellowship with known sinners. He conveyed hope to those in despair and inspired faith in those dispirited by shameful deprivations. He did this in spite of the scandal his manner of living and healing aroused in the self-righteous religious leaders who controlled the rubrics of behavioral propriety in Israel. His freedom to be a loving brother toward all, especially the victims of poverty, disease, and social ostracism, gnawed at the self-satisfaction of those who had dominated the lowly. Jesus was notably free from an over-reverence for the status quo and even personal survival. His attitude, which seemed to declare the relativity of law and order in his own rigidly structured society, brought him into ineluctable conflict with the religious and political authorities, and eventually led to his arrest and execution. Far from being the placid, haloed figure of saccharine holy cards, Jesus threatened the whole system of slavish dependence on legalistic control, a system that paraded under the enticing guise of security and order. Small wonder that Bonhoeffer saw in Jesus' life and death the courageous moral leadership that might jolt the German generals out of their "duty-oriented," stiff obedience to their military oath and their bellicose dictator.

Bonhoeffer's spirituality pivoted on courageous deeds in imitation of Christ as well as on the trustful prayers that emanated from his personal piety. For Bonhoeffer, truly mature spirituality manifests itself above all in love of one's neighbor and working for peace and justice in one's spheres of influence in a society that often fails to provide for the common good of all its citizens. This was his gauge of the quality of effective moral leadership. As he pointed out to his fellow conspirators, the Christian moral leader needed the vision and imagination of Jesus Christ to see history from the perspective of those who were living in the shadows of human existence, society's despised outcasts and throwaways.[10] True moral leaders had to look to remedy the ills and heal the brokenhearted of any society whose policies left victims suffering in their wake.

Faith as Service and Action for Justice: A Critique of Religion

In Bonhoeffer's spiritual outlook, the only faith that reflects one's deepened relationship with Jesus Christ is that inspirited by compassion and shaped in service. Anxiety over security, survival, and even self-respect were hardly the marks of the freedom of Christ, who could move openly with sinners and with his healing mercy touch the leper, the insane, the epileptic, and all those beyond the margins of "respectable society." Moreover, despite the cajoling counter-persuasions by family and followers and threat of imprisonment and death, Jesus condemned the hypocrisy of Jerusalem's powerful religious leadership. The Christic parallels with Bonhoeffer's ethical decisions to break with his church, so comfortably stuck in the web of national heartlessness, and to enter the conspirators' "fellowship of guilt" are apparent enough in his final writings.[11] The war years were, as he put it in his sermon on the occasion of the baptism of his grandnephew and godson, Dietrich Bethge, the time for prayer and "action for justice."[12]

This baptismal sermon, sent in a letter to his godson, not only provides many insights into Bonhoeffer's feelings about the future direction of church leadership, but it also exposes the core of his own Christ-centered spirituality: "Our being Christians today," he wrote, "will be limited to two things: prayer and action for justice on behalf of people. All Christian thinking, speaking, and organizing must be born anew out of this prayer and action." The churches, he said, needed a new way of speaking. "Till then the Christian cause will be a silent and hidden affair, but there will be those who pray and act for justice and wait for God's own time. May you be one of them."[13] Indeed, prayer and action for justice stand out as the most distinctive characteristics of what we have called Bonhoeffer's spirituality. Above all, Bonhoeffer emerges from his writings as a person who, despite his personal flaws, seems to have been led by

God's Spirit into a deep, prayerful faith to undertake great risks to his life in working for the restoration of justice in a society befouled by systemic immorality.

Bonhoeffer also spoke in that sermon of the need for a "new language, perhaps quite non-religious, but liberating and redeeming — as was Jesus' language; it will shock people and yet overcome them by its power; it will be the language of a new righteousness and truth, proclaiming God's peace with people and the coming of God's kingdom."[14] The clue to what Bonhoeffer meant by the "new language" that both liberates and shocks might lie in the words immediately following that passage in the letter and in the context of his vision of a "non-religious" Christianity.

Bonhoeffer was wary of a church rising high from the rubble of the Second World War and once again exerting clerical dominance over a sinful world. This was not the moral leadership he had in mind. He spoke of his misgivings about a future church's scramble to recover its privileges and convince itself that it was without blame for the atrocities of the Hitler years. His statements about the coming of a non-religious Christianity are a caution to the church to convert to Jesus Christ and patiently wait with perseverance in prayer and courage in deeds until it can "once more be called so to utter the Word of God that the world will be changed and renewed by it." His aversion for an aristocratic Christianity is made clear when, almost immediately, he adds that the Christian cause will be a *silent* and *hidden* affair. But "there will be those who pray and act for justice and wait for God's own time."[15] In two related passages from letters sent around the same time as the baptismal sermon, he mentions a "discipline of the secret" *(disciplina arcani)*, a reference to a practice of the ancient church that was aimed at safeguarding church integrity against pagan corruption. The first reference brings out some of his intent behind that phrase as Bonhoeffer invokes the "discipline of the secret" in the context of asking what meaning worship and prayer will have in a non-religious, non-triumphal Christianity.[16]

According to Bonhoeffer, religion was never to be equated with faith as God's gift; religion, with all its institutional structures and laws, was all too human, flawed, and prone to sin. The religious trappings of faith were never the same as the gift of faith whereby God saves God's sinful children and bestows the genuine holiness that flows from that faith. Bonhoeffer spoke of the mysteries of faith that had to be protected from profanation. Hence the restoration of the early church's practice of the "discipline of the secret."[17] Bonhoeffer was all too painfully aware of the cavalier way the churches of Germany had transformed the ultimacy and wholly otherness of God into an icon of their own making and turned the "sacred" into empty religious jargon. The words of the churches had lost any claim to moral credibility in that era of gospel spoliation. The acts of injustice perpetrated by so-called Christians seemed to be abetted by their churches beaming with the nationalistic pride engendered by Adolf Hitler.

The practical question thus became for Bonhoeffer how, in a non-triumphal Christianity, to prevent Christians and church communities from squandering their identity with Jesus Christ in the midst of their involvement with the secular. This is in essence the fundamental question of how one's spirituality can be integrated into one's everyday life. Bonhoeffer viewed discipline as essential, but, as in the early church, this was not to be brandished imperiously before a hostile society or forced upon an unwilling citizenry. A discipline of modesty in claims and humility in action was called for to help the church become liberated from itself and delivered from the stagnation of less-than-Christian forms of religious expression. The church had a mandate to preserve the mysteries of the Christian faith proclaimed by God's Word, not with a pathetic defensive frenzy, but with prayer, worship, and Christlike example.

Ethicist Larry Rasmussen has with characteristic insight described the implications of this discipline for American society. This discipline "means in part that the church and worship in a world-come-of age is not for everyone. It is only for the small groups of clearly committed Christians who comprise an intense community on the basis of their common, intense loyalty to Christ; and their expression of the meaning of that loyalty and community is communicated to and with one another in worship. . . . [This] worship . . . is not for the streets, for the posters, for the media, for the masses. It is certainly not Hollywood Bowl and Drive-in Easter sunrise services, nor Sunday East Room exercises in American civil religion, nor Astrodome rallies or religiosity. . . . It is not bumper sticker and slick-paper Christianity. The church, if Bonhoeffer has his way, will be rigorous in its membership stipulations and devout in its practice of disciplines. It will also give up its property for the sake of the needy."[18] According to Bonhoeffer, no proclamation of God's enduring goodness carries any cogency without this renewed form of prayer, worship, and example in a society where human malevolence predominates. Bonhoeffer's cryptic allusions to the "discipline of the secret" were intended to preserve the Christ-centered perspective in all vicarious action of the church on behalf of the least of Jesus' brothers and sisters.

To extrapolate from Bonhoeffer's Christocentric spirituality, we can affirm that Christ is as much the center of this "discipline" as he is the

43

structure of all reality and the inspiration behind what Bonhoeffer made the central theme of his *Ethics:* Christians are called to exercise responsibility for the well-being of the society in which they live. Christians are to pray and worship in a community of like believers and thus be strengthened in those attitudes that enable them to serve others who may have experienced only destitution and sorrow. If the same Christ-oriented outlook is not shared by everyone, Christians and their churches are nonetheless to trust that the Holy Spirit will eventually give revelatory sound to their prayer and example and bring the church once more to speak God's word effectively to those who are brothers and sisters to them in Jesus Christ. They are to speak anger against the forces of injustice; they are to do those actions necessary to secure justice for those who have been victimized by the oppressions that morally corrupt, ideologically cruel governments have sanctioned throughout human history.

Jesus and the Mission of the Church to be a Voice of the Oppressed

As we have seen time and again in examining Bonhoeffer's spirituality, the silence of the churches while evil was done — at times in Christ's name — was particularly vexatious to him. To be sure, the Confessing Church exhibited courage in fighting for its proper space against the control of the Nazi government. But in Bonhoeffer's opinion, even here it failed as church through its timidity in not resisting more forcefully those government policies that victimized Jewish citizens. From the moment of the anti-Jewish legislation in April 1933 and throughout the church struggle, Bonhoeffer was nearly without support in defending the Jews. He frequently cited the passage from Proverbs 31:8 ("Speak up for those who have no voice") as a God-given mandate to oppose energetically the anti-Jewish policies of the nation. Bonhoeffer himself had urged his church to enter into solidarity with the Jews dispossessed by bigoted laws and Nazism's dehumanizing tactics of repression; this was the central feature of his essay on "The Church in the Presence of the Jewish Question." The three steps he advocated could very well spell out what Bonhoeffer had in mind when he wrote to his godson that being Christian in the future would be limited to prayer and action for justice.[19]

In face of the civil legislation that in its malicious intent had targeted Jewish citizens for persecution, Bonhoeffer said that, at the very least, the church had to question the policies of the state and protest against them.

Secondly, the church had to aid the victims, and not limit that help to those of the Christian faith. Finally, the church was obliged to oppose the government — as Bonhoeffer put it, "jam a spoke in the wheel" of state.[20] These three steps are the hallmarks of a spiritual life and moral leadership in keeping with Jesus' beatitudinal demands on his followers. It is interesting to note that two of the martyrs honored with Bonhoeffer at Westminster Abbey in the summer of 1998, Martin Luther King and Archbishop Oscar Romero, both led their people in the same three steps urged by Bonhoeffer. Action for justice, whether for the beleaguered peasants of El Salvador or for the disenfranchised blacks of the United States, was as much a part of their love for and obedience to Jesus Christ as it was for Bonhoeffer.

But Bonhoeffer's own church did not enter into battle for the Jews, not even to defend with any noticeable vigor its pastors of Jewish blood. By the time the early loss of their civil rights had escalated into full-scale genocidal extermination of the Jews of Europe, the church's silence had itself become not merely a failure of nerve but also, in Bonhoeffer's eyes, a sinful denial of Jesus Christ present in those weakest among his brothers and sisters. The total silence of the churches on Crystal Night, November 10, 1938, presaged its feckless silence and failure to take effective counteraction during the coming horrors of the death camps. In prison he penned his acidic judgment that his own Confessing Church seemed interested more in its own prosperity and survival because it had "little personal faith in Christ," adding that Jesus was "disappearing from sight."[21]

It is evident from Bonhoeffer's bitter criticism of the church's moral leadership that the churches of Germany did not always speak with prophetic candor or engage in courageous action for justice during the Hitler era. They had managed with theological adroitness to find reasons not to interfere with the Nazi government over the anti-Jewish legislation. Endorsing the synodal declarations of Barmen and Dahlem without any effective follow-through in concrete actions of protest and civic disruption seemed to be the extent of the church resistance. Bonhoeffer's was a lonely voice crying in the Nazi wilderness against injustice and idolatry. In 1935 he reminded the Confessing Church of Saxony of its call to action. "The service of the church has to be given to those who suffer violence and injustice. The Old Testament still demands righteousness from the state, the New Testament no longer does so. Without asking about justice or injustice, the church takes to itself all the sufferers, all the forsaken of every party and of every status. 'Speak up for those who have no voice' (Prov. 31:8). Here the decision will really be made whether we are still the church of the present Christ. The Jewish question."[22] If we can put aside his spurious differentiation between the Old and New Testaments, Bonhoeffer is saying that the test case of whether the church is the church of Jesus Christ lies in its willingness to serve "those who suffer violence and injustice." Speaking out for those deprived of a voice in their own destiny is one way the church community can demonstrate its fidelity to Jesus Christ and the movement of his Spirit and a significant way in which the church can exercise moral leadership.

Bonhoeffer was all too well aware of the cowardly retreat of the churches in the face of swift Nazi sanctions for any act of defiance against its policies. The Hitler government had inoculated itself against opposition through Gestapo terror and cruel reprisals. For Bonhoeffer, the fear of repression served as no excuse for the church's widespread failure to act; the silence and inaction of the churches made them accomplices in the crimes of the government. In his judgment churchgoing Christians, intoxicated with pride in the commendable truth of their own glorious history, remain entombed in some nostalgic past if they fail to be the church of the present through fidelity to their prophetic mission in each succeeding generation. It was right action for the church publicly to oppose the Nazi government as it did through the Barmen Declaration of faith;[23] it was wrong to have kept silent during the genocidal persecution of the Jews. As we will see later, nowhere was this judgment more forcefully leveled against church smugness than in Bonhoeffer's "Confession of Guilt" on behalf of the church.[24]

For Bonhoeffer, the moral issue of a church becoming an outspoken advocate of the civil rights of Jews in Germany was of a piece with the related issues of justice and peace. In each instance it is a question not of orthodoxy but of action. His 1942 Christmas letter to his family and fellow conspirators declares what it takes to be genuine Christians obedient to the teachings of Jesus Christ. "We are not Christ," he wrote, "but if we want to be Christians, we must have some share in Christ's large-heartedness *by acting with responsibility and in freedom* when the hour of danger comes and by showing a real compassion that springs, not from fear, but from the liberating and redeeming love of Christ for all who suffer. Mere waiting and looking on is not Christian behavior. *Christians are called to compassion and action,* not in the first place by their own sufferings, but by the sufferings of their brothers and sisters for whose sake Christ suffered."[25] The words "compassion" and "action" are repeated here like a theme. Here as in Bonhoeffer's previous writings Christ is his exemplar of what a church community should be even when the risks of fidelity to

God's call to compassionate action are persecution and even death. The willingness to suffer for justice became for Bonhoeffer the hallmark of his spirituality and moral leadership as well as the test case of whether the church was really free.

Whether Christians and their churches are capable of fostering the kind of spiritual renewal and moral leadership needed to eradicate the injustice and bloodshed for which the past century has been infamous remains a moot question. Will the churches in the twenty-first century be able to speak God's word with credibility and dare to do those courageous deeds that can even liberate a church from itself? Bonhoeffer argued that his own church was not only *not* free, but worse, was so interested in its own survival and its own continued enjoyment of privilege that it had become a sop to the ideology that filled people's hearts with dreams of racial superiority and militaristic glory. Bonhoeffer bristled at the church's mediocre implementation of God's Word that had made the church such an ineffective counterforce to the turbulent evil of a nation trapped in its own nationalistic schemes. The peace of 1945 was hardly a complete liberation of the church, if the continued pursuit of institutional self-aggrandizement is any measure of a church's professed dedication to the gospel. The "bourgeois church" hankering after the security of a guaranteed status quo and fearful of any prophetic voice that might threaten its peace is very much with us. The stated priorities of churches at local and international levels are often a witness to the manner in which religious denominations can appear to serve only their own security needs or become preoccupied with trivia.

Bonhoeffer was gifted with an extraordinary ability to recognize and expose the moral obtuseness and political opportunism behind self-serving assertions that Christian faith was congruent with the dictates of Adolf Hitler. Having witnessed the nazification of countless churches, Bonhoeffer was angered by the obvious repudiation of the gospel by a so-called Christian society. He often wrote of his suspicions that church life and the profession of one's faith had been cheapened by an easy accommodation to a paganized ideology. The ecclesiastical endorsements of Nazism's promise for a more law-abiding, orderly society had alerted him to the churches' proclivity for entering into unholy alliances with tainted political systems.

Even a seemingly harmless sermon, such as he described in his diary in 1939, could stir up his inner malaise over the church's failure to be Christ to the world. On that occasion Bonhoeffer lamented that a worship service he had attended in a prominent Riverside, New York, church was nothing more than "a respectable, self-indulgent religious celebration" bereft of the cutting edges of God's Word. For Bonhoeffer, that service, full of self-satisfied praise for the freedoms of America, represented the "sort of idolatrous religion" that "stirs up the flesh which is accustomed to being kept in check by the Word of God." He complained that the sermon reeked of "libertinism, egotism, and indifference," qualities that he knew all too well from similar church services in his native Germany.[26]

Everywhere Bonhoeffer turned in the 1930's it seemed that an easily led citizenry was content to bask in the Teutonic pride that Hitler was proclaiming to mesmerized audiences all over Germany. The churches, supposedly representing Jesus Christ, were neither the voice of compassion nor the conscience of their nation in all the crises churned up by Hitler's stifling of individual freedom and denial of dignity to those dehumanized by Nazi ideology. Churches survived by cleverly separating the sacred side of their activities from the secular, the religious from the profane, retreating behind the protection offered them in political-ecclesiastical concordats or in the ersatz safety of Luther's doctrine of the two kingdoms.

But, as Bonhoeffer reminded the Christians of Germany, Luther's teaching on the relationship between "the sword and the gospel," state and church, was never intended to be a severance of one from the other, as if churchgoers had to accept without contention whatever a political government decreed. The playing-it-safe tactics of the churches were, in Bonhoeffer's opinion, a dishonoring of the faith in Jesus Christ religious people so cheerfully professed. The churches had given the impression to many Christians that it was common prudence to cordon off the demands of their everyday, secularized life from the more rigorous demands made on them as followers of Jesus Christ. And they, in turn, were allowed to prosper in Nazi Germany so long as they did not question political decisions, even if this meant shirking their responsibility to promote justice and to defend human rights in the name of Jesus Christ.

Bonhoeffer harshly criticized those religious leaders who encouraged such "thinking in two spheres," keeping the issue of human rights violations apart from their personal devotions and worship services. Bonhoeffer accused them of denying to people "that community with the world into which God entered in Jesus Christ."[27] Bonhoeffer maintained that the reality of Jesus Christ extends to his human solidarity with all peoples, including Jews, socialists, gypsies, and homosexuals — all objects of Nazi hatred. In Christ, God invests the world with a commonality in which one's faith and one's "worldly" concerns must be reconciled. Bonhoeffer offered what he believed to be the true interpretation of Luther's doctrine of the two kingdoms, that of a mutually supportive yet critical relationship in which Christians may and at times should oppose the secular "in the name of a better secularity."[28] Bonhoeffer was aware that interpreting Luther in this way and invoking the example of Jesus Christ in "opposing the secular" could bring the wrath of the Nazi empire on the person of faith. The "cost" of Christian discipleship in Bonhoeffer's spirituality soon became the "cup of suffering" and even an inglorious death in one of those twentieth-century Golgothas, the Nazi extermination camps.

Throughout his life Bonhoeffer urged the churches to live up to their social responsibilities, to care for the poor, to take risks for the cause of peace, to live daily the Sermon on the Mount, to profess solidarity with the Jews, and even to confront malice in government head-on. His was a spirituality immersed in acts of responsibility and sustained by an intense respect for God's Word. The Spirit's powerful presence in the prayers and community life were his sustenance. Passages stand out again and again in Bonhoeffer's collected writings in which he reminds the churches in many different ways of what he had advanced in an early essay, that "God wants us to honor God on earth; God wants us to honor God in our fellow man and woman — and nowhere else."[29] The Hitler years were not the time for church leaders to assess the political advantages and disadvantages of resistance to systemic evil in government. For Bonhoeffer, genuine Christian spirituality and moral leadership demand that one accept the call to follow Christ in full awareness of the dangerous consequences so graphically depicted in the crucifixion. Christian discipleship was never for him the easy path reached only after endless calculation of the personal or social advantages of being Christian in a troubled time. Without any doubt, to be led by Christ's Spirit into modern-day deserts or into cities where the enemies of Christ lurked was risky. But the command of Jesus Christ to follow him was as clear as the gospel story of Jesus going up to Jerusalem to confront the religious and political leadership knowing full well the dangers faced by those who speak the word of God to the powerful of this earth. As he put it in *Discipleship*, "whenever Christ calls us, his call leads us to death."[30]

In retrospect, Bonhoeffer's dream of a renewed, Christ-orientated church may have been too upsetting and too demanding for the churches and their bourgeois parishioners. Bonhoeffer himself took the Sermon on the Mount seriously. He also wanted to hold the churches to their claims that they were an *alter Christus* to the world. In this lay both his disappointment and his hope. While in prison he longed for the rebirth of Christianity in nations where the gospel's mandate of love for all people had been thwarted. He had come to the sobering conclusion, as we saw in his baptismal sermon from prison, that the church had been largely fighting only for its own survival, as though that were its sole purpose. Such priorities rendered the church almost incapable of proclaiming the Word of God with any compelling conviction to an unbelieving world.

CHAPTER THREE

The Holy Spirit and Christian Discipleship

The Prophetic Dimension of Moral Leadership

> The Holy Spirit and not some human rationality is the church's teacher. . . . The Holy Spirit is the living God, not some inert concept. The church community has to trust the Holy Spirit in every decision and believe strongly that the Spirit continues to be present in the community and at work in it. The Spirit will not permit our community to grope about in darkness, if only we are willing to take the Spirit's teachings seriously. But every lesson of the Holy Spirit remains conjoined to the words of Jesus.
>
> *From Bonhoeffer's sermon for Whitsunday, 1940*[1]

At the Eighth International Bonhoeffer Congress in August 2000, we were surprised to find that several of the participants had little idea there were so many references to the Holy Spirit in Bonhoeffer's writings. These were not beginners in Bonhoeffer studies but scholars who, for the most part, had spent considerable time researching Bonhoeffer's theology. Their astonishment is understandable; Bonhoeffer's theology is so Christocentric that it is easy to ignore or skip over the many passages in which Bonhoeffer connects his admiration for and relationship with Jesus Christ to the empowerment he experienced through the Holy Spirit. We noted in our presentation, however, that even when there is no explicit mention of the Holy Spirit in Bonhoeffer's texts, there is the tacit understanding that God is present in a trinitarian outreach in which Father,

Son, and Spirit act as one. A study of Bonhoeffer's spirituality leads directly to his acknowledgements of the ways in which God's Holy Spirit opened his mind and heart to the paths of life along which he was led. What happened to Bonhoeffer is not all that different from the fate of the prophets in crisis moments of any historical period. At issue here is the manner in which the Holy Spirit raises up prophetic figures as moral leaders.

Bonhoeffer does not often use the word "prophecy." Nor does he speak directly at any length of the prophetic vocation of the Christian church community. Yet the Pauline pneumatological imagery that he uses connects the Spirit's gift of freedom from law, sin, death, and secular idolatries with the prophetic vocation to speak with outrage against those secular powers that have oppressed those most vulnerable. Essentially, when Bonhoeffer urged his church to take a practical stand against Nazism he became indirectly an advocate of the radical prophetic vocation of the Christian church. The Spirit's gift of prophecy is an endowment of freedom enabling community leaders and individual Christians to proclaim God's word against evil entrenched in systems masquerading as utopist visions of prosperity. Most Germans hailed the promises of Adolf Hitler as the beginning of a new millennium of unparalleled Germanic achievement. But Bonhoeffer believed that if a church claims to honor Jesus Christ and the Holy Spirit yet fails to speak up for the oppressed, it ceases to follow Jesus. In the traditional biblical depiction of prophecy it is the role of the prophet to speak truth on behalf of the exploited poor against the affluent and the politically powerful.

Our contention is that the Spirit of God touches people of faith like Bonhoeffer to sting the conscience of religious and secular authorities with judgments that are, like the cutting edges of God's prophetic word, encouraging, reproving, warning, and when necessary condemning the rampant infidelity and mean-spiritedness toward the poor that are a betrayal of God's covenant. In the case of the gospel mandate to learn of Jesus Christ, those actions that constitute an explicit or implicit repudiation of Jesus Christ run parallel to what aroused the prophets of old to convey God's anger to a faithless people. One pays homage to the Spirit of truth by speaking truth to political and religious falsehood. One honors the Spirit of love by acts of compassion on behalf of those whom the agents of falsehood hate and oppress.

Without alluding specifically to the prophetic dimension of being the church, Bonhoeffer was incessant in his badgering the church to speak up and act in the manner of Jesus, who was fearless in defending the poor and outcasts of Israel. The silence of the churches while evil was being done, at times even in Christ's name and under the banner of a twisted cross, was particularly vexatious to Bonhoeffer. At one time he reproved the church for its self-serving evasions in not rejecting the oath of allegiance required of all German clergy. Bonhoeffer saw the synodal decision to leave this oath to the individual conscience as avoiding taking a decisive stand against the attempt to infuse Nazi ideology into the ordained ministry. He asked, "Will Confessing Synods learn that it is important to counsel in the peace and patience commanded and to decide in defiance of all dangers and difficulties? Will they ever learn that majority decision in matters of conscience kills the Spirit?"[2]

It is evident from Bonhoeffer's life and spirituality that, guided by this Holy Spirit, he had strong convictions about what was, indeed, the proper way of living one's faith and exercising moral leadership. He had an equally strong detestation of other, less truthful, even pernicious modes of being "Christian" that he considered to be deviation from faith in Jesus Christ. He was moved to anger at what he detected as a distortion of the Word of God by so many church leaders and their clergy. He rejected self-serving compromises and deceitful accommodations to the regnant political ideology. He was outspoken in a way that was considered by many to be unreasonable, over-demanding, stubborn, and offensive. He was unwilling to strike compromises with churches that had adopted the Nazi line. One has only to read the lamentations of Jeremiah to see in Bonhoeffer's complaints an echo of the prophet's frustration that few were listening and too many had rejected God's judgment against a sinful people. This is a frustration that many Christians today experience when their church leaders seem unresponsive to their needs for protection from ruthless politicians and greedy corporate policymakers.

The issues that Bonhoeffer addressed were controversial: peace, poverty, the idolatry of national security, the Jewish Question, the struggle against the heretical Reich Church, the denunciation of government malevolence, the overthrow of that government, the no-compromise demands of the Sermon on the Mount, the reform of the church, and no-excuses obedience to the teachings of Jesus Christ. Strong stands on these issues could be risky under a government whose *modus covivendi* was uniformity through coercion and hasty, barbaric punishment of every deviation from its dictates. Each issue in turn required the kind of spiritual discernment in which Bonhoeffer placed himself in the power of God's Word to be decisive through the movement of the Holy Spirit. In many respects his life became an unending effort to convince others, particularly those who were called to be the moral leaders of the community, to do the same. For this purpose he attempted to derive a spiritual, pastoral meaning from the scriptural word, an approach more dependent on faith in the teaching power of the Holy Spirit than in the less soul-nurturing rules of historical criticism. This mode of reading and interpreting the Bible would never cease to captivate him.

Beginnings: A Spirit-Inspired Interpretation of the Scriptures

Bonhoeffer's earliest foray into this innovative interpretation of the Scriptures, a student essay on their spiritual interpretation, would unnerve his mentors at Berlin University, suspicious as they were of Karl Barth's pungent challenge to the liberal theology for which Berlin was noted. While the language of Bonhoeffer's essay is not consonant with the typical style of exegesis throughout most of Germany, the idea of separating the scientific exegesis in vogue at Berlin University from a more spiritual, pastoral interpretation was attractive to Bonhoeffer as early as 1925. The title of his paper was "Can a Distinction Be Drawn between a Historical and a Pneumatological Interpretation of the Scriptures, and How Does Dogmatic Theology Regard This?" The title suggests that the controlling differential between the two modes of interpretation in Bonhoeffer's mind is pneumatological, or the meaning-for-life implanted by the Holy Spirit both in the text (even if that meaning was not the primary intent of the writer) and in the mind of the believer. The historical approach that searches out the most accurate text as well as the original intention of the writer appears to be secondary in importance in Bonhoeffer's analysis. The study was turned in on July 31, 1925. It was not well received by his mentor, Reinhold Seeberg, who had sniffed out the Barthian influence and assigned the paper only the mediocre grade of "satisfactory."

The opening words of Bonhoeffer's essay expose his problematic. Does one read the Scriptures in a purely scientific mode or in a spirit of prayer and faith with the mind opened to what God, and not the skilled scientific exegetes, may be saying? "The Christian religion," he wrote, "stands or falls by belief in the divine revelation that became historically real, tangible and visible — that is, to those who have eyes to see and ears to hear — and thus in its very essence contains the question that we ask ourselves today about the relationship between history and spirit, or applied to the Bible, between letter and spirit, scripture and revelation, man's word and

God's."[3] By this time Bonhoeffer was already captivated by the exciting new theology of Karl Barth, leaving him disgruntled with the textual criticism of his mentors, Adolf von Harnack and Karl Holl. Bonhoeffer had acquired enough expertise in textual criticism to satisfy his mentors, but they were not friendly to Barth's mode of searching the Scriptures with what they saw as an a priori pastoral bias. For someone like Reinhold Seeberg, the teacher for whom Bonhoeffer wrote this paper, the essay appeared to be open rebelliousness on the part of the university's most promising young student, now in danger of being "seduced" by Barthianism. Bonhoeffer countered his critics with the assertion that the textual criticism then in vogue left only "rubble and fragments."[4] He now felt that historical criticism had failed to appreciate the biblical sources as agents of revelation and sacred canon, not to be handled merely as a literature, picked apart and finely honed for textual accuracy.

Bonhoeffer did not repudiate the historical-critical method — in fact, he insisted it was still necessary. He thought, however, that the scientific approach had to give way to the pneumatological, which inevitably became "prayer, . . . *supplication to the Holy Spirit* which alone, as it pleases, gives it the hearing and understanding *without which the most highly intellectual exegesis* is nothing. Textual understanding and interpretation, preaching, that is the realization of God, is contained in the prayer: *Veni creator spiritus* [Come, creator spirit]."[5] Bonhoeffer seemed to be struggling at this time between the lure of academe and his personal attraction to the Word in which God is made known through the enlightening inspiration of the Holy Spirit. The historians at the university would surely not be comfortable with Bonhoeffer's acerbic judgment on their efforts at textual accuracy: "For history, scripture is only a source; for pneumatology, it is testimony."[6] Later, a more mature Bonhoeffer would again turn his attention to the interpretation of the Christian Scriptures during the more crisis-conditioned period of the church struggle and against the misuse of the Bible by the heretical Reich Church. By that time Bonhoeffer would also be heavily involved in the training of seminarians for a pastoral mission in opposition to the churches infected with Nazi ideology.[7]

The Holy Spirit in the Berlin
Dissertations and Early Writings

To judge from his essay promoting a spiritual interpretation of the Scriptures, as well as letters he wrote that speak of his change of heart toward

academe, one might suspect that Bonhoeffer had become openly diffident of the intellectual side of doing theology. His Christology lectures
would further show a teacher anxious to move away from the more
philosophical-theological issues of conciliar Christology into the existential, pastoral question of where this Jesus was to be found in 1933 German
society. And, despite the compelling theological-philosophical insights incorporated into his two Berlin dissertations, Bonhoeffer seemed supremely uninterested in contributing to their publicity. Neither book sold
well during his lifetime. Bonhoeffer had moved on to more pressing, practical concerns related to the church struggle.

Yet Bonhoeffer's doctoral study of the sociality of Jesus Christ become
unending reality through human believers brought together in Christian
church communities does connect the giftedness of individual believers
with the emergence of faith communities through the mysterious, tran-
scendent bonding force of the Holy Spirit. The Spirit creates the communion of individual believers with God and with each other. Bonhoeffer
does not aver that this force is palpable enough to be empirically evident.
Yet for Bonhoeffer the confession that God's Spirit makes possible the
birth, growth, and enhancement of individuals and their church communities is a matter of undeniable truth. His pneumatological claims are far
ranging. They are the outgrowth of his reflections on the direct act
whereby God's Spirit accomplishes the astounding transformation of ordinary people into determined, even heroic believers. To say that the
church community exists in the power of the Holy Spirit is more than a
lifeless line from a creedal litany. Every church community in Christianity
today claims its foundational bondedness to the Holy Spirit. What that
means in the practical living out of gospel mandates is the question that
Bonhoeffer continued to address in the crisis years of Hitler's tightened
control over the German nation.

The two converging dynamics Bonhoeffer isolates as his study of the
church community unfolds are the deepened relationships between individual believers and the building up of a community that both represents
Jesus Christ to the world and through its actions demonstrates that God
in Jesus Christ is confessed, worshipped, and obeyed. To have the kind of
social relationships in which genuine human personhood can grow calls
for a willingness to accept the gift of God's pulling individuals out of
their innate self-centeredness to a sense of their being for and belonging
to others. The unique personal dignity of every individual has to be affirmed, enveloped in the confession that each person is an image of God,
a brother or sister of Jesus Christ and of all those claiming to be Christian.

Other persons are never to be looked on as things to be disdained or manipulated. It is in the powerful grip of God's Holy Spirit that the absurdity of assuming responsibility for others is overcome.[8]

The Holy Spirit, Bonhoeffer says categorically, "establishes community and is presumably also the spirit of unity."[9] God, now revealed as Holy Spirit, is the gathering force of those who have become the church community. This same Spirit is the cohesive web that supports the unity of Christians despite the disparate personalities that compose an "actualized church." Bonhoeffer eschews the idealization of the church community and rejects it as a vaporization of reality or a wishful utopian dream. This community exists in historical concreteness and not merely as some future possibility of a "perfect" church. Bonhoeffer argues that the church community is actualized by the Holy Spirit as "the reality of revelation in Christ."[10] Nor is this reality established when the church "assumes empirical form, when the Holy Spirit does God's work." The reality of this "church of the Holy Spirit" is at bottom "a revelational reality" to be believed as such.

What the Spirit is accomplishing in individuals can never be isolated from the church community of the here and now. Bonhoeffer's argument on this point is circular; his distinctions, finely drawn. The Spirit's work and the reality of Jesus Christ existing in the church community are in their essence divine revelation. Its counterpart is the confession of faith in what God is making known in and through the church community on this less-than-perfect earth. For Bonhoeffer, the Spirit exists "only in the church community; and the church community exists only in the Spirit."[11] In the church, as in individuals, the Holy Spirit's presence is accommodated to the flawed reality. The role of church leaders in this perspective is not to preside over cadaverous dogmatic formulae, nor is it to hold out to a hurting congregation the promise of an abstract, idealized future life in a sorrow-free heaven. Moral leadership in the church community must deal with every present reality in which God's communion with humanity is denied in the denial of compassion and help to those who have become the least of God's children. One honors the Holy Spirit in the church community only in honoring the needs of God's people.

Bonhoeffer traces that distinction between the empirical church, in which all the dynamics of social relations are operative, and the church community, actualized in the Holy Spirit, to the founding of the church at Pentecost. "The church," he claims, "originates only with the outpouring of the Holy Spirit, and so too the Holy Spirit is the spirit of the church community of Christ."[12] In his lectures on "The Essence of the

Church," Bonhoeffer distinguishes between the work of the Spirit and the deeds of Jesus with the simple assertion that "The Holy Spirit actualizes what has been accomplished in and through Christ." In this perspective, the resurrection becomes present in the history of believers through the Holy Spirit, who is the empowering force in the later preaching and extension of what has already been brought into being by Jesus Christ.[13]

The distinction is crucial for Bonhoeffer in order to avoid the ambiguity attached to the assertion that none other than Jesus Christ himself founded the church. Bonhoeffer is aware of the pathologies that can ensue when arrogant and even idolatrous sacralizations of what is human take place, such as one can detect in the corruption in pre-Reformation Christendom or when religion is hijacked by fundamentalism. Over the centuries the religious trappings of churches and facile invocations of Jesus' approval of less-than-Christian actions have been used to cover up ecclesiastical abuses of God's Word and Jesus' name. Such abuse is weighty evidence that the church in question has ceased to be a prayerful listener to what God is saying through Jesus Christ. It is the Holy Spirit, speaking through the scriptural word, who becomes the judge of fidelity or infidelity within the community that is supposed to listen to and prayerfully proclaim that word in all its demands on Christian faith.

What makes possible the actualization or palpable reality of God's presence through Christ's word in the church community is, for Bonhoeffer, "the Spirit-impelled word of the crucified and risen Lord of the Church." In an unqualified overstatement he adds that, "the Spirit can work only through this word." Nonetheless, for Bonhoeffer, it is the word of Christ himself, brought into the heart of every believer, that engenders the astounding diversity of hearers of this word becoming one in Christ. Christ wins hearts by his Spirit and the church community comes into being as communion with God. The action of the Spirit, Bonhoeffer concludes, is simultaneous. The Spirit moves the believers who are themselves already in the church community in a communion of hearts pulsating in unison with the Spirit-filled word of Jesus Christ. "The church," he writes, "does not come into being by people coming together, rather its existence is sustained by the Spirit who is a reality within the church community."[14] He extrapolates from this affirmation of the Spirit's mission to the church community the conclusion that Christ and the Holy Spirit "are inseparably linked."[15] They are linked, moreover, in the spiritual life of the individual called by God into a communion of inexpressible intimacy. Leadership in the church community is unfaithful to the Spirit if this intimacy is not fostered in Word, sacrament, and action for justice.

The prime action of the Holy Spirit in Bonhoeffer's scenario of how God creates a Christian church community is ultimately the divine process of conveying "to human hearts God's love, which has been revealed in the cross and resurrection of Christ." Bonhoeffer makes the extraordinary confession of his conviction that the Holy Spirit brings people into community with God "by putting Christ in our hearts, creating faith and hope." This Spirit incites Christian love "as the love or the heart of Christ in us, . . . given to us as a new heart, as the will for good."[16] How the Spirit uses that "will for good" to impel the believer to make the right decisions and to engage in correct ways of acting in ethical murkiness will be examined below. What Bonhoeffer elaborates on in this early pneumatology is reinforced in *Life Together*. There he directs his seminarians to explore the manifold contours of the Christian love that alone can vivify the togetherness of the Christian church community. In that practical context Bonhoeffer contrasts spiritual love *(geistliche Liebe)* centered in Jesus Christ and self-serving, emotional, manipulative love *(seelische Liebe)* as prelude to his placing love in the context of each member's service to the others. In this section of his study Bonhoeffer praises Augustine for his helpful portrayal of the community of saints, "the core of the church, as the community of loving persons who, touched by God's Spirit, radiate love and grace."[17]

One notable offshoot of this Spirit-driven core of concern for others within the Christian community is the gift of love in which one surrenders one's self for others for the sake of Jesus Christ. Nowhere does Bonhoeffer depict this gift of the Spirit more graphically than in his appropriation of the Lutheran understanding of how the holy sacrament can affect the love Christians are to have for one another. Bonhoeffer calls this being "in the power of Christ and the Holy Spirit." He proclaims that "whoever lives in love is Christ in relation to the neighbor." He then paraphrases Luther, who declared that "we are God through the love that makes us charitable toward our neighbor." Ever practical, Bonhoeffer adds the note that in a community, patience and forbearing are essential virtues if peace is to be sustained: "Christians can and ought to act like Christ; they ought to bear the burdens and sufferings of the neighbor."[18] Forgiveness of petty grievances and of one another's sins is, for Bonhoeffer, a vital part of Christian life together in Jesus' name. In his opinion, Christian faith without a spirit of forgiveness is bereft of the Spirit of Jesus Christ.

Bonhoeffer continues in the same vein to designate the mutual love generated by the Holy Spirit as the primary bond that marks church communities bearing their pledge to follow Jesus Christ. While God's gift of faith is the ground of Christian community life, love for others, he insists, is its very soul. Bonhoeffer addresses this distinction in his analysis of the church community's need to radiate unity of spirit. It would be a deception for such a community merely to exhibit unanimity, uniformity, or a fluffy congeniality — qualities often held up for admiration as outward signs of a successful community — rather than their common bonding in the one Lord and the one Spirit. "The Christian church," he writes, "is usually called a community of faith. Sociologically, this is at least an abbreviated way of saying it. The Christian community rests solely on the fact of faith, i.e., the acceptance of God's Spirit, source of Christian faith in the service of love. Considered as a concrete community, however, it is not a community of faith, but rather a community of love and of spirit. . . . Faith is acceptance of God's sovereign will, submission to the divine truth. Love is the application, effected by the Spirit, of this faith." He ends by reminding readers not to forget Augustine's teaching that "caritas [love] is the *bond* of the unity of the church."[19] Later, in drawing distinctions between this church community whose core is the Holy Spirit and associations of kindred spirits or associations of force dominated by authoritarian structures [*Herrschaftsverband*], Bonhoeffer concludes that the acts of love which the Holy Spirit brings about are "the very heart of community of spirit." Those so touched by this Spirit organize their relations to others "with a single end in mind, namely to fulfill God's will by loving the other."[20]

Bonhoeffer is also aware of the ethical potholes that can open up when the Holy Spirit is so identified with the church community. It has happened in times past that the Spirit has become a cover for the sin and imperfections of these church communities, however touched they may be by the divine presence. Human sinfulness is the everyday reality of the Christian; Christ entered into a sinful world. While the church is "Christ existing as church community," to reiterate Bonhoeffer's now celebrated phrase, nonetheless, the church always exists in its empirical form as a concretion of Christ present in history. As historical and empirical, the church is, like its individual believers and leaders, *"simul iustus et peccator,"* paradoxically a community of sinners and a community of saints. Lutheran Bonhoeffer is well aware of the possibility that any church community's "objective spirit" could contain elements that risk becoming a corrosive repudiation of the gospel and a breeding ground for the estrangement and indifference to others that the Holy Spirit must overcome. Bonhoeffer sees this aspect of the Spirit's mission to the community as that of moving believers in their sinful state to see others "as love, as Christ."[21] The church is composed of people who are varied, flawed, broken, and fickle. These are the untoward strains against which the Holy Spirit struggles in order to heal the sinful brokenness of the community and to renew the community's allegiance to Jesus Christ.

The implications of this distinction for preaching the Word within the community are enormous. Here too the action of the Holy Spirit can transcend the human sinfulness of the preacher. The Holy Spirit uses humans as instruments in extending the preached Word into the hearts of the church community, and in that mysterious reciprocation described by Paul in Romans, elicits the response in faith of the believer touched by the Word, which the Spirit has vivified and made meaningful.

Bonhoeffer returned to this metaphor of the Spirit of God touching the hearts of the faithful in and through the church community in his first London sermon and later in his second draft of a catechetical preparation for Confirmation. In the London sermon, based on 2 Cor. 5:20, Bonhoeffer speaks of the role of the Holy Spirit in the interpretation of the sacred scriptures: "When the sacred scriptures are interpreted in a church, the Holy Spirit comes down from its throne *into our hearts,* while the busy world outside sees nothing of this; nor does it know that here is where none other than God is to be found."[22] In the simple language of the catechism Bonhoeffer writes, "the Holy Spirit bestows on me forgiveness of all my sins. The Holy Spirit teaches me to detest sin with all my heart. The Holy Spirit *makes my heart willing to obey* and leads me through death into everlasting life."[23] Bonhoeffer's pneumatology appears to draw heavily from this metaphor: the Spirit touches the hearts of the faithful, wins over hearts that otherwise are closed to God's Spirit, and moves Christians to heartfelt compassion for those who become Christ in the neediest of God's children.

There are many passages in Bonhoeffer's writings where it is difficult to distinguish between the role of Jesus Christ and the role of the Holy Spirit. The two are one God, to be sure; they act together in creating and sustaining the Christian church community. While developing his understanding of the church as "Christ existing in the church community," brought into being by the Holy Spirit at Pentecost and in every succeeding age, Bonhoeffer tries at several junctures to lean toward either Christ or the Holy Spirit in his acknowledgements of who does what in order to maintain the orthodox distinction of persons and the theological certification of the "ad extra" functions within the Trinity. In the matter of the church community, Bonhoeffer tends to blur the distinctions between the role of the risen Jesus and the work of the Spirit.[24] In one lengthy footnote he plays on the Pauline image of Christ the head who governs the *body* of the church community, which the Holy Spirit makes possible by leading individuals to Christ and bringing Christ to individuals. He notes the identification between Jesus Christ and the church community. Yet he also sees the ensuing reality as the creation of the Holy Spirit, whose mission is to gather the faithful and unify them through Word and sacrament and all those acts in which it can authentically be said that "the church is the presence of Christ in the same way that Christ is the presence of God."[25] In the "Catechism" of 1931 that Bonhoeffer and Franz Hildebrandt composed for his Confirmation class, we read the following in their answer to the question: Who is the Holy Spirit? "No spirit of the world, but the Spirit of God and Christ, who is present in the church. Without the Spirit we would know nothing of Christ, just as without Christ we would know nothing of God."[26] For all of Bonhoeffer's sound theological maneuvering, however, the distinctions between Christ and Spirit that he puts forward seem arbitrary.

This ambiguity is, however, shared within the Christian Scriptures themselves. Except as attested in John's Gospel, Jesus' preaching made little mention of the Spirit, though both Matthew and Luke are clear that Jesus was a Spirit-filled prophetic preacher of God's kingdom, who entered into the lives of his followers and through them became known to the wider world itself.

The doctrine of the Holy Spirit seems itself to have emerged in the context of the apostolic experience of Jesus' resurrection appearances. When Jesus was not physically present as during his pre-Calvary ministry, the Spirit of Jesus continued to be evoked and honored. Jesus had never left them. That was the meaning of that poignant phrase in John's Gospel: "If I do not go away, you will not receive the Comforter . . . the Spirit of truth [who] will guide you into all truth" (John 16:7, 13). The "truth" was that Jesus would always be among them, but from that time on his presence would be enveloped into the church community. Phrases abound in which the Spirit of God is the Spirit of Christ. By reason of its unique relationship with the risen Christ, the early Christian community became the locus where the Spirit's activity became evident and acknowledged in subsequent gatherings of Jesus' followers.

The Pauline metaphoric interplay is also intriguing, culminating in the memorable phrase in 1 Corinthians that, by his resurrection, Jesus had become "a life-giving spirit" (1 Cor. 15:45). Paul speaks of the "Spirit of Christ" in his letter to the Romans: "Anyone who does not have the Spirit of Christ does not belong to him" (Rom. 8:9). He likewise writes of "the Spirit of [God's] own son" whom the Father sends into the hearts of the faithful (Gal. 4:6), and "the Spirit of Jesus Christ" whose help together with the prayers of the believers in Philippi will lead to his deliverance (Phil. 1:19). No one utterance of Paul, however, is so explicit in identifying Jesus and Spirit as his extolling of the freedom of the Christian in 2 Cor. 3:17-18: "Now the Lord is the Spirit, and where the Spirit of the Lord is, there is freedom. And all of us, with unveiled faces, seeing the glory of the Lord as though reflected in a mirror, are being transformed into the same image from one degree of glory to another; for this comes from the Lord, the Spirit." In John's Gospel, the Holy Spirit as Paraclete is "the personal presence of Jesus in the Christian while Jesus is with the Father" or the presence of Jesus where Jesus is not empirically present.[27] All of these citations point up the inevitable ambiguity in differentiating the functional roles of Jesus, the Spirit of Jesus, and the Holy Spirit in ascribing the effects of God's actions and presence among Christians in the Christian church community.

However this might be, what takes place spiritually in those who belong to the church community as well as their actions on behalf of others constitute the only credible evidence that God's Holy Spirit is bestowing and enhancing their personal faith and Christ-centered relationships. Bonhoeffer traces even the act of believing to that reciprocal interplay of God as the subject of all revelational cognition and the human ability to say "I believe" and "I will obey." As the subject of all revelation God speaks to the Spirit within, so that the ensuing knowledge of God's ways "is called 'believing,' what is revealed is called Christ, and the subject of understanding is God as Holy Spirit." It is in the act of believing, he says, that "the Holy Spirit attests itself."[28] This is a claim that totally eludes empirical certification. It is God as Holy Spirit who arouses and sustains the gift of faith in believers gathered to become a church community. Faith in all its giftedness and process is, as Bonhoeffer insists, a direct act, given independent of any theological correctness or control. In this divine action the Spirit moves the believer through Word and sacrament toward Christ and facilitates the commitment to follow Christ in the way of the gospel and along the way to the cross. The act of reflection that takes place at a secondary level, in which faith seeks to understand theologically what has happened, can never substitute for the Holy Spirit's ineffable impact on the members of the church community.

In turn, Jesus makes possible a newness of being "by being the one who creates within me the act of faith by granting me the Holy Spirit who hears and believes within me, [and] thereby proves to be also the free lord of my existence."[29] The stilted phraseology here is deliberately close to Paul's famous exclamation of the Spirit's role in Christian prayer: "Likewise the Spirit helps us in our weakness; for we do not know how to pray as we ought, but that very Spirit intercedes with sighs too deep for words. And God, who searches the heart, knows what is the mind of the Spirit, because the Spirit intercedes for the saints according to the will of God" (Rom. 8:26-27). Christian prayer thus unfolds into the prayer of Christ in the prayer of the Holy Spirit.

In his meditation on Psalm 119, written during the first winter of the war years, Bonhoeffer depicts the role of the Holy Spirit in prayer as twofold. He points out that not only does the Holy Spirit speak in believers "in a totally new and different way," but the Holy Spirit also "makes true for me what was only true for Jesus Christ," namely, the conforming of our human will to God's will. The prayer that one be not forsaken does not beg the question of God's ever abandoning the believer. Rather, it is the cry of one whose faith is being tested. All the while the Holy Spirit through Word and sacrament creates the renewal, freedom, and strength to keep God's commands no matter what the misfortune or misery.[30] The implications of this for Christian spirituality and moral leadership are far reaching.

One unmistakable effect of this power of the Holy Spirit is the gift of freedom that comes when one gives oneself totally to the following of Jesus Christ. As Bonhoeffer points out in his lectures on "Creation and Fall," it is erroneous to say that God in some deistic whim decided merely to launch creation on its way, unattended by any subsequent divine intervention and protection; God also gives us freedom. To believe that humankind, unlike any other creatures, is fashioned in the very image of God is to proclaim that the freedom of the creator must be reflected in the freedom of human beings in whom the Trinity dwells. For Bonhoeffer this "divine indwelling" is not a mere metaphor. In sentences of uncommon insight, extrapolated from the Pauline passage cited above, he writes, "In the free creature the Holy Spirit worships the Creator; uncreated freedom glorifies itself in view of created freedom. The creature loves the Creator, because the Creator loves the creature."[31] This "created freedom" he goes on to attribute to the abiding presence of God as Holy Spirit within the human spirit. It "is freedom in the Holy Spirit, but as created freedom it is *humankind's* own freedom," through the continued and sustained outpouring of the mercy of God. How God's creating freedom within the believer expresses itself is Bonhoeffer's question. He replies in words that define the core of Christian togetherness in community. "The creature is free," he says, "in that one creature exists in relation to another creature, in that one human being is free for another human being."[32] Bonhoeffer insists in these same remarks that freedom must be defined in terms of how human beings exist in interrelationship with one another. Moral leadership has to be expressed in compassionate, sensitive service of others, particularly those unable to help themselves, or it is estranged from Christ and his church.

This, in turn, becomes his opening to contend that all language about God can only be by an analogy of relationship, because God, who can be entirely self-sufficient, chooses instead to exist for the creature and to be known only through the relationships established with creation, highlighted by God's own word in Jesus Christ. Language about God is necessarily language about faith within the church community. God's freedom has been forever bonded to humankind. Bonhoeffer concludes in his lectures on "Creation and Fall" that "God is the one who in Christ attests to God's 'being for humankind.'"[33] His words here echo his earlier description of God's mysterious freedom in *Act and Being*. There he argues emphatically that the strongest evidence of the nature of God's own freedom lies "in that God freely chose to be bound to historical human beings and to be placed at the disposal of human beings. God is free not from human beings but for them. Christ is the word of God's freedom."[34] How that became acted out in Bonhoeffer's fearless — his enemies might say "rash" — outspokenness and courageous actions is the story of what Bonhoeffer described, in a poem from Tegel Prison, as the path to freedom eternal.[35]

Bonhoeffer's earliest pneumatology did not change drastically in the years that followed. Bonhoeffer never ceased to attribute the continued presence of Jesus Christ in the church community to the life-giving power of the Holy Spirit. At times he did not distinguish between the work of Jesus' post-resurrection presence as church and the extraordinary mission of the Holy Spirit, without which there would be neither church community nor any possibility that Jesus' words, teachings, and personal presence would ever reach his followers. It is the Holy Spirit that emanates from the one God, Father creator and Word become flesh, in God's trinitarian outreach to hearts and minds in God's gift of faith. Bonhoeffer connects this Holy Spirit of God with the Pentecostal impetus that began the church and turned quite ordinary, inept disciples of Christ into determined doers of God's Word, servants and lovers of all peoples — including their avowed enemies and willing executioners. The Holy Spirit of God symbolizes in Bonhoeffer's pneumatology the complex dynamics of

God's grace justifying sinful human beings and sanctifying them in the church community. Bonhoeffer's claim that Jesus Christ exists as the church community in and through the power of the Holy Spirit does not yield to empirical analysis in terms of its material tangibility. Any evidence is a derivative of the way Christians act toward one another and toward those not belonging to the church community. Christian behavior alone becomes the most convincing attestation of Christ's followers' true transformation.

In his sermon for Pentecost 1940, when Germany was already at war, Bonhoeffer declared categorically that "Jesus' coming in the flesh was for the world, while his coming in Spirit is for those who love him." Pentecost was not for him a one-time occurrence. Indeed, he insisted that "even today Pentecost exists in all places where the love of Jesus is found."[36]

In his earlier pneumatology and his later theology, three aspects of Bonhoeffer's belief in the Holy Spirit remain constant. The first is that every referent is always to Jesus in his human ministry as a man in whom the Spirit of God dwells in its fullness. Secondly, the Holy Spirit brings about a freedom for Christians to overcome their sinful turning in on themselves in order to live for others and to proclaim the Word of God, even when it could lead to persecution. Thirdly, the Holy Spirit is the life-giving soul of the Christian church community, transforming disparate individuals into a community united in one mind and one spirit, all bringing their special gifts to each other in their evangelizing mission to the wider world. We turn now to Bonhoeffer's spiritual classic, *Discipleship*, to examine the way he incorporated his doctrine of the Holy Spirit into a book written in the context of the church struggle and his training of seminarians for a subversive ministry within Nazi Germany.

Following after Jesus: Christian Discipleship in the Holy Spirit

As we will see in detail in Chapter Six, Bonhoeffer's spiritual classic *Discipleship* is from beginning to end a lucid explanation of and an impassioned exhortation to follow Jesus Christ, guided by Jesus' own teachings and empowered by the Holy Spirit's call to genuine faith. Throughout the pages of *Discipleship* we see a vivid challenge to Christians to take seriously their profession to follow Jesus Christ. Bonhoeffer asks what such a profession means in a nation racked with idolatrous attachments to a way of life that either explicitly or implicitly denies Christ. Readers of this book encounter the powerful words of Jesus himself in his Sermon on the Mount. They are asked to pit the teachings of Jesus and Paul against the materialism, militarism, and ruthless denial of human dignity in a country bent on domination and the extermination of those deemed inferior. Bonhoeffer reminds Christians of the nature of the church community in which faith in Christ is proclaimed from pulpits but denied in practice. The book is a study in the nature of Christian discipleship and the power of the Holy Spirit, through the biblical word, to inspire believers to be willing to follow Jesus even to political reprobation and death. It also acknowledges the work of the Holy Spirit to elicit Christian action on behalf of the downtrodden and the victims that define the truth or falsity of professed discipleship.

Bonhoeffer makes a direct connection between his insistence on doing what Christian faith demands (orthopraxis) and professing that faith with creedal accuracy (orthodoxy) within the church community. The fidelity to Jesus, made possible by the presence and guidance of the Holy Spirit within the community, is much more than purity of orthodoxy. Bonhoeffer builds his argument on Paul's exclamation of 1 Cor. 12:3: "no one can say 'Jesus is Lord' except by the Holy Spirit." He pairs this tribute to the Holy Spirit with the warning in Matthew's Gospel that "not everyone who says to me, 'Lord, Lord,' will enter the kingdom of heaven, but only the one who does the will of my Father in heaven" (7:21). Bonhoeffer notes the orthodox naming of Jesus as Lord holds little weight with Jesus. Claims that honoring Jesus with titles is the prime requisite of belonging to the Christian community are based, according to Bonhoeffer, only on a skewed sense of self-righteousness. People who limit their faith to such acclamations are, he says, "without love, without Christ, without the Holy Spirit."[37] They are guilty of a fundamental infidelity to the guidance of the Holy Spirit, who brings to life the gospel teachings that are to guide the church community to action for others in Jesus Christ.

The same line of thought came out even more forcefully in Bonhoeffer's sermon on the German Memorial Day in 1935. There, basing his remarks on Rev. 14:6-13, and speaking of death and God's judgment, he asked his seminarians what God would demand of them on the impending day of judgment. His rhetorical reply: "At the judgment, God will ask us solely about the everlasting gospel: Did you believe and obey the gospel? God won't ask whether we were Germans or Jews, whether we were Nazis or not, not even whether we belonged to the Confessing Church or not; nor whether we were great and influential and successful, nor whether we have a life's work to show for ourselves, nor whether we were honored by the world or unimportant and insignificant, unsuccessful and unappreciated. All persons shall be asked by God one day whether they could risk submitting to the test of the gospel. The gospel alone shall be our judge."[38] Given the political climate of 1935, Bonhoeffer's words were a bracing reminder to his seminarians of the need to preach the Word fearlessly in what he referred to as "the Babylon" of Nazi Germany. His words, too, are a statement that those called to exercise moral leadership in a troubled society are judged by their fidelity to the gospel and not by their self-aggrandizing political schemes.

The threat of arrest, interrogation, and imprisonment hung heavily on those seminarians. Knowing this, Bonhoeffer urged them in this sermon never to forget the promise of resurrection and the blessedness of martyrdom. "To die in Christ — that this be granted us, that our last hour not be a weak hour, that we die as confessors of Christ, whether old or young, whether quickly or after long suffering, whether seized and laid hold of by the lord of Babylon or quietly and gently — that is our prayer today, that our last word might only be: Christ."[39] The thought of such a death in consequence of one's fidelity to Jesus Christ is repeated in *Discipleship* in Bonhoeffer's stark phrase: "Whenever Christ calls us, his call leads us to death."[40] And if they were to be subjected to the brutal interrogations associated with arrest by the Gestapo, Bonhoeffer, citing Luke 21:15, reminded them of the presence of the Holy Spirit, who would "be with them at that time" and "make them indomitable," giving them "a wisdom that none of your opponents will be able to withstand or contradict."[41] By their fearless suffering, Bonhoeffer preached, they would witness to the gospel and, indeed, engage in a paradoxical form of evangelization.

The support they received from the Holy Spirit in standing firm in their commitment to follow Jesus even to the cross was augmented by their solidarity with those who share a common faith in the church community. Bonhoeffer's pneumatology in *Discipleship* retrieves his reflections on the Body of Christ of *Sanctorum Communio*. It is through the Holy Spirit, he writes, that "the crucified and risen Christ exists as the church community, as the 'new human being.'"[42] Here he adds the nuance that Christ's presence is his resurrection existence in the unparalleled newness the Pentecostal Spirit turns into a lived reality. The church, he says, is one, but that oneness is achieved out of a multiplicity of disparate believers shaped by the Holy Spirit into a community that serves all its members. Bonhoeffer specifies the work of the Holy Spirit in the creation of this oneness in a series of laudatory confessional affirmations. "It is the Holy Spirit who brings Christ to the individuals (Eph. 3:17; 1 Cor. 12:3). It is the

Spirit who builds up the church by gathering the individuals, even though in Christ the whole building is already complete (Eph. 2:22; 4:12; Col. 2:4). The Holy Spirit creates the community (2 Cor. 13:13) of the members of the body (Rom. 15:30; 5:5; Col. 1:8; Eph. 4:3)."

Once again Bonhoeffer fortuitously blurs the distinction between Christ and Spirit in his concluding statements: "The Lord is the Spirit (2 Cor. 3:17). The church of Christ is Christ present through the Holy Spirit. The life of the body of Christ has thus become our life. In Christ we no longer live our own lives, but Christ lives his life in us."[43] Bonhoeffer's identification of Christ with the Spirit is not accidental. Both represent the continuing mode of God's personal outreach to those who commit themselves to follow Jesus Christ. This is the work of God's powerful Spirit breathing new life into the hearts of the faithful; it is also the presence of Jesus Christ, the center of all history, the person whose presence is continually acknowledged through Word and sacrament.

Bonhoeffer ends his observations in *Discipleship* on the Body of Christ with two of his earlier metaphors, that of the church community as a spiritual temple and the human heart as the dwelling place of God's Holy Spirit. "Christ is the sole foundation and cornerstone of this temple (Eph. 2:20; 1 Cor. 3:11); at the same time he himself is the temple (Eph. 2:21) in whom the Holy Spirit dwells, filling and sanctifying the hearts of the believers (1 Cor. 3:16; 6:19)."[44] Here Bonhoeffer commingles the justification by faith alone that begins the process of sanctification with the holiness that becomes a human possibility through the trinitarian outreach to those gathered in the church community. It is not an exaggeration to claim that those called to Christian moral leadership are at the same time called to holiness of life nurtured in Jesus through the Spirit.

This "filling of the hearts" of the followers of Jesus Christ cuts to the primary mode of Christ's abiding presence in the church community. Bonhoeffer is emphatic that the same Word made flesh lives in the church community through the Holy Spirit: "But in and with this Word comes none other than the Holy Spirit, revealing to the individual and to the church community as a whole the gifts they have already been given in Jesus Christ. The Holy Spirit bestows faith on the hearers, enabling them to believe that, in the word of preaching, Jesus Christ himself has come to be present in our midst in the power of his body. The Holy Spirit likewise enables me to trust that Jesus Christ has come to tell me that he has accepted me and will continue to do so again today."[45] Bonhoeffer declares that the Spirit reveals to believers the wondrous presence of Christ in their midst. The Holy Spirit gives faith and enables believers to trust the astounding news that they are accepted and loved by Jesus Christ himself.

Even when Bonhoeffer addresses the more administrative structures of leadership through various offices within the community, it is again in submission to and under the guidance of the Holy Spirit. Though this "guidance" seems vague and may even be questioned by those who have chafed under a less than holy, less than competent, moral leadership in the church, the point Bonhoeffer wishes to make here is that every administrative office is solely for service. He concedes that the appointments are subject to the at times flawed judgment of the church community. Nonetheless the appointments, made for order and peace, have a connection to the Holy Spirit. "Therein," he says, "the Holy Spirit becomes visibly present by the fact that everything is done for the benefit of the church community."[46] In short, it is in the testing ground of altruistic service that the guidance of the Holy Spirit is actualized. Bonhoeffer's argument here is dependent on the understanding of "service" in a manner consonant with the gospel and not in the sense of exercising self-gratifying dominance over others.

Bonhoeffer is explicit in his relating Christian leadership to compassion and charity. The evidence of the Spirit's guidance is in the comportment of the community itself in all those areas of life that are to reflect the mode of Jesus' community with his original followers. The elements of Word, sacrament, worship, and material priorities have a place. "Here," Bonhoeffer writes, "a perfect community is *established freely, joyfully, and by the power of the Holy Spirit,* a community in which 'there was not a needy person,' in which possessions were distributed 'as any had need,' and in which 'no one claimed private ownership of any possessions.' The fact that this practice was commonplace reveals the community's complete freedom, a freedom grounded in the gospel, and which requires no coercion. They were indeed 'of one heart and soul.'"[47] This nostalgic portrait of the early church community, based on Acts 2 and 4, is not totally an exercise in idealism. Bonhoeffer was offering his seminarians and the readers of *Discipleship* a retrieval of their Christ-Spirit origins, the church community that sprang up under the fiery presence of God's Holy Spirit. In Jesus' resurrection the disciples had discovered anew the source of the peace that was his promised legacy as he prepared to leave them physically. The contrast with the Christian churches of the 1930s is obvious. The church communities in Nazi Germany had drifted far away from the spirit of that first community living in the conscious awareness of Jesus' resurrection and the Pentecostal continuation of Jesus' presence as the life-giving Spirit. Moral leadership under Hitler's dictatorship had drifted into unconscionable accommodation to the will of a merciless secular lord.

The question that emerges from Bonhoeffer's euphoric representation of the church community at its best is how God creates a "community of saints" out of the flawed grist of sinful human beings. Bonhoeffer's answer is, as expected, in the paradoxical life-giving death of Jesus enabling sinners to be released from their bondage to self-serving, willful sinfulness with its concomitant indifference to the least of Jesus' brothers and sisters. In the teachings of Jesus Christ, even sinners belong to God. Their growth in holiness, on the other hand, is "brought about by God the Holy Spirit and in it God's work finds its completion. . . . Just as before they had been held in bondage under the law as in a locked prison (Gal. 3:23), so now the believers are locked 'in Christ,' marked with God's own seal, the Holy Spirit."[48] The pledge for the preservation in faith and in community of those who follow Christ's way to his Father God, despite the hatred of ideologues and the destructive coercions of those in power — Bonhoeffer invokes the metaphor of Noah's Ark — is "none other than the Holy Spirit."[49] Bonhoeffer does not advocate here an insularity of non-involvement in the world in which his seminarians and fellow Christians exercise their ministry. The "seal" of the Holy Spirit is the Spirit-energized determination not to be absorbed into a world dominated by the anti-Christian forces that sadly had attracted masses of less-than-critical German citizens. It is also a "seal" of the unique Christ-like conduct that, as Bonhoeffer says, "is worthy of God's place of holiness." Finally, this is a sanctifying process that remains tacit or hidden; it is not to die the death of a holier-than-thou self-righteousness in which the so-called "virtue" of moral leaders is paraded before an admiring public.[50]

Bonhoeffer brings out another significant aspect of the Spirit's mission in this process: to fortify the faith of the believing Christian against the vices of the flesh that erode the human body, corrupt the will, and maliciously attack the Body of Christ. These reprehensible forces that can wither the resistance of believers are counterattacked in the church community by the transformation that takes place in the power of Christ's Spirit. He insists that it is under the sanctifying impulses of God's Spirit that the "fruits" of this Spirit — "'love, joy, peace, patience, kindness, generosity, faithfulness, gentleness, and self-control' (Gal. 5:22)" — become commonplace in the community.[51] Bonhoeffer is also quick to add that all this transformation in holiness occurs only as a tacit reality of which the person of faith is unaware. The Spirit of God works quietly to bring about Christians who, despite their past wandering away from the gospel,

are able to love even their enemies, to exercise patience in the midst of ordinary vexations, to respond with kindness and generosity to those in
need, and always to be gentle, not governed by the angry outbursts that
can hurt a community.

The ensuing transformation that takes place is the great accomplish-
ment of the Holy Spirit in God's great gift of the faith that saves. "The
only thing they are aware of," according to Bonhoeffer, "is the power of
Christ from whom they receive their life. There is no room for glory here,
but only the ever more intimate union with the source, with Christ."[52]
Even in death, as in their life, the followers of Jesus see strife, hardship,
weakness, and sin, to be sure, but "their whole life must now be an act of
faith in the son of God who has begun his own life in them (Gal. 2:20)."
Bonhoeffer reiterates his heartfelt conviction that the death of the saints,
whether placidly or through violence, is but a veiled glorification: "The
dying of the saints according to their flesh is grounded solely in the fact
that, through the Holy Spirit, Christ has begun his own life in them."[53]
His claim here applies whether it is that daily dying to self in which the
Spirit creates space for Jesus Christ or the death of the martyr.

The Spirit of God in the Church
Struggle and the War Years

During the turbulent debates and political upheavals that gnawed at
Christian faith during the Nazi dictatorship and the church struggle,
Bonhoeffer seemed to speak and act with an uncommon certitude that
the way he chose to follow was faithful to the guidance of the Holy Spirit
and the teachings of Jesus Christ. The issue for him was never to achieve
some kind of peaceful truce with those German churchmen who saw no
problem in their political accommodation to Hitler's absolute rule and
who had without opposition accepted the infusion of Nazi ideology into
church policy. For Bonhoeffer, this caving in to what he viewed as unchristian, hate-mongering, divisive forces smothering his nation and terrorizing his church, was a betrayal of Jesus Christ and an unconscionable infidelity to the Holy Spirit. The struggle, as Bonhoeffer saw it, was for the
truth of the gospel and the soul of the nation.

In relation to the conflict between his Confessing Church and what he
judged to be the heretical Reich Church, Bonhoeffer concentrated on the
interconnected, decisive issue of the creedal affirmation of "filioque [and
the Son]" — a reference to the Holy Spirit's proceeding from the Son as

well as from God the Father. For Bonhoeffer the Holy Spirit, not rationalized, racially conditioned biblical exegesis, offered the only correct interpretation of the Bible. The issue of the doctrine of the Holy Spirit's being sent by the Father and the Son, referred to as "filioque," loomed large, therefore, in Bonhoeffer's conflict with the nazified Reich Church. The "filioque," that traditional creedal article of faith that the Holy Spirit proceeds from the Father and the Son, was more than a traditional dogmatic statement for Bonhoeffer; it was the crux of his argument that the philosophical and theological protagonists of the nazified Reich Church had polluted the Scriptures with their ideological insistence on special orders that emanated from God's own creation. Those "orders of creation" were said to have antedated the moment of the Word of God become flesh, orders that were not cancelled out by Jesus sending the Spirit in that privileged moment of time, the resurrection. That twisted reasoning was invoked to permit political and church leaders to ignore the teachings of Jesus in formulating their policies of eliminating all the "undesirables" from the German earth and expropriating territories then populated by those deemed to be inferior to the pure Aryan race. Moral leadership in Nazi Germany was therefore divested of its connection to Jesus Christ.

In late summer of 1933 Bonhoeffer and a minister colleague, Hermann Sasse, were commissioned by the anti-Nazi "Young Reformers Movement" to retire to the pastoral center of Bethel to compose a Confession of Faith against what they surmised to be the budding heresy of the Reich Church. The "Young Reformers" were still smarting from their defeat in the July elections, outmaneuvered as they were by the "German Christians" who had themselves endorsed the core of Nazi ideology, the leadership principle and racial conformity. Bonhoeffer soon recognized the major crack in the Reich Church's line of battle: the crude, dangerous emphasis of Nazi sympathizers among churchmen on a revelation in creation itself outside of what Bonhoeffer insisted was the inseparable communion of Jesus Christ and the Holy Spirit from the moment that the Word was made flesh. If the German Reich Church leaders had their way, Christianity would be reduced to a lumpy blandness. Bonhoeffer looked forward to using the Bethel Confession as an opportunity to smoke out the protagonists of the nazified church and to unmask their reductionisms.

In the first form of this Bethel Confession it is clear that Bonhoeffer wanted to launch an attack against the Nazi philosophers and theologians who claimed there was a revelation in creation itself that established divine orders of race and peoples, enabling church leaders to pander to the baser instincts of their people. The language of the first draft is crystal clear: "We reject the false teaching that the Holy Spirit may be known in the creation and the orders of creation without Christ. This is because the Holy Spirit always proceeds from the Son in whom this fallen world is judged, in whom the new order of the church as the people of God is set over the people. Only because the Holy Spirit proceeds from the Father and the Son is the task of the church become its mission to all peoples."[54] It is clear that Bonhoeffer was convinced that the Reich Church had no intention to engage in open, prayerful discernment of the gospel or to permit the Holy Spirit to teach them the judgment of Jesus Christ against the kind of secularized, Germanistic salvation preached in their churches.

The notes of Bonhoeffer's input into this document show his insight into the importance of the "filioque" doctrine. Bonhoeffer interpreted this traditional article of the creed in terms of how the Spirit's mission was to stir the teachings of Jesus Christ into the hearts of the faithful. This was, in his opinion, absolutely contrary to the wave of populist "Germanism" threatening to swallow up the church in a new, more facile mode of being Christian. "It is decisive," Bonhoeffer is reported as having said, "that the filioque is lacking. The German Christians want to incorporate a populist spirit [Volksgeist] into the church which is not submitted to the judgment of Christ but justifies itself. . . . Is there a revelation of God disconnected from the revelation of Christ in the scriptures and in the proclamation of the church? Nature, blood, race, individual character-istics of people [völkische Eigenart] do not justify. To be sure, they are valid aspects of people but they are not definitive [for justification]."[55] Bonhoeffer was convinced that the German Christians were in uncon-scious denial of the Holy Spirit of Jesus Christ, discarding God's Spirit of truth in favor of the more popular Nazism, with its national pride and racism. The German Christians, he felt, had ceased to be excited about Je-sus Christ and the words of Jesus spoken through God's Holy Spirit in the church struggle. Moral leadership had been abandoned to the political watchdogs of Nazi correctness and to a nazified clergy lost in naïve admi-ration of the accomplishments of Adolf Hitler.

Despite its original incisive directness and its pungent criticism of the "German Christians," the Bethel Confession failed to represent in any compelling way the dissenting movement soon to be known as the Con-fessing Church. It died the death of the many qualifications cut into it, softening it to such an extent that in the end Bonhoeffer himself refused to sign its final overwrought, toothless version. The Barmen and Dahlem Synods were to produce the major confessions on which the Confessing Church finally took its stand.

Bethge reports that Bonhoeffer's growing awareness that unchristian Germanism was the church's main danger had reached a feverish level following the failed Bethel Confession. He saw no room for compromise. Bonhoeffer spent a great deal of time urging his fellow churchmen to resurrect the traditional weapons of former ecclesiastical crises: councils, clearcut exposition of authentic doctrine, isolation of heresies, and confessions of faith. His enthusiasm carried him to such an extent that, as Bethge remarks, "his elders looked upon the younger man as a mere visionary."[56]

Bethge adds the somber note that Bonhoeffer put more faith in these synods than those who had contributed to them by their presence. Bonhoeffer was vexed at those who sheepishly seemed content that they had composed the correct words but saw no need to follow up their words with concrete, effective actions to restore human dignity and civility in the German nation. For Bonhoeffer it was a question of a prayerful acceptance of the fact that the Holy Spirit had spoken definitively in those synods and should therefore be obeyed. Bethge offers this analysis of Bonhoeffer's dedication and adherence to the synods of Barmen and Dahlem: "Personally Bonhoeffer's commitment was made possible by his own decisiveness; theologically it was fostered through his faith in the Holy Spirit. He may also have believed that once decisions had been made, only by adhering to them could the valuable tradition of liberalism be preserved throughout a period of tyranny."[57] The Confessing Church had, in Bonhoeffer's opinion, resisted by its confession but failed to confess by its resistance.

Bonhoeffer's no-compromise championing of these synods became well known in Confessing Church circles. Bonhoeffer was forced to defend the Confessing Church against the charge that it was instigating unholy divisions in the church. Not so, Bonhoeffer replied. What they had done was to discern the truth, guided by the Holy Spirit, who brought the biblical word to their decisions. Bonhoeffer's words were an expression of his deepest convictions about the direction his church should go in fighting this latest heresy. "There is no greater service of love," he wrote, "than to put people in the light of the truth of this Word, even where it brings sorrow. The Word of God separates the spirits. There is no vindictiveness here, but only the humble and truly dismayed recognition of the way which God will go with God's Word in the church. The bounds of this Word are also our bounds. We cannot unite where God divides. We can only bear witness to the truth, remain humble, and pray for each other. *I now believe that the Holy Spirit spoke at the synods of Barmen and of Dahlem,* which bound themselves to scripture and confession alone, a word that is at the same time binding on us. . . . *We can no longer free ourselves from the direction of the Holy Spirit.*"[58] Toward the end of the same letter he added, "The Confessing Church would surrender the promise given to it if any other factor were introduced alongside *obedience to the truth achieved through the Holy Spirit,* in order to give the church new life."[59]

Nonetheless, the debates raged on and Bonhoeffer's own positions became ever more harshly worded as his frustrations grew. As unmistakably as possible, Bonhoeffer intensified his opposition to the Reich Church, even accusing it of endangering the very salvation of its members. Whether knowingly or not, he said, the German Christians had cut themselves off from the church of Jesus Christ. In an essay on "The Nature of the True Church" he spelled out the reasons why he believed the Reich Church could not be considered the true church of Jesus Christ. In aligning themselves with Adolf Hitler, he argued, they were rejecting "the testimony of God, *of the Holy Spirit itself,* which requires obedience." He went on to say that Barmen was the test case of why the Reich Church had been waylaid by its politicization under Nazism, leading it to ignore the truth of the Barmen Synod: "Either the Declaration of Barmen is a true confession of the Lord Jesus Christ *which has been brought about through the Holy Spirit,* in which case it can make or divide a church, or it is an unofficial expression of the opinion of a number of theologians, in which case the Confessing Church has been for a long time on the wrong track."[60]

But Bonhoeffer was adamant that the Confessing Church was on the right track even though its very existence was causing a sharp division within the Protestant churches of Germany and heartache to those who wanted to work out some accommodation for the sake of the peaceful coexistence of the two churches. Bonhoeffer never ceased to inveigh against any fuzzy tendency to smooth out the differences between the Reich Church and the Confessing Church, even if such actions were intended to maintain the union of the churches. He refused to waver on what to him was a matter of truth and conscience. It did not bother him that the churches were in full combat regalia if the issue was as important as the true teaching of Jesus Christ and the teaching authority of the Holy Spirit or that some of the simpler faithful were confused. The people had been deceived by the hapless leaders of the Reich Church. In the face of such obstinacy, he argued, the Word of God itself, even with its teaching on forbearance, still insists on brotherly warning, admonition, and even exclusion of those who persist stubbornly in their errors, should their errors be a danger to the community. Again, Bonhoeffer saw himself taking a stand on an issue of truth versus falsehood at a time when people were being misled by Nazi deceptions that affected the churches' allegiance to Jesus Christ. The divisions in the churches were already there; the culprits were those who had spliced Nazism into church life. Hence his question to the church leaders: "*Is there community in the Holy Spirit without the Holy Spirit at the same time having the power to separate and to divide?* Are we ready to hear what was justified in detail in the previous article, that the dissolution of the community is the 'strange' work of the church which it does in order to be able to fulfill its proper function, that the dissolution of the community is the last offer of the community?"[61] True to his no-compromise attitude, Bonhoeffer states here his strong belief that it is better to have a church divided than a church trying to merge two diametrically opposite views of Jesus Christ and his Holy Spirit, especially when one side is clearly in God's own truth as expressed in the sacred Scriptures.

Bonhoeffer's confident outspokenness on the theological and ethical issues that divided the Reich Church from the Confessing Church never abated as the church struggle continued. He knew that the Reich Church had been born out of Hitler's appeal to the baser feelings and instincts of the German people and that the popular drift of the people was toward the political, materialistic promises of the new age under Nazi rule. But that in turn could only endanger the Protestant reliance on the Scriptures alone, since for so many, including clergy and theologians who should have known better, the lure of National Socialism evidently rendered the New Testament irrelevant. The lust for relevance, to interpret the New Testament to make it fit into all the contours of the new wave following Hitler, was, in Bonhoeffer's opinion, a wrong-headed menace to the biblical foundations of Christian faith.

> The intention should be not to justify Christianity in this present age, but *to justify the present age before the Christian message.* . . . Where Christ is spoken of in the word of the New Testament, relevance is achieved. The *relevant* is not where the present age announces its claim before Christ, but where the present age stands before the claims of Christ, for the concept of the present age is determined not by a temporal definition but by the Word of Christ as the Word of God. *The relevant has no feeling of time, no interpretation of time, no atmosphere of time, but the Holy Spirit and the Holy Spirit alone. . . . The Holy Spirit is the relevant subject, not we ourselves, so the Holy Spirit is also the subject of the interpretation. The most essential element of the Christian message and of textual exposition is not a human act of interpretation but is always God; it is the Holy Spirit.*[62]

This invocation of the authority of the Holy Spirit is typical of Bonhoeffer's unbending belief that Jesus Christ, the biblical Word, and the Holy Spirit share in God's being present in every relationship that emanates from God's gift of faith. For Bonhoeffer, therefore, it was not a question of adapting the New Testament to make the teachings of Jesus more palatable to the undiscerning masses. This to him would be an unconscionable watering down of the demands of Christian faith. It would also ignore the essential fact in question: it is the Holy Spirit who speaks the words of Jesus Christ to the faithful, not the ideologues who have softened the cutting edges of God's will for those who claim to follow Christ. The factual content of the New Testament should be clear enough if one is open to the Holy Spirit of truth. Bonhoeffer tells his audience that "Christ speaks to us through his Holy Spirit. . . . But what is factual in this matter is the Holy Spirit who is the presence of both God and Christ."[63] Bonhoeffer concedes that there is a method to such interpretation, but this method must also include obedience to and trust in the Holy Spirit. Of the troubled present age, he says that the "present" is defined from without and not by those involved in that "present"; it "is defined not by the past" — perhaps an allusion to the Nazi nostalgia for the Teutonic heroes of old — "but by the future, and this future is Christ, it is the Holy Spirit."[64] For Bonhoeffer, the correct interpretation of the Scriptures was infinitely remote from making the Word of God more relevant, more "present time" for the whims of a particular audience.

What we read of his ideas on how to properly interpret the New Testament in 1935 retrieves some elements of Bonhoeffer's earliest foray into a spiritual interpretation of the Scriptures, the Barthian turn examined above. In this later time of the church struggle Bonhoeffer also spoke from his personal experience of an earlier change of heart — the moment when, as he put it, he became a Christian.

A letter he wrote to his brother-in-law, Rüdiger Schleicher, is significant because of the insights Bonhoeffer gives into his personal way of reading the Bible. The letter also confirms that what he taught and preached on the interpretation of the New Testament, he practiced in his own spiritual life. In the letter he confided to Schleicher that, for him, the power of the Holy Spirit was always linked to the inspiration of the Word of God in which the Holy Spirit was the tacit guarantor of truth and the scriptural word the backbone of one's decisions, way of life, and resistance to evil in high places. He wrote, "I ask God to show us what God wants to say." He then added that he wanted to avoid the temptation of making the Bible conform to his own self and his own ideas of life everlasting. Rather, "God's word . . . begins where God points us to the cross of Jesus at which all our ways and thoughts . . . converge. . . . I won't at any point be willing to sacrifice the Bible as this strange Word of God, that, on the contrary, I ask with all my strength what God wants to say to us here. Everything outside the Bible has become too uncertain for me. I am afraid only of running into a heavenly double of myself. Is it also comprehensible to you that I am rather ready for a sacrifice of my intellect *(sacrificium intellectus)* even in these matters and only in these matters, that is, in the sight of the God of truth?" In a very personal admission, he went on to tell Schleicher that, by reading the Bible in this way, "it becomes more wonderful to me every day. I read it every morning and evening, often also during the day." He described how he studied one passage for an entire week in order to immerse himself in it and listen to that word. He made it clear that this habit of reading the Bible daily maintained the strength of his decisions and of the way of resistance he chose: "I know that without this I would no longer be able *to live properly*. Or, even before that, to believe in the right way."[65]

It is this prayerful reliance on the Scriptures that helps explain how Bonhoeffer could be self-assured and fearless enough to state categorically that one course of action was acceptable to God while another way of living was an implicit denial of Jesus Christ and a failure to listen to the Holy Spirit. It is not out of order to speculate about the quality of the moral leadership that had failed the Christians of Germany during the Hitler era and that may fail Christians in any age of church history. Did the church leaders project their own biases into their reading of the Bible, or did they permit themselves to be addressed critically by biblical judgment on all human pretentiousness, idolatry, and hypocrisy?

The Holy Spirit and the Right Way for Christians to Live Their Commitment to Follow Jesus Christ

Neither in the traditional origins of the doctrine nor in Bonhoeffer's pneumatology is the Holy Spirit merely some laid-back, ephemeral, divine control factor pleased to be confessed in a correct creedal declaration — as in "I believe in the Holy Spirit" — or honored only on that special day of Pentecost. The Bible attests to the many wonders accomplished by the Holy Spirit in the believing community. These coalesce in action for justice, compassion, peace, courage, and the love that can transform individuals and church communities into a Jesus-like force for good in a perennially troubled world. Through the Holy Spirit there is, in short, a ministry and mission for every Christian who is genuine in proclaiming "I believe in Jesus Christ" and "I believe in the Holy Spirit."

We have seen how in Bonhoeffer's theology the mission of the Holy Spirit is always a function of Jesus' resurrection and ascension. The Spirit is never apart from Jesus in the creation and sustenance of individual faith and the church community in which that faith is expressed. This is in keeping with the Christian tradition in which the Holy Spirit emerged in the context of Jesus of Nazareth and the extraordinary transformation of the disciples into intrepid apostolic evangelizers and martyrs. Bonhoeffer depicts the church community, by reason of its unique identity with the crucified and resurrected Jesus, as the unique locus of the presence and actions of the Holy Spirit to create a better world for all God's children. The "directness" of the Holy Spirit's intimacy through grace, beyond orthodox theological, creedal claims, would later move Bonhoeffer to make his radical call for a non-religious, "worldly" Christianity.

The Spirit of God in Bonhoeffer's theology, as in the biblical imagery, is likewise the inspiration behind the "action for justice" that Bonhoeffer wrote about to his grandnephew, Dietrich Bethge. Such action, along with prayer, would be the future of a church chastened by its failures in the Hitler era.[66] Action to achieve justice would in part be accomplished through the prophetic voice of those unique individuals through whom the Spirit of God voices God's judgment on a sinful nation. Bonhoeffer retains the tensive Pauline imagery in depicting not only the prophetic vocation of the church community but also the prophetic vision of a future in which honest, heartfelt prayer and compassionate deeds to create the just society constitute the ministry of Christ's followers. In short, Bonhoeffer uses the example of Jesus Christ and the Pauline exhortations to delineate the obedient willingness to continue Christ's original ministry as word, truth, and life in a sinful world. Those called to moral leadership in societies troubled by dehumanizing criminality are asked to enter into the patterns of Christ's life, speaking the gospel word to the people and standing up for the truth about God's love for his people in Jesus Christ.

Following Jesus is, in Bonhoeffer's theology, more than mere orthodoxy. It is doing the right thing under the tacit, steady guidance of God's Word and Spirit conjoined. It is not that in each instance of Christian action to achieve peace and justice the followers of Jesus Christ must consciously tell themselves, "I do this because God's Holy Spirit commands it." The Holy Spirit's way is to embody itself in the person of faith and in the spirit of the church community. The movements of the Holy Spirit are subtle, gentle, forceful, persuasive, compelling, and if so willed by God, irresistible.

In his last homiletic meditation on John 14:23-31, prepared for Whitsunday 1940, Bonhoeffer emphasized in the strongest possible language the importance to individual Christians and their churches that they be led by none other than God's Holy Spirit. He points out that for the church to make its proper way in the tumultuous era of Hitler's dictatorship it must be willing to receive the Spirit's renewed guidance and understanding. In coping with new enemies, new questions, and new needs, he writes, "the church has the Holy Spirit as its teacher." He goes on to say that the church should never lose sight of the guidance and insight that is its divine endowment, for "the Holy Spirit, and not some human rationality, is the church's teacher. . . . The Holy Spirit is the living God, not some inert concept. The church community has to trust the Holy Spirit in every decision and believe strongly that the Spirit continues to be present in the community and at work in it. The Spirit will not permit our community to grope about in darkness." Bonhoeffer is confident of the reasons to trust in the Holy Spirit, but only on condition that the church community is "willing to take the Spirit's teachings seriously." He notes in conclusion that the lessons of the Holy Spirit have not changed since the days of Jesus' preaching. But the church community has to keep in mind, then as always, that "every lesson of the Holy Spirit remains conjoined to the words of Jesus."[67] This dramatic expression of the need for Christians and their churches to trust in and obey the Holy Spirit in a period of persecution and confusion of loyalties has few parallels among theologians and church leaders who wrote during the war years.

Only in moments of reflection was there conscious awareness on Bonhoeffer's part that Christian action for justice, peace, and freedom is in reality the tacit action of the Holy Spirit. The Holy Spirit creates a church community united under the words of Jesus Christ; the Holy Spirit gifts individuals like Bonhoeffer as well as the community itself to exercise moral leadership with prophetic outspokenness and the freedom to act in Jesus' name to achieve a Christ-centered society. Bonhoeffer's prayer to the Holy Spirit, written for his fellow prisoners, is revealing of how he acknowledged in God's Holy Spirit the source of his faith, love, hope, and courage:

O Holy Spirit,
Give me faith that will protect me
from despair, from passions, and from vice;
Give me such love for God and people
as will blot out all hatred and bitterness;
Give me the hope that will deliver me
From fear and faint-heartedness.[68]

CHAPTER FOUR

Bonhoeffer's Spirituality of Liberation

Solidarity with the Oppressed

"The truth shall set you free." Not our deed, not our courage or strength, not our people, not our truth, but God's truth alone. Why? Because to be *free,* does not mean to be *great* in the world, to be free *against* our brothers and sisters, to be free *against* God; but it means to be free from ourselves, from our untruth, in which it seems as if I alone were there, as if I were the center of the world; to be free from the hatred with which I destroy God's creation; to be free from myself in order to be free for others. God's truth alone allows me to see others. . . . The people who love, because they are freed through the truth of God, are the most revolutionary people on earth.

*From Bonhoeffer's sermon marking the end
of the academic semester, Ninth Sunday
after Trinity Sunday, July 24, 1932*[1]

It is ironic that Dietrich Bonhoeffer, a pastor theologian from an elite, affluent family high in the social circles of Berlin, should have such an impact on liberation movements among the impoverished masses of Latin America, the victims of apartheid in South Africa, the socialist revolutions in Cuba and Nicaragua, and the beleaguered churches in those countries that endured a shaky existence under the suspicion and tight control of communist regimes. Despite his privileged upbringing, Bonhoeffer had an uncommon ability to empathize with those disadvantaged and oppressed people in every area in which he ministered, whether it was to the ragged poor of Barcelona, the poverty stricken blacks of Harlem, hungry teenagers in the slums of Berlin, or the persecuted and endangered Jews of his native land. Bonhoeffer has been quoted extensively by those who have championed the cause of freedom for the exploited peoples of those regions of the world where coping with systemic injustice has become a way of life.[2] They are inspired not only by his theology from that "underside of history" but also by his actions against Nazism.

Influence among Latin American Liberation Theologians

In Latin America, Dietrich Bonhoeffer continues to be an inspiration to the advocates of the social liberation of oppressed peoples. According to Gustavo Gutiérrez, Bonhoeffer, like the many liberation theologians inspired by his example, "had moved toward a theological outlook whose point of departure is in a faith lived by exploited classes, condemned ethnic groups, and marginalized cultures. Those heretofore 'absent from history' are making the free gift of the Father's love their own today, creating new social relationships of a communion of brothers and sisters. This is the point of departure for what we call 'theology from the underside of history.'"[3] Similarly, Jesuit missionary Jon Sobrino praises Bonhoeffer for his intuitive, poetic insistence that "only a God who suffers can save us." Sobrino is fascinated not only by Bonhoeffer's theology of the cross but also by the way Bonhoeffer did theology "from below," from the perspective of those who are the victims of political, military, and economic callousness.[4] Bonhoeffer's encouragement to those who defend the downtrodden of underdeveloped countries against violations of their dignity and of their right to a better quality of life has opened up a fascinating new dimension in Bonhoeffer studies, particularly in Third World countries.

Liberation from Injustice in the United States: Political Deceptions

In the United States, too, Bonhoeffer is seen as a beacon of hope for church people who work to defend the poor. The euphoric promises of skilled politicians continue to pander to big business interests and plutocratic supporters filled with dreams of unparalleled wealth. For many church workers, however, these dreams of the prosperous are nightmares for the have-nots of American society. Too many Americans see freedom from want as the only "freedom" that really counts. But is that true freedom? Or does its pursuit dishonor the "freedom" that has been the boast of the nation?

Two additional phenomena might be laid on the scales weighing the harm done to the less fortunate in the United States in recent years: the shrinking of the middle class in terms of growth in income, and the shrinking of a working class able to reach middle-class standards of living. Furthermore, though the production of material wealth across the world is booming, billions of human beings are still sinking into the economic quicksand of a demeaning poverty. Nearly a billion people, mostly children, live at the edge of starvation; and an estimated 30,000 children die each day because they lack sufficient food and clean water. In the midst of all this, the steps taken by politicians to address budgetary allotments in the richest nation in the world continue to cause pain and diminish the quality of life of the many trapped in pockets of economic hopelessness.

This less-than-optimistic state of affairs is precisely where Bonhoeffer's message and example can serve as a prophetic critique not only of American consumerism and militarism but also of the false freedom they promise. Certainly one of the reasons so many Germans paid homage to Hitler during the 1930s was that he had delivered them from the economic deprivation hanging over from the "Great War" and the ravages of the depression. Bonhoeffer's liberating spirituality serves as a warning against inaction in the face of inflated promises of prosperity contingent on absolute trust of domineering political leaders. The attractiveness of Bonhoeffer's spirituality to those who are involved in self-sacrificing labors to rescue the impoverished is his willingness to make himself a nuisance to those who kept alive the Nazi machinery of oppression. Bonhoeffer's spirituality challenges Christians and their churches to be genuinely Christian and to act as the true church of Jesus Christ through their willingness to suffer for those bereft of power.

Bonhoeffer's Critique of Americans' Boasts about Their Freedom

There is no doubt that Bonhoeffer is looked on by many Americans familiar with his story as an exemplar and inspiration in their own efforts to be free and to promote freedom in troubled spots around the world. Though their ideas of freedom are not always rooted in serious, spiritually sound convictions, Americans rightly take pride in what the United States did to defeat the Nazi armies and to liberate the captive nations and the inmates of the concentration camps during World War II. Some Americans have, in fact, turned Bonhoeffer into a folk hero with whom they can identify, knowing that their cause was the same during that agitated period of twentieth-century history.

Yet Bonhoeffer himself was diffident about the boast of America that it was the land of the free. Nor can his writings be used to support America's militarism or unexamined patriotism. His theology exposes the fraud of politicians who play on their citizens' basic insecurity to justify obscene spending on weaponry to solve problems seen as inimical to the business interests of the nation. He berated the churches for their lack of vigilance over criminality in government. A page from his 1939 diary indicates that he considered the churches of America mired in the same self-serving religiosity he later would denounce in Germany as unchristian, escapist, and playing into the hands of a manipulative, criminal government. In that diary entry he bemoaned the fact that a worship service he had attended in a very prominent Riverside church in New York was merely "a respectable, self-indulgent, self-satisfied religious celebration. This sort of idolatrous religion," he wrote, "stirs up the flesh which is ac-customed to being kept in check by the Word of God. Such sermons make for libertinism, egotism, indifference. . . . Perhaps Anglo-Saxons are really more religious than we are, but they are certainly not more Chris-tian, at least, if they still permit sermons like that."[5] His complaint about that sermon was of a piece with his observations that America's inveter-ate boasting about its freedom tended to blind the people to their na-tion's own sinfulness.

Not long after that Sunday in June 1939, he jotted down in his diary that Americans speak "much about freedom in their sermons. Freedom as a possession is a doubtful thing for a church; freedom must be won under the compulsion of necessity. Freedom for the church comes from the ne-cessity of the Word of God. Otherwise, it becomes arbitrariness and ends in a great many new ties. Whether the church in America is really 'free,' I doubt it."[6] For him, a church that prizes fidelity to destructive political policies out of a misplaced sense of loyalty to either party or nation is a church enchained to an idol. Nonetheless, such loyalty linked to love of country soon became the trademark of the good citizen well beyond World War II and is particularly evident today in the public's uncritical reaction to the United States' record of bullying, belligerent, often covert incursions in Latin America and other troubled regions of the world. Those who publicly disagree with United States military interventions over the last several years have often been branded as soft on communism and terrorism, left-leaning liberals, or simply unpatriotic citizens. Managers of political campaigns are careful to drape their candidates in the American flag and to make an issue of the constitutional right to bear arms at home, to pile up weapons of massive destruction in the mightiest of all arsenals on this earth, or to trumpet the sacredness of the American flag and any foreign policy that leaders declare to be a guarantee of national security. Manipulative politicians have learned the art of identifying the idol of national security with the nation's pursuit of freedom and prosperity. These leaders are thus able to sway unwary citizens to their way of thinking with easy solutions to the complicated problems of insuring a better life for themselves and their children.

Following his second trip to the United States in 1939, Bonhoeffer composed an essay on the state of the American church entitled "Protestantism Without Reformation." There he laid bare what he had detected from his exposure to Americanized churchliness. The churches of the United States, he argued, lacked both the cutting edge of the Reformation and a courageous confession of faith that could challenge their prideful pretentiousness. He chided the American churches for their failure to reach out to their black brothers and sisters and to counteract in any effective way the racism and even lynchings they faced daily in discriminatory, intimidating actions designed to keep them in a constant state of repression. Churchgoing Americans, gloating over their supposed freedom, were hardly free from the hubris that had rotted out church resistance to Hitlerism in Germany. One particular passage hits on the question central to Bonhoeffer's thoughts on moral leadership: the source and experience of genuine freedom.

> The American praise of freedom is more a praise which is directed to the world, the state and society, than a statement about the church. Such freedom may be a sign that the world truly belongs to God. But whether it belongs to God in reality [depends] . . . on freedom as reality, as constraint, as actual event. Freedom as an institutional possession is not an essential mark of the church. It can be a gracious gift given to the church by the providence of God; but it can also be the great temptation to which the church succumbs in sacrificing its essential freedom to institutional freedom. Whether the churches of

God are really free can only be decided by the actual preaching of the Word of God. Only where this word can be preached concretely, in the midst of historical reality, in judgment, command, forgiveness of sinners and liberation from all human institutions is there freedom of the church. But where thanks for institutional freedom must be rendered by the sacrifice of freedom of preaching, the church is in chains even if it believes itself to be free.[7]

Bonhoeffer had seen all too well how pastors were terrified to preach prophetic words of judgment against the blatant wrongdoing of the Nazi government. They were not free, nor were the churches of Germany free, despite their gratitude for having been liberated through Hitler from what they viewed as the more serious menace to faith — atheistic Bolshevism.

The Liberating Effect of Bonhoeffer's Ministry to the Blacks of Harlem

It comes as no surprise that Bonhoeffer identified with many of the impoverished blacks of Harlem during his stay at Union Theological Seminary in the academic year 1930-31. That decisive year in America was his first indication of how poverty could be tied into racism. Through his close friendship with African-American student Frank Fisher, Bonhoeffer became attached to the Abyssinian Baptist Church in Harlem. Indeed, he called his association with that community "one of the most decisive and delightful happenings of my stay in America." But while he admired the deep, liberating spirituality of their hymns at worship, Bonhoeffer also noticed the impatience of young African-Americans at their elders' stoically enduring injustice in a country that bragged of its love of freedom. He believed strongly that, if these young people were ever to become godless because of the cruel racism they encountered and the absence of any real church support on their behalf, "white America would have to acknowledge its guilt."[8] He was mystified at the silence of the churches during the lynchings perpetrated by the Ku Klux Klan against blacks in the South.

Bonhoeffer's Struggle against Racial,
Religious Discrimination in Nazi Germany

Bonhoeffer took back to Germany a disgust with the racism to which his friends were subjected and which he himself had witnessed. One of his students in Berlin remembered that "it [the Negro Spirituals and the stories of racial discrimination in America] was for us an entirely unknown, strange and frightening world." Before Bonhoeffer introduced his students to that "strange new world," he prefaced his remarks with the poignant statement that telling them about the racist downside of his American experience was a fulfillment of a promise to his friend, Frank Fisher. "When I took leave of my black friend, he said to me: 'Make our sufferings known in Germany, tell them what is happening to us, and show them what we are like.'"⁹ Having absorbed from Fisher a sensitivity to the economic and psychological misery of America's blacks, and having tracked their woes not only to racism but also to ecclesiastical apathy, Bonhoeffer was doubly alert to the menace of Hitler's racist ideology. He recognized that in the laws then being concocted to deny the Jewish citizens their fundamental human rights, a contemptuous gauntlet was being thrown down at the churches.

It was in character with Bonhoeffer's spirituality, then, for him to hold the churches responsible for their cowardice in failing to respond to Hitler more vigorously on an issue so close to Jesus' own identification with and compassion for the poor and afflicted of first-century Jewish society. The Gospels make it clear that Jesus will continue to identify himself with the least of his brothers and sisters of all ages. Bonhoeffer therefore could declare that the churches of Germany had jeopardized their Christian integrity by having forsaken their Jewish brothers and sisters in their time of greatest need. His demands for critical questioning of the Nazi government, for a decision to aid the Jewish victims of the repressive laws, and even for direct acts of opposition to such a criminal government, belong to this period.¹⁰ Bonhoeffer's statement, mentioned above, that white people would have to acknowledge their guilt should the racism of Americans push blacks beyond the brink of their trust in God came in 1939. In 1940, at the height of Hitler's popularity with the German masses and in the glow of Hitler's greatest military achievements, Bonhoeffer crafted a "confession of guilt" charging the churches with complicity in the sufferings inflicted on the innocent victims of Nazi ideology. His words are a stark reminder of how churches have often been willing to surrender their prophetic freedom of speech and to sell their souls for the porridge of institutional survival.

Part of the German church's caving in to the dictates of the state included permitting the demonization of the nation's so-called enemies by callous propagandists of war. This had its counterpart in the demonization of the poor, the "racially inferior," despised outcasts, and non-productive citizens. In Nazi Germany this underclass of people included Jews, gypsies, homosexuals, the mentally and physically handicapped, and anyone judged not to meet the Nazi standards for a pure Aryan race. Bonhoeffer never ceased to pester the church to make common cause with Nazism's list of *"Untermenschen,"* the sub-humans that were destined for extermination in Hitler's scheme to create a master race. The euthanazing of those labeled unfit and the murder of Jews and other "sub-humans" were closely related steps toward acts of war in the name of domination, *Lebensraum* (expansion space for Germany's purified but still growing population), and vengeance on Germany's enemies. Bonhoeffer asserted the responsibility of the churches to defend those most vulnerable to oppression from Nazi ideology. Here again, church action to defend human rights was, in Bonhoeffer's opinion, not something apart from the central mission of the church to be a place of worship. In Bonhoeffer's spirituality, worship itself is never separated from the Word of God and the actions for justice that the Spirit arouses in people who obey that Word. The essence of Christian faith, according to Bonhoeffer, is never encased in sacred rituals or accurate catechetical manuals unrelated to fundamental human needs.

Ministry to the Poor of Barcelona, to the Jews of Nazi Germany

As early as his Barcelona ministry, Bonhoeffer wrote of the paradox of Christianity's attitude toward those of high or low station in life. "Christianity," he told his parishioners, "preaches the unending worth of the apparently worthless and the unending worthlessness of what is apparently so valuable. The weak shall be made strong through God and the dying shall live."[11] It is well for religious and political leaders to keep this in mind in assessing fidelity to Christ's mandates in countries where the "worthless" are objects of abuse. And when the churches do not raise their voices in prophetic protest against the injustice done to the weak, the condition of oppressed peoples is all the more exacerbated.

In Bonhoeffer's spirituality, churches turned in on themselves in beautiful ritual and inspiring hymnody can still fail to be the church of Jesus

Christ in the power of the Holy Spirit. His retort to church gatherings for discussions on forms of worship and even new church music in the Hitler era needs to be reiterated here: "Only those who cry out for the Jews may sing Gregorian Chants."[12] His conference for the week of repentance in 1932 is a jolting reminder to the churches that "God wants us to honor God on earth; God wants us to honor God in our fellow man and woman — and nowhere else."[13] He then explained that this "honor" is to be connected to the judgment scene in Matthew's Gospel, where Jesus identifies with the least of his brothers and sisters in need of food, drink, and human solace.

Bonhoeffer's Christology lectures are equally emphatic that Christ can be found on the factory floor in the worker's world. Jesus' earthly appearance in the post-resurrection era is not, Bonhoeffer contends, in some kind of kingly glory. Jesus "goes incognito, as a beggar among beggars, as an outcast among outcasts, as despairing among the despairing. . . ."[14] This statement illustrates one of the main characteristics of Bonhoeffer's spirituality of liberation, namely, solidarity with oppressed peoples.

Solidarity with the Oppressed

Those who have looked to Bonhoeffer for inspiration in dedicating their lives to free oppressed peoples from the abusive conditions of their oppression often cite that dramatic passage from the Christmas 1942 exhortation he had sent to his family and fellow conspirators. In it Bonhoeffer tells of their need to view the happenings of history not so much from their noble, commanding position, but with the eyes of the victims. "There remains an experience of incomparable value," he writes. "We have for once learned to see the great events of world history from below, from the perspective of the outcast, the suspects, the maltreated, the powerless, the oppressed, the reviled — in short, from the perspective of those who suffer."[15] He goes on to say that personal suffering would be more effective in understanding the world than their own "good fortune." It is this "view from below" integrated into his spirituality that has endeared Bonhoeffer to those who minister to the downtrodden of Third World countries.

Bonhoeffer's words, written shortly before his arrest by the Gestapo, do not represent a sudden turn in his life's path. As we have seen, he was able as early as 1928 during his "internship ministry" in Barcelona to remind his people that, through their Christian ministry, God's light shines down on "those who are ever neglected, insignificant, weak, ignoble, unknown, inferior, oppressed, despised," because these people are of infinite worth to God.[16] These sentiments were echoed in an Advent sermon in which he asked his people to accept a Jesus who "asks you for help in the form of a beggar, in the form of a ruined human being in torn clothing."[17] Christ's coming was not, for Bonhoeffer, a once a year reaching out at Christmas to the cuddly babe of Bethlehem, but an everyday opportunity to welcome Christ in the person of the outcast in torn clothing or the homeless beggar in need of shelter.

As we have seen above, Bonhoeffer's love for those in need extended to his ministry among the blacks of Harlem. He accused the white churches of apathy in permitting the racism that had boxed so many of these people into ghettos of economic desperation. His solidarity with the economically depressed blacks as with the hated Jews of Nazi Germany was of a piece with his conviction that Christ himself lived anew in these peoples. The task of Christians was unchanged from gospel days: to confess Jesus Christ in the "least of people, those deprived of their basic human rights in societies bereft of compassion." His biographer reports that Bonhoeffer upset many synodal delegates, smug in their well-crafted pronouncements, if they failed to take up the cause of the Jews. "Where is Abel, your brother?" he wanted to know.[18] Opposing the popular mood meant entering into a fellowship of rejection and adversity. Bonhoeffer believed strongly that for Christians it also meant entering into that mysterious communion of suffering with Jesus Christ. In his *Discipleship,* therefore, he saw the bullying and brutalizing of Jews as directed against Christ himself: "Whoever from now on attacks the least of the people attacks Christ who took on human form and who in himself has restored the image of God for all who bear a human countenance."[19]

Bonhoeffer was aware of the enormous cost of defending this underclass of people in terms of losing "respectability" and being called unpatriotic. For Bonhoeffer the true patriots were those struggling against the Nazi government. As Bonhoeffer put it to his seminarians, genuine followers of Jesus Christ are those who "share in other people's need, debasement, and guilt. They have an irresistible love for the lowly, the sick, the suffering, for those who are demeaned and abused, for those who suffer injustice and are rejected, for everyone in pain and anxiety . . . those who are compassionate give their own honor to those who have fallen into shame and take that shame unto themselves."[20] For Bonhoeffer, as for today's Christians, following Christ along the path of Christian discipleship requires no less than embracing God's own vulnerability in caring for those whom hard-hearted governments have made an object of contempt.

Bonhoeffer had insisted that the conspirators stand firm in their resolve to overthrow the Hitler government despite the shame of being condemned as traitors should the plot fail. His words in that letter sent to them at Christmas 1942 are striking for their realistic assessment of what a spirituality of liberation demanded of them. His answer to the question "who stands firm?" reveals his own sympathy for the resistance movement: "Only the persons who are ready to sacrifice all . . . when they are called to obedient and responsible action."[21] Bonhoeffer had insisted that the claim of so many churchgoers that they "stood firm" in the faith was a pretension unless they did the concrete deeds necessary to overcome systemic injustice. The men and women of the resistance had to be willing to risk losing their freedom and their reputation as loyal citizens. Those who would deliver their nation from fascist cruelty were not allowed to retain their high standing in German society. They were entering into a world where all the choices of action were morally distasteful. Their only recourse was to trust in the understanding and forgiveness of Jesus Christ, who had taken on himself the guilt of a sinful world. They would die shameful deaths on Nazi gallows. Only later would their nation bestow honor on them for having sacrificed their lives to overthrow the cruel dictatorship of Adolf Hitler.

This belief in God's vulnerability in a world of sorrow and compassion for the victims is at the core of Bonhoeffer's theology of the cross. It is why those involved in missions to the destitute of Latin America and elsewhere find in Bonhoeffer's writings and the example of his life a liberating solace for the wounded victims under their care. Bonhoeffer's emphasis on God's power in human weakness sends an unmistakable message of hope to those societies where militarism has metastasized and where dictators still use their might to crush the lowly. We will examine in a separate chapter how Bonhoeffer integrates his strong Lutheran theology of the cross with a spirituality in which he affirms God's sharing in human suffering together with the Christian calling to share in the pain of God.

The Spirituality of Liberation and This-Worldly Christianity

Bonhoeffer's spirituality and moral leadership likewise profoundly disturb those who view their religion as an otherworldly affair in which political, economic, and social problems can be comfortably separated from religious performance, usually Sunday worship, safe prayers, and periodic gorging on cheap grace. Bonhoeffer's spirituality is itself intertwined with the concrete problems of those denied human dignity. In their plight they long not for slick prattle about Christian forbearance and heavenly bliss from unctuous pastors, but for prophetic outrage and practical action on their behalf. To accept the status quo and to counsel patience when human rights are being violated was considered by Bonhoeffer to be infidelity to the gospel.

In sentiments close to the liberation theology of Latin America, Bonhoeffer made the connection between permitting poverty and injustice to fester and the difficulty Christians have fulfilling the gospel mandate to be Christ to those in need. For a political or religious leader "to allow the hungry to remain hungry would be blasphemy against God and one's neighbor, for what is nearest to God is precisely the need of one's neighbor. It is for the love of Christ, which belongs as much to the hungry as to myself, that I share my bread with them and that I share my dwelling with the homeless. If the hungry do not attain to faith, then the guilt falls on those who refused them bread."[22] Bonhoeffer wrote this remarkable passage from his *Ethics* while fully involved in the conspiracy to overthrow the Nazi government. For him, Christians must assume responsibility for turning history in a more humane, Christlike direction. He argued that ecclesiastical quietism coupled with the apathy of several church leaders and their directives to obey their government's laws, however unjust, were tantamount to a complicity in the sins of the government.

Bonhoeffer was further infuriated by the escapist practice among Christians of compartmentalizing their Christian faith, separating it from their secular lives and careers. This had created a space for keeping religion as otherworldly, pertaining to personal salvation unrelated to one's everyday actions as, for example, a politician proclaiming that his was a political decision, not a moral one, as if the two could be separated. The waging of war, as we will see in the next chapter, demanded such segmenting of one's actions as a good soldier from the commands of Jesus Christ to love one's enemies. The Nazi deities were not the Christian Trinity but blood and battle, national security and blind patriotism.

These were the very same deities invoked by United States–supported security forces of Central America to exonerate the killing of opposition politicians, labor leaders, catechists, missionaries, nuns, brothers, priests, and even an archbishop. "Be a patriot, kill a priest," read posters and right-wing graffiti in El Salvador before the assassination of Archbishop

Romero, once it was evident that he had sided with the poor and posed a threat to the cheap labor force exploited by the wealthy oligarchy of that country.[23] The irony that the people behind the murders considered themselves good Catholics because they were avid churchgoers was not lost on the archbishop.

Nor did Bonhoeffer miss that same irony in Nazi Germany. In assessing the failure of Christians to generate any effective resistance to the ideology of Nazism, Bonhoeffer expressed again his longstanding suspicion of institutionalized religiosity and its potential to distort genuine faith. This attitude reached a climax in his prison letter of July 18, 1944. "The 're-ligious act,'" he wrote, "is always something partial, 'faith' is something whole, involving the whole of one's life. Jesus calls us not to a new religion, but to life."[24] In his very next letter he confided to his friend Bethge that he was "still discovering right up to this moment, that is only by living completely in this world that one learns to have faith."[25] Well before those letters he had written in a similar vein to his fiancée Maria,

> When I also think about the situation of the world, the complete darkness over our personal fate and my present imprisonment, then I believe that our union . . . can only be a sign of God's grace and kindness, which calls us to faith. We would be blind if we did not see it. . . . This is where faith belongs. May God give it to us daily. And I do not mean the faith which flees the world, but the one that endures the world and which loves and remains true to the world in spite of all the suffering which it contains for us. Our marriage shall be a yes to God's earth; it shall strengthen our courage to act and accomplish something on the earth. I fear that Christians who stand with only one leg upon earth also stand with only one leg in heaven.[26]

Few expressions in the literary lore of love letters can match this letter for the way Bonhoeffer blends his love for Maria with his this-worldly spirituality even in the midst of the tragedy of his imprisonment, the allied destruction of Berlin, and the uncertainty over his personal fate. It is likewise evident that his love for Maria reinforced his convictions about the necessity for Christians to integrate into their spiritual life a commitment to make this earth a more humane place for coming generations.

Bonhoeffer's statements about a "this-worldly" Christianity are a significant key to the interpretation of his call for a "non-religious Christianity." For him, "religionized" Christianity was adept at divorcing itself from involvement in the real problems of people forced to endure injustice, while sanctimonious church people turned their gaze away or were paralyzed into inaction by their own cowardice. In short, Bonhoeffer's spirituality, like the liberation theology of Latin America, is unabashed about crossing into that combat zone where politics and militarism are said to command obeisance.

According to Bonhoeffer, if Christians of the post-Hitler future wanted to regain their credibility, they had to be persons whose lives of prayer were conjoined to concrete action on behalf of social justice.[27] And the question was not what they were obliged by authority to believe or what their intellectual prowess could accept as orthodox, but the real question Bonhoeffer poses to those who claim to be genuine followers of Jesus Christ: "What do we really believe? I mean, believe in such a way that we stake our lives on it?"[28] Bonhoeffer's impact on a Christian spirituality and moral leadership is all the greater today because his personal life was a mirror of his faith and because he became a victim in the heroic effort to overthrow a powerfully entrenched oppression.

Bonhoeffer's Spirituality of the Servant Christ and the Servant Church

One of the reasons for liberation theology's unpopularity among several of America's mainline ecclesiastical institutions and in some Vatican circles is the way theologians like Leonardo Boff, Pedro Casadaliga, Juan Segundo, Gustavo Gutiérrez, and many others have castigated the churches for appearing to favor their rich congregants over the poor. Liberation theologians have asserted that the churches are often part of the problem rather than a consciousness-raising ally of the oppressed. Bonhoeffer too had a knack for annoying the leadership of the mainstream German churches in the 1930s, accusing them of reluctance to fully integrate practical action on behalf of justice into their regular church life. During the dictatorship of Hitler and the storm troopers' enforcement of the most outrageous anti-Jewish legislation, the churches seemed to look out mainly for their own survival. Even amidst the atrocities of the war years, when the horrors of the death camps were at crescendo pitch, the silence of the churches was ominous. Hence, in the "Outline for a Book" appended to his letter of August 3, 1944, Bonhoeffer noted poignantly that the church was good at protecting its own petty interests but it had "little personal faith in Jesus Christ."[29]

He had heralded this Jesus in the prison letters as "the man for others" who challenged his followers themselves to "a new life in 'existence for others' through participation in the being of Jesus." If Jesus was that man who lived to serve others, then, Bonhoeffer argues, it follows that "the church is the church only when it exists for others." What he observed in his own church in the Nazi era, however, was not a self-sacrificing community of Christ's followers, such as he had experienced in his seminary of Finkenwalde, but a "church on the defensive," refusing to take "risks for others."[30] In his opinion, the churches of Nazi Germany were hardly faithful to their calling to preach and to be Christ to the world.

Bonhoeffer's unyielding criticisms of church cowardice in the Hitler years have their counterpart in the accusations of liberation theology that the problems of the poor in Latin America have been exacerbated by church officialdom's having become too long identified with the rich and powerful in all the centuries from the Conquest to the modern-day enigma of economic servitude.[31] The churches taught the poor forbearance and resignation in their misfortunes. The resulting docility of the peasantry and their non-resistance to systemic evil, garnished with the religious spin put on their misery by some church leaders, was ideally suited to the affluent oligarchy's strategy for keeping these masses under control. When the churches began to take the side of the poor, however, the venom of rulers, wealthy landowners, and business leaders, abetted by ruthless national security forces, was directed against them. Representatives of the church working with the poor and catechizing them through the Bible to their basic human rights were targeted for kidnapping, torture, and extermination. Unexpectedly, the church of Latin America has today, to a great extent, "come out of its stagnation" and risked "saying controversial things" and gotten "down to the serious problems of life," to borrow the phrases Bonhoeffer used to challenge the churches of Germany in his letter of August 3, 1944.[32]

Bonhoeffer had little idea in 1944 that the churches were capable of such a turnabout in the defense of human rights. What he demanded of the churches in the Nazi years was nothing more than that they live up to their claim to be where Christ would be and to teach Jesus Christ by their own example. It irritated Bonhoeffer that the church, which continually proclaimed its faith in the resurrection, lacked the courage to follow Jesus to the cross, preferring instead the cheap grace of accommodation to political overlords. His question from the prison letter of April 30, 1944 — "What is bothering me incessantly is the question what Christianity really is, or indeed, who Christ really is, for us today"[33] — had its answer "in the long lines of Jews herded to their death in the extermination camps, in the tortured limbs and haggard faces of those imprisoned for daring to criticize the criminal regime, and in the bodies of the innocent victims of Nazism's fantasies of bloody conquest and military glory."[34] These acts of ideological malevolence need not have been.

As early as the first anti-Jewish legislation of 1933, Bonhoeffer goaded his church to do more than offer rhetorical lamentation over the fate of the Jews. It was the mission of the church, he said, to confront the state boldly and to demand an explanation for the unjust laws. Secondly, the church had to do more than pray for the victims; Christians had to rush to their aid, "even if they do not belong to the Christian community." Their motive had to spring not from concern for only those Jews who had accepted baptism, but out of compassion for any victims of injustice quite apart from their religious affiliation.

Finally, the church had to take concrete action against the state should the injustice continue — it had to bring down or overthrow the repressive government.[35] No church was willing to go that far in Nazi Germany. Yet these steps, so often cited in analyses of Bonhoeffer's spirited defense of the Jewish people, are a compelling public policy for churches eager to do battle against a given country's violation of human rights. When Bonhoeffer presented his thoughts on the matter to a group of clergymen, many walked out in anger. Later, when he and his Jewish-Christian friend Franz Hildebrandt urged the churches to use the ancient weapon of spiritual interdict to pressure the Nazi leaders to retract the anti-Jewish legislation, they were scoffed at and accused of meddling in politics.[36]

When the war had broken out and the deportations of Jews had begun, Bonhoeffer crafted that "confession of guilt" on the part of the churches to which we have already alluded. Now an integral part of his *Ethics,* these caustic statements castigating the churches for their self-seeking and apathy stand as an indictment of these same churches for their complicity in the evils done by the Nazis. This was a church that shrank from getting involved in the cause of justice but had little hesitation in bestowing approval and respectability on the Nazi cause. The "confession" included the unforgettable phrase that acknowledged the church's guilt in the Holocaust: The church "is guilty of the deaths of the weakest and most defenseless brothers and sisters of Jesus Christ."[37] What is additionally noteworthy about this "confession" is that it was composed at the height of Germany's military success, the fall of France. Church bells rang out the joy of the populace. For Bonhoeffer, however, the bells only symbolized a church enchained to the idols of militaristic glory and national pride. "Freedom," he wrote in his famous poem from prison, can only come about from "what is braved in the bold deeds of justice."[38]

CHAPTER FIVE

The Spirituality That Dares Peace

The Great Venture in Moral Leadership

These brothers and sisters in Christ obey his word; they do not doubt or question, but keep his commandments of peace. They are not ashamed, in defiance of the world, to speak of eternal peace. They cannot take up arms against Christ himself — yet this is what they do if they take up arms against one another! Even in anguish and distress of conscience there is for them no escape from the commandment of Christ that there shall be peace. . . . Peace must be dared; it is the great venture.

From Bonhoeffer's sermon "The Church and the People of the World," August 28, 1934[1]

S tudents discovering Dietrich Bonhoeffer for the first time are fascinated by the fact that this moral leader who involved himself in a plot to kill Adolf Hitler was not only an ordained minister, but also throughout most of his professional career an avowed pacifist. In this chapter we will examine the events, crises, and turns in his life through which Bonhoeffer gradually integrated pacifism into his spirituality and moral teaching. Even when he abandoned his non-violence to join the conspiracy, pacifism always remained his ideal. Only with a troubled conscience and the acceptance of guilt could he abandon pacifism. Before the conspiracy entered its critical phase, there were identifiable moments when Bonhoeffer publicly taught that the only way to follow Jesus Christ was to live out Jesus' teachings on non-violent resistance to societal and governmental injustices.

The Beginning of Bonhoeffer's Pacifism

While it is difficult to pinpoint the precise time when Bonhoeffer began to see war and pacifism in an entirely new light, there is clear evidence that the most significant shift in his attitude came in 1930-31 as a result of his close friendship with the pacifist Jean Lasserre, founder of the "Movement for Reconciliation" in his native France. Lasserre prompted his German friend to reread and reexamine the challenges of the Sermon on the Mount. He and Bonhoeffer engaged in long discussions over how war and the gospel were clearly contradictory. Gradually, Bonhoeffer came to understand more personally the absurdity of Christians killing people for the sake of national pride, economic advantages, hatred, revenge, or territorial ambitions, the most common reasons for nations' declaring war on one another.

In private interviews, Lasserre told us that he was drawn to Bonhoeffer and to a third foreign student, the Swiss seminarian, Erwin Sutz, because they were Sloane Fellows at Union from abroad, but also because they represented for him the more serious European approach to theology. Lasserre suspected that his convictions on social Christianity and pacifism may have shocked Bonhoeffer at first because Bonhoeffer was, like most Germans, resentful of the harsh conditions imposed on Germany by the Treaty of Versailles following the Great War. In an interview just before his death, Lasserre described an important aspect of his initial attraction to Bonhoeffer: "He never crushed us with his theological superiority. He never let us feel that he disapproved of something in us or our behavior. He totally respected our freedom, that of living as well as thinking."[2]

Under the impact of Lasserre's unwavering dedication to pacifism, Bonhoeffer the German began to recognize the need to transcend the national setting of his faith and loyalty. It was a struggle with his own attachment to Germany, but eventually the struggle wrung from him a deeper commitment to the principles of the Sermon on the Mount and a firm devotion to the cause of world peace. Paradoxically, this commitment led to a truer loyalty to Germany in the higher integrity of the service to country he and his fellow conspirators would exemplify.

Lasserre believed the turning point in Bonhoeffer's own pacifism came on a Saturday afternoon when together they viewed the film "All Quiet on the Western Front." They were aghast and saddened to the point of tears at the lighthearted reaction of the young children in the theater to the killing portrayed on screen. Lasserre said that this was a shocking, even tragic, experience for both of them. "I think it was there both of us discovered that the communion, the community of the church is much more important than the national community." Lasserre adds in his recollection of the event: "I think this has been very important in his path toward pacifism because he has discovered that war is not the most important thing from the church's viewpoint. The important, the only really important thing, is that the church . . . keep in fellowship all Christians. And what is absolutely awful and unacceptable in war is that Christians are compelled to forget their Christian faith."[3]

Under Lasserre's pacifist influence, Bonhoeffer's rediscovery of Jesus' words on peace and justice became for Bonhoeffer what Eberhard Bethge has called a "momentous change."[4] In three significant letters he described the shift in his thinking as a great liberation. To his friend Elizabeth Zinn he confided that the Sermon on the Mount had freed him from being a self-serving theologian and helped him finally to become a Christian who was enabled to pray and rededicate himself to his ministry with the church.[5] To his brother-in-law, Rüdiger Schleicher, he spoke of his having learned from Jesus' words not to fashion a god of his own selfish choosing but to let God be God and show him where he, a Christian, and God were to be found together — namely, with Jesus under "the cross of Christ . . . just as the Sermon on the Mount demands . . . for this is the very place God has chosen to encounter us."[6]

Earlier he had acknowledged to his brother, physicist Karl-Friedrich, that the Sermon on the Mount had set him straight for the first time in his life. "I believe that inwardly I shall be really clear and honest only when I have begun to take seriously the Sermon on the Mount." Even his hopes for the future restoration of the church would depend on "the uncompromising attitude of a life lived according to the Sermon on the Mount in the following of Christ." He added the memorable words that reveal to what extent Jesus' sermon had captivated his heart. "At present there are still some things for which an uncompromising stand is worthwhile. And it seems to me that peace and social justice or Christ himself are such."[7]

Becoming a Witness for Peace

Peace and social justice soon became the main focus of Bonhoeffer's spiritual energies. Speaking before the German Student Christian movement in Berlin in 1932, for instance, he linked following Christ with "becoming witnesses for peace." He jolted his youthful audience with his sharp, uncompromising insistence on uniting a professed faith in Christ with the bringing about of peace. In the talk he dismissed the phoniness of so many peace treaties in which considerations of national security dominated the more important issues of human dignity and the gospel demands. Among the memorable phrases, the following cuts to the heart of his argument: "So long as the world is without God, there will be wars. For Christ, rather, it is a matter of our loving God and standing in discipleship to Jesus in whom we are called with the promise of blessedness to become witnesses for peace."[8] He rejects the political ethic that in time of war one is justified in stepping around the command of God that "you shall not kill," and the word of Jesus to "love your enemies." This sort of stepping around, he says, cheapens grace.[9] The commands of Christ are clear in this regard, and they are given to be obeyed. Bonhoeffer's denunciation of the ethic of the just war that could so easily be twisted to justify hatred and killing of one's enemies along with acceptance of "collateral damage" to civilian life would return with even more insistence in his more developed *Discipleship*.

The vehemence of Bonhoeffer's resistance to the glorification of war is seen further in a sermon on the "Day of National Mourning." Speaking to a congregation gathered to commemorate the war dead in February 1932, and with several of those in attendance wearing their military uniforms bedecked with medals of honor, Bonhoeffer spoke the daring words that, in the name of Jesus Christ, Christians must reject war as one of the insidious powers attempting to wipe the spirit of Jesus Christ from Christian consciousness and to replace that spirit with the language of political expediency. Knowing that soldiers are thrilled by allusions to Christ, as their leaders pep them up to shed their blood "for God and country," Bonhoeffer called the deceitful tactic a confusion of fighting "in the name of Christ against the true Christ." That, he said, is when the "powers of the world are revealed" as those who deny Jesus Christ, wanting only "to snatch the disciples from him, . . . to show them that it is madness to go with him, that Christ has no power or authority, only words; that they, the powers of reality, speak the language of facts and this language is more convincing than the language of Christ. The world bands together against the spirit of Christ, the demons are enraged: it is a revolt against Christ. And the great power of the rebellion is called — war!"[10] In those words ringing with indignation at the tragedy of the war dead and before a congregation honoring their memory and grieving their loss, Bonhoeffer exposed the fraud behind the political propagandizing of soldiers. He insisted that in the call to arms the teachings of Jesus Christ have utterly no relevance. Soldiers are told to purge their minds of Jesus Christ in order to do the murderous work of an army in battle. His critical exposure of these militaristic attitudes could attest to the truth of Chesterton's complaint that Christianity has not failed; it has never even been tried.

The Call to Pacifism in Bonhoeffer's Ecumenical Activities

Although in earlier discourses Bonhoeffer recognized the possibility that war might be justifiable and individual Christian participation in such wars morally acceptable,[11] by the end of 1932 his attraction to non-violence and his rejection of war had grown close to the position of absolute pacifism. Nonetheless, his continued aversion for crafting absolutist principles led him to consider war as a mere extreme that is at best possible but always exceptional, and in any case a grievous violation of the overarching Christian mandate to preserve life and to follow Jesus even to the cross. We can detect the spiritual strength of his ever-growing pacifism in his address at the ecumenical conference in Gland, Switzerland, during the summer of 1932. There he challenged the ecumenical delegates to take seriously the teachings and example of Jesus Christ. "And this cross of Christ now calls wrath and judgment over the world of hate and proclaims peace," he said. "Today there must be no more war — the cross will not have it. . . . War in its present form annihilates the creation of God and obscures the light of revelation. . . . The church renounces its obedience [to Christ] if it should sanction war. The church of Christ stands against war and for peace among peoples, between nations, classes, and races."[12] He goes on to say that the peace of Christ depended on truth in government and justice in society. Because of his strong belief that this longed-for peace is an impossible dream "unless justice and truth can be preserved," he shared with the delegates his conviction that it was better to suffer in the struggle for peace than to accept the false calm of a troubled status quo. "But the church also knows," he said, "that there is no peace unless justice and truth are preserved. A peace which does damage to justice and truth is no peace, and the church of Christ must protest against such peace."[13]

In that same summer Bonhoeffer argued even more vehemently for a no-compromise stance on behalf of pacifism. The setting of his address,

"The Theological Basis for the World Alliance [for Promoting International Friendship through the Churches]," was the Youth Peace Conference in Czechoslovakia on July 26, 1932. For Bonhoeffer, one of the primary tasks for the ecumenical movement at that time was to condemn war in all its destructive forms and promote pacifism as its official policy. "War today," he declared, "destroys both soul and body. Now because we can in no way understand war as one of God's orders of preservation and thus as the commandment of God, and because on the other hand war needs idealizing and idolizing to be able to survive, war today, and therefore the next war, must be utterly *rejected* by the church. . . . Nor should we shy away from using the word pacifism today."[14] He felt compelled to make that final remark in the light of Germany's exaltation of the military hero and its inveterate contempt for pacifists. Bonhoeffer shared with these ecumenical leaders his fears that the ecumenical movement would be content with pleasant socializing, finding only friendship and fellowship among themselves, but with no concrete move toward the most pressing issue directly and indirectly affecting the credibility of the church. Not without irony he alluded to Jesus' admonition that "even the heathen and the tax collectors do that."[15]

Peace with Justice

Here too, as in the ecumenical address in Gland, Bonhoeffer made it clear that, as a moral leader, he was not interested in a peace that is only the absence or renunciation of armed conflict. The peace he envisioned was the peace of Jesus Christ, in which justice and truth are the *sine qua non* hallmarks of a decent society. Where peace and justice are absent, then a struggle must be joined. If the struggle for justice disturbs the peace, then so be it. "Where a community enjoying peace endangers or chokes truth and justice," he said, "the community of peace must be broken and battle joined." This is the same rationale that revolutionary movements have invoked in their battles against the systemic injustice that oppresses and exploits the poor. Bonhoeffer specified the peace he was advocating was not mere illusory orderliness but the "reality of the gospel, of the kingdom of God,"[16] which means the truth of Jesus' teachings and the justice that promotes human dignity. Law and order and the semblance of peace in the streets did prevail in Hitler's Germany, but at the cost of truth, justice, and freedom.

Throughout the 1930s Bonhoeffer had to contend with church leaders who had made unholy compromises of their integrity in exchange for the dictatorial government's approval and their continued privileges. Many churches seemed so eager to insure their survival as solvent institutions under Hitler that they were willing to overlook the Nazi security forces' patent abuses of human rights and to submit to governmental infringements on their ministry and their freedom to criticize the government. Those pastors who resisted often felt themselves left dangling in a lonely struggle without the support of their leaders. The violence from which they and their people suffered was, in Bonhoeffer's opinion, the inevitable outcome of the churches pursuing the cheap grace that he so angrily excoriated in his most famous book, *Discipleship*.

The Challenge of Peace

Bonhoeffer again put the cost of living that gospel squarely to the delegates of the ecumenical conference in Fanø, Denmark, in 1934. The setting was a morning sermon in which he asked these church leaders not to miss a serious opportunity to act as the one church of Jesus Christ in addressing an issue as clear as the promotion of peace and the condemnation of war. As in the conference in Czechoslovakia in 1932, he pushed those present to abandon their usual staidness and stop couching their resolutions in inoffensive, polite, and easily ignored platitudes. Bonhoeffer's sermon on peace supports the observations of historians of the ecumenical movement that Bonhoeffer's "Ecumenical Youth Commission" was the most radical of all the groups at Fanø.[17] In that sermon he attacked attempts to downplay or ignore the teachings of Jesus Christ on peace by appealing to national security needs to defend one's country. God was not to be identified with the idol of national security. And the church, to be true to its claim to radiate the presence of Jesus Christ to the world, had to be in the vanguard of the peace movement, or otherwise risk falsifying the gospel.

Bonhoeffer went on to point out that "this church of Christ exists at one and the same time in all peoples, yet beyond all boundaries, whether national, political, social, or racial." When nations take up arms against one another they are in reality taking up arms against Jesus Christ, who lives in the German, the English, the French, and in all those who are the targets of militarized annihilation. And so he beseeched the ecumenical council to speak out, "so that the world, though it gnash its teeth, will have to hear, so that the peoples will rejoice because the church of Christ in the name of Christ has taken the weapons from the hands of their sons, forbidden war, proclaimed the peace of Christ against the raging world." A significant sentence from that sermon remained forever emblazoned in the memories of Bonhoeffer's students: "Peace must be dared; it is the great venture."[18] The effect of Bonhoeffer's words on that congregation of eminent church delegates was electrifying.[19] His student, Otto Dudzus, later testified in his reminiscences of that sermon, "From the first moment the assembly was breathless with tension. Many may have felt that they would never forget what they had just heard. . . . Bonhoeffer had charged so far ahead that the conference could not follow him. Did that surprise anybody? But on the other hand, could anybody have a good conscience about it?"[20]

Evidently, the great majority of German church leaders neither followed Bonhoeffer nor seemed ready to confess to a "bad conscience" in their later support of the war that ensued. The enthusiasm he generated at Fanø was short-lived. The ecumenical movement, which Bonhoeffer regarded as the most powerful source of hope for the preservation of Christianity in Germany and the world, eventually became indecisive and unwilling to interfere further in Germany's "internal ecclesiastical affairs." At the International Bonhoeffer Conference held at the World Council of Churches in 1976 to commemorate the seventieth anniversary of Bonhoeffer's birth, the then-General Secretary, Willem Visser 't Hooft, told the assembled delegates it was because of Bonhoeffer's influence and example as well as his sharp criticism that the World Council of Churches had resolved in the postwar years "to live up to their main obligation, which is to be the church, and to announce the Lordship of Jesus Christ over the world." He acknowledged Bonhoeffer's insistence that "the church . . . be truly the church for others." According to Visser 't Hooft, this was Bonhoeffer's way of calling the church back to its true mission. He went on to say, in keeping with Bonhoeffer's earlier critique of the World Alliance for Promoting International Friendship through the Churches, the forerunner of the WCC, that "an ecumenical movement which is simply another United Nations with a religious varnish cannot help the world. What the world does need is . . . an ecumenical council . . . which does not only witness with authority to the truth and unity of the church of Christ, but also renders witness against the enemies of Christianity everywhere and speaks a word of judgment about war, racism and social exploitation."[21] One can only wonder what the history of the Third Reich would have been had the World Alliance put Bonhoeffer's exhortations into practice in 1934.

Bonhoeffer and the Pacifist Non-violence of Gandhi

Some of Bonhoeffer's words from that sermon at Fanø are reminiscent of the pacifist tactics of Mohandas Gandhi. "Which of us can say he knows what it might mean for the world," Bonhoeffer speculated, "if one nation should meet the aggressor, not with weapons in hand, but praying, defenseless, and for that very reason protected by the only defense and weaponry that is any good?"[22] Several letters written prior to the Fanø gathering do indeed reveal Bonhoeffer's growing interest in visiting India and learning firsthand Gandhi's way of life and the successful tactics of his pacifist, nonviolent resistance. Bonhoeffer was interested, too, in exploring with Gandhi the political implications of the Sermon on the Mount. His teacher at Union Theological Seminary, Reinhold Niebuhr, tried to dissuade Bonhoeffer from becoming a disciple of Gandhi, saying that the tactics of non-violent, pacifist resistance to Hitler were hopeless; they would not work in Germany. Although later Bonhoeffer's ethics would lean very heavily on Niebuhr's "Christian Realism," in the early 1930s Gandhi offered the greater attraction to Bonhoeffer. As ethicist Larry Rasmussen has pointed out: "Gandhi, and not Niebuhr, offered the more probable political articulation of the gospel. For the pacifist of the Church Struggle, nonviolent resistance seemed the political *Gestalt* that . . . [in that day] conformed to Christ's form in the world."[23]

Bonhoeffer spent part of 1934 preparing for such a journey to India, not only procuring letters of introduction but also seeking out British disciples of Gandhi to discover more about life in the East and about a method of pacifist resistance closer to Christ than the bellicose accommodation of the Christian churches in Europe to the political expediency he so openly abhorred. "Must we be put to shame by non-Christian people [*Heiden*] in the East?" he asked at Fanø.[24] Bonhoeffer had already alluded to this "shameful" discrepancy in a letter to his grandmother informing her of his plans for travel to India. "Sometimes it even seems to me that there's more Christianity in their 'paganism' than in our entire Reich Church. Of course, Christianity did come from the East originally. But it has been so westernized and so permeated by civilized thought that, as we can now see, it is almost lost to us. Unfortunately, I have little confidence left in the church opposition. I don't at all like the way they're going about things, and really dread the time when they assume responsibility and we may be compelled yet again to witness a dreadful compromising of Christianity."[25] Bonhoeffer pushed ahead with his travel plans. The invitation from Gandhi finally arrived. Bonhoeffer was invited to share in Gandhi's community life, living at his ashram (temple), accompanying him on journeys throughout India.

The encounter with Gandhi was, however, a dream that was never to be realized. More important considerations made it necessary for Bonhoeffer to return from London to take over the directorship of one of the seminaries of the Confessing Church. In this seminary in Finkenwalde he would lecture extensively on following Jesus Christ, lectures that were to be integrated into *Discipleship*. At that time his spiritual outlook, as the world edged toward war, leaned toward a Gandhian non-violent resistance, knowing this would exact a willingness to suffer for that cause. This was the risk that he believed Christian discipleship demanded of Jesus' followers. The cross of Christ, experienced by all those whose lives incarnated Jesus' Sermon on the Mount, offered only costly grace to those called to be peacemakers.

The Pacifism of *Discipleship*

We find articulated in the pages of *Discipleship* Bonhoeffer's understanding of the Christian vocation to follow Christ in the way of making peace. Bonhoeffer extends to his readers the challenge to take to heart Jesus' praise of those whom he calls peacemakers, notwithstanding the sufferings peacemaking enjoins. It is not mere coincidence, he says, that this beatitude lies between the praise for those with "purity of heart" and those willing to suffer persecution for justice and peace. Those involved in the peace movement, then as now, must allow none other than Jesus Christ to rule over their hearts. Christ's paradoxical command is to love one's enemies and, thereby, through that "extreme" of nonviolence, extend his peace to the world. Bonhoeffer urges genuine followers of Jesus to remember that they are "called to peace":

> Jesus is their peace. Now they are not only to have peace, but they are to make peace. To do this they *renounce violence and strife.* . . . Jesus' disciples maintain peace by choosing to suffer instead of causing others to suffer. They preserve community when others destroy it. They renounce imperious self-assertion and are silent in the face of the hatred and injustice done to them. That is how they overcome evil with good. That is how they are makers of divine peace in a world of hatred and war. But their peace will never be greater than when they encounter evil people in peace and are willing to suffer

from them. Peacemakers will bear the cross with their Lord, for peace was made at the cross.[26]

These extraordinary words reveal the beatitudinal center of Bonhoeffer's spirituality. The crises of the Hitler years had only strengthened his commitment to follow Jesus along the paths illuminated in the Sermon on the Mount though they lead to the cross of imprisonment, torture, and death. Bonhoeffer likewise counseled his seminarians that those who follow Christ must be willing to endure suffering in order to restore peace in a world of hatred, vengeance-seeking, and unbridled violence.

Bonhoeffer risked being misunderstood when he observed that the process of being a peacemaker demanded that one be "silent in the face of hatred and injustice." Certainly the expression fits with the pacifism he preached. But, in this instance, Bonhoeffer was also addressing one of the major causes of the violence that regularly shatters the peace of a community or of a nation, namely, the harsh words and reprisals that quickly escalate into vengeance and desires to obliterate the enemy. Bonhoeffer's spirituality, in the context of *Discipleship*, obviously included not only the words of protest against injustice but also the enlisting of church influence against the Hitler government's dehumanizing policies. He even urged the mobilization of the churches to use coercive tactics against state policies inimical to human dignity and infringing on the right of all peoples to live in peace with one another. Here, as in his other writings of the period, he was still attempting to preserve the best features of Luther's doctrine of the two kingdoms, in which the church, while respecting the territorial province of the state, nonetheless lives in a prophetic, even polemical relationship with the state, and when necessary is obligated to intervene to remind the state of its duties to protect and provide for the well-being of all its citizens.

Bonhoeffer was well aware that the subterranean hatred nurtured by Nazi ideology was the root impetus for the wanton acts of terror whereby the Nazi government maintained its control over the large population of Germany. Hence Bonhoeffer spoke not only of suffering in the cause of peace in his troubled land, but also of the need to forgive enemies. His words fly in the face of the nationalistic, popular sentiments that offered pragmatic justification for hating the enemy while loving only one's friends. For Bonhoeffer, this ideological ignoring of one of Jesus' hardest sayings amounted to a sinful denial of a central tenet of Christian discipleship, love of one's enemies. Bonhoeffer reiterated his conviction that love of enemies flowed directly from the will of Jesus. He did not want it to be seen as an impossible ideal to be ignored for the sake of self-defense or, worse, the compulsion to "get even." Bonhoeffer made it clear that when he spoke of enemies, he was talking "about those who will remain our enemies, unmoved by our love; those who do not forgive us anything when we forgive them everything; those who hate us when we love them; those who insult us all the more, the more we serve them. . . . But love does not ask if it is being returned. Instead, it seeks those who need it. But who needs love more than they who live in hate without any love? Who, therefore, is more worthy of my love than my foe? Where is love praised more splendidly than amidst one's enemies?"[27]

These words were published just before he began writing his *Ethics* and at a time when Hitler was busy pumping life into his plans to reverse the shame of losing the First World War. Hitler harped on his long list of grievances against the neighboring nations now become the targets for conquest and territorial expansion, his coveted *Lebensraum*. As the rhetoric of nationalistic vengeance-seeking reached a fever pitch, just two months before Germany annexed Austria, Bonhoeffer returned to the theme of loving one's enemies in a moving sermon. Taking as his theme Paul's dramatic advice to the Christians of Rome (Rom. 12:17-21), he reminded his congregation of Christ's way with the enemy:

> God gave God's life, God's all, for your enemies; now you, too, give them what you have: bread if they are hungry, water if they are thirsty, aid if they are weak, blessing, compassion, and love for your enemy. Are they worth it? Who, indeed, could be more worth our love, who could stand in greater need of our love than those who hate? Who is poorer than those, who is more in need of help, who is more in need of love than your enemy? Have you ever looked upon your enemies as those who, in effect, stand destitute before you and, without being able to voice it themselves, beseech you: 'Help me, give me the one thing that can still help me out of my hate; give me love, God's love, the love of the crucified Savior'? . . . When you reject your enemy, you turn the poorest of the poor from your door.[28]

Such a love, brimming with the example given by Jesus Christ of forgiveness and unconditional love, is a centerpiece of Bonhoeffer's spirituality, and his challenge to those who exercise moral leadership within the nations. In the entire history of Christian spirituality, no words rise to the heights of the eloquent reiteration of Jesus' teaching on love of enemies that one finds in *Discipleship* and in Bonhoeffer's sermons. What is remarkable is that his words were not composed from a safe distance, where no enemies could touch him. He lived and wrote in a time when hatred of the enemy was the popular mood, and when the Nazi security forces had no qualms about arresting and imprisoning, and later murdering, those considered hostile to the Nazi government. Bonhoeffer himself would fall victim to this hatred.

By the time he had joined the anti-Hitler conspiracy and was working on drafts of his *Ethics*, however, we see a change in his outlook toward the pacifism he had advocated so eloquently in *Discipleship*. The stakes in terms of human lives had mounted to new heights, and the survival of Christian faith in Germany seemed to be at its most precarious. The war had begun; the killing of Jews and other "undesirables" was underway. Hitler's popularity, bubbling up from the people's lust for military success, was at its peak, as his armies were subjugating nearly all of Europe with negligible loss of German lives. Even the churches were joining in the wild celebrations of Germany's dominance over its erstwhile conquerors and reveling in having finally exorcised the shame of having lost the Great War.

Bonhoeffer's Pacifism and the Political Conspiracy

If in *Discipleship* Bonhoeffer offered a compelling argument on behalf of pacifism as blessed in Jesus' beatitudes, his thoughts in composing his *Ethics* became conditioned by the reality of an entrenched, seemingly insurmountable evil that no ordinary means, least of all that of pacifism, appeared capable of nullifying. The times called for another approach, one inspirited by his practical sense of responsibility for the victims of Nazism and his trust in the incarnate presence and forgiving power of Jesus Christ. We still see traces of how the Sermon on the Mount and the letters of Paul conditioned and even modified Luther's teaching of the two kingdoms. But now Bonhoeffer focused more clearly on Nazism's deceptive promotion of Hitler's kingdom of the gun over Jesus' appeal to follow him to the cross. In his *Ethics* Bonhoeffer excoriates the living in two spheres in which churchgoing Christians thought they could march lockstep with the German military. Throughout the text of *Ethics*, Bonhoeffer's main focus still remained that of conforming to Jesus Christ.

Single-minded obedience to the commands of Jesus Christ on nonviolence is no longer the unshakable rule of conduct in the *Ethics*. All the qualms about killing even the malicious, powerful enemy of humanity give way in the *Ethics* to the personal freedom of the Christian called to take self-sacrificing initiative to confront head-on the massive force of governmental malevolence. In his *Ethics* Bonhoeffer now followed a middle course in which freedom, responsibility, and trust in the forgiving mercy of Jesus Christ became conscience-alleviating motives for those plotting the long-awaited coup d'état.

Bonhoeffer's *Ethics* covers the wider moral dilemmas faced by a church whose country was ruled by a savage dictatorship dragging the nations of the world into mortal combat. The senseless bloodshed of that war, together with the genocidal atrocities committed by ruthless SS troops, impelled Bonhoeffer to shift his moral focus more intensely toward the affirmation of the Lordship of Jesus Christ while advocating pragmatic ethical structures in which Christians were enabled to take personal responsibility for eradicating evil from their nation. Here Bonhoeffer's obvious concern is to be for others, in this case the victims in whom Jesus had taken form in the shooting pits and gas chambers. His ethical judgments helped his fellow conspirators to engage courageously in actions that held the hope of restoring peace, freedom, and justice where war, oppression, and injustice had prevailed.

Although the peacemaking dimensions of Bonhoeffer's Christian spirituality seem muted by his arguments in *Ethics* in favor of tyrannicide and violent interventions to end the war, in truth Bonhoeffer's reliance on Jesus Christ's example and mandates of responsibility never ceased to be his primary motivating force. Here, however, it is the Christ who lives and acts for others, to take on the guilt of sinners, and to extend the forgiveness of his Father God to those sinners. He who did not hesitate to place his healing touch upon the rotting skin of lepers, to associate with the hated Samaritans, to become one with society's deviates and outcasts of all sorts, now sets the example for those who must enter into the sinful, guilt-ridden world of a political conspiracy. To act on behalf of the victims of the widespread suffering inflicted by Nazism's militaristic bloodletting meant that truthful people had to learn to maintain a deceitful front, and law-abiding citizens had to be willing to break the laws and plan the violent death of a dictator. Being for others in the manner of Jesus Christ meant more for Bonhoeffer in writing his *Ethics* than mild, convenient acts of charity.

The abandonment of the ways of non-violence that Bonhoeffer had advocated earlier did not come about without considerable pondering of the alternatives. The deeds of free responsibility that could include violence were not justified by either convenience or mere pragmatism.

Breaking the civil laws of a nation was not a common undertaking for the people of the German resistance. But for Bonhoeffer, common sense and personal faith dictated that the laws set by the dictatorial state were infringing on the rights and dignity of ordinary citizens and instigating the extermination of innocent victims robbed of their human dignity by those laws. Germany had reached an extraordinary situation, the point where war and a coup d'état were the inevitable last resort and only responsible initiative of those who resisted evil structured into their criminal government. No other responsible actions had been able to topple the Hitler regime. There remained now only the question of how the conscience, liberated by a renewed sense of the compassion and confrontational courage of Jesus, could free the conspirators to perform acts that in themselves were treasonous and sinful. And yet, murdering the criminals who had engineered the genocidal bloodshed was the taking of human lives. Here Bonhoeffer invoked the presence and example of Jesus Christ, saying that "the law is no longer the last thing; there is still Jesus Christ; and for that reason in the contest between conscience and concrete responsibility, the free decision must be given for Christ. This does not mean an everlasting conflict, but the winning of ultimate unity; for indeed the foundation, the essence and the goal of concrete responsibility is the same Jesus Christ who is the Lord of Conscience."[29] Bonhoeffer bemoaned the prevailing attitude of so many Germans that, in their acts of violence, their "conscience is Adolf Hitler." Bonhoeffer claimed, on the contrary, that in the regrettable abandonment of the non-violence of his pacifism, "Jesus Christ has become my conscience."[30]

What is important from Bonhoeffer's perspective is that abandoning non-violence is not without its own ambiguity, sin, and guilt. Breaking the law for the sake of the law, lying for the sake of the truth, and violence for the cause of restoring peace all bring on the healthy guilt that requires repentance, forgiveness, renewal, and the justification that can come from God alone. The Pauline, Lutheran emphasis on justification by faith alone is crucial to Bonhoeffer's ethical reflections on how Christians are to restore peace and justice in Nazi Germany. The necessity of stopping the slaughter of the innocent may require violent deeds, as one's conscience moves the resister to act against both civil and religious laws, hoping only for God's compassion and forgiveness.[31] The guilt Bonhoeffer experienced in joining the conspiracy and participating in the deceit and violence needed to stop Nazism brought on the unavoidable guilt that good people must endure if they are to oppose systemic evil in any effective way. But even here Bonhoeffer invoked the encouraging example and redeeming love of Jesus Christ, who "is not concerned with the proclamation and realization of new ethical ideals; [who] is not concerned with himself being good (Mt. 19:17); [but who] is concerned solely with love for real human beings, and for that reason he is able to enter into the fellowship of the guilt of humans and take the burden of their guilt upon himself."[32] In no way did Bonhoeffer concede that the violent deeds planned by the conspirators escaped the guilt for what they had to do in attempting to free the world from the sinister, lethal grip of Adolf Hitler.

Terrorism and the War in Afghanistan

As this book was reaching its final stages of production, the United States military was fully engaged in waging war against the Taliban rulers of Afghanistan. The war itself was the nation's response to the September 11, 2001, attack on the United States that killed innocent men, women, and children. A fanatical group of Islamic terrorists had hijacked four commercial airplanes loaded with fuel and unsuspecting passengers, both young and old, and flown these planes against the World Trade Center and the Pentagon, causing the deaths of over 3,000 people. A fourth attack was averted when some heroic passengers fought the hijackers and caused the plane to crash outside Pittsburgh, sacrificing their lives in order to keep the hijackers from a fourth target. This terrorist "bombing" of America was carefully organized by members of the al Qaeda network under the direction of Osama bin Laden, then living under the protection of the Taliban rulers of Afghanistan. This "invasion" of American soil and the murder of so many civilians in the buildings and the airliners were universally denounced as despicable acts that constituted, in the judgment of an overwhelming majority of political and church leaders, an armed aggression against the United States.

What is more, the investigation that followed uncovered evidence of the involvement of Afghanistan, not only in harboring the leaders of the al Qaeda terrorist organization and providing training camps for their followers, but also of a worldwide network of fanatical Islamic fundamentalists out to destroy the United States and slaughter as many Americans as possible. In short, the terrorist acts of September 11, 2001, were exposed as an undeclared war on America and a prelude for even more murders of innocent civilians. For the protection of its citizens and defense of the inner fabric of American society, as well as the safety of other allied nations also targeted for terrorist attack, the United States had to respond.

It came as no surprise to us that, when the subsequent air strikes against Afghanistan began, we were beset with questions about how Bonhoeffer would have reacted to this latest of the wars in which the United States had participated. Could we extrapolate an adequate answer to that question from his pacifist ideals and ethical reflections? Applying Bonhoeffer's writings to the United States' bombing campaign against the Taliban rulers of Afghanistan, depicted originally as an effort to capture and bring Osama bin Laden to justice, would be as completely unlike our judgments on the Persian Gulf War as the terrorist acts of September 11, 2001 were unlike the Iraqi seizure of Kuwait.

When Bonhoeffer crafted his *Ethics*, Germany was locked into bloody battles on every front. Millions were dying on the battlefields, in bombed-out cities, and in the notorious Nazi gas chambers. In fact, Bonhoeffer's hopes for the liberation of his nation from the existing government, as well as the deliverance of the victims then languishing in the death camps, depended in large measure on the successful military efforts of the allies. He had himself joined the conspiracy to overthrow Adolf Hitler and thus hasten the defeat of his own country. While Bonhoeffer condemned what he called the "arbitrary killing" that happened in every war, he recognized that the justifying circumstances of self-defense as well as the compassionate concern to liberate a terrorized people could necessitate killing the enemy. But this killing could be countenanced morally only in order to protect the lives of a nation's innocent civilian population including the victims of systemic genocidal terror. Here he reminds his readers that "the sparing of life has an incomparably higher claim than killing can ever have."[33] He adds that, nonetheless, it remains the duty of the moral leader as well as the "strong" and those hailed as "socially valuable" to defend even those whom class-conscious societies have labeled "less valuable," in the name of the right to life of all those created by their Father God to be brother and sister of Jesus Christ.[34] It is clear that the war Bonhoeffer had in mind was directed against Nazism's immoral destruction of Europe's *"untermenschen,"* the less productive, less genetically fit of the masses in Germany and the occupied territories. If war was what it took to protect and liberate such helpless people, then so be it! His previous pacifism seemed no longer realistic enough in the changing context of Nazi terror.

The key to Bonhoeffer's shift to non-pacifist statements in his *Ethics* in favor of limited war as a Christian's last recourse lies in his endorsement of the principle of self-defense. He couples this with his abiding insistence that Christians must remain in communion with Jesus Christ, who alone can set one's conscience free to do deeds of unavoidable violence that otherwise Christians would never countenance. At this juncture of his ethical guidelines, he recognized that, in justifying sinners by the gift of faith and bearing their guilt, Jesus Christ frees the human conscience by permitting the Christian moral leader to accept responsibility for decisive actions against human malevolence. Such actions can never be isolated from the context of defending the innocent in a nation under attack from without or subjected to tyrannical rule from within. "Thus responsibility is bound by conscience," he wrote, "but conscience is set free by responsibility." Knowing full well the reverberations in one's conscience of the guilt that ensues in acts of self-defense with violent, military means, he added the observation that the Christian moral leader remains "dependent on grace. Before other people the man of free responsibility is justified by necessity; before himself he is acquitted by his conscience; but before God he hopes only for mercy."[35]

Given the circumstances under which the armed attack was launched on Afghanistan, Bonhoeffer's ethical reflections offer helpful guidance for a qualified assessment of the United States' armed response to the terrorist attack on innocent civilians. Bonhoeffer invokes the need for a nation to preserve the freedom of its citizens and to exercise civic responsibility, all in an overarching conformation of one's life to Jesus Christ and Jesus' solidarity with the victims of violence. This is the Jesus who himself exercised the freedom to speak out against repressive power structures on behalf of the downtrodden and to act with responsibility in confronting the sources of evil in his society. "The action of the responsible [Christian] person is performed in the obligation which alone gives freedom and which gives complete freedom, the obligation to God and to our neighbor as they confront us in Jesus Christ."[36] Understood in this statement is the ever-present sense of personal sin, in which there can be neither justification through some legalistic stratagem (perhaps laws passed by a willing Congress or even an approving consensus among church leaders!), nor gloating over the destruction of the enemy, nor an unchristian desire for revenge, but only a surrender to God's justifying grace "of the deed which has become necessary and which is, nevertheless, or for that very reason, free; for it is God who sees the heart, who weighs up the deed, and who directs the course of history."[37] Bonhoeffer sees no alternative for the Christian except to face up to one's human condition and to intensify one's relationship with Jesus Christ, sorrowing when the situation of war as *ultima ratio* or last resort is reached.

Even with the noble aim of protecting from harm the innocent or liberating victims of tyrannical repression, Bonhoeffer cautions Christians to avoid the self-deception of elevating the war once justified into an endorsement of any war as the first tactic to achieve one's ends as a nation or as an exercise in national security. War is not supposed to be the hiding place for any would-be moral leader behind which the divine law against killing is proclaimed no longer binding. The moral constraints that God has placed on human behavior and God's judgment against human arrogance and pretentiousness must also be affirmed.

It would seem that, in the context of war and Nazi genocide, Bonhoeffer's moral leadership allowed ample room for the use of force to retrieve truth, justice, and peace from the ruins of a Nazi world where lies, injustice, and war were the standards of excessive nationalism. The recent war against terrorism elides well with Bonhoeffer's own decision to join a violent conspiracy, not as a virtuous decision in keeping with the gospel, but as a sinful, albeit tragic, necessity in order to protect the lives of the innocent. Bonhoeffer invoked the responsibility to defend those unable to protect themselves, which is the hallmark of Jesus' mandate to care for the most vulnerable of his brothers and sisters. The moral leaders' sense of responsibility for the common good of society and their obligation to protect the innocent from lawless violence can demand the response to terrorist attacks in measured ways that include war. The comments of historian and Bonhoeffer scholar Jean Bethke Elshtain on the justice of the United States' war against terrorism are timely in this regard: "If evil is permitted to grow, good goes into hiding."[38]

Bonhoeffer, who struggled passionately on behalf of rescuing Jews and whose motive for joining the conspiracy included freeing the victims of the concentration camps, offered supportive ethical comment on the use of violent means to liberate the innocent from terror and death.[39] In his essay, "After Ten Years," Bonhoeffer asked his fellow conspirators to see reality through the experience and eyes of the victims as he also declared that merely looking on and waiting while people were made to suffer was an unchristian attitude.[40]

In this instance, however, as in so many of his ethical judgments, Bonhoeffer remained critical of the unlimited use of coercive force to achieve even the good aims of self-defense and liberation from oppression. He rightly condemned "total war," where the killing of noncombatants through errant bombs has now been callously dismissed as collateral damage. He called total war a threat to Christian unity and denounced it as a "war of destruction, in which everything, even crime, is justified if it furthers our own cause, and in which the enemy, whether he be armed or defenseless, is treated as a criminal."[41] The constraints he advocated on military conduct in conquering the enemy were guided by the same respect for life that must be invoked as a nation claims justice in its resort to war to protect its citizens or to solve its problems. For Bonhoeffer, as for Christians who are defending themselves and their nation against aggression, the obligation to maintain justice in the course of military operations was paramount. To abide by these limits is to accept the Christian obligation to conform to Jesus Christ even in relating to one's enemies. Hence to kill civilians wantonly, to abuse conquered peoples, to practice cruelty in combat with the enemy is to deny one's responsibility to God, the creator of life, and to Jesus Christ, still brother and sister of one's enemy. Bonhoeffer insisted that killing in war is never without its guilt and regret: guilt in disobeying the divine injunction against killing, and regret that citizens of a beleaguered country are forced to "sin bravely" in order to restore peace and justice to a people victimized by systemic injustice.[42]

This is the same concern that Bonhoeffer had when he began writing his *Ethics*. How does one remain loyal to Jesus Christ while leaving aside all considerations of one's personal virtue, one's aversion for deception, for violence, for armed combat, in order realistically to confront entrenched evil? In every contour of his ethical decision-making, the life and commands of Jesus were Bonhoeffer's guidelines. To be conformed to Jesus Christ, which is the center of his ethical reflections, meant maintaining the ideals of peace and justice while following Jesus in declaring solidarity with innocent victims and risking one's life to restore the kind of order in which human life and civil rights are respected. Bonhoeffer did not endorse war uncritically; nor did he accept that the exceptional war effort be universalized as the most ready-at-hand weapon in a nation's pursuit of self-interest.

What is more, Lutheran Bonhoeffer never loses sight of the sinfulness that can be present in every decision to engage in actions that in themselves and out of their practical moral context would be reprehensible. In the case of the United States' military actions against terrorism in its Afghanistan setting, he would ask the tough questions: What actions or attitudes on the part of the United States led to such an intense hatred that the terrorists felt justified in the mass murders they perpetrated on September 11, 2001? Were the foreign and economic policies of the United States responsible in any way for the helplessness, hurt, and anger experienced by those who were allied to the terrorists or in sympathy with their aims to kill Americans and destroy America? These critical questions are not asked to exculpate the terrorists. But they should lead to serious reflection on how, in the aftermath of the initial military actions of the United States, the nation had to reassess its policies in an effort to alleviate the poverty, injustice, and violence in which that terrorism had found its breeding grounds. The challenge Bonhoeffer posed to the delegates of the World Alliance to Promote International Friendship through the Churches in his sermon at Fanø, Denmark, still holds. Winning the armed conflict was the relatively easy part; then the question became whether the United States had the courage to create peace with justice. This phase of peacemaking is what Bonhoeffer called "the great venture."[43]

In all his ethical reflections Bonhoeffer strove to maintain what is so often denied in national security states: the ideal of Jesus' gospel. Christians are to conform themselves in faith and obedience to none other than Jesus Christ. Christians are to follow Christ, not some earthly leader who claims their unquestioning patriotic allegiance, or some powerful state that offers prosperity but demands unwavering loyalty even in blatantly immoral actions. Bonhoeffer's question from prison persists even as a nation marches to a war that political and church leaders proclaim to be just: "Who really is Jesus Christ for us today?"[44]

Bonhoeffer's Spirituality of Peace and the United States' Militarism

Because so many Americans have turned Bonhoeffer into a folk hero and modern martyr, they seem to expect that Bonhoeffer would have been proud of the way in which the United States has been a force for peace in the world ever since the allied victory in World War II. If they would examine Bonhoeffer's writings more carefully, however, they might find a withering condemnation of any political system, including that of the United States, that engages in ideological, domineering, manipulative attitudes toward vulnerable peoples and nations. During the period of the Persian Gulf War, for example, we spoke in several churches on the prophetic theology and Christ-centered spirituality of Bonhoeffer. Our audiences, many of whom had been led to believe that Saddam Hussein was another Hitler, saw themselves in the same patterns as the allies lined up against the Nazi war machine. These congregations were for the most part surprised to find that the writings and actions of Bonhoeffer could just as well be directed against the American overkill of Iraqis and the massive destruction, unrelated to the liberation of Kuwait, that took the lives of countless civilians, including an estimated 49,000 children. Using documentation readily available in several newspapers and journals, we tried to point out that the continued bombing of and economic sanctions against that pathetic country had cost an additional half a million lives of Iraqi civilians. Indeed, Bonhoeffer's spirituality that challenges us to "dare peace" stands as a bracing reminder to America's gung-ho "patriots" that war, however well orchestrated by skilled politicians, brilliant military strategies, and smooth spinners of presidential policies, is still a denial of the gospel teachings of Jesus Christ.

The dulling downplay in the churches of America of moral sensitivity for the people of Iraq made palatable to many Christians the destructive bombing of defenseless villages and the consequent killing of innocents either through the bombing itself or through the lingering effects of having obliterated the industrial infrastructure needed to provide for the weakest citizens of Iraqi society. That massive terrorizing of the civilian population was, of course, dismissed by the Orwellian doublespeak of the Pentagon spokesmen as merely unfortunate accidents that happen in wartime. Such doublespeak was typical of how Jesus' preaching of agapeic love for and sensitivity toward one's supposed enemies could be suppressed by Christians who should know better and by churches that neglected their duty to proclaim the prophetic words of Jesus with any vehemence.

It is all too easy to avoid prophetic critiques of government even when news of war does not fill our headlines. Whatever became of the "peace dividend" that was supposed to come with the end of the Cold War? Was it used for the tax cut that has benefited the wealthiest of Americans? It seems that far from decreasing the military budget in favor of spending on education and other projects more promotive of human well-being, particularly among the destitute of American society, the United States Congress persists in bestowing on the military even more than they ask for. Some members of Congress will admit that, if they vote to cut some defense appropriations they know in their hearts are an unnecessary drain on the limited resources even a rich nation like the United States can afford, they will lose both campaign contributions and votes. So they most often will vote according to whatever helps them get reelected.[45] One can only wonder about the morality of their leadership!

Applying Bonhoeffer's spirituality in its pacifist dimensions to the cause of peace in the United States exposes three myths about America and Americans that this spirituality challenges. The first is that America has always been a peace-loving nation; second, that Americans have always respected the freedom of other nations and have not imposed their will on them; third, that Americans have always hated dictatorships. Unfortunately, our national penchant for comparative morality helps us reinforce these myths. Surely, we are not so grandiosely miscreant as, say, Hitler and the Nazis. Nor are we on the same level of international troublemaking as was Joseph Stalin and his evil empire. As the myth would have it, we liberate while other nations have colonized and tyrannized.

In face of this, Bonhoeffer's spirituality, so emphatic on the issues of obeying Christ's commands to love our enemies and to be people of peace, can help Americans admit that their respect for the freedom of other nations to be themselves is, at best, an abstract notion. The attitude that we have done no wrong blithely ignores our invasion and occupation of Haiti, Nicaragua, and Panama in this past century. It overlooks the CIA's toppling of democratically elected governments in Chile and Guatemala and subsequent propping up of their repressive governments, and our cozy ties to brutal dictatorships, such as in Samozan Nicaragua and the Dominican Republic. It glides over our myopic backing (at over a million dollars a day) of a Nazi-like Salvadoran military, trained first in Panama, and later in Fort Benning, Georgia, at the "School of the Americas." The name of this school has recently been sanitized to read "The Western Hemisphere Institute for Security Cooperation," but it is more accurately dubbed by peace activists the "School of Assassins." Graduates have created "death squads" in an attempt to defeat popular movements for liberation from systemic injustice — especially from the poor being exploited for their cheap labor. These American policies and actions hardly constitute the posture of a nation willing to allow people of other countries the freedom to choose their own form of government.

Peace and the Idolatrous National Security State

It is not possible to account for the militarism and barbarity that have characterized the suppression of dissent and the annihilation of enemies in both Nazi Germany and modern-day El Salvador without reference to the national security state. The invocation of the needs of national security has often been the justifying rationale behind the deceptions, lies, and violence engineered by the Central Intelligence Agency and the U.S. State Department in the nation's recent past to offset conjectured threats to the United States' political and business interests, whether from countries declared to be terrorist or from an unruly peasantry angrily threatening the cheap labor on which corporations have feasted. National security ideology is not a new phenomenon. Nor is it surprising that national security is still invoked by many in Congress to justify outlandish funding of expensive weaponry, even if such spending compared with that of other nations suggests not only that we are wasteful but also that we are in a ludicrous one-nation arms race.

Bonhoeffer's denunciation of the churches' unholy alliance with such an ideology came early on in his contribution to the ecumenical movement. In a disturbing talk at the ecumenical conference of Gland, Switzerland, in 1932, he succeeded in goading the assembled delegates to take another look at the consequences of their having uncritically honored the "idol of national security," accepting its violent side as the inescapable price of maintaining a peaceful status quo at home and national interests abroad. Bonhoeffer drew their attention to the power this idol exerted over the churches, deterring them from their mission to preach without flinching the gospel mandate of peace. His remarks on that occasion, fittingly entitled "The Church Is Dead," are uncanny in their attunement to the problems faced by the people whom Archbishop Romero would later defend against the mistreatment they suffered because of their supposed threat to "national security."

Bonhoeffer's words are likewise remarkably perceptive of the suffering to befall the German people on Hitler's accession to power through the promise of revenge on enemies and making Germany a proud, secure nation once again. Bonhoeffer warned the church delegates of the danger of this "national idolatry": "It is as though all the powers of the world had conspired together against peace: money, business, the lust for power, indeed, even love for the fatherland, have been pressed into the service of hate . . . and behind it all a world which bristles with weapons as never before, a world which feverishly arms itself to guarantee peace through weaponry, a world whose idol has become the word security — a world without sacrifice, full of mistrust and suspicion, because past fears are still with it."[46]

Bonhoeffer's views are surprisingly similar to sections from the bristling denunciation of this same idolatry in Archbishop Romero's Fourth Pastoral Letter, "The Church's Mission Amid the National Crisis." In his pastoral Romero complained that "peoples are put into the hands of military elites and are subjected to policies that oppress and repress all who oppose them, in the name of what is alleged to be total war. . . . the omnipotence of these national security regimes . . . turn national security into an idol, which, like the god Moloch, demands the daily sacrifice of many victims in its name."[47] When one ponders the number of times United States politicians and political candidates have trotted out national security needs to justify the CIA's secret budget of $30 billion with no accountability, the military's share now at over $300 billion per annum and climbing, the billions to be invested in "Star Wars," the additional 70 percent of all research directed toward military weaponry, the money poured into arms sales as the core of foreign aid to despotic leaders, and the denial of funds for the more pressing "war zones" at home, Bonhoeffer's words have a perennial accuracy about them.

Judging from acceptance of such annual budgets, national security is surely one of the altars where politicians and many church people burn a large portion of their incense. But such obscene budgetary allocations are not just limited to the United States. It is estimated that the nations of the world together spend close to two and a half billion dollars a day on military expenditures while nearly fifty thousand children die daily for lack of proper nourishment and medicine. And over forty million Americans, many of them children, suffer from relentless poverty. Dan Maguire has exposed the depths of this quasi-religious attitude toward national security, stating that the nation's well-being tied tightly into military might "is the credo of modern faith in America." He calls this a "twisted religion. Its believers are fervent, and empirical evidence that undermines their creed is dismissed as an irreverent irrelevance."[48]

This disparity in priorities for congressional funding has prompted Barbara Bennett Woodhouse, author of *Honor Thy Children*, to ask: "why is Congress so moved by the suffering of Bosnian children and so hardened to the suffering of our own? Is it because Bosnian children are so white, so innocent and so far away?" Despite the untold suffering of urban children in America, "the plight of these children seems unable to move those lawmakers who talk of 'hard fiscal choices,' oppose gun laws, seek to cut child nutrition and safety programs, and block grant children's services to states whose past records are abysmal."[49]

Bonhoeffer's Denunciation of War and the Church's Complicity

Bonhoeffer takes his own criticism of the idolatry of national security a step further by not only opposing a criminal government but also by blaming the churches for their complicity in the moral and physical devastation caused by Hitler and his fellow ideologues. Bonhoeffer was himself frustrated by his inability to convince the churches of Germany and the ecumenical churches abroad that they had the power to mobilize the people in a counterforce to Nazism and to save innocent victims from the aggression Hitler was preparing to unleash on Europe. Yet he saw these same churches in Germany pandering to the popular mood of the vast crowds of ordinary citizens enamored of Hitler's achievements and lost in admiration for his promotion of strong families, law and order in the streets, toughness on the "criminal element" (atheistic Bolsheviks and political dissenters), and national pride. Throughout the years of the tight Nazi grip on Germany, the majority of the churches continued to provide the moral support Hitler needed to rally citizens to back his master plans for the conquest of Europe, the extermination of enemies, and the establishment of a new world order, the much vaunted Nazi millennium.

It is no wonder, then, that Bonhoeffer directed most of his anger against these same churches. Bishops and clergy alike should have been a more vibrant moral force in Germany. Given the power of the Word of God in Jesus Christ, in whom Bonhoeffer believed so ardently, the churches, in his opinion, bore the greater guilt for not seeing through the "masquerade of evil" and not opposing Hitler with sufficient fortitude and consistency.

The same churches that claim Bonhoeffer as one of their own because of his struggle against fascism might be disconcerted to see themselves bitterly denounced by him for their unwillingness to reform themselves in light of that tormented period of Christian history. Bonhoeffer's indictment of the churches for their failure either to prevent or to bring to an end the repression of human rights and senseless, insane killings offers a lesson on how even well-intentioned churches can lose their vocation to be the prophetic Christ speaking peace against the demonic spirit of warlords. In his prison letters Bonhoeffer demanded that the churches once again become, as they had always boasted they were, the presence and word of Christ for their people.[50]

In short, Bonhoeffer's opposition to dictatorships and the wars they spawn constitutes a challenge to the churches to become, like Jesus, the protector of the outcast and the "voice of those who have no voice." That expression, now associated with the martyred Archbishop Romero, was in fact used by Bonhoeffer to explain why he had entered into solidarity with the Jewish victims of Nazi hatred. As we have seen, he cited Proverbs 31:8 ("Speak up for those who have no voice") as a biblical mandate to offset the unjust laws that denied Jews their human and civil rights in Nazi Germany. The church failure to defend the Jews, apart from a few non-offensive resolutions and toothless, indirect words of disapproval, was for him a weakness that permitted the brutal crimes perpetrated against that people.

Bonhoeffer's demands that the church rush to the aid of the victims, even to take steps to directly oppose the government, went largely unheeded. If Christians in America claim Bonhoeffer as exemplifying American ideals in the struggle for freedom, they should ask who among American church leaders publicly demonstrated anything resembling Bonhoeffer's outrage at the violence unleashed by Hitler and Nazism during the wild celebration of the American military victory in the Persian Gulf. Only a handful of editorial writers complained about the huge costs of the parades while official government decrees were quietly moving to cut the stingy benefits already allocated to war veterans. Other mischievous editorials dared point out the billions spent on weapons of death while the inner cities of America, looking war-torn themselves, suffered from poverty, decay, and crime. The cartoonist Tony Auth drew a satirical political cartoon depicting in opposite panels the "wars fought but not declared: Korea, Vietnam, Nicaragua" and the "wars declared but not fought: war on poverty and war on drugs." No matter! Many churches still hastened to offer prayers of thanks for the fact that so few American soldiers had been killed. Some included prayers for the Iraqi dead. Few saw the moral implications of killing an estimated 200,000 people, soldiers and civilians, to achieve political goals in an awesome display of overwhelming military supremacy over a smaller nation. Moral theologian Dan Maguire was prompted to point out the irony for Christians snug in their faith: "We are enthralled with war. We have parades for military killers, but not for peacemakers or healers."[51]

Where was the outcry of the church leaders when Generals Schwartzkopf and Powell were greeted as the new saviors of freedom and feted in all corners of America by adoring crowds, despite the reports of atrocities filtering through the Pentagon's iron curtain of news control? And given the poverty on the home front, did any church leaders protest with moral indignation the outlay of money siphoned from social programs to finance the excessive military expenditures? Where were the cries of anguish and the prophetic contestations when the extent of the killing and destruction of Iraq's industrial infrastructure (with cruel consequences to Iraq's children) was made known, when we could see more clearly the "collateral damage" of the war? One might also ask to what extent the teachings of Jesus, rather than the more abstract, arguable principles governing the declaration that a war was either "just" or "unjust," were invoked in those churches that registered their opposition to the war. The American church leaders sounded more like phlegmatic lawyers than outraged prophets. Here are the principles behind our judgment, now make your intelligent choices, they seemed to say! And most Americans reacted predictably with indifference. In a strange inversion of the foundation spirit of Christian faith, few, if any, of these "moral leaders" cited Jesus Christ in their message against the impending war.

One contemporary ethicist, Stanley Hauerwas, himself strongly influenced by Bonhoeffer, has thrown down his own gauntlet on the issue of pacifism and nonviolence. In an interview following the tragic events of September 11, 2001, Hauerwas voiced his "disappointment with an American Church that fails to instruct its adherents in basic gospel values." Called a "Christian contrarian" because of his courage in disputing popular assumptions and trends in ethical decision-making, Hauerwas has been consistently anti-war, anti-death penalty, and anti-abortion. He, like Bonhoeffer in the 1930s, has denounced the way Americans continue to invoke God's approval for their self-declared "just wars" and their bullying militarism. Hauerwas also rejects the naïve notion that God is always on the side of the United States, or that enemy nations are in league with the demonic. The invocation of God in "God and country" (ever together) is not, he says, an affirmation of the God of Jesus Christ. For him, no war has met the stringent standards required for it to be labeled "just." No war is in accord with the teachings of Jesus Christ. In rejecting the now-fashionable postwar congratulatory celebrations and patriotic displays of the symbols of military victory, Hauerwas offers his own chilling jeremiad: "In the past when Christians killed in a just war, it was understood they should be in mourning. They had sacrificed their unwillingness to kill. Black, not yellow, was the appropriate color. Indeed, in the past when Christian soldiers returned from a just war, they were expected to do penance for three years before being restored to the Eucharist. That we now find that to be unimaginable is but an indication of how hard it is for us to imagine what it might mean to be Christian."[52] Statements like these do not appeal to the popular mood. Nonetheless, Hauerwas's critique of militarism and of the churches' failure to emphasize the teachings of Jesus Christ in assessing moral issues is uncannily reminiscent of Bonhoeffer's own unpopular, lonely struggle for a restoration of gospel values in the Hitler era.

Suffering and Serenity in
Bonhoeffer's Spirituality of Peace

What is needed to counteract the world's continued attraction to and fascination for war and the heroism displayed only on bloody battlefields is something of Bonhoeffer's unrelenting efforts to inspire church leaders to more prophetic, self-sacrificing actions on behalf of peace. The deceptions he exposed within the churches of Nazi Germany were many. He bemoaned the fact that evil had appeared in their nation "disguised as light, charity, historical necessity, or social justice,"[53] a begrudging tribute to the propagandistic prowess of Joseph Goebbels. Bonhoeffer noted that the manipulative skills of Adolf Hitler often bewildered gullible church leaders trained in traditional ethics. Their favored method of reasoning with the enemy — single-mindedness in pursuit of their goals, invocation of conscience, fidelity to duty, cherishing the freedom of the Christian, and especially the practice of "virtuous patriotism" — were all co-opted by Hitler.

Bonhoeffer insisted that claiming to stand firm in one's faith is a sham unless accompanied by concrete action to overcome the barbaric injustices of the Nazi government. The men and women of the resistance had to risk losing their reputations as loyal citizens. Those who would deliver their nation from Fascist cruelty were not allowed to retreat into a sanctuary of unsullied virtue. The conspirators had entered a murky world where courage to undertake a violent coup d'état mingled with the guilt that prompted them to cry out for mercy and forgiveness from the Christ who had taken on himself the guilt of a sinful world. The only persons who could persevere in resistance to that inglorious world of twisted morality were those whose faith rested not on preserving their virtue, purity of conscience, obedience to duty, and personal freedom, but on Jesus Christ alone. They would die lonely deaths on Nazi scaffolds, branded as traitors to their country. Only years later would they be recognized as patriots and exemplars of Christian martyrdom in the cause of justice.[54]

CHAPTER SIX

Discipleship and the Cross

Following Christ in Bonhoeffer's Spirituality

> Like ravens we have gathered around the carcass of cheap grace. From it we have imbibed the poison that has killed the following of Jesus among us.[1]

At the outset of *Discipleship,* Dietrich Bonhoeffer declares that he wants to get behind the battle cries and catch words of the church struggle and to turn to the one person who ought to be the center of their concerns, Jesus Christ. Bonhoeffer's questions, shocking in their directness, set the tone for all the disturbing passages that follow. "What did Jesus want to say to us? What does he want from us today? How does he help us to be faithful Christians today?" As a caution against what the average German was hearing in church, Bonhoeffer concludes in this opening section, "It is not ultimately important to us what this or that church leader wants. Rather, we want to know what Jesus wants."[2] *Discipleship* is a book in which Bonhoeffer, using Jesus' own words and the exhortations of the Apostle Paul, confronts readers with uncushioned challenges to all their distortions of what it means to be a follower of Jesus Christ. The original German title, *Nachfolge,* is elliptical, meaning simply "following after," with "Jesus" being understood.[3] Bonhoeffer probes the seemingly "impossible demands" of Jesus' Sermon on the Mount against the economic materialism, patriotic militarism, and ruthless racism to which Christians and their churches had succumbed in Nazi Germany. What Jesus was commanding his followers thus became the guideline of every chapter of this book.

The Churches and the Nazi Menace to Christian Faith

Although the book was published in 1937, the words that have excited each new generation of readers were actually spoken or written much earlier, during Bonhoeffer's work as a young teacher in Berlin and as a seminary director in lectures to his seminarians. In *Discipleship* Bonhoeffer crafts a Christ-centered spirituality that incorporates the insights of his earlier writings on church, faith, community life, and gospel truth into the practical level of Christian life. As we have seen, Bonhoeffer himself was one of the leading theologians of the Confessing Church, which had come into being as a result of pastoral outrage at Hitler's subversion of the established Protestant churches in Germany. Those churches, dominated by the faction of the so-called "German Christians" (emphasis on "German" rather than "Christian"!) and known for their undivided loyalty to Adolf Hitler, had become united under a national Bishop sympathetic to the Nazi cause. Bonhoeffer and his Confessing Church colleagues refused to compromise with this far more extensive Reich Church. They manifested their open hostility to the domineering Nazi ideology behind this "national church" with the weapons at hand: synodal declarations and confessions of faith. The Barmen Declaration of May 1934 had become the founding document of this Confessing Church. In it the Confessing pastors stated their repudiation of "the false doctrine, as though there were areas of our life in which we would not belong to Jesus Christ, but to other lords — areas in which we would not need justification and sanctification through him."[4] The allusion to the rejection of Adolf Hitler's lordship over the churches is unmistakable, even though Hitler is not named. The Nazi government, in turn, through its ministry for church affairs, reacted by enacting ever more stringent regulations that squeezed the Confessing Church into narrow pockets where the dissident pastors could be smeared with accusations of disloyalty to Germany. The more uncompromising pastors were subjected to demeaning psychological and economic coercion and harsh imprisonment. The Nazis thus stymied an effective church opposition to the government even as German citizens were themselves subjected to strangulating control in every aspect of their daily lives. It soon became apparent to Bonhoeffer that Christian civilization, the faith of his people, and even world peace were in jeopardy if the criminal excesses of the Nazi government were not opposed and uprooted.

It was also clear to Bonhoeffer that throughout the whole sordid history of Nazi domination of the German nation, the churches themselves were either witting or unwitting accomplices. He became convinced that more daring strategies had to be set in motion to snap these churches out of their standard mode of compromise and accommodation with political powers for the sake of their own survival and the retention of their clerical privileges. For Bonhoeffer, the puffy statements of so many church leaders at every stage of Hitler's rise to power were in sharp contrast to the fearless castigation of systemic evil one finds in the inspiring words of Jesus Christ.

Cheap Grace and Costly Grace in the Church Struggle

During his years as director of the illegal Confessing Church seminary at Finkenwalde in Pomerania, Bonhoeffer presented his thoughts on "Following Christ" in the paths of Christian discipleship, which later became this book. Bonhoeffer's biographer, Eberhard Bethge, called Bonhoeffer's reflections on the Sermon on the Mount the "nerve center" of the seminary and the book that ensued, "Finkenwalde's own badge of distinction."[5] In these lectures he opened to his seminarians the personal heart of his own spirituality: discipleship and the cross, living out the teachings of Jesus Christ even if that led to their persecution and martyrdom. The opening passages of his book expose his deeply felt chagrin at the church's watering down of Jesus' teachings and example. He shares his conviction that too many church leaders had cheapened themselves and misled their parishioners. The Protestant principles of faith alone, Scripture alone, and giving glory to God alone now had deteriorated into mere boorish churchgoing, easy procurement of sacramentalized grace, and reduction of the Bible to legalisms and routine rituals. In the opening pages of *Discipleship,* Bonhoeffer plunges straightaway into what he views as the real source of the crisis generated by the collapse of any effective resistance to Nazism: "Cheap grace is the mortal enemy of our church. Our struggle today is for costly grace."[6]

Bonhoeffer then moves to the problem of following Jesus Christ when so many pastors and churchgoers lived comfortably in thrall to a seductive political dictator. He alerts his readers from the outset that Christian discipleship has to be lived with utter seriousness. Christian life was at a crossroads, and the direction Christians took would determine whether or not they and their churches were true or false followers of Christ. In typical German church life Bonhoeffer detected only "cheap grace." This expression, which to this day theologians associate with Bonhoeffer, represented his dismay at the easygoing displacement of genuine Christian faith in the crisis years of Hitler's rise to absolute power. As he put it, "Cheap grace is that grace which we bestow on ourselves. Cheap grace is preaching forgiveness without repentance; it is baptism without the discipline of community; it is the Lord's Supper without confession of sin; it is absolution without personal confession. Cheap grace is grace without discipleship, grace without the cross, grace without the living, incarnate Jesus Christ."[7]

For Bonhoeffer, the spirituality of "costly grace" is to be found only along the obedient ways of following Jesus Christ. This spirituality, he insists, offers no set program, no set of principles, no elitist ideals, and certainly no new set of laws to preserve purity of doctrine. Christian discipleship means simply Jesus Christ alone. "It is costly," he admits, "because it calls to discipleship; it is grace, because it calls us to follow Jesus Christ. It is costly, because it costs people their lives; it is grace, because it gives them their lives. It is costly because it condemns sin; it is grace because it justifies the sinner."[8] In Bonhoeffer's spirituality this call to follow Jesus is the unique experience of both liberating grace and Christ's command, devoid of legalism yet binding. "It is," Bonhoeffer observes, "nothing other than being bound to Jesus Christ alone. This means completely breaking through anything preprogrammed, idealistic, or legalistic. No further content is possible, because Jesus is the only content."[9]

Bonhoeffer laments in *Discipleship* the loss of a sense of Jesus' presence in the churches. He notes that monastic spirituality once held the promise of preserving genuine Christian discipleship, as those involved left everything for the purpose of following Jesus' commands more strictly. But this development was doomed. It was suffocated at the hands of the very church it had protected from the decay of creeping secularization. The church, which had grown affluent and comfortable, manipulated monasticism to justify its own addiction to a status quo of wealth and privilege. It relativized monastic life by declaring it fit only for a specially graced elite but not for the average churchgoer. Monastic spirituality was thus saddled to the easier ways of being Christian.

When Martin Luther unraveled this ironic distortion of Christian life by leaving the monastery and preaching against the monastic repudiation of the sinful world, Lutheran spirituality was put on course to be the leaven of faith that made worldly holiness possible. Luther had geared this development in his spirituality into a "frontal assault" on the false values that had enslaved people in the chains of materialism, lasciviousness, and worldly indifference to the teachings of Jesus Christ. In

Bonhoeffer's opinion, if such was the original effect of this aspect of the Lutheran Reformation, its noble aim had deteriorated in the modern world into a justification not of the sinner, but of sin. During the crisis years of the Hitler era, Christians had become, in Bonhoeffer's caustic judgment, "like ravens . . . gathered around the carcass of cheap grace," imbibing "the poison which has killed the following of Jesus."[10] The spread of this poison would cause the loss of discipleship in Christ as Christian life itself was handed over to legalists, fanatics, and cynical secularists. Jesus' call to follow him was seldom heard and the light of Christian discipleship "mercilessly extinguished."[11] Bonhoeffer proposed to his seminarians that they encourage their parishioners to follow Christ with more pristine fervor and to "live in the world without losing themselves in it."[12] This to him was closer to the original intent of Luther in extending God's gift of faith as a mandate, not to be overcome by the world's easygoing ways of being Christian, but to Christianize their world with all the graced energy of Jesus' own life and example.

Christian Obedience to the Word of Jesus Christ

Bonhoeffer detected a complication in the modern-day rejection of Christian discipleship: the failure to take Jesus Christ at his word, still less to obey Jesus' commands in all their forthrightness and simplicity. The question Bonhoeffer hoped to resolve through a renewed sense of discipleship was how to bring self-seeking and self-centeredness under the authority of Jesus Christ and his standards of Christian conduct in the Sermon on the Mount. His search for an answer brought him to affirm the single-minded obedience to Christ that he believed to be the essence of Christian faith. *Discipleship* is as much a communication of his own shift from being a "self-serving theologian" to the reality of following Christ as it is a challenge to the German church in its struggle against Nazism.

In an ironic way Bonhoeffer considers the act of inconveniencing oneself to serve others as a liberating force in one's spiritual life. In Bonhoeffer's spirituality, Christian freedom must include utter devotion to those in need after the manner of Jesus, whose cross is the ultimate symbol of being for others. The example of Jesus Christ prompted Bonhoeffer to insist in his lectures on Genesis that freedom is not something people have for themselves alone, but a quality they extend in serving those beyond themselves. Christians are truly free only in relationship with others.[13] This is how Bonhoeffer interpreted the gospel message that as Christians we are bound to the very self-sacrificing freedom of the God who in Christ became "weak" for our sakes. Christians, touched by God's grace, become free inasmuch as they are dedicated to those who also may address God as Father and to whom Christ is brother — even though they may not be conscious of it.[14]

This kind of freedom presupposes, however, that people are also liberated from the disorderliness that impedes wholehearted commitment to the gospel teachings of Jesus. Again, Bonhoeffer's spiritual outlook attempts to preserve the paradox of Christian discipleship: the faith of the disciple of Jesus Christ is truly liberating only if joined with the obedience to Christ's word that appears to limit one's freedom to do as one pleases. Hence Bonhoeffer's injunction: "Only the believers obey and only the obedient believe."[15] He is not arguing that faith in its freeing dynamic needs to be supplemented by some obedient action. Rather, he saw the whole sphere of obedience to God's will in any age inextricably bound to the gift of faith and to the gospel of what God has done for us in Jesus Christ. Faith and obedience are linked together in a dialectical and indissoluble unity in which willingness to serve God by obeying the gospel mandates is the natural and spontaneous note of Christian life governed by the person and mission of Jesus Christ. Earlier, in urging Christians to do their part in bringing about peace on their turbulent earth, Bonhoeffer spoke words that exude the simplicity of his spirituality. It is a matter, he says, of simple obedience to God's Word: "The command, 'You shall not kill,' and the word, 'love your enemy,' are given us simply to obey."[16] Bonhoeffer's friend Eberhard Bethge once recalled that the pairing of those reciprocal concepts seemed "rather shocking" to Lutherans wary of any hint of salvation-by-works doctrine. "There was hardly a German theologian who hadn't left the world of 'simple obedience,' that is, the world of understanding the Sermon on the Mount literally, to the pietists, the enthusiasts and the radicals. But he tried to win it back for a liberated faith."[17] To illustrate the need to conjoin absolute obedience to one's professed faith in Jesus Christ, Bonhoeffer took his seminarians and readers back to the apostolic age in order to see how the first followers of Jesus reacted to his teachings. Without looking back, the disciples gave themselves unstintingly to live as Christ counseled them. Despite the personal sacrifices demanded of them, Jesus' way of being the truth compelled them to love their Lord and Savior.

Obedience to the Call to Follow Christ Even to Death

Bonhoeffer used the apostles' eagerness in answering the call of Jesus Christ to expose the subterfuges and rationalizations of those who avoid the call. Christians evade the exigencies of their professed faith when they proclaim their pride in being disciples of Christ but are totally ignorant of the utter poverty it may require, or when they slavishly let obeying the law interfere with Jesus' call, or when they set their own conditions for following Jesus.[18] Peter, on the other hand, for all his blustering, is willing to take that first step at Jesus' call, even though from a human point of view his walking on the sea of Galilee is both impossible and irresponsible.[19] It is Jesus alone who turns his seeming recklessness into an act of faith. Bonhoeffer dwells on the need for followers of Christ to take the first step like Peter into the unknown. At stake for Bonhoeffer is the obedience to Jesus' call and acceptance of his demands without which faith becomes entangled in a lethal self-centeredness. On this point Bonhoeffer's spirituality is akin to Kierkegaard's observation that the leap of faith is the risk of love, and the only certitude we can enjoy is trust in the one we love.[20]

Bonhoeffer compared the rich young man of Mark's Gospel with the lawyer's self-justifying query about the neighbor we are supposed to love in the parable of the Good Samaritan. In each instance, the answer to the question is simply Jesus Christ, whether it be the voluntary poverty Jesus counsels or the compassionate neighborliness that asks no reward.[21] Uppermost in Bonhoeffer's intentions is to restore the biblical connections between the life, death, and resurrection of Jesus Christ and the present-day call to a new life of genuine Christian discipleship. He believed that what Christians needed desperately in the Hitler era was to recover true communion with Jesus Christ, to commit themselves "solely to the person of Jesus Christ." The dogmatic systems then in vogue were, in fact, mere ideas about Jesus unrelated to the personal obediential relationship to which Jesus calls his followers. "Christianity without the living Jesus Christ," he wrote, "remains necessarily a Christianity without discipleship, and a Christianity without discipleship is always a Christianity without Jesus Christ."[22]

At the same time, Bonhoeffer acknowledged that following Christ in full obedience to the gospel call is to endure suffering patterned after Jesus' own experience of rejection, condemnation, and the cross. He cited Jesus' searing reminder to would-be disciples: "If any want to become my followers, let them deny themselves and take up their cross and follow me"

(Mark 8:34). In unforgettable, sobering words, Bonhoeffer told his readers that every Christian worthy of the name must bear the cross: "Whenever Christ calls us, his call leads us to death."[23] This "death" of the Christian assumes all the forms one finds in belonging to a genuinely Christian church community, from the daily struggle against sin to acts of forbearance and mutual forgiveness, and even to open persecution and martyrdom. "Discipleship," he said, "is being bound to the suffering Christ."[24] Even this, he argued, is made possible by the indescribable confidence in Jesus' spiritual nearness transforming even grotesque torments into the blessed joy of knowing one is suffering in union with Jesus Christ.

Christian Discipleship as Living the Beatitudes

Bonhoeffer's many years of interaction with and reflection on the Sermon on the Mount reach their fullest expression in those sections of *Discipleship* that challenge Christians to follow Christ wherever they may be led. In Bonhoeffer's spirituality, being bonded to the sufferings of Jesus Christ extends not only to the ultimate sacrifice of one's life but to the daily acts of renunciation that define discipleship as described in the beatitudes. Bonhoeffer declares at the outset of his commentary that the beatitudes are the point of convergence where discipleship and the cross, the sufferings of Jesus and the Christian community, come together. Jesus proclaims his followers to be blessed in what the world would call misery: poverty, meekness, sorrowing, rejection, sufferings, persecution, even death. This is the paradox of joy in suffering, life in death, that only intimacy with Jesus, not any political or social program, can bring about.

In offering unique observations about these dimensions of the Christian spiritual life, Bonhoeffer indirectly provides guidelines for genuine moral leadership. Those who mourn are blessed, for example, because they are not caught up in the world's definitions of happiness and peace. They mourn the idolatries of their secularized world. They are unwilling to conform themselves to society's standards or to join in celebrations while the country parades its own economic prowess, military might, and futuristic achievements as the real kingdom of God. Christians, he points out, are to be strangers in that phony world and, in the name of the only true peace of Jesus Christ, disturbers of false peace based on a belligerent order. They give witness to this peace by bearing the sufferings the idolatrous, security-minded world inflicts on them: "As bearers of suffering, they stand in union with the Crucified. They stand as aliens in the power of him, who was so alien to the world that it crucified him. This is their comfort, or rather, he is their comfort, their comforter."[25] Bonhoeffer sees the strength of Christians in the midst of their sufferings in the sustaining power of Jesus Christ. In the face of their enemies they can be neither worn down nor embittered. They remain at peace with the blessed calm that comes from obedient faith to their crucified Savior. They endure the violence done to them, leaving ultimate justice to God alone. If they hunger and thirst for righteousness, they know that they cannot achieve this by themselves. Only the Lord in God's own time and ways can bring it about. Their consolation is the cry of Christ rejected and dying in desperate longing for the vindication denied him.[26] It is not surprising that in prison Bonhoeffer continued to derive intense comfort in pondering this cry of Jesus: "My God, my God, why have you forsaken me?" (Matt. 27:46).[27] In Bonhoeffer's spiritual outlook and because of the sacrificial death of Jesus, what people fear as death is in reality resurrection. To those who knew Bonhoeffer it came as no surprise that his last recorded words before his execution were: "This is the end; but for me, also the beginning of life."[28]

Bonhoeffer wrote that the death of Jesus paralleled the death to self endured by those who would be merciful. In Bonhoeffer's spiritual outlook, following Jesus to death entails a renunciation even of one's own personal dignity. Those who embrace the beatitudinal way of compassion, he said, "share in other people's need, debasement, and guilt." Christians join the ranks of the disenfranchised by making common cause with those reprobated and marginalized by their government. He praised those who, in the face of their own needs, "have an irresistible love for the lowly, the sick, the suffering, for those who are demeaned and abused, for those who suffer injustice and are rejected, for everyone in pain and anxiety."[29] Even more painful than the sacrifice of their lives, the followers of Jesus give away their greatest possession, "their own dignity and honor," in order to be compassionate. Bonhoeffer assured his readers, some of whom had already experienced the indignity of being branded unpatriotic, disloyal Jew lovers or enemies of the Nazi party, that God took on their shame and would eventually deliver them from evil.

Bonhoeffer applied the beatitude in which Jesus blesses the pure of heart to those who, in all childlike simplicity, depend solely on Jesus Christ and not on some idolatrous substitute. He was uncompromising in his opinion that genuine Christians must belong wholly to Jesus and not some deceptive earthly lord or to some materialistic icon of their own success story. Those who have looked only to Jesus in the twists and turns of their lives will alone receive the ultimate grace of seeing God, because they have been purified of the defiling images that deaden the conscience. "They will see God," he writes, "whose hearts mirror the image of Jesus Christ."[30]

As we have seen in the previous chapter, the Christian whose soul is centered on Jesus Christ's gospel commands must be ranged among the peacemakers of this world. Christians "are not only to have peace, but they are to make peace." They do this by courageously "choosing to suffer instead of causing others to suffer." In Nazi Germany, about to unleash the military against its neighboring nations with all the murderous targeting of civilian life that comes with war, Bonhoeffer's words stood out as a critical exception to the popular mood. The world of discipleship, he observed, is a world already torn by hatred and violence. It is the Christian's task to preserve and restore community despite the destructiveness of ideologues against those who attempt to make peace in the name of Jesus. Those who work for peace are God's children because they work in communion with God's own son Jesus, "bearing the cross with their Lord, for peace was made at the cross."[31]

The Community of Suffering
for the Sake of Christ's World

Bonhoeffer wondered aloud what his readers might be thinking: where in the world does such a community of genuine followers of Jesus Christ exist? Only in one place: "the place where the poorest, the most tempted, the meekest of all may be found, at the cross of Golgotha." The kind of spirituality Bonhoeffer espoused in *Discipleship*, if followed, exposes Christians to slander, revilement, and persecution. Those responsible for the systemic injustices that spawn destitution and death are disturbed by the negative judgments, sometimes spoken but often simply implied, in the example of Christians who live their faith in open contradiction to the values espoused by their society. This is to be expected, for "Things cannot go any other way than that the world unleashes its fury in word, violence, and defamation at those meek strangers." The witness of Christians comes across as threatening to those ensconced in a comfortable status quo and as "too strong a witness to the injustice of the world."[32]

Despite the dangers and threats of persecution, Bonhoeffer urged the Christians of Germany to be that "salt of the earth" and "light of the world" that Jesus enjoins on his followers, even as their discipleship in its visibility separated them from the secularized misconduct around them. Although Bonhoeffer advocated a definite demarcation of Christian church life from the world with its festering, dehumanizing ideologies, this is neither promotion of otherworldly dualism nor avoidance of the call to improve society. Bonhoeffer's initial audience was a church under attack by the state. He was also writing in the political ambience of a ruthless, powerful government that had abrogated all criticism and pre-empted to itself control over the conduct of church affairs, forcing acceptance of racist, bellicose, and nationalistic policies as the price for the church's continued existence. It is not astonishing that he avoided here many of his previous positive assessments of the world, and even his references to the Lutheran doctrine of the two kingdoms in his early theology — in short, anything that could add to the incense church leaders were busily burning at Nazi altars — in favor of a more eschatological perspective. Nonetheless, in *Discipleship* there is no question of a "flight from the world." On the contrary, Bonhoeffer was struggling to establish a critical church presence in the world. He was a vigorous critic of the church's apparent yielding to the seduction of the Nazi millennium. If in the context of such church-state conflict Bonhoeffer stressed the ultimate significance and present role of the church, it was for the sake of the church's penultimate loyalty to the earth. Even while distinguishing church and world, he insisted that, through them, God's Word must go forth from the church into all the world. Disciples are called to follow Jesus; their discipleship, Bonhoeffer noted, must be "as visible as light in the night, as a mountain in the flatland."[33]

As we have seen in the previous chapter, that light included what in Nazi Germany was considered highly suspicious and unpatriotic: pacifism. Bonhoeffer insisted that Christians are not to repay in kind the evil done to them. Instead, evil is to be overcome by suffering without retaliation. The followers of Jesus are sustained by their communion with his cross; suffering is their freely chosen mode of discipleship. His conviction that injustice is overcome by nonviolence led Bonhoeffer to several radical statements that are in turn a challenge to Christians today. Americans live in a culture that is dominated by vengeful, violent attitudes toward personal enemies, incarcerated criminals, and unfriendly, ideologically opposed nations. Yet from the gospel evidence, Jesus does not tolerate the nursing of hateful, revenge-laden feelings. Bonhoeffer insisted, therefore, that the Christian attitude toward enemies reflect the extraordinary love that Jesus manifested and enjoined on his followers. With this in mind, he asked the extraordinary question about loving one's enemies: "Who, therefore, is more worthy of my love than my foe? Where is love praised more splendidly than amidst one's enemies?"[34]

As revolutionary as that notion is, he added one even more revolutionary: if Christians are to share their possessions and life with their brothers and sisters, even more so are they obliged to share with their enemies. Bonhoeffer's cue for these claims was Paul's injunction to provide food and shelter to those who have made life a misery for Christians (Rom. 12:20-21). Bonhoeffer did not promise that these enemies would thereby cease their abuse of Christians. But he was convinced that, following the example of Jesus Christ, the bearing of violent persecution can only move the enemy closer to reconciliation with God, as Christian love in the face of violence becomes ever more irresistible and the enemy is eventually won over.

This is why Bonhoeffer continued to remind his readers that Jesus commands his followers to "pray for those who abuse and persecute" them. Such forbearance and love is what Jesus had asked of his disciples in declaring that their righteousness had to be different from and more than the so-called goodness of the Pharisees and Sadducees, with their legalistic, minimalist approach to religious faith. In commenting on this difficult command of Jesus, Bonhoeffer noted that what is distinctly Christian is the extraordinary love, self-denial, truthfulness, and espousal of non-violence that set Christians apart from the ordinary believers in their society. "What is unique in Christianity," he wrote, "is the cross, which allows Christians to transcend what the world does and gives them victory over the world."[35] But this victory needs to be visible, out in the open, just as Jesus was crucified in a mocking public display of his helplessness. The suffering in the disciples' decision to follow Jesus was paradoxically their joy and the inner core of their holiness.

Following Jesus in the Hiddenness of Christian Discipleship

Yet despite this need to be a disciple publicly, Bonhoeffer added, the disciple's visibility also has a hidden dimension. The moral righteousness of Christians, like their freedom, taps into the humility of Jesus Christ, who did not brandish his unique powers before an unbelieving world. Christians are not to do their extraordinary works of love in order to be seen and admired. Their focus is not even on their own goodness, but on Jesus, whose own goodness seemed as natural as it was obvious. Christians are to act in simple obedience to their Lord, whose divinity was hidden before the wise and powerful of this world and whose own life was beset with insult and reprobation. Christians cannot afford to tarry in self-satisfying reflections on their accomplishments, lest they be tempted to trumpet their own goodness as a holier-than-thou status well above those they disparage. The hiddenness of their virtue, Bonhoeffer says, is for Christians a death of the "old self" in which "the love of Christ crucified . . . lives in Christ's followers."[36] Their existence is not in the glorious starburst of moral superiority but in the shadow of Jesus Christ's cross. Bonhoeffer shows how not only their prayer but also their lives are directed solely to their Father God, who knows their needs, and their brother Jesus, who tells his followers to forgive as they have been forgiven. Entrusting their hearts to God, as Bonhoeffer counsels his readers, makes possible the simplicity and happiness of the carefree life that Jesus exalted when he pointed to the birds of the air and lilies of the fields. Followers of Jesus are called to joy by sharing in Jesus' own freedom from materialistic domination. The simplicity Bonhoeffer idealized is not a mindless naiveté, but a refusal to succumb to the lure of greedy materialism.

That lure was part of Hitler's winning pitch with the German masses. Bonhoeffer argued here that the followers of Jesus Christ could not go along with the mainstream of German society in its support of the dictator, even though powerful people in their society would resent them. Bonhoeffer's question is as emphatic as it is rhetorical: "How could they suffer need who in hunger and nakedness, persecution and danger are confident of their communion with Jesus Christ?"[37] Jesus often told his followers not to be afraid of their enemies' power, which stops at their physical death. Disciples overcome their fear of death with reverence for God's presence; Jesus stands with them, giving them the Spirit to speak through them in time of turmoil. Bonhoeffer's words were timely in a period when Nazi agents were arresting pastors and terrorizing potential dissenters with no respect for either civility or law. Bonhoeffer neither softened nor minimized the difficulties of following Jesus. He did not deny that following Jesus leads to the cross and the cup of bitterness. But he stressed the focal point of their hope: "Those who have held onto Jesus in this life will find that Jesus will hold onto them in eternity."[38]

The Demands of a Christian's Baptismal Consecration

Bonhoeffer next turned to the Apostle Paul's teachings on the need for Christians to live and die in Christ conscious of their baptismal consecration. Here as elsewhere, Bonhoeffer's writings are infused with Luther's theology of the cross and Paul's preaching solely Christ crucified. With Luther he insists that all individual as well as ecclesiastical goodness can come only through Christ's salvific death. Bonhoeffer made it clear that those who follow Jesus Christ must live a special kind of worldliness that casts a critical judgment on human pretentiousness. He viewed the Sermon on the Mount as a worldly document, not a retreat from Christians' visible witnessing in and to the world. In the second part of *Discipleship,* he depicted Paul's understanding of baptism and his directives for the practical everyday living out of the gospel as a dying to a world that, without Jesus Christ, is itself dying the death of ideological corrosion. In effect, Bonhoeffer's spirituality is grounded in Christ's mandate to break with any civil rule that denies the dignity of people for whom Jesus Christ died and with whom Jesus Christ has identified as his brothers and sisters.

The human dignity of the "least" of those brothers and sisters was for Bonhoeffer a natural consequence of living in communion with Jesus Christ. Resistance to the ideological perversion that dehumanizes those in whom Christ dwells beyond all boundaries of color, blood, religious, and national differences is a vital aspect of Bonhoeffer's spirituality. Such resistance is the only practical way Christians of Nazi Germany could confess that "in Christ we no longer live our own lives, but Christ lives his life in us."[39] To suffer for this crucial act of faith in the Body of Christ extended to include those with whom Christ identifies is the privilege of suffering for and with Christ. Bonhoeffer invoked Paul, who tells Christians that their own sufferings complement the sufferings of Jesus in every society where Christ identifies with the least of his people. Bonhoeffer called this demand on Christian faith the "miracle and grace" of living in communion with the body of Christ.[40] Such communion is a grace because it is made possible by God alone, and a privilege because Christians are permitted to proclaim Jesus Christ in their suffering and dying for the "least," most impoverished, most oppressed members of Christ's body.

Despite the risks of defying Nazism's threats against dissenters, including clergy who dared criticize official government policies, Bonhoeffer never backed down from his demand that Christians and their churches step up their visibility in witnessing to Jesus Christ. Bonhoeffer acknowledged the presence of Jesus' body in the twentieth-century community of those reaching out in Word and sacrament to their fellow human beings as they would to their needy Lord. Those who in goodwill and compassion live for one another in the manner of Jesus' earliest followers are those who co-create "a perfect community . . . established freely, joy-fully, and by the power of the Holy Spirit, a community in which 'there was not a needy person,' in which possessions were distributed 'as any had need,' and in which 'no one claimed private ownership of any posses-sions.'"[41]

Bonhoeffer understood the spiritual call to be part of this community as an invitation from Jesus Christ to become his communal form in every generation, suffering from the same rejection he experienced at the hands of a hostile world. Thus Bonhoeffer wrote of Christ's community assum-ing "a 'form' that is different from that of the world" because it is inspired to be increasingly transformed into Jesus Christ. A true Christian commu-nity is, in fact, "the form of Christ himself" who "came into the world and in infinite mercy bore us and accepted us. And yet he did not become con-formed to the world but was actually rejected and cast out by it. He was not of this world."[42] Though the tone of his remarks here seems other-worldly, Bonhoeffer simply intended a more correct perspective on the vo-cation of Christians who, like their Lord, are attacked precisely because their actions are seen by the enemies of God for what they are: an un-abashed solidarity with the underclass of society and a protest against the mistreatment of the most vulnerable.

What Christians do, Bonhoeffer said, must be qualitatively different from the actions of their counterparts in all areas of their secular profes-sions. This element in his spirituality may lead to Christians being es-tranged from and even hated by their own society. Yet, in a completely ironic way, their alienation from the anti-Christian values of their world and their suffering at the hands of the godless may be the only shield that preserves the world from God's wrath. "Christians are," he wrote, "poor and suffering, hungry and thirsty, gentle, compassionate and peaceable, persecuted and scorned by the world. Yet it is for their sake alone that the world is still preserved. They shield the world from God's judgment of wrath. They suffer so that the world can still live under God's forbearance. They are strangers and sojourners on this earth."[43] This element of the vi-carious sufferings of Jesus and his followers offers a view of suffering as salvific expiation for the sins of the world that extends from the theology of Jesus' death on the cross to the deaths of modern-day Christians in the killing fields of the twenty-first century.

Christian Holiness in Conformity with Jesus Christ

Even with his insistence on the need for Christian witness to be public and visible, Bonhoeffer also pointed out that Christian holiness is at its greatest intensity when hidden from Christians until the day Christ will reveal that their good works were done to him and were in themselves the work of the Spirit of God. That depth is unveiled only at the moment of Christian resurrection when, as Bonhoeffer wrote, "Without knowing it, we have fed him, provided him with drink, given him clothes, and visited him."[44] The astonishment of that moment gives way to the realization of what was confessed only in faith: our goodness is ultimately the work of God.

Bonhoeffer closed *Discipleship* with a remarkable plea for Christians to be conformed to the image of Jesus Christ. He said that such conformity is not something we accomplish on our own; rather, it is the impact in our lives of God's design "to take shape within us."[45] "In Christ's incarnation," Bonhoeffer argued, "all of humanity regains the dignity of bearing the image of God. Whoever from now on attacks the least of the people attacks Christ, who took on human form and who in himself has restored the image of God for all who bear a human countenance."[46] This subtle reference to the Jewish victims of Nazi genocide has far-reaching implications for the Jewish-Christian dialogue after the Holocaust. "Jesus Christ was a Jew," he would write in his *Ethics*.[47] Bonhoeffer called the Christian conformity to Jesus Christ the exterior sign of Christ's dwelling in the hearts of his followers. To be like Christ is to follow his example; it is, as Bonhoeffer concluded, to be "able to do those deeds, and in the simplicity of discipleship, to live life in the likeness of Christ."[48]

CHAPTER SEVEN

Christian Community

Strength for Moral Leadership

The church-community is so structured that wherever one
of its members is, there too is the church community in its
power, which means in the power of Christ and the Holy
Spirit. . . . Whoever lives in love is Christ in relation to the
neighbor. . . . Christians can and ought to act like Christ;
ought to bear the burdens and sufferings of the neighbor. . . . It must come to the point that the weaknesses,
needs, and sins of my neighbor afflict me as if they were my
own, in the same way as Christ was afflicted by our sins.[1]

One of the main reasons why readers find Bonhoeffer's writings so
compelling lies in the inner strength and intensity of his relationship with Jesus Christ developed in the practical everyday life of a Christian community. When he wrote his account of his community-sustained
spiritual life in the Finkenwalde seminary, he was not reminiscing about
an agreeable, idyllic experience of a like-minded group of dedicated seminarians. He intended to share with others this experience, with its joys
and trials, its mutual support and enduring friendships, that it might
serve as a model for forming moral leaders and for the creation of new
forms of church community throughout Germany. With vivid memories
of how he and his seminarians were able to form a supportive community
for each other in Finkenwalde, he wrote that what they accomplished
could become a possibility for the church as a whole. In fact, it was entirely possible, he said, for the creation of communities like these to be-

come a bona fide "mission entrusted to the church."[2] In depicting that community in *Life Together,* Bonhoeffer also acknowledged the urgent need for the church to discover new and different ways to be the church. He thus emphasized the courageous following of Jesus Christ within a genuine community formed along the lines of the gospel, not the typical kind of church gatherings where strangers met and remained strangers, and whose dull blandness offered little resistance to the political ideology that had successfully gained the allegiance of most churchgoers. In Bonhoeffer's spirituality, effective moral leadership and one's personality strengths are supported in and through the sharing of convictions that takes place in genuine Christian communities where the teachings of Jesus Christ, not political ideology, should inspire believers.

Early Attempts to Form Community

From his biographer we learn that Bonhoeffer harbored a desire to live in and help shape a Christian community from his first days as a student at Berlin University.[3] He was intrigued then, as he was in the years that ensued, by the mystery of how God in Jesus Christ becomes present in and among those who gather to profess their faith together and celebrate through Word and sacrament their oneness in the Lord. His earliest attempts to put into practice his ideas on Christian community, however, began in the circle of his admiring students. At Berlin University his seminars, evening discussions, and country excursions brought him into closer contact with like-minded students, some of whom later became his colleagues in the church struggle. Several would enter the seminary to study under him. Together with these students of theology he organized frequent weekend trips to a rented cottage in the hilly countryside well beyond the outskirts of Berlin, where they could discuss theology, work into their day some spiritual exercises, and enjoy long walks and pleasant hours of listening to Bonhoeffer's collection of the spirituals that had so enthralled him during his pastoral ministry at the Abyssinian Baptist Church in Harlem. During these times apart from the hubbub of university life, these young men thought seriously about how to form enduring Christian communities through a structured spiritual life and assist people in need. Though these beginnings in community life were informal and spontaneous, they provided some of the sparks for the creation of the kind of community life that Bonhoeffer presented in *Life Together* with a view to reanimate the Christian churches in Germany and withstand the lure of Nazism.

The events of the church struggle that began in earnest in 1933 were to hinder Bonhoeffer from developing this early, more casual experience of community with his students into something more permanent. Yet by the end of 1932, most of the conceptual underpinnings of the community life he would develop in detail in *Life Together* were already in place. Aside from his analysis of Christian church community in his Berlin dissertations, there are additional declarations in his lectures on the nature of the church and in the conferences of that period that show how the idea of belonging to a genuine Christian community continued to dominate his thinking. Bonhoeffer was interested not in merely theologizing about church, but in being part of a church community committed to God's Word in service of others, particularly society's unfortunates, and willing to make the sacrifices embodied in truthfully following Jesus Christ, even though that way might lead to the cross. He left no doubt about his desire to enter into a community life that, with the courage of Jesus Christ and in obedience to Jesus' teachings, could live out the gospel more intensely and thus cope more courageously with the crises then overwhelming the German people and their churches. In hindsight, one wonders whether the slaughter that took place in the war and the death camps could have been avoided had the Christians of Germany professed their faith in truly Christian communities like that directed by Bonhoeffer.

In his lectures on "The Nature of the Church" presented during the summer semester of 1932, Bonhoeffer succeeded in developing along more practical lines the finely honed analyses of church that one reads in *Sanctorum Communio*. The language of his lectures is obviously trimmed of the heaviness of his doctoral dissertation, though he speaks essentially of the same reality. The church, he argued in these lectures, is not called to be a tiny, sacred haven from secular turmoil, but like Jesus himself it has to be a visible presence in the midst of the world. Everyday life, not some heavenly realm, is the only locus of church life for Bonhoeffer, even though this way of understanding its mission could propel the church into controversial areas of conflict with government. The church required visibility for the carrying out of its Christ-given mandate to be salt and light for the world. To his audience of university students Bonhoeffer excoriated the church for its tendency to seek out the privileged places while trying to be everywhere and ending up "being nowhere," neglecting the very ones that the church was called to serve. This church was to be neither a church clamoring for its privileges nor a church totally absorbed into the secularisms of the day. It was called instead to be the community of Jesus Christ serving the world, yet being free enough from the world to

oppose its secular idolatries and to be engaged in practical deeds to protect the vulnerable and to defend the victims of harsh governmental policies. It is not surprising that students of Bonhoeffer's thought today see
so many parallels in his challenges to the churches of Germany and their
own churches' efforts to promote, peace, justice, and liberation among
the people they represent and among those who have no one to speak up
for them.

In his lectures at the university one can see formulated, even before
Bonhoeffer's experiences of community life at Finkenwalde, his conviction that the church had to be thoroughly involved in and for the world,
and not given over to forms of ecclesiastical escapism from the problems
that bedevil ordinary people. Fortified with the Word of Jesus Christ, this
same church was likewise obligated never to yield to the popular ideologies that paraded themselves as wholly congruent with Christian faith. He
told his students that this was not an "ideal church, but a reality in the
world, a bit of the world reality." Adding that this church can never be reduced to a domesticated abstraction, he went on to say, "this means that
it is subjected to all the weakness and suffering of the world. The church
can, at times, like Christ himself, be without a roof over its head. . . . Real
worldliness consists in the church's being able to renounce all privileges
and all its property but never Christ's Word and the forgiveness of sins.
With Christ and the forgiveness of sins to fall back on, the church is free
to give up everything else."[4] These words to his students in 1932 would
find their echo in one of his last writings from prison, the "Outline for a
Book" that promised to be a "stocktaking of Christianity" with an explo-
ration of "the real meaning of Christian faith." There, in the last year of
his life, he dared the church to be like Jesus Christ and to peg its existence
solely to the service of others. The church, he said, should make a start by
giving away "all its property to those in need."[5] The renunciation of privileges, the liberating Word of Jesus Christ, and the forbearance needed to
forgive sins would also be in the forefront of Bonhoeffer's concerns for his
community of seminarians. His words on the self-sacrifices required of
the churches continued to reverberate in his seminary lectures on following Jesus Christ, whom he regarded as the binding force that held the
Christian community together in fidelity to the gospel and in mutual service to the Word of God.

Most of Bonhoeffer's theological reflections on Christian community
focused on the question of how God's gift of faith to individual believers
assumes concrete form in a world of astounding diversity. He also pondered the question of how the individuals whose personalities shape their

communities undergo a spiritual growth through the sharing of their faith and through their mutual service and forbearance. One's faith in Jesus Christ expressed through the bonding of Christians with each other was more than an abstract, rationalized theory to Bonhoeffer the young student, and later to Bonhoeffer the mature theologian drawn into a bitter struggle over whether the churches of Germany were truly representing Jesus Christ in the Hitler era. Hitler's popularity with the masses generated a dilemma for the churches. Afraid to contradict what the people so enthusiastically applauded, in spite of their own misgivings, most of the churches went along with the popular mood. Bonhoeffer was convinced that the failure of the churches to become prophetic communities contributed to the perverse attractiveness of National Socialism. He criticized the churches for being turned in on themselves, lost in a kind of sanctimonious narcissism. When composing his doctoral dissertation he complained of a very obvious example of that self-centeredness, namely, that the churches had disdained the poor working class. He warned that any renewal of the church would succeed only if it could win over these workers who were then drifting into the camp of Bolshevism with nowhere else to turn. These same workers would later fall into the ideological clutches of National Socialism. Those in the working class, he argued, dreaded only their isolation, and longed only for community.[6] He believed the churches had, with disastrous consequences, failed to extend their compassionate outreach to those at the lowest level of German society.

Community in and through the Person of Jesus Christ

It comes as no surprise that Bonhoeffer's reflections on community converge on the person of Jesus Christ, whom he depicts as gracing people in their common humanity with dignity and a sense of purpose. He was endlessly trying to understand where the present reality of Jesus Christ could be found and invoked in that turbulent world. In Bonhoeffer's theology, the human person always exists in some form of relationship, whether with itself, with others who become part of an individual's personal growth, or with the communities and associations that become integrated into one's social life. He does not hesitate to claim that the moral demands of Jesus define all relationships.

Bonhoeffer's unwavering Christocentrism moved him further to assert that what may be the strength of all other forms of community becomes qualitatively different in communion with Jesus Christ within the

Christian church community. His most extensive study of the Christian church community roams widely around his claims that human life itself can be understood only through one's social relations with others in those communities which shape one's personal world of meaning. In like manner he sees God's revelation, the ultimate source of that meaning, reaching people only through their corporeal and communal reality. In Jesus Christ, God not only entered human history, but in a striking way God has directed that history by becoming inextricably bound up with human beings in all their concreteness. Bonhoeffer asserts his conviction that Christ's role in human history lies in the divinely enabled integration of our personal and social existence by standing as our vicarious representative at the point where human community has been disrupted by sin and healed through redemptive forgiveness. Jesus, in Bonhoeffer's theology of the "communion of saints," is the Lord through whom God's love, the foundation and binding force of all humanizing community, overcomes sin and brings about the reconciliation of individuals with themselves and with others, even those at the farthest reaches of one's personal existence: one's enemies.[7]

If, as Bonhoeffer insists in his analysis of the church, Christ's presence does indeed transform communities into spiritual centers for God's healing power in the world, then through Christ God's Word for the world assumes not mere hazy visibility but incarnate nearness within the church. God's otherness is not, he contends, that of an eternal being aloof in a distant heaven. Rather, God has become in Jesus a Father God for people in the context of their social existence as followers of Jesus Christ. Christians in church communities are called to reflect in their brotherly and sisterly love for others the everlasting relationship of God to God's people in the course of human history. In turn, Christian communities become the stories of how God in Jesus Christ has entered into a unique solidarity with human beings. That is the immediate context for Bonhoeffer's claim that to be truly the church, those who claim to follow Jesus Christ must become themselves "Christ existing as the church community."[8]

Bonhoeffer writes glowingly of Christ's vicarious action as the soul of that community of believers whose oneness would be structured by unconditional, other-centered love, their living and acting for others rather than for themselves. It is this self-sacrificing love that shapes the community into concrete resemblance to Jesus Christ. Bonhoeffer's distinction between being *with* and being *for* the others in community is apropos here. The churches of Germany were filled with parishioners who were merely occupying pews in proximity one to another; very few were there in any real sense to form a genuine community in love and service for the others. It has been said that in American churches, people come together without knowing each other, they live without loving each other, and they die without grieving for one another. A cynical statement, to be sure, but with an element of truth if the sole extent of parish life is simply to be bodily present during the Sunday services. For Bonhoeffer, the Christian community must proceed to the next stage, where the believers are there in order to be with Christ as they become Christ for others. He writes of that stage with an evident passion: "Whoever lives in love is Christ in relation to the neighbor. . . . Christians can and ought to act like Christ; ought to bear the burdens and sufferings of the neighbor. . . . It must come to the point that the weaknesses, needs, and sins of my neighbor afflict me as if they were my own, in the same way as Christ was afflicted by our sins."[9] His later statements on the necessity of forbearance have their foundation in this powerful exhortation to act like Christ toward one's fellow Christians.

In Bonhoeffer's analysis of the "communion of saints" we see too his laying of the groundwork for advocating actions on behalf of the oppressed. Bonhoeffer writes glowingly of Christ's vicarious action as the basis of that communion of people whose oneness would be structured by unconditional love, living and acting for others rather than for themselves. The attitude of giving the Christlike service he idealizes here can never be restricted to one's own circle of like-minded believers. Bonhoeffer sees the Christian community more as the vortex of that new existence in which sociality would be delivered from the evil of those human introversions that destroy community. As we will see, he returns to this theme time and again in *Life Together*.

Throughout his foundational study of the "communion of saints," Bonhoeffer takes issue with those ideologies that tend toward exclusivity and divisiveness precisely because he is convinced that such ideologies negate community in favor of a self-assured, self-centered, triumphalist isolationism. His reaction to any narcissistic turning in on oneself extends to the self-serving egocentrism that effectively reduces God to a "heavenly double" of corporate ideology and personal ambitiousness. For Bonhoeffer, it is Jesus Christ, not the self-seeking, self-gratifying individual, and not the ecclesiastical establishment in its pompous triumphalism, that is the center of the Christian church community.

Catechizing the Young through
Christian Community Life

Bonhoeffer's convictions about the need for this kind of community explains why later, in teaching catechism to a group of slum-dwelling teenagers he was preparing for Confirmation, he resolved to emphasize not the catechetical correctness then in vogue, but community spirit. As best as he could, he gave them some experience of what a real life community could be like, even if it meant moving from his spacious suburban home to the seamier side of Berlin to be near these students and their families. He described his approach in a letter to Erwin Sutz, a Swiss friend from his year at Union Theological Seminary:

> Since New Year I've been living here in north Berlin so as to be able to have the young men up here every evening. In turns, of course. We eat supper and then we play something — I've introduced them to chess, which they now play with great enthusiasm. In principle anyone can come, even unannounced. And they all love coming. So I don't have to go on prodding them. Then at the end of each evening I read them something from the Bible and after that we have a short spell of catechizing, which often becomes very serious. . . . It has been really possible to talk to them and they have listened, often with mouths wide open. It is something new to them to be given something other than learning the catechism. I have developed all my instructions on the idea of the community, and these young men, who are always listening to party political speeches, know quite well what I'm getting at.[10]

What he was "getting at" was their budding relationship with Jesus Christ to whom they were about to profess their allegiance in accepting Confirmation. In his sessions with them he emphasized the love Jesus embodied for them and with whom they could find the fulfillment to which they aspired.

One of the students would later mention in a letter that Bonhoeffer "was so composed that it was easy for him to guide us; he made us familiar with the catechism in quite a new way, making it alive for us by telling us of many personal experiences. Our class was hardly ever restless because all of us were keen to have enough time to hear what he had to say to us."[11] That "new way" was his emphasis on forming among themselves a Christian community enlivened by the personal approach in which Bonhoeffer excelled. What he had to say about Jesus was appealing even to a class of ordinarily restless teenagers because they were enabled to see Jesus in an entirely new light, that of a faith community.

In many ways Bonhoeffer's experiences in preparing this class of teenagers for Confirmation reinforced his conviction that the wordy, ponderous world of academe in which he had been steeped in Berlin University was not where his pastoral ministry would be most effective. His biographer recalled Bonhoeffer's having distanced himself from his heady, footnote-heavy Berlin dissertations even though the conceptual foundations of his research in these two books return time and again in all of his later writings. In each instance, whether it be the reality of revelation, the essence of freedom, the sociality of Christian faith, or the contemporary encounter with Jesus Christ, the church community is not only the prerequisite for theological reflection, it is also the concrete locus for encountering the continuing presence of God with God's people. Revelation, faith, and worship converge for him where Jesus Christ exists as the faith community.[12]

Creating Community with the
Seminarians at Finkenwalde

The opportunity to organize, with church backing, the kind of community he had in mind came in 1935, when Bonhoeffer accepted the directorship of the Confessing Church seminary for the region of Berlin-Brandenburg. He had been approached in the summer of 1934 with the offer to be part of the Confessing Church's training of its future ministers. At the time he continued to maintain his hope of traveling to India to learn from Mohandas Gandhi about "community life as well as [Gandhi's] methods of training."[13] With a view to loosening Hitler's vise-like grip on the German nation, he also desired to learn more about "Gandhi's exemplification of the Sermon on the Mount — in the spiritual exercises aimed toward a certain goal, and the Indian ways of resistance against a tyrannical power."[14] With these words Bonhoeffer revealed his interest in the Gandhian tactics of nonviolent passive resistance that were so successful against imperialist Britain. Despite Niebuhr's attempts to drum into him the futility of nonviolence against a powerful, unprincipled dictator like Hitler, he did not immediately abandon his plan to use Gandhi's strategy of resistance against Hitler and the Nazi government. Indeed, he had obtained letters of reference from both

Bishop Bell and Reinhold Niebuhr and had been formally accepted into Gandhi's ashram.

However, the trip to India and the encounter with Gandhi never materialized, because in the meantime Bonhoeffer accepted the leadership of the seminary to be established in Pomerania in northern Germany. Writing from London, he confided to his Swiss friend, Erwin Sutz, his misgivings about this decision: "I am . . . struggling over the decision on whether I should go back to Germany as director of the new Preachers' Seminary (still to be established) or whether I should remain here or whether I should go to India. I no longer believe in the university and never really have believed in it — a fact that used to rile you. The entire training of young seminarians belongs today in church-monastic schools in which the pure doctrine, the Sermon on the Mount, and worship can be taken seriously — which is really not the case with all these things at the university and, in present-day circumstances, is impossible."[15]

In preparation for this task he used his final months as pastor of two German-speaking parishes in London to visit Anglican monasteries and seminaries of other denominations to examine their "monastic training" programs and their different modes of community life. After studying the varied ways in which Christian faith was lived in these institutions, Bonhoeffer became even more resolved to establish the kind of training center for these future moral leaders where everyone would be fully committed to incorporating Jesus' Sermon on the Mount into their daily life. This commitment would in turn be sustained by community structures based on the gospel, structures that emphasized their togetherness as well as their need for prayerful time alone in order to foster the mutual support they needed and their service of one another as a prelude for serving the wider church community. He wanted also to have incorporated into their lives a daily routine with regular spiritual exercises and hours of worship, manual work, classes on discipleship, and ecumenical dialogue, all to reinforce their resistance to the systemic evil that had been the original raison d'être of the Confessing Church seminaries. In a memorandum to the Ecumenical Youth Commission meeting in Paris on January 29, 1935, Bonhoeffer made it clear that even before the appointment he and several compatible students had wanted to start "a small Christian community in the form of a settlement or any other form on the basis of the Sermon on the Mount" and where "only by a clear and uncompromising stand [could] Christianity be a vital force for our people."[16]

The community life Bonhoeffer set in motion at Finkenwalde, however, soon put him in violation of the laws of the Nazi government relating to the regulations for church affairs. It was not something he wanted the seminarians to dwell on. He kept the seminarians focused not on their dissident status, but on the purpose for their training by imposing a daily schedule and by the example of his own intense way of working, always leaving room for prayer and leisure. We read in *Life Together* his detailed account of how the day was to be spent in a structured balance of devotions, study, classes in discipleship and preaching, service of one another, common meals, and hours of worship, leisure, and play.

What is not so clear in *Life Together* are the tensions Bonhoeffer had to endure in directing the seminary his way and in setting up a "Brothers' House" to provide continuity to what was in practice an experiment in community living. He lectured extensively on what being disciples of Jesus Christ entailed for Christians eager to practice their faith in obedience to the gospel. These lectures later became his spiritual classic, *Discipleship*. For the seminarians, the following of Jesus Christ Bonhoeffer's way meant beginning each day with prayer and private meditation, for which they had little or no preparation. In those first meditation times, some read, some slept, some smoked, some allowed their minds to wander. Some voiced their resentment at being the butt of jokes from ordinands at other seminaries about their "unevangelical monasticism."

All this was brought out in an evening discussion they had with Bonhoeffer on his return from a protracted absence from the seminary. He listened with sympathy to their complaints, but did not waver about their continuing to practice the daily meditation. Instead, he suggested that they have a communal meditation once a week. The public sharing of their meditation, in which Bonhoeffer himself took the lead, proved so helpful that gradually their opposition ceased. Most of them continued the practice after their seminary training. The daily meditation brought home to them that their faith had to be centered in God's Word as a gift given to them in their relationship with God and not as a personal skill acquired for the sole purpose of doling out spiritual tidbits in their preaching.[17]

With the intention of helping them in their practice of meditation, Bonhoeffer introduced his seminarians to the *Losungen*, or short daily texts drawn from the Bible that the Moravians had been using and making available to a wide variety of interested people. In his circular letters both before and during the war, Bonhoeffer called his seminarians' attention to these texts, especially those that were appropriate for the time and the circumstances of their ministry. In Tegel Prison he declared that these daily texts had opened for him a whole new world of meaning. Before his imprisonment he included the weekly texts in his letters to the seminarians, reminding them of the "precious gift which is given us in meditation . . . which brings inward and outward order into my life [and] gives our life something like constancy. It maintains the link with our previous life, from baptism to confirmation, to ordination. It keeps us in the saving community of our congregation, of our brothers and sisters, of our spiritual home."[18] During the war years, these reminders from their beloved director brought back poignant memories of Bonhoeffer's lessons on prayer, taught as much by his example as by his classroom instructions. Many years later one of Bonhoeffer's "inner circle" of Finkenwalde students, Winfried Maechler of Berlin, commented: "When I was on the Eastern front, in Russia, in the German army, my mind went back again and again to this experience of meditation. That is what really fortified me during the painful ordeal of serving in the army. I have never forgotten it."[19]

The Community Life in and through the Brothers' House

Bonhoeffer's desire that his seminarians live a common life with some continuity from year to year prompted him to explore the possibility of arranging for some of them to remain beyond their customary training period in order to form a more tightly knit community. He had in mind a "Brothers' House" whose members could serve as a leaven for the incoming students, helping them to adjust to the ways of forming community, to the practice of prayers in common, and to the various ways in which one ordinand served another. Bonhoeffer sent a proposal along those lines to the synodal council, asking for the release from their ordinary duties of some of the young ordained ministers whom he wanted to be involved in this enterprise. Among those six approved for this extraordinary ministry was Eberhard Bethge, Bonhoeffer's closest friend and future biographer. The proposal is informative for the kind of community Bonhoeffer was attempting to create for his seminarians and, indirectly, for the church at large. Bonhoeffer argued that Christian life could never be lived in the drab abstraction experienced in the typical German parishes of the day; the people needed a genuine Christian community. He was certain that the authentic profession of one's faith required living in community and developing a sensitivity to one another. Further, he pointed out that clericalism and the pursuit of clerical perquisites distracted church leaders from their calling to serve not themselves or their buildings, but the needy people entrusted to their care. He challenged the churches, therefore, to renounce their clerical privileges and make themselves more available for generous, self-sacrificing service to the most vulnerable of God's people. This giving of themselves to others through whole-hearted living in a Christian community would focus the ministers on the Christ-centeredness of their calling. Finally, Bonhoeffer made it clear that the community life he envisaged could provide pastors with a spiritual refuge where they could renew and refresh themselves for further service in the church. Concerning the details of their daily life, Bonhoeffer described a simple life in common, a daily schedule of prayer, meditation, mutual encouragement, common studies suitable for pastors in training, and worship together. He pledged the availability of these pastors to answer any emergency call. They would have full freedom to leave the community should the need arise.

In some respects, Bonhoeffer's vision of the kind of community life needed in the church can still serve as a gauge of whether a Christian community is on the right track in its ability to live according to the gospel mandates.

> There are two things the brothers have to learn during their short time in the seminary — first, how to lead a community life in daily and strict obedience to the will of Christ Jesus, in the practice of the humblest and the noblest service one Christian brother can perform for another. They must learn to recognize the strength and liberation to be found in their brotherly service and their life together in a Christian community. For this is something they are going to need. Secondly, they have to learn to serve the truth alone in their study of the Bible and its interpretation in their sermons and teaching.[20]

It came as a major disappointment to Bonhoeffer when the Gestapo closed down the seminary. His attempts to continue the training of seminarians through clandestine meetings were fraught with obstacles. They were unable to form communities such as existed in Finkenwalde. In the difficult, lonely days of his imprisonment, however, Bonhoeffer would derive solace from the lingering memories of community life in the seminary, with its nurturing prayers and warm expressions of brotherly love.

Because the community life at the Finkenwalde seminary was structured by a disciplined life not common to the Protestant tradition in Germany and a daily schedule that resembled somewhat the regimen of Catholic monasteries, Bonhoeffer had to fend off accusations that he was catholicizing the seminary or introducing a hothouse atmosphere that was both esoteric and impractical. He was able to win over his critics and the seminarians themselves by the introduction of several counterbalancing aspects of their life together. First and foremost, he enabled the seminarians to experience, many for the first time, the sustaining power of a life in common in a faith-filled, caring community. Second, the ordinands were given a rigorous theological, spiritual training that helped them to distinguish between the task of theological reflection and the demands of their ministry of pastoral care. Third, their daily routine was punctuated by periods of recreation, music, sports, and other forms of lighthearted relaxation. Bonhoeffer's biographer reports that Bonhoeffer was adept at organizing these periods of physical and mental renewal. Finally, Bonhoeffer was able to convince his ordinands and the church authorities that the life together he had set in motion was not a withdrawal from the arena of combat against Nazism in the churches. On the contrary, he intended their life together to be a unique, more effective way of preparing these young ministers to enter that struggle as moral leaders, and in the process to revitalize their church.[21]

Life Together: The Structured Community of Finkenwalde

Bonhoeffer's community at Finkenwalde lasted only a little more than two years before the Gestapo closed it down. Prior to the Gestapo action, he had been reluctant to publicize the remarkable common life he and his seminarians had experienced. But in 1938 and at the urging of Eberhard Bethge, his best friend and one of those who had stayed on at the Brothers' House, he felt compelled to record for posterity what took place at Finkenwalde and to again state his conviction that the wider church needed to develop a similar mode of Christian community. With a new sense of urgency during the tensions of the Sudetenland crisis, he and Bethge went in late 1938 to the home of his twin sister, Sabine Leibholz, in Göttingen to work on the text of *Life Together.* Earlier in the month the two of them had helped the Leibholz family — Sabine's husband, Gerhard, though baptized, had been certified a Jew by the Nazi authorities — to escape Germany into Basel, Switzerland, from which they would later emigrate to a safe haven in Oxford, England.

Bonhoeffer completed work on *Life Together* in a single, hurried stretch of four weeks. The book itself was published in 1939; within a year it had reached a fourth printing. Since then this spiritual classic has been through twenty-four reprints in addition to the new critical edition and thoroughly revised translation for the Dietrich Bonhoeffer Works English Edition series.[22] The book itself is divided into five interrelated sections: Community, the Day Together, the Day Alone, Service, and Confession and the Lord's Supper.

1. Community

Bonhoeffer's *Life Together* reprises many of the themes on the nature of the church already enunciated in *Sanctorum Communio*, but in a more lucid language shorn of the ponderous, heavily footnoted analyses of the dissertation. This section begins and ends with a passage from the Psalms proclaiming how good and pleasant it is when kindred people can live together in unity (Ps. 133:1). He explained that the "unity" of which the Psalmist speaks is now made possible through Jesus Christ, because "he is our peace."[23] He was not claiming that the "peace of Christ" is without its tensions. Bonhoeffer was mindful of his own sense of frustrations in the church struggle and of the Nazis' persecution of any and all that dared resist their policies. Citing Luther, he forewarned his seminarians that their community life was set in the midst of their most intractable enemies. He wanted anyone embracing Christian community in fidelity to Jesus Christ to be resigned to the inevitable antagonisms generated by self-proclaimed, well-armed enemies who demanded absolute loyalty to their own ideology. This being said, Bonhoeffer emphasized the reasons why a Christian community can be an indomitable defense against those who would destroy both their church and their nation, namely, "the incomparable joy and strength" given to the person of faith through "the physical presence of other Christians." He alluded to the examples of Paul and John, who were consoled in prison by thoughts of the presence of their fellow Christians whose nearness was "a physical sign of the gracious presence of the triune God."[24] To live in community with other Christians is, he insisted, a privilege, an "inexpressible blessing," a gift all too easily forgotten but one that should prompt a daily prayer of gratitude to God. For Bonhoeffer, Christian community is nothing less than "community through Jesus Christ and in Jesus Christ in which we belong to one another only through and in Jesus Christ."[25] He added that those who in coming together want more than what Jesus Christ has promised do not really want community. Christian community cannot find its validation in the extraordinary, rhapsodic experiences that people might desire. Nor should believers confuse Christian community with their wishful thinking and their personal pious projections. According to Bonhoeffer, those who declare their willingness to form such a community are not called to create a utopian ideal or to enjoy a self-centered reality. He insists that the Christian community is fundamentally a divinely established, spiritual reality in its very core, but with all the practical challenges that God gives to individual Christians and their communities.

Life Together moves from this sturdy affirmation of the divine Christ-centered core of Christian community into a series of cautions against the subtle forces that can quickly shatter the common life. Bonhoeffer singled out for rejection the "wishful thinking" that evades the demands of Jesus Christ and the self-centeredness that masquerades as the love one needs in Christian community. Both dangers in their own way are insidious in their ability to erode community life. "Wishful thinking," for example, is Bonhoeffer's phrase for those who ruin community togetherness by projecting their own image of what they imagine the common life should be. They are dreamers who pester others in their insistence on having things their way, with little room for compromise. Their idealized image is puffed up with their pride and pretentiousness. Ultimately, Bonhoeffer saw "wishful thinking" leading to disillusionment. With uncommon harshness Bonhoeffer laid bare the flaws in those who bring down the community with the weight of their own visions and ideals. These "wishful dreamers" make impossible demands on others, establish their own laws, and engage in caustic reproaches against those unwilling or unable to conform to their individualized way of living. Even though they may be responsible for the breakup of community life, they accuse the others and even blame God for the failure of the community life they embraced on their own flawed terms.

Instead of permitting those "wishful dreamers" from dominating the common life believers have embraced, Bonhoeffer countered with a call to forego one's wishful projections in favor of courageously accepting the reality of what God has *actually* accomplished in Jesus Christ. Gratitude for what God has done, not embittered carping over the failure of others to cooperate in one's unreal vision, should mark the attitudes of those who agree to share their faith in the unique ways of the Christian community. For Bonhoeffer, this must include gratitude for the supportive presence of others, forbearance and forgiveness, and compassion for the weaker members of the community. He would outlaw any whining complaints about what God and one's fellows have not done. As for the inevitable gap between one's ideals and the reality of everyday living in community,

Bonhoeffer asked, "Therefore, will not the very moment of great disillusionment with my brother or sister be incomparably wholesome for me because it so thoroughly teaches me that both of us can never live by our own words and deeds, but only by that one Word and deed that really binds us together, the forgiveness of sin in Jesus Christ? The bright day of Christian community dawns wherever the early morning mists of dreamy visions are lifting."[26] In essence Bonhoeffer was calling those who commit themselves in faith to form a community life in union with Jesus Christ to engage in heartfelt gratitude for everything small or great. He asked, "How can God entrust great things to those who will not gratefully receive the little things from God's hand?"[27] He counseled the community members not to be constantly complaining. He warned too against gauging the worthiness of spirituality on the artificial standards of grandiose achievement. Only God, he said, knows the true depths of the community's growth into Jesus Christ.

According to Bonhoeffer, the quality of that love can either empower the community members to live for each other or it can stifle community spirit and ultimately prove fatal to the survival of their common life. As a forewarning against this danger, Bonhoeffer contrasted what he called "spiritual love" with what he wanted to expose and counteract for its lethal flaws: the self-centered, purely emotional, self-gratifying giving in to one's urges under the guise of genuine love. Self-centered love, he said, is calculating, manipulative, and domineering. Spiritual love, on the contrary, is humble, deferential, submissive to the guidance of God's Holy Spirit and God's Word. This spiritual love is agapeic, capable of loving the other without preset conditions for the sake of Jesus Christ. Self-serving love, he said, is incapable of loving one's enemies. Those addicted to it long for other persons in a mushy emotionality that will use the others for their own purposes and often as objects of "uncontrolled and uncontrollable dark desires."[28] It can lead to lustful enslavement and psychic domination for the sake of the pleasure one can derive from another. Bonhoeffer was convinced that this kind of false love can lead to the exclusion from the community of the handicapped, the weak, and those labeled as insignificant and non-productive. Ultimately, self-centered love can cause the exclusion of Jesus Christ, who in the person of those rejected as less than desirable begs the believer's compassion. He reminded those who would form themselves into a Christ-centered community that they "must release others from all [their] attempts to control, coerce, and dominate them with [their] love. In their freedom from [them], other persons want to be loved for who they are as those for whom Christ became a human being, died, and rose again, as those for whom Christ won the forgiveness of sins and prepared eternal life. . . . Spiritual love recognizes the true image of the other person as seen from the perspective of Jesus Christ. It is the image Jesus Christ has formed and wants to form in all people."[29]

Finally, Bonhoeffer noted that the euphoric thrill of experiencing the kind of love that genuine Christian community makes possible is an unpredictable extra and not the sole purpose of community. Faith, not fleeting emotional satisfaction, is what holds the Christian community together, engendering the more lasting joy and happiness that comes through living in communion with Jesus Christ and in Jesus Christ with one another.

2. The Day Together

Bonhoeffer was all too aware of the importance of structure for a community of like-minded Christians. To that end, his practical side came through in the careful daily schedule of time together for him and his seminarians. From rising in the morning until the public evening prayer, there were always things to do. He offered practical directions in order to encourage their mutual support and to insure continuity in their common life. He insisted on an early hour for communal worship, with time given to the singing of hymns, the reading of Scripture, and prayer. That morning hour, he wrote, "does not belong to the individual; it belongs to all the church of the triune God, to the community of Christians living together, to the community of brothers."[30] Having been preserved through the night and granted an awakening to the new day dawning, Christians in turn are to begin their life together each morning by gathering for worship with their prayers of praise and thanks, their scriptural readings, and their hymns breaking the silence of the nightly darkness.

Bonhoeffer considered this morning time sacred. He admitted very frankly that he did not want those living in the community of faith to "be burdened and haunted by the various kinds of concerns they face during that working day."[31] In these moments of worship they experience anew the mediation of Jesus Christ and the light of "his awakening word."[32] Bonhoeffer followed this exhortation with a lengthy explanation of the beauty and power of the Psalter.[33] He declared that in the Psalms the community is drawn into the prayer of Jesus Christ, who as vicarious representative of all Christians stands with the individual and the community, praying on behalf of all the needs that their own prayers can ever express.

To this prayer Bonhoeffer conjoined the common reading of the Scriptures. He believed such reading would have the effect of drawing the community into the stories of Israel and of Jesus, and in this way help the members of the community to learn more about their own stories. The reading of Scripture permits believers "to be found in Jesus Christ — in the incarnation, cross, and resurrection — [they] are with God and God with them."[34] In effect, Bonhoeffer asked the Christian community to know the Scriptures the way the great reformers did. For them, the Bible was a privileged gift from God for the salvific nurturing of the people. Bonhoeffer conceded with dismay that too often the Scriptures are excluded when one's practical course of action is to be determined. The subtle reference to the manner in which ordinary Germans and many of their churches hailed Hitler and the Nazi ideology without any reference to the biblical judgment or the teachings of Jesus is unmistakable here. For Bonhoeffer, even when the biblical word goes against the grain of one's own selfish inclinations, it is not to be discredited in favor of what one's so-called experiential wisdom or the popular mood might dictate. What is more, Bonhoeffer questioned whether Christians, especially the leaders of Christian communities, can be of help to one another except through God's own Scripture. He notes that human words fail to alleviate one's troubles and temptations. He likened the savoring of the scriptural word to reading to another a personal letter from a friend.

Bonhoeffer found the singing of hymns in unison a pleasant spiritual exercise in which one's voice is united to others' as the voice of the church itself. The words, together with the music, extend the spiritual horizons of the community just as this mode of music making enhances the Word of God and brings a unique dimension to community praise, thanksgiving, confession, and prayer. Feeble though the quality of the music or the quality of the individual voice may be — and here Bonhoeffer poked fun of the show-off basso profundos and quivering tenors who like to dominate, and the moody members who in their hurt feelings refuse to sing — nonetheless, Bonhoeffer joined the unison singing of hymns to the essential structures of the community. It helps the community joyfully and with melody to become one with the song of the church.

At the closing of the service Bonhoeffer strongly recommended that the members of the community bring up their requests, expressions of gratitude, and intercessions in a common prayer. He believed this practice has within it the power to break down one's fears of the reactions of others and the inhibitions one feels against praying freely and publicly in the presence of others. For Bonhoeffer, this common intercessory prayer in the name of Jesus Christ is "the most normal thing in our common Christian life."[35] Bonhoeffer would cap this common worship service with extemporaneous prayer led by an individual in the community, often the head of the house or director of the group. He adds the cautionary word, however, that the individuals who close the daily worship with a spontaneous prayer must be aware that they pray for the community as a whole and not in place of that community. Hence they have to share in the common life and know firsthand the community's needs and concerns, its joys and requests, its gratefulness for favors received and its hopes. Nor must they confuse the possible chaos of their own heart with the more ordered hearts of those who compose the community. He advises too against the temptation to substitute the profound, well-crafted, prefabricated prayers of the universal church for the more personal, though perhaps fumbling, confused prayer one must offer to God every day. On this point, he argues that "here the poorest stammering can be better than the best phrased prayer."[36] God is more moved by sincerity of heart than by impressive words, however well honed for a particular theme or service.

Finally, Bonhoeffer turned his attention to the "breaking of bread together," the meals, the Lord's Supper, and the heavenly banquet. The first of these is his main concern in their "day together," namely, the role of the table fellowship in binding Christians to one another both spiritually and physically. The fostering of community at the hours of table repast serves to remind Christians of the providential care God takes of God's children and of the ways in which God has blessed God's people with the good gifts of food and drink. Bonhoeffer states clearly that he does not want to see these gifts spiritualized through misplaced begrudging of the body's need for comfort. Nor does he countenance eating in a somber, sullen, or too-busy-to-celebrate manner. The call to table fellowship, he says, is an invitation to be festive even in the midst of or at the end of one's working hours. In their enjoyment of these "good gifts of this physical life, Christians recognize their Lord as the true giver of all good gifts. And beyond this, they recognize their Lord as the true gift, the true bread of life itself, and finally as the one who calls them to the joyful banquet in the reign of God. So in a special way, the daily breaking of bread together binds Christians to their Lord and to one another."

Bonhoeffer concluded this description of the community's day together with the structure of evening prayer, a brief daily worship service with song. This is the moment when Christians can lay aside their work and entrust their cares to God. Most important of all, it seems, is his plea that at the close of their day the members of a Christian community ask forgiveness of their sins against God and one another and express their forgiveness of any wrongs done to them. He counseled this practice vehemently, perhaps conscious of the vindictiveness then encouraged in government circles and accepted in resigned silence by the churches. "It is perilous," he writes, "for the Christian to go to bed with an unreconciled heart. Therefore, it is a good idea especially to include the request for mutual forgiveness in every evening's prayers, so that reconciliation can be achieved and renewal of the community established."[37] For Bonhoeffer, the day together ends the way it began, with prayers to the God who in Jesus Christ has made the Christian community possible and, for nations and individuals in turmoil, necessary if one is to remain united in spirit with Jesus Christ.

3. The Day Alone

To claim as Bonhoeffer did that living together with others in community is actually strengthened by individual time alone strikes many readers as a paradox. For Bonhoeffer, solitude in community is neither paradoxical nor a contradiction. He goes so far as to declare that "whoever cannot be alone should beware of community."[38] Community is not an escape route for those unable to cope with life on their own, or for those who desire to bury bad experiences of their past with help from the companionship of gracious people. "The Christian community," he points out, "is not a spiritual sanatorium" where one's sense of isolation can be healed.

But Bonhoeffer also insisted that if people can't endure living in community, they should also be wary of being alone. The Christian calling, he said, is to enter into a community of faith; it is not a call to isolated exercise of one's faith or a call suitable for the rugged individual who craves to be left alone at all times. Christians genuine in their profession of allegiance to Jesus Christ pray, act, and struggle with difficulties always in the sustaining communion with Jesus Christ and with other Christians. Bonhoeffer recognized, therefore, "that only as we stand within the community can we be alone, and only those who are alone can live in the community. Both belong together."[39]

What did Bonhoeffer intend by correlating the time set aside for being alone with the times spent with others in the personal exchanges that are part of every thriving community? He expanded the concept of "being alone" with the adjunct ideas of beneficial solitude and silence. In his opinion, both the individual believer and the community need the solitude and silence out of which comes the deepening of one's appreciation for true community living. Bonhoeffer's affirmation of the need for solitude is similar to John Selby's observation in his book *Solitude:* "the most lonely, frustrated people I have worked with have not been the loners but people who are addicted to social interaction. Afraid to encounter themselves in solitude, they fill their lives with shallow social interactions that keep them from ever coming face to face with their own solitary spirit."[40]

The silence of which Bonhoeffer speaks is required to listen prayerfully to the Word of God and to the words of those who share life in community. This is the silence needed to let God have the first word in the early morning hour and the last word as one ends the day in sleep. It helps the members of the community to avoid idle chatter and misuse of speech that can wound the most vulnerable members of the community; it helps people to manage their speech during their daily conversations. There is power, Bonhoeffer says, in this kind of silence, "the power of clarification, purification, and focus on what is essential" that contributes "to proper speaking of God's word at the right time."[41] Such silence, which Bonhoeffer wishes to protect by adopting it into a daily discipline, insures not only a fresh renewal of the ways in which individuals are respected in the community encounters, but also the right of privacy.

For Bonhoeffer, the silence structured into their daily schedule is vital to that encounter with God's Word that shapes the community. To protect this silence, Bonhoeffer advocated regular times for being alone: meditation on God's word in the Scriptures, hours of prayer, and moments of intercession, all converging in the daily period of quiet meditation. This meditation, he insisted, serves the purpose of bringing order into one's daily life as it provides the "solid ground on which to stand and clear guidance for the steps we have to take."[42] This is the time for God's Word to enter into human hearts to remain as an empowering, guiding force for the entire day. Bonhoeffer eschews any expectation of extraordinary, blissful experiences that might or might not occur in the period of silent meditation. On the other hand, neither spiritual aridity nor occasional listlessness should dissuade Christians from persevering in their meditative attention to the Word of God spoken in silence.

Bonhoeffer depicts one's effective prayer life itself as an offshoot of this meditative listening to God's Word. "Prayer," he claims, "means nothing else but the readiness to appropriate the Word, and what is more, to let it speak to me in my personal situation, in my particular tasks, decisions, sins, and temptations."[43] This personal prayer thus complements what one may feel as an individual need but, for various reasons, can never enter it into the community prayer; instead, one makes these personal problems known to God alone in silent prayer.

Equally important for Bonhoeffer is intercessory prayer for one another. He sees intercession as a natural outcome of the agapeic love whereby "Christians [bring] one another into the presence of God, seeing each other under the cross of Jesus as poor human beings and sinners in need of grace."[44] When this intercessory attitude can be fostered, the antagonisms that can tear a community apart are tempered. In the midst of the Nazi world where hurting the enemy was held up as deserving of medals of honor Bonhoeffer offered the following extraordinary reason for intercessory prayer:

> A Christian community either lives by the intercessory prayers of its members for one another, or the community will be destroyed. I can no longer condemn or hate other Christians for whom I pray, no matter how much trouble they cause me. In intercessory prayer the face that may have been strange and intolerable to me is transformed into the face of one for whom Christ died, the face of a pardoned sinner. That is a blessed discovery for the Christian who is beginning to offer intercessory prayer for others.[45]

For Bonhoeffer, forbearance and forgiveness intersect at the point of intercessory prayer.

4. Service

Bonhoeffer looked on the diversity of those who belong to Christian communities as another aspect of God's blessings and another way in which the spirit of Christ is enfleshed anew in the loving presence of Christians one to another. "People," he wrote, "are talented and untalented, simple and difficult, devout and less devout, sociable and loners. Does not the untalented person have a position to assume just as well as the talented person, the difficult person just as well as the simple one?"[46] Bonhoeffer knew firsthand the dynamics of community living. People come together in faith, but soon enough there follow the observations about those who share the common life, judgments of their character, and classifications of people according to standards that can plunge the community into a life-and-death struggle. Bonhoeffer warns the community against the competitiveness, domineering tendencies, exploitation of the weak and untalented, and invidious comparisons that are abhorrent to the spirit of Jesus Christ.

Instead, he counsels the community to look on the diversity not as an enemy of the common life, but as a cause for rejoicing and an opportunity to tighten community bonds. Individuals should not look on the presence of so many others in the community as an occasion for self-promotion, but as a call to service. Bonhoeffer implies that the community's strength lies in the care it takes of its weakest members. Hence the vigor of his statement: "Every Christian community must know that not only do the weak need the strong, but also that the strong cannot exist without the weak. The elimination of the weak is the death of the community."[47] These are words written in the face of the Nazi determination to euthanize the mentally and emotionally weak and physically handicapped.

The practical directives that Bonhoeffer issues in *Life Together* are all related to the manner in which a community's diversity provides an opportunity for individuals and the community itself to grow in the love of Jesus Christ and in their love and esteem for one another, especially the most vulnerable of their brothers and sisters. He speaks out against "vain glory" on those occasions of feeling angry or disappointed when one's achievements are not honored enough by the community. Bonhoeffer's advice rings with the simplicity of the example of Jesus, which teaches believers to remain silent in the face of humiliations. He knows that inordinate ambition can only sow the seeds of irritability and carping about real and imagined injustices. In the same spirit Bonhoeffer asks the community not to be overly judgmental, especially in the matter of the annoying sins of others that are sometimes used as a pretext to overlook one's own sins and failings.

The core of Bonhoeffer's concerns is to integrate diversity into the formation of a community faithful to Jesus Christ in the promotion of the mutual service that, like common worship, Scripture reading, table fellowship, and holding to the daily schedule, is necessary for the community to grow in love for one another and into the image of Jesus Christ. Bonhoeffer listed three kinds of services that one Christian must offer to another for the sake of Jesus Christ and to keep the ideal of agapeic love alive within the community.

The first service mentioned in Bonhoeffer's directive is that of listening to others; this, he says, is the work of God, who is the great listener. Bonhoeffer was aware that preachers often overwhelm their people with words when the people crave nothing more than the sympathetic ear of someone willing to listen to their problems. If we can't listen to one another, he asked, how can we listen to God? "The death of the spiritual life starts here, and in the end there is nothing left but empty spiritual chatter and clerical condescension which chokes on pious words."[48] Bonhoeffer was equally vehement that if a person's time is too important to allow listening with patience to others, then that person really has no time for God. Effective moral leadership demands this ability patiently to listen to others in their needs.

The second great service for Bonhoeffer is active helpfulness. He is not advocating here those grandiose deeds that are often used to measure human greatness, but the simple help in the little things that can become bothersome in a community. Here Bonhoeffer focuses on an attitude fairly common in a structured life where some people may be engaged in important tasks that do not tolerate any interruption. Often Christians may think their time or their plans too vital to what they hope to accomplish in any given day and so they may resent the knock of a needy brother or sister on the door or the intrusion into their plans for the next couple of hours. Bonhoeffer's counsel is that Christians must look on those unforeseen moments as opportunities to respond to none other than God, who sends those needy people to busy Christians, however preoccupied they might be: "Nobody is too good for the lowest service. Those who worry about the loss of time entailed by such small, external acts of helpfulness are usually taking their own work too seriously. We must be ready to allow ourselves to be interrupted by God, who will thwart our plans and frustrate our ways time and again, even daily, by sending people across our path with their demands and requests."[49] Bonhoeffer concludes that, if we fail to make ourselves available for these small acts of service, we may be passing by the cross that God has raised across our lives to tell us that God's ways, not our own ways, are what count in the Christian community.

In a final segment, Bonhoeffer speaks of the service of forbearance. Drawing from Paul's advice to the Christians of Galatia, "bear with one another's burdens, and in this way you will fulfill the law of Christ" (Gal. 6:2), he explains that Paul's words would never be a problem to pagans, because pagans could simply stay away from burdensome people. Not so with Christians living in community! Bonhoeffer proposes as their example not a proponent of secular wisdom in how to deal with others, but Jesus Christ himself, in whom God suffered by bearing with and enduring the sinfulness of humans. Bearing with human sin and forgiving sinners, he says, was the mission of Jesus Christ. Can it be otherwise for Christians?[50] For Bonhoeffer this forbearance is also how God draws Christians into a saving community in and with God's son Jesus. Only in this way can the freedom of others, including difficult sinners, be made possible. The implications of this attitude for moral leadership are enormous. In Christian forbearance, the strong help the weak, the healthy help those who are ill, the talented help the untalented, the righteous help the fallen-away sinner — always in a Christlike manner that is humble, patient, gentle and friendly. Even the sinners must be forgiven on a daily basis.[51]

Bonhoeffer concludes that listening, helping those in need, or bearing with others is ultimately the service that Christians are called to give by the Word of God. That Word, in turn, must be uttered freely to one another. To be the instrument of God's accepting, forgiving, peace-giving Word is to give comfort as well as forgiveness, admonition as well as consolation, all the wondrous light of the Word of God, to allow God to speak that Word through one Christian to another. In this way Bonhoeffer discerns the deepening of personal relationships that are integral to our common life. The Christian moral leader becomes, in effect, God's own gracious outreach to all those who comprise the Christian community.

5. Confession and the Lord's Supper

In this last segment of Life Together, Bonhoeffer emphasizes the need for Christians to confess their sins to a representative of the Christian community. He states unequivocally his belief that the call to confession is essential for those living together, that they might confront their sins directly, particularly the sins and failings that have impacted on the community's well-being. Despite the fact that the practice of confession had fallen into disuse in Protestant Germany, Bonhoeffer took seriously the scriptural injunction to "confess your sins to one another" (James 5:16). He also invokes John 20:23 in directing the members of the Christian community to admit their sins in confession to another member of the community. On the practical level, Bonhoeffer looks on this confession as an opportunity for Christians to drop their masks, their pretenses, and their denials, and to acknowledge what they are in God's sight: sinners who have experienced God's mercy. "In Christ," he writes, "the love of God came to the sinner. In the presence of Christ human beings were allowed to be sinners, and only in this way could they be helped. Every pretense came to an end in Christ's presence. This was the truth of the gospel in Jesus Christ: the misery of the sinner and the mercy of God. The community of faith in Christ was to live in this truth."[52] Bonhoeffer notes further that in the act of confessing our sins, other Christians have the occasion to become Christ for us. They are now the sign of God's gracious, caring, forgiving presence. They are, in effect, sent by God to help us. The other Christian to whom we go to confess sins hears us "in Christ's place, forgives our sins in Christ's name. Another Christian keeps the secret of our confession as God keeps it. When I go to another believer to confess, I am going to God."[53]

Bonhoeffer hails the confession of sins as achieving a fourfold blessing: a breakthrough to community, a breakthrough to the cross, a breakthrough to new life, and a breakthrough to assurance.[54] The confession exposes sins to the light, as the sinner no longer has to hide from sight or harbor the evil which can smolder in the human heart. Relieved of the burden of sin, the Christian now stands relieved in the community of sinners, living by the forgiving grace of God in the cross of Jesus Christ. Sin exposed and forgiven loses its power.

Confession provides a breakthrough to the cross because of the Christlike humility one must have to approach another Christian to ask for forgiveness in Jesus' name. Confession of sins effects a kind of death to the old self, mired in pride, a death not unlike the humiliating crucifixion that Jesus suffered in our place. Bonhoeffer points out another reason for his strong advocacy of personal confession: it is a unique way for Christians vicariously to experience the cross of Jesus Christ as they themselves, with some pain, contribute to their deliverance from the sins that could tear a community apart.

Bonhoeffer wrote that confession is also a breakthrough to new life in its providing a necessary opportunity for sinners to break with their past. The renunciation of sin shatters sin's power, delivers the Christian believer from the darkness of inner evil, and brings with it the conversion and the longed-for new life in which one's baptism is renewed and the following of Jesus Christ reaffirmed. This ensuing reassurance is, however, far removed from the self-delusion that is inevitable with those who excuse and forgive themselves. When we are turned in on ourselves and evasive in dealing with our inner sinfulness, there can be none of the assurance that comes when the Christian who hears our confession "breaks the circle of self-deception."[55] The other Christian is God's agent for the assurance that God has forgiven the sins confessed.

In his direction of their life together Bonhoeffer was trying to reinforce a consciousness of personal sins as well as of the sins that threatened community. This was one of the reasons why he linked the confession of sins to preparation for the celebration of the Lord's Supper, the sacrament that celebrated their common life and their communion with one another. The reconciliation that is the outcome of having their sins forgiven was, in his opinion, the best preparation for those who desired to receive the body and blood of Jesus Christ and, in that communion, to renew their commitment to one another, symbolized in the Lord's Supper. One must not approach the table of the Lord unprepared. Hence all anger, envy, contention, hurtful gossip — in a word, any sin detrimental to those who composed the community — had to be eliminated. The Lord's Supper, he notes, "is a joyous occasion for the Christian community. Reconciled in their hearts with God and one another, the community of faith receives the gift of Jesus Christ's body and blood, therein receiving forgiveness, new life, and salvation."[56] Bonhoeffer's closing words are a fitting summary of the kind of Christian community that is at once faithful in practice to the teachings of Jesus Christ and the source of strength for moral leadership and of that joy which Christians are called to find and enhance in one another. "Here joy in Christ and Christ's community is complete. The life together of Christians under the Word has reached its fulfillment in the sacrament."[57]

CHAPTER EIGHT

Bonhoeffer's Spirituality and God's Vulnerability

Compassion for Those in Suffering and Sorrow

> God suffered on the cross. Therefore all human suffering
> and weakness is a sharing in God's own suffering and weak-
> ness in the world. We are suffering! God is suffering much
> more. Our God is a suffering God.[1]

D ietrich Bonhoeffer stands out as a moral leader and influential spiritual guide because of his willingness to suffer the harshness of imprisonment for his faith and to endure the loss of his freedom. He was
destined to die a martyr's death. On April 9, 1945, Bonhoeffer, having been
found guilty of taking part in the plot to assassinate Adolf Hitler and
bring about the defeat of Germany, was executed by hanging in the concentration camp of Flossenbürg. Only later would his deeds in the German resistance movement be acclaimed for their heroism in his native
country.

Bonhoeffer's execution was, in a way, his own answer to the question of
faith that he posed from his prison cell. There he declared that the question
of faith is neither what we *can* believe intellectually nor what we *must* believe
out of obligation and fear. The question of faith for him could only be,
"what do we really believe? I mean, believe in such a way that we stake our
lives on it?"[2] Bonhoeffer had himself staked his life on the Sermon on the
Mount and the gospel commands of Jesus Christ who was demanding of
him a faith lived out in an active responsibility to extricate his church and
his nation from the war into which they were plunged and in which millions were being killed on bloody battlefields and in hellish death camps.

In a letter from prison that his best friend, Eberhard Bethge, would treasure for its words of faith and courage, Bonhoeffer shared one of the sources of the faith that led ineluctably to his arrest by the Gestapo and his imprisonment. To learn more fully what God has promised to those who love and serve God, he said, one has to "persevere in quiet meditation on the life, sayings, deeds, sufferings, and death of Jesus."[3] He went on to declare that living close to God and in the light of God's presence was an entirely "new life," because in God all things had become possible.

Bonhoeffer was not speaking here of the unleashing of human potential for the grandiose, extraordinary deeds that are often invoked to judge human greatness and rewarded in ceremonies honoring the military heroes of a nation. Rather, he was coming to grips in Tegel Prison with the fearful reality of his own death. The July 20, 1944 plot against the life of Adolf Hitler had failed, as had all the other numerous attempts.[4] The noose of the Gestapo was drawing ever more tightly around his band of conspirators. Soon Bonhoeffer, cut off from any contact with his family, would be transferred, first to the dreaded Gestapo prison in Berlin, and then, just a few short weeks before Hitler committed suicide, to the death camp at Flossenbürg in southern Bavaria.

But Bonhoeffer's words, smuggled out of prison by a friendly guard, were not those of a man in despair over his fate. Instead they were as death-defying as those words Paul spoke in declaring that nothing in this world or beyond could ever separate him from the love of God that he had experienced in Christ Jesus (Rom. 8:28-39). To Bethge, Bonhoeffer confided his conviction that "no earthly power can touch us without God's will and that danger and distress can only drive us closer to God. It is certain that . . . our joy is hidden in suffering, and our life in death." That certainty, he said, came from communion with Jesus Christ, whose death on the cross Bonhoeffer saw as God's "Yes and Amen" and "the firm ground on which we stand."[5]

A God Wounded and Oppressed

In prison Bonhoeffer had come to experience more deeply the pathos of God's "weakness" and "foolishness" that Paul made the leitmotif of his first letter to the Christians of Corinth. While the warring world was refining its destructive technology and Christ was being tortured and crucified anew on Nazi Golgothas, Bonhoeffer was entering into the last phase of his young life, a prisoner whose final writings would inspire countless

Christians to reexamine their own commitment to Jesus Christ and to renew their determination to live their faith in greater fidelity to the gospel. Bonhoeffer now saw the extent of God's love for God's people not in the power of God to eradicate evil and to permanently assuage all grief, but in the way God had made divinity itself vulnerable in the stark, unfathomable reality of Jesus' humanity. When hopes for his release from prison dimmed, Bonhoeffer took comfort from Mark 15:34, in which Jesus cries out in despair from the cross, "My God, my God, why have you abandoned me?" This passage became a word from God telling Bonhoeffer that not even Christ could avoid the human consequences of self-sacrifice for the sake of others, sharing both the earthly blessings of God's providential care and the inevitable sufferings of his people. "Like Christ," Bonhoeffer wrote, "Christians must drink the earthly cup to the dregs, and only in doing so is the crucified and risen Lord with them, and they crucified and risen with Christ."[6] Bonhoeffer firmly believed that Christ was not like a god who came to earth from on high, to remain supremely aloof except to intervene at certain dramatic moments with opportune miracles, and then depart virtually untouched by the world's harshness and life's tragedies. Christ experienced the absence of God at the very moment when he veritably ached for deliverance. In the gospel story of Jesus Christ, Bonhoeffer could see that God does not offer any glib answers to the agonizing problem of human grief. Instead, from every vantage point of faith, God has freely chosen to suffer *with* those who suffer. This realization of God's eloquent silence in the midst of the sufferings of God's children and Jesus' brothers and sisters became at once Bonhoeffer's greatest consolation and most demanding challenge as he came to grips with his own death.

This sense of God's solidarity with the weakest of God's children in their distress, in fact, inspired Bonhoeffer to compose one of his most moving poems from prison, "Christians and Pagans." In the opening lines of this poem Bonhoeffer describes how people, both Christians and unbelievers, go to God when they are troubled, pleading from God the liberation and peace for which they long. But the second verse abruptly tells Christians that they paradoxically must stand with God to help a needy God who can only share the pain of those who cry out for deliverance from their suffering.

> But some [people] turn to God in God's need and dread,
> A God poor, despised, without roof or bread.
> By sin's harm weakened and by death distressed,
> Christians stand steadfast by their God oppressed.[7]

In the concluding verse Bonhoeffer writes of how God goes to every person, pagan and Christian, with the bread that feeds the human spirit. For both, God hangs in death, and for both God offers pardon and solace. God has, in short, become in Christ a wounded God, vulnerable to all the pain that people endure in life's journey back to God. The thought that God too bears the hurts and rejections of the innocent, that God suffers with all God's children, and is a hidden presence even in their lonely, degraded deaths at the hands of a criminal dictator, inspired in Bonhoeffer that extraordinary peace of mind admired by both his fellow prisoners and wardens.[8]

Jesus Humiliated and Crucified

In many ways his understanding of how God in Christ accepts the pain of God's victimized children with all the intensity of divine love became the motivating force in Bonhoeffer's own decisions to make common cause with the outcasts of Nazi Germany. Even before his involvement in the church struggle and the conspiracy, Bonhoeffer saw that God had proclaimed an irresistible oneness with the destitute and fully shared in the sorrows and joys of those trapped in poverty. As early as his Barcelona ministry in 1928, he had attempted to sensitize his affluent parishioners to the plight of the poor in the dingy slums of the city, telling them that Christianity subverts the systems of society and preaches the "unending worth of the apparently worthless and the unending worthlessness of what is apparently so valuable."[9] The paradoxes of that statement were intensified in the way he asked his students and seminarians to seek and find Christ in those in their society who were the most despised and rejected. He pointed them to the poor worker on the factory floor, the homeless beggar, and the ragged human being, who had so little to offer them in return but who could provide a more intimate encounter with Jesus. Bonhoeffer played on the theme of Jesus challenging his followers to see him not primarily in the privileged people of this world but in the lowly and abandoned, those who were the object of God's special predilection and outreach through the compassion of Christians. In the lowly, vilified outcasts of this world Bonhoeffer could affirm both the woundedness of God and the risk of being a Christian. Christians had to follow Christ even when it cost them status and respectability to be one with the despised Jews and the unwanted castaways of a heartless society.

For Bonhoeffer, it was not sufficient merely to label oneself a church-going Christian or fulfill the minimal requirements for membership in a parish. Bonhoeffer argued that the Christian church's boast of being the herald of God's love and instrument of salvation was empty if its credibility was not grounded in a Christlike solidarity with the oppressed and in willingness to endure persecution for them. He even claimed in *Discipleship* that Christians would even have to abandon their own dignity in order to reach out in compassion to those who suffer the murderous rejection of their society. Faithful followers of Jesus Christ must be careless of the shame they incur; in fact, they "take that shame unto themselves." To be compassionate, they "give away anyone's greatest possession, their own dignity and honor." They can do this because their dignity and honor come from their solidarity in compassion with Jesus Christ.[10] Bonhoeffer's words and example are particularly apropos for churchgoers who may fear "suffering persecution for the sake of justice." In Bonhoeffer's spiritual reflections, fidelity to one's Christian vocation entails the closest possible communion with the suffering Christ. For Bonhoeffer, Christian faith demands that we accept God's own vulnerability in embracing those to whom society deals destructive poverty, vicious enslavement, and malicious neglect. Reaching out to these victims of societal violence is the only way Christians can bring God's healing presence into the lives of those in whom Jesus Christ is bruised and rejected anew.

It comes as no surprise to discover that Bonhoeffer's decision to make common cause with the enemies of the Nazi government is inspired by Martin Luther. Luther's own life underwent a dramatic change when, moved by God's Word, he based his reform on the experience of God's encountering him in Jesus Christ. This took place not in a theology of triumphalism, but in pondering the lowliness and sufferings of Christ, becoming one with people in their weakness, guilt, and pain. The Christian believer, Bonhoeffer noted in words that echoed Luther, must live "by the grace of God which comes to people and comes to every person who opens his or her heart to it and learns to understand it in the cross of Christ. And, therefore, the gift of Christ is not the Christian religion, but the grace and love of God which culminate in the cross."[11] Luther's attraction to God's paradoxical "strength in weakness and wisdom in foolishness" was itself drawn from the salvific death of Jesus Christ depicted in Paul's letter to the Christians of Corinth.

This is the same cross of Christ that Bonhoeffer said was blocking the paths of otherwise comfortable Christians, interrupting their lives and disrupting their well-set plans for their future. He reminded his seminarians that their main preparation for ordination to the Christian ministry was in their generous, self-sacrificing service for others, the lot of any minister dedicated to helping people in the name of Jesus Christ. The followers of Jesus Christ had to be like the Good Samaritan, who was willing to comfort and heal the wounded traveler brutally beaten and robbed by highway thugs. No follower of Jesus was permitted to pass by the needy preoccupied with so-called "more important tasks," as the priest passed by the victim lying bloody and wounded — indeed, Bonhoeffer suggests in a phrase filled with irony that the priest may have been reading his Bible. To ignore the person in need was, in Bonhoeffer's opinion, to ignore the sign of the cross that God puts in the paths of Christians to remind them that God's will, not theirs, must be done.[12]

Suffering is the way the cross of Jesus Christ comes to Christians who might religiously kiss a replica of the dying Christ but shrink from personal encounters with the real Jesus — a victim who may be a fearsome prisoner on death row or a terminally ill patient making demands on their kindness and faith. According to Bonhoeffer, the cross of Jesus Christ is the only way for Christians to discern what Christ is demanding of his contemporary followers and to discover, in the alleyways of destitution and the shadowy recesses of poverty and despair, Christ's contemporaneous presence.

Speaking on the theology of the great Reformed theologian Karl Barth, Bonhoeffer turned to the same theme. On that occasion he told his fellow students at Union Seminary that Christians, who should be attentive to human misery, must recognize God in an unheard-of way. This is a God, Bonhoeffer said, "revealed in the poor life of a suffering man; God revealed on the cross; God revealed in . . . sin and death. . . . Faith sees God coming most closely . . . where a man hanging on the cross dies in despair. . . . This is the real world of biblical faith, which sees God's work not on the top, but in the depth of mankind."[13] If God's way of being with God's children is epitomized in the brutal anguish and death of Jesus, then the Christian path to God means sharing the suffering of Christ. In his lectures on following Christ, Bonhoeffer could say quite simply that "Discipleship is . . . having to suffer." He went on to make the following stark declaration: "Those who do not want to take up their cross, who do not want to give their lives in suffering and being rejected by people, lose their community with Christ. They are not disciples. But those who lose their lives in discipleship, in bearing the cross, will find life again in following in the community of the cross with Christ. . . . Discipleship is being bound to the suffering Christ."[14] Bonhoeffer understood from his own experience that the cross of Jesus Christ can interrupt the best-planned career in order to invest the Christian vocation with its most genuine meaning, God's love shown paradoxically in the ever-escalating demands God makes on the Christian.

What should result is not the predictable trademarks of well-organized religion, with its emphasis on orthodoxy in creeds and correctness in worship that made little impact on dedicated Nazis, but the willingness to make common cause with every victim struck down by oppressive governments. Hence Bonhoeffer's sobering phrase that the gift of Christ to people is not organized religion, but rather "the grace and love of God which culminate in the cross."[15] Embracing the cross of Jesus Christ is not necessarily an idealistic blueprint with which to construct a better world. Jesus' cross, which Christians are also asked to carry, offers instead liberating reassurance to the wounded victims of this world who continue to cry out for a God who cares and who call out to Christians for help.

When Bonhoeffer speaks of Christian suffering and moral leadership, he is thinking of those qualities that Christians are called to bring into the lives of the many people who seek solace from their afflictions. For Bonhoeffer, God graces Christians first with the fortitude to engage themselves in voluntary suffering. Though this sounds like something spectacular and attention-getting, he addresses more the everyday, ordinary suffering that Christians must accept for the sake of the community to which they belong — the quirks, annoyances, and petty squabbles that would otherwise erode the common life of faith. Secondly, Bonhoeffer points to the motivation that should inspire Christians and their leaders to enter into solidarity with those whose setbacks and grievances are their human lot: their suffering must be accepted for the sake of Jesus Christ. John Godsey has very perceptively commented on this aspect of Bonhoeffer's observation that the Christian life is intimately connected as a *conditio sine qua non* to the willingness to suffer for the sake of Jesus Christ. "As such," Godsey writes, "it is nothing other than answering the demands of Christian discipleship. According to Bonhoeffer, this suffering entails the abandoning of earthly attachments and the active following of Jesus into a hurting and often hostile world, doing the 'extraordinary,' not from some heroic impulse but from the prompting of the Spirit of Christ."[16]

Godsey's colleague Josiah Young takes this insight into the more shadowy world of American racism in arguing that theologians miss the point if they fail to see Bonhoeffer's martyrdom unrelated to the lifelong struggle for justice and equality for people of color and racial minorities. "Bonhoeffer brings to light that a genuinely anti-racist theologian is bound to suffer when he can't capitulate to racist forces (for Christ's sake!). Bonhoeffer's point, particularly during the time he was in prison — and it came to light there that he was part of a conspiracy to kill Hitler — is: only the suffering God can help. You have to suffer yourself, take the side of the victims, to see, and really see, that Christ is a fellow-sufferer. Only he knows how alienated we are from God and each other."[17] As a person of color himself, Young has a unique appreciation of the influence of the black community on Bonhoeffer's development as a theologian, pastor, and champion of human rights in both Germany and the world of his ecumenical activities.

Standing Firm in the Faith: Bonhoeffer's Exhortation to His Fellow Conspirators

In assessing the deleterious effects on the nation of the fecklessness of those who were then waging an unjust, destructive war and with an aim to boost the spirits of the resistance movement, Bonhoeffer included in the essay he sent to the conspirators not long before the first assassination attempt a short section asking the question, "who stands firm?" Bonhoeffer bemoaned the fact that Hitler's popularity had wreaked havoc with all their usual ethical concepts. Evil had been disguised as good, and many reasonable people of Germany had failed to detect the full depths of Hitlerism and the injustice that Nazism was inflicting on the masses. His answer to his own question helps to unpack just what bearing the cross of Jesus Christ meant to him and to his fellow resisters. The world at war needed those "whose final standard is not their reason, their principles, their conscience, their freedom, or their virtue, but who are ready to sacrifice all this when they are called to obedient and responsible action in faith and in exclusive allegiance to God — the responsible persons, who try to make their whole life an answer to the question and call of God." But "where are these responsible people?" he asked.[18] Except for the handful of those involved in the conspiracy and the few who were able to rescue Jews, not many moral leaders were to be found in Nazi Germany!

Bonhoeffer's discourse on the firmness he was seeking in those who would assassinate Hitler and overthrow the Nazi government has its parallel in Paul's parting exhortations to the various communities he had evangelized to "stand firm" in their faith if his best hopes for them were ever to come true. And those hopes included letting the mind of Jesus Christ into their own way of thinking (Phil. 2:5). In his letter to the Christians of Philippi, Paul expresses his hope that they were "standing firm in one spirit, striving side by side with one mind for the faith of the Gospel" (Phil. 1:27). Given the fearful persecutions Christians had to endure from the Roman Empire and the worldly seductions they were supposed to reject, Paul's exhortations were timely. One is tempted to ask whether the enticements of the Roman Empire were any different from the allurements of huckstering commercials and clever political sloganeering in Bonhoeffer's time, or even in our own circumstances? All the ethical principles that had guided and defined Christian behavior seemed woefully inept when stacked up against the Nazi ideal of the "good German" and Hitler's manipulative, mesmerizing mastery of the German nation. Bonhoeffer was distressed at the lack of courage in those who were supposed to be the moral leaders of the nation. By 1942 it seemed that only a coup d'état offered any promise of deliverance from Nazism. Bonhoeffer was insistent: the claim that one stood firm in the faith was a sham unless so-called believers did the concrete deeds necessary to overcome systemic injustice and criminality in government. Those who would deliver their nation from fascist cruelty were not allowed to retreat into the private sanctuary of an unsullied virtue. Only those who relied on Jesus Christ alone could stand firm in that inglorious world. Bonhoeffer was unbending in his belief that those who preferred to look on as innocent, uninvolved bystanders and who were waiting to see how the winds of war were shifting could in no way be considered genuine in their professed allegiance to the cross of Jesus Christ. Again and again those who would stand fast in their Christian faith are reminded of Bonhoeffer's chilling remark in *Discipleship:* "whenever Christ calls us, his call leads us to death."

Bonhoeffer and Modern Martyrs

That death to which Bonhoeffer refers and to which he himself succumbed on April 9, 1945, has led him to be numbered among the martyrs of the twentieth century. Westminster Abbey so honored him in the summer of 1998 when the authorities at the Abbey decided to fill ten niches on the West Façade, empty since the fifteenth century, with statues of outstanding Christian martyrs of the twentieth century. They commissioned artists to create the statues of ten modern martyrs under the general theme that the sacrifices of these revered exemplars of faith served to define the Christian experience in a century riddled with war, persecution, and oppression. In the words of Canon Anthony Harvey, Sub-Dean of the Abbey and a principal organizer of the event, they wished "to proclaim a message of which too few people are aware: the twentieth century has been a century of Christian martyrdom. The cost of Christian witness, and the number of Christians willing to die for what they believed (alongside others of different religious faiths or none), has been greater in this century than in any previous period in the history of the church."[19]

In the statuary commissioned by the Abbey, Bonhoeffer stands next to the saintly Roman Catholic Archbishop Oscar Romero, defender of the oppressed poor of El Salvador, murdered by the death squads of the affluent Salvadoran oligarchies and the ruthless military. Romero stands near Martin Luther King, Jr., the Baptist preacher killed for his work in the Civil Rights Movement in the United States. All these martyrs had one quality in common: they were moral leaders willing to stand firm in their faith against the perpetrators of the acts of violence and injustice dominating their world.[20] There are, in fact, numerous affinities between Bonhoeffer's struggle against Nazism and the missions of liberation engaged in by Archbishop Romero and Martin Luther King against the injustices of Salvadoran and American societies.

Bonhoeffer's pastoral work in Harlem, for example, had sobered him to the realities of American racism and made him doubly alert to the dangers of Hitler's own hate-filled speeches. Like Bonhoeffer, Martin Luther King had to sustain himself and his people against the ideology of racial supremacy and racial hatred, those nagging contradictions of the United States' promise of equality. Having organized a peaceful civil rights march in Birmingham, Alabama, and suffering imprisonment, King was urged by several white ministers not to stand firm in this dangerous cause, not to set the bad example of being jailed for breaking the statutes of Birmingham. He was advised to accept the status quo for the present and wait until the slow gradualism of the United States legal system could inevitably take hold and the civil rights of blacks eventually be guaranteed. His reply parallels Bonhoeffer's own call to action in his essay to the conspirators. Imprisonment was painful, to be sure, but King could never stand firm in his resolve to pursue justice unless he was also willing to risk being beaten and jailed for breaking unjust, racist laws. In his now celebrated "Letter from a Birmingham Jail," he reminded his self-righteous fellow ministers of the situation that Bonhoeffer himself had faced: "We can never forget that everything Hitler did in Germany was 'legal.' . . . It was 'illegal' to aid and comfort a Jew in Hitler's Germany. But I am sure that if I had lived in Germany during that time I would have aided and comforted my Jewish brothers even though it was illegal."[21] As we have seen, Bonhoeffer did, in fact, speak of the churches reaching the point where they could "jam a spoke" in the wheel of state if that was necessary to coerce the government into repealing its unjust laws against the Jews.[22]

Called an extremist, King cited several examples of how the extremists of yesterday become the revered prophets of today. From Amos, to Paul, to Luther, to John Bunyan, to Jefferson (who dared to affirm that all people were created equal), and, finally, to Jesus, who "was an extremist for love, truth and goodness," we have need of such extremists, King wrote. He decried those more devoted to law and order than to the cause of justice. Echoing Bonhoeffer's own distrust of and contempt for the "neutral bystanders," King excoriated the white churches who "stand on the sideline and merely mouth pious irrelevancies and sanctimonious trivialities."[23] Standing firm in the faith entailed more for both King and Bonhoeffer than belonging to a contemporary church that is "so often the arch-supporter of the status quo" and the "silent and often vocal sanction of things as they are."[24] For King, standing firm in his peaceful advocacy of civil rights destined him, as it did Bonhoeffer, to vilification by politicians and church leaders alike; King and his followers were subjected to brutal beatings by angry policemen, incarceration in "filthy roach-infested jails," and, finally, King himself was murdered. But the pursuit of justice had become the ultimate core of his faith-filled ministry and the heart of his personal faith, never allowing him to "sit idly" in comfortable Atlanta when what was happening in Birmingham affected him and his people personally, and indeed menaced human dignity everywhere. As he proclaimed so eloquently, "injustice anywhere is a threat to justice everywhere."[25] Standing firm had become in the life of Martin Luther King, as it was to Dietrich Bonhoeffer, a call to action on behalf of justice and compassion for the victims of unjust, repressive systems.[26]

The story of Archbishop Oscar Romero, martyred by the security forces of El Salvador for his daring solidarity with the oppressed poor of his country, seems of a piece with those of both Bonhoeffer and King. Their common sensitivity to the problems besetting the underclass of their countries was exemplary. For Romero, it was his choice to be "the voice of those who have no voice,"[27] while Bonhoeffer could justify his defense of the Jews by asking in the spirit of Proverbs 31:8: "Who will speak up for those who have no voice?"[28] The "death squads" that enforced order and conformity among the peasants and poor of the country's work force, who had been exploited for the cheapness of their labor, were the Salvadoran counterpart of the Gestapo of Nazi Germany. Once Romero was able to appreciate the true condition of his people, his prophetic words of protest stamped him as a leader to be reckoned with by those who subjugated the poor. The oligarchs and their "death squads" cruelly suppressed any dissent, especially from "upstart" church people whose loyalty and patriotism had heretofore been unquestioned. Peasants, labor leaders, and religious activists who protested the injustice had either been openly murdered or had been made to "disappear."

In many ways, Romero's experience was not unlike that of Bonhoeffer, who mentioned in the closing section of his essay to the conspirators that it was a valuable experience to have been able to see the events of their history "from the perspective of those who suffer."[29] Romero could point to the church's having finally adopted as its own that "view from below," declaring in his own words that, "once again it is the poor who bring us to understand what has really happened. That is why the church has understood the persecution from the perspective of the poor. Persecution has been occasioned by the defense of the poor. It amounts to nothing more than the church's taking upon itself the lot of the poor."[30] Archbishop Romero had decided that the church would accompany the people in their poverty. He himself set the example. Bonhoeffer, on the other hand, was frustrated in his efforts to muster the support of church leaders for a more concerted resistance to the political perversions of Nazi Germany.

Solidarity with the Least of Jesus' Brothers and Sisters

God's vulnerability in the crucifixion of his son Jesus can be seen in tandem with the martyrdom of moral leaders like Bonhoeffer, King, and Romero. These martyrs lived in solidarity with the least of Jesus' brothers and sisters. Bonhoeffer's convictions about God's woundedness in the most defenseless of God's children help explain why he could state so matter-of-factly from prison that the way of God's weakness and powerlessness in the world "is precisely the way, the only way, in which God is with us and helps us. Matt. 8:17 ["This was to fulfill what was spoken by the prophet Isaiah: 'He took up our infirmities and bore our sorrows.'"] makes it quite clear that Christ helps us, not by virtue of his omnipotence, but by virtue of his weakness and suffering."[31]

Bonhoeffer's willingness to enter into solidarity with those branded as less than fully human was inspirited by the example of Jesus, who dared his followers to search for him not in the clouds of heaven, or on the thrones of earthly majesty, or at the banquet tables of the affluent, but in the places where ordinary people can only cry out to God in their distress. To be one with the oppressed of Nazi Germany, as Bonhoeffer was, made him a sharer in God's own vulnerability. The mystery of personal suffering is not that God permits it, but that God suffers in the loneliness, anguish, and tragic deaths that scream out their denial of any belief in a God who cares. In their pain, those who suffer call out to the Spirit of Christ in those who hear, not the lament of strangers, but the heart-rending cry of brothers and sisters who may otherwise be as remote as the despised psychotic on death row or the maggot-laden untouchable in the stinking streets of Calcutta gasping out his dying breath. God's communion with people is never so intense as when human suffering seems to belie the existence of the goodness, justice, and hope we confess to be the qualities of the loving God in whom we trust.

It is at this troubled point of human pathos that Bonhoeffer recognized his own calling as a moral leader to be an instrument "in the hand of the Lord of history." Knowing that "we can share in other people's sufferings only to a very limited degree," Bonhoeffer nonetheless insisted it was the vocation of all who would be like Christ to share in Christ's own compassion, and to act despite the dangers, and to be for those who suffer the embodiment of Christ's own liberating and redeeming love and his abiding presence in service of others. Christians are expected to be moved not primarily by their own sufferings, "but by the sufferings of the brothers and sisters, for whose sake Christ suffered."[32]

Bonhoeffer's spirituality impelled him to embrace the Christian life as a call to suffer with and to respond with courage to those in whom Jesus Christ was experiencing a modern-day crucifixion. The cost of making common cause with Jesus Christ in the countless victims of Nazi brutality would be his freedom and his life. The liberating and redeeming words of Jesus Christ reach people through preaching of God's Word and the celebration of the Lord's Supper, to be sure. But that Word is also spoken in the Christ who has entered into communion with the most downtrodden and helpless of his brothers and sisters for whom, in the compassionate outreach of their fellow Christians, the cross of Christ has become what it has always been: the light shining in the darkness of human malevolence and personal tragedy.

Sharing in God's own compassion, followers of Jesus Christ are called to an extreme sensitivity to human suffering. Their personal gifts are always at the disposal of the most needy and, at times, the least grateful.

The challenge of Christian faith is to combat the multiple causes of suffering, to avoid compromise with evil, to embrace the solitude of the prophetic moral leader, all the while longing for the peace, justice, and freedom that are Jesus' legacy to his followers.

CHAPTER NINE

Preaching the Spiritual Life

Bonhoeffer's Sermons and Insights on Moral Leadership

For the sake of the proclaimed word the world exists with all its words. In the sermon the foundation for a new world is laid. Here the original word becomes audible. There is no evading or getting away from the spoken word of the sermon, nothing releases us from the necessity of its witness, not even worship or liturgy. Everything revolves about the accepting and sustaining witness of Christ. This is the way we must learn to look at the sermon again. . . . The preacher should be assured that Christ enters the congregation through those words that he or she proclaims from the Scripture.[1]

Dietrich Bonhoeffer has been quoted as having said that every good sermon should have a shot of heresy in it. In his view sermons needed to be challenging, exciting, encouraging, at times disturbing the peace, but always grounded in the love for and service of Jesus Christ. On several occasions his biographer, Eberhard Bethge, has emphasized the significance of preaching in Bonhoeffer's exercise of moral leadership. "Preaching," Bethge wrote, "was the great event for him; his very strong theologizing [*harte theologisierung*] and critical love for his church were all for its sake, for preaching proclaimed the message of Christ, the bringer of peace. For Bonhoeffer nothing in his calling competed in importance with preaching."[2] We subtitled this chapter "Insights on Moral Leadership" in order to highlight the importance of Bonhoeffer's sermons in illustrating his challenges to Christians and their churches through comments on God's Word that he shared in this unique way with his various communities. His sermons reveal the kind of moral leader and Christ-centered man his family and friends remembered him to be.

Bonhoeffer's dedication to preaching is evident from his earliest experience as a young interning pastor in Barcelona. In a letter to his parents, written in 1928, he mentioned that every day he devoted hours in preparation for a single sermon. The sermons from that period and throughout his career as a minister that have been preserved in volumes of his collected writings and attested to by his students and friends were not stuffed with the pietistic blather and uncritical stroking of comfortable churchgoers enjoying the status quo that were so typical of the time. His homiletic extensions of the Word of God to his people were likewise remote from the typical serving up of placid conundrums that marked those church services in Germany, where priests and ministers quaked at the thought of offending the Nazi government and jeopardizing their respectable standing in the community. Bonhoeffer's sermons were deliberately relevant to the moral and human struggles of real people trying to cope with the concrete problems of their everyday lives. He detested those common, self-serving bromides of the preaching clergy as much as the pompous display of their rhetorical skills in the pulpit. These sermonizing tactics were for him nothing more than the self-centered huckstering of cheap grace.

Bonhoeffer's effectiveness as a preacher of God's Word was enhanced by the obvious sincerity of his words and the concrete deeds of concern and kindness that made him known among his parishioners and students as a dedicated pastor and teacher. They remembered him as someone who was willing to listen and be a presence in their hopes and successes as well as in their troubles and sorrows. In essence, what people noticed in this young pastor-preacher was the way he himself lived out the observations that later became his published description of the spirit that must bind members of a Christian community together. As one commentator on his life has put it, although Bonhoeffer admitted he was less enthused about routine parish meetings, "preaching was his finest hour." He cites one elderly parishioner from Bonhoeffer's London pastorate: "I never fell asleep while Pastor Bonhoeffer was preaching!"[3]

During his stay in the United States in 1930-31, Bonhoeffer was shocked at the emptiness of the preaching there. In his opinion, which he was not reticent in voicing, the preachers had degraded this crucial aspect of Christian ministry, turning it into superficial observations about the daily happenings or inflated narrations about their personal experiences with little connection to the Scriptures. On his return to Germany, Bonhoeffer's preaching took on an uncommon urgency. "Every sermon must be an event," he wrote to his friend, Franz Hildebrandt.[4] Germany was then shaken by the crises generated by the rise to power of Adolf Hitler and National Socialism. Bonhoeffer wanted to preach in an entirely different way to a people experiencing the turmoil, insecurity, and fear that erupted in the wake of the Hitler takeover. Bethge reports that Bonhoeffer "avoided modernist tricks," and while not commenting directly on political events, his references to what was taking place in Germany were unmistakable.[5] The collection of these sermons reveals his concern for unemployment, hunger, poverty, peace, war, Nazi blasphemy, martyrdom, freedom, marriage, family strife, baptism, forgiveness of enemies, and resistance to evil in all its insidious forms. As the occasion demanded, he made sure the congregation knew the targets of his biblically based criticism.

In training his seminarians to preach the Word of God in this way and to subvert the Nazi ideology, Bonhoeffer insisted that they steep themselves in the Bible and meditate every day on the Word and the daily texts. The preacher, he said, needed to be a person of prayer, not only before every decision, but also in tandem with the Scriptures, as God's Word "drives us to the cross that Christ bore and brings that which bothers us and from which we suffer into proper perspective." He adds the following advice: "Every day should begin with meditation on the Scriptures. Before we meet others, we should meet Christ. Before we decide something, his decision should have confronted us."[6] In his lectures on preaching Bonhoeffer offered ten points that every minister should take to heart. Nearly all of these pertain to the presence of Jesus Christ in the proclamation of the Word of God. That "Word," he writes, "is not a medium of expression for something else, something that lies behind it, but rather it is the Christ himself walking through his congregation as the Word." It is that "Word" that "makes individuals part of one body." That "Word" is "the historical Jesus Christ, who bears humanity upon himself with all its sorrows and its guilt. The sustaining Christ is the dimension of the preached word." That "Word" is, further, "the creating, accepting, and reconciling Word of God, for whose sake the world exists." Everything in the congregation should turn on the sermon's bringing the people to the "accepting and sustaining witness of Christ." The preacher must be convinced that "Christ enters the congregation through those words that he or she proclaims from the Scripture." In extending that "Word" to the congregation, he goes on to declare, "the foundation for a new world is laid." To ignore the sermon is to "ignore the living Christ."[7] All of Bonhoeffer's statements about the ordained ministry and the proclaimed Word show how he relied heavily on preaching in encouraging his seminarians to resist the systemic evil represented by Nazism and to work for the reconstruction of Christianity in Germany after the war. He prepared his sermons with meticulous care, going so far as to type out the finished copy from which he would speak in the pulpit.

We are fortunate to possess copies of the drafts of most of his sermons and to see revealed in them not only his personal spirituality but also the manner in which he exercised moral leadership and exhorted the Christians in Germany to remain steadfast in their own faith. In the sections that follow we will examine these sermons under the following headings: Words on Faith, Words on Hope, Words on Love, Words on Truth and Freedom, Words on Peace, Words on Justice for the Poor, and Words on Suffering and Death.

Words on Faith

As the university semester closed in 1933, Bonhoeffer delivered his first sermon since Hitler's accession to full dictatorial powers. He took as his point of departure the biblical story of Gideon. The real theme, however, was faith when we are confronted with overwhelming odds against us. Gideon's faith is terribly tested; he is outnumbered and over matched against a mighty army. He is, nonetheless, told by God to pare his army down to a mere handful and, instead of force of arms, to trust in the Lord. Weapons, armies, huge numbers are not to be counted on. "Let the armies return," comes God's crazy command. "God is with you; God is victorious, not your army." In the light of the reliance on the size of an army and the weaponry at one's disposal, both then and in today's world, God's order seems insane. In the context of German history and the endless posturing of political parties, it also contradicts common sense. Bonhoeffer attempts to show that this is the essence of faith: not following conventional wisdom, but trusting in the Word of the Lord, taking, as Kierkegaard put it, a "leap of faith" into the unknown, where the only certitude is trust in the beloved.

It is a difficult problem for Gideon, as it is for Christians up against the might of empire. Gideon's problem, not uncommon among the Christians of Bonhoeffer's day, is that he craves the fame of victory and doesn't want God to take any credit for his success. But Gideon finally obeys and an astounding victory is secured. Bonhoeffer remarks that, in effect, God has stepped into Gideon's paths and crossed up all his fine schemes. He has God say: "Let my grace suffice you. My strength is powerful among the weak."[8] The words could have come from Paul's letter to the Christians of Corinth. They are also reminiscent of the passage in Bonhoeffer's *Life Together,* where he tells his seminarians that God will frustrate their plans time and again, sending them people with uncommon demands on their time and energy, intruding into their lives as God's cross standing athwart their paths, reminding them that God's ways and not their own are to be followed.[9]

Bonhoeffer's conclusions were apropos of the people and churches of Germany in the grip of Nazism's stranglehold over their lives. The call to rescue the people from their new enchainment "frightens and disturbs the church to the utmost; it [has] no influence [and is] weak, without particular distinction. . . . It sees the hopelessness of its proclamation, the apathy and the wailing of those who should hear its message, and it realizes that it is not able to stand against them. It sees its own emptiness and desolation and so it speaks full of fear and reproach." Few, if any, of the sermons in that season of Germany's enchantment with its great dictator spoke with such critical perception of the lack of moral leadership on the part of the churches. The victory, Bonhoeffer tells his people, comes about because "faith alone is victorious." It is not the work of Gideon, nor is it the work of the churches. "The church does not overcome, we do not overcome, but God shall overcome." And that means the defeat of human pride, crossing up our own stratagems along with our trust in all the idolatries of this world. The faith of Gideon in its Christian context is, in Bonhoeffer's sermon, nothing less than "the cross of Jesus Christ." And this "means the bitter mockery of God over the height of all human achievements, the bitter suffering of God in all human depths, the Lordship of God over all the world."[10]

Bonhoeffer's words have a contemporary application in a world where the voice of the church seems so inept against the militarism, oppression, and exploitation of the little people and smaller, underdeveloped nations. Is Christians' security based on the weight of their armaments and weapons of mass destruction? Is their security enhanced by their ability to threaten nations and peoples to do things their ways? What can restore the credibility and influential power for good of Christians and their churches except the kind of faith that God demanded of Gideon?

Less than two years later, Bonhoeffer preached a sermon on Reforma-

tion Sunday, November 4, 1934, in which his springboard verse was from
1 Cor. 13:13, "So faith, hope, and love abide, these three; but the greatest of
these is love." Acknowledging that, while the church, in line with the
abiding guidance of Martin Luther, had been great in faith, Bonhoeffer
declared it had to be even stronger in love. But Bonhoeffer then expressed his desire to go back to the only faith that counts, that inspirited
by love. Is it faith to proclaim Jesus Christ as the Lord of one's faith but
to refuse to do his will? "Such faith is not faith at all," Bonhoeffer told
the congregation, "but hypocrisy. It is of no use to us for us to confess
our faith in Christ if we have not gone first and reconciled ourselves to
our brothers and sisters, even to the godless, racially different, ostracized,
and outcast." The reference to Hitler's policies against the "racially different, ostracized, and outcast" was as clear as Bonhoeffer's words were
opposed to the popular trend in his country. And the role of the church,
he insisted on this day of special commemoration, was to be a force for
reconciliation, where the fires of hatred and national pride could be
transformed into love. Was Bonhoeffer indicating the failures of the
churches or stating an ideal and mission? Perhaps both. He brought back
an insight from his sermon on Gideon, namely, the church's tendency to
measure its success by its grandiose deeds. The same measure is often
used by Christians to gauge their success as human beings and believers.
However, Bonhoeffer reminded his congregation that the preeminent
deed, the greatest achievement, is that of the cross, the wondrous act of
God that is unseen and hidden in the world. If churches fall into the trap
of flaunting their "mighty deeds" before an applauding world, they "become a slave to the laws and powers of this world. The *church of success*,"
Bonhoeffer said, "is far from being the church of faith." He added this
jolting rejoinder against pretentiousness: "The deed God has done in this
world, the deed the whole world has lived on since then, is called the
cross of Golgotha. These are God's successes."[11]

Bonhoeffer notes further that the Protestant church was built on the
affirmation that faith alone justifies. He uses this to invert Paul's exhortation in 1 Cor. 13 to read: "And if I have all love so that I do all good works
but have not faith, I am nothing. Faith alone justifies. But love perfects."
He witnessed in Nazi Germany the gradual erosion of faith and the reliance on vapid religious jargon mixed with political slogans proclaiming
love of the German earth and family values, when the real problem lay in
their lack of faith. Hence he informed his people of their need for faith as
much as their need for hope and love: "A humanity that has been deceived
and disappointed thousands of times needs faith."[12]

In his lectures on "Following Christ in Discipleship" to his seminarians in Finkenwalde, he returned to the theme of faith but in the context of what he knew had been the national ecclesiastical neglect to conjoin obedience to the gospel commands of Jesus Christ with saving faith. Otherwise Christians and their churches fell into the trap of believing in a salvation with neither a genuine faith nor any of the works that should flow from a commitment in faith to Jesus Christ. For Bonhoeffer, there could be no true Christian faith without obedience to the mandates in Jesus' Sermon on the Mount. Jesus' call to discipleship is a calling to be conformed to Jesus Christ by living in full communion with him, including acceptance of Jesus' cross. Faith, to paraphrase Bonhoeffer's poignant question from prison, is what we really believe, such that we stake our lives on it.[13] In a letter to his agnostic brother, Karl Friedrich, Bonhoeffer spelled out what he considered the crucial issues of faith in which he was willing to invest his own life's energies: "At present there are still some things for which an uncompromising stand is worthwhile. And it seems to me that peace and social justice or Christ himself are such."[14] When we examine the reasons why Bonhoeffer eventually joined the political conspiracy, the central motivation in many ways was his commitment to work for the restoration of peace and social justice, and, in the name of Jesus Christ, to make common cause with the oppressed of Nazi Germany.

Bonhoeffer's reasoning here is important in assessing the qualities that make for effective moral leadership. The moral leader must, above all, be a person able to trust in the Lord, like Gideon, and to acknowledge the providential care of God in all his or her attempts to uproot evil from society. Moral leaders who profess faith in Jesus Christ are hypocritical if, at the same time, they do not obey the gospel commands of Jesus Christ. Politicians who claim to be Christian but who are supporters of murderous policies counter to Jesus' teachings, for example, may be politically astute but inwardly they exude the duplicity that Bonhoeffer denounces.

Church leaders who lack the moral fiber to confront the state for its failures to take care of the weakest of citizens likewise fail in their allegiance to their crucified savior. As Bonhoeffer put it in a Confirmation sermon in 1938, at the height of Hitler's excesses and at a low depth of church resistance, "Belief is a decision. We can't get away from the fact. 'You cannot serve two masters'; from now on you serve God alone or you don't serve God at all. You have only one master now — that is the world's master, that is the world's redeemer, that is the world's re-creator. It is your highest honor to serve God."[15] He goes on in this sermon to speak of the Christian leadership that the sacrament of Confirmation enjoins on them and the troubles they must endure to be faithful to Jesus Christ. "Your faith," he said, "will be led into severe temptations. . . . It must all come to pass, so that your belief is tested and fortified, so that you become equal to ever greater challenges and struggles."[16]

What Bonhoeffer seems to fear is the way so-called moral leaders often invoke the name of God or, in the case of Germany, the name of Martin Luther, but only in a self-serving way to exculpate themselves from their own failures. To them Bonhoeffer adds in his Reformation Day sermon, "this God looks back in accusation." He declares that church leaders will often refuse to "leave old Luther in peace. He suffers the indignity of being called as a witness in behalf of all the bad things that now are happening in the church. The dead man is hauled into church, his hand is propped up to point at today's Protestantism, and in a perfect pathos of self-reliance he is made to say, over and over again, 'Here I stand, I cannot do otherwise.'" But, as Bonhoeffer argues, this is using Luther and the name of God to evade the responsibility that moral leaders have for the waywardness of their charges. Quoting the Word of God as a cover for fecklessness in leadership is a species of blasphemy. Citing the words of Luther as a pretext for reprehensible actions that impact adversely on the most hurting and defenseless people in a society rings false in the presence of God. This God is not fooled; this God will only look back in accusation and reply to the leader who betrays faith in Jesus Christ, "But I have this against you." Bonhoeffer thus changes the celebration of Reformation Day into a protest against the failure of both church and nation to live up to the promise of Luther and the gospel to which the leaders swore loyalty. God is a God of promise and fidelity; the moral leader must be a person of genuine faith, even to the point of opposing the public sins of both church and state.

Words on Hope

Several of Bonhoeffer's sermons were delivered in the midst of heightened expectation of what the future would bring; some were given to comfort those experiencing sorrow and grieving. He knew firsthand what sorrowing over the loss of a loved one meant for one's faith and emotional trauma. As a teenager he mourned the death in battle of his older brother, Walter, and witnessed the ensuing depression of his mother. He himself underwent severe depression at the outset of his imprisonment. Yet throughout the worst moments of the church struggle and in his resistance activities for the conspirators as well as during the last days before his execution, he was able to maintain a steady, trusting outlook that they and their work were in God's hands and not solely dependent on their own frustrated efforts; he was able to use this hope in God's protection and assistance to keep up the spirits of many others. Nowhere is this more forcefully proclaimed than in his "Exaudi Sermon."

In this sermon preached on May 8, 1932, in the midst of the agitation that preceded the eventual Nazi takeover of the German government, Bonhoeffer reflected on how Christians and their churches might handle the pressures of the political turmoil that would eventually permit Adolf Hitler to be named chancellor of Germany. He leaned on the passage from 2 Chronicles 20:12, which reads like prayer in the midst of personal doubt: "We do not know what we should do, but our eyes are fixed upon you."[17] The setting is the king of Israel facing the prospect of a bloody war and feeling the urgency to have decisive strategies for the impending battles. Suddenly the plans fade into an expression of confidence, not in humanly programmed tactics, but in God alone. Bonhoeffer mused about how badly that attitude would float in the political climate of 1932. A politician expressing trust in the Lord and acknowledging that he didn't know what to do would be so politically outrageous that such an honest leader would run the risk of being derided and rejected, first by the media, and then by the voting public. Would the moral leader of today have the kind of courage and faith that the Bible holds up for emulation?

Bonhoeffer admitted that with politicians God is often cynically added to political planning only as a shield or cover for the already-decided-upon course of action. Why not in all honesty admit that the invocation of God in most decision-making is mere propaganda to gain added respectability for dubious policies? Bonhoeffer noted the divisive ideologies that were tearing his nation apart and plunging people into confusion without any certain path to follow. He asked if anyone really knows the thrust of Jesus' command to love our neighbor. What does the command mean to the politician, the educator, the businessman, the parent? "We are," he said, "seized by the terrible fear of decision because we know that what we decide must be done under God's eyes, and we do not know what to do."[18] For Bonhoeffer, the only solution and the source of their hope in the midst of chaos lies in the death and resurrection of Jesus Christ. In the cross there is the life in which God has accomplished what no human ingenuity could achieve, the bringing of people through death to new life. The cross tells the uncertain Christian, not what precisely to do in the uncertainties of life, but that the gracious God forgives sins and

Christians can know they are held safely back by God from the emptiness that otherwise would torment their hearts.

Knowing not what to do, nonetheless, Christians do know that they are under Christ's judgment. Bonhoeffer closed his sermon with a moving prayer that hope could be sustained in a world of increasing doubt:

> Do not let us sink with these bits and pieces upon which we are drifting. Do not let it be eternally foggy and cold around us. Show us the light of your Resurrection in all of the darkness of the cross .... We who are children of the world, men and women of work, of action, we stand before you, God, and pray. We do not know what to do, but our eyes are fixed upon you. . . . Hear us, O Lord.[19]

But it seems the eyes of most Germans were fixed more on Adolf Hitler than on Jesus Christ.

In another sermon, Bonhoeffer likened hope to the expectation of miners trapped underground by a mining disaster. Suddenly they hear the tapping and hammering of their rescuers as the moment of deliverance draws near and they are encouraged to hold out. He likened hope also to prisoners who have failed to escape their cells but who hear the message ringing in their prison that very shortly they will be freed. These analogies were incorporated into his Advent sermon of December 3, 1933. Christian hope, he said, longs for the liberation that Advent stirs in human hearts, because it betokens the daily coming of Jesus Christ into the lives of his brothers and sisters as redemption draws near. Bonhoeffer's message is clear: Christians are to look upward, to take courage, to listen to the tapping of Jesus at the door of their hearts. "'Look up and raise your heads.' Advent creates new men and women. Look up, you whose eyes are fixed on this earth, you who are captivated by the events and changes on the surface of this earth. Look up, you who turned away from heaven to this ground because you had become disillusioned. Look up, you whose eyes are laden with tears, you who cannot lift up your eyes because you are so laden with guilt."[20]

In an earlier Advent sermon set in Barcelona in 1928, Bonhoeffer turned the hope with which Jesus supports Christians in their impoverishments and imprisonments into a call for Christians to share that hope with those who live deprived lives in their troubled world. In effect, he told his congregation that they were to give hope to the Jesus who stands at their doors and pleads for help. "We are faced with the shocking reality: Jesus stands at the door and knocks, in complete reality. He asks you for help in the form of a beggar, in the form of a ruined human being in torn clothing. He confronts you in every person that you meet. Christ walks on the earth as your neighbor as long as there are people. He walks on the earth as the one through whom God calls you, speaks to you and makes his demands."[21] In the lives of Christians, Bonhoeffer said, every day is an Advent of the Lord Jesus.

Five years later in a sermon delivered in London on Reformation Sunday, November 4, 1933, Bonhoeffer explored the inner connection between hope and faith and love. Even agreeing with Paul that love is the greatest of the "theological" virtues because it abides eternally, nonetheless, Bonhoeffer commented with a certain dismay that in the Nazi era their Reformation churches had failed all three. Their adherence to creedal correctness was besmirched by the hatred and failures to do Christ's will that he detected in the lives of Christians. What does it mean, he asked, for a church to call a nation to faith if there is no reconciliation, but lots of hate-filled people? What does it matter if a church dwells on the glory of its past instead of the unseen acts of God? What good is a church of success if that church fails to live by that which is unseen? The church of faith, hope, and love, according to Bonhoeffer, "never ever lives by its deeds, not even by its deeds of love. Rather it lives by what it cannot see and yet believes. It sees affliction and believes deliverance. It sees false teaching and believes God's truth. It sees betrayal of the gospel and believes God's faithfulness."[22] The paradoxes of these words recall Kierkegaard's insistence that personal truth always lies beyond mere appearances. Moral leaders must have the ability to look beyond the appearances of persons and things as they appeal to those who depend on them for guidance.

Bonhoeffer likened this hope with which people continue their struggles for survival and for meaning in their lives to the hungry child promised bread, or the music aficionado who can wait out the disharmonies in anticipation of their resolution later in the score, or patients waiting for the medicinal alleviation of their pain. Christians, he admitted, hope for what is beyond all measure and human reach, the vision of God, the peace and love of eternal life. He pointed out that hoping for what seems impossible is nothing to be ashamed of; instead, Christians should be ashamed if, in their fear-filled lives, they lack hope in the graciousness of their God always faithful to the divinely promised Word. In Bonhoeffer's sobering words, "A faith that does not hope is sick."[23]

Indeed, even while he agreed with St. Paul that love is the greatest of the theological virtues, he also argued that without hope, the love praised by Paul cannot exist. If faith alone justifies and love perfects, hope focuses us on the beatific end to which we aspire. Such hope Bonhoeffer saw as particularly important in its necessary congruence with faith and love. He concluded his sermon with this remarkable insight not only on the intimate connection of faith, hope, and love, but also on the vocation of Christians to extend their practice of these virtues to the impoverished human beings entrusted to their care through the churches: "A humanity that has been deceived and disappointed thousands of times needs faith. A wounded and suffering humanity needs hope. A humanity that has fallen into discord and distrust needs love. And if we no longer have any compassion on our own poor soul which truly needs all this too, then at least have compassion on a poor humanity. It wants to learn from us to believe, hope, and love anew. Don't deny it to them."[24] Two weeks before preaching those words Bonhoeffer concluded in another sermon that hoping for results, whether political or spiritual, without love amounts to naïve, foolish optimism. On the other hand, hoping and working for the desired results out of motives of love "is the power from which a nation and a church can take courage." He added, "It is our task to hope so unconditionally that our hope in the spirit of love may be a source of strength for others." Maintaining this kind of determined hope may expose Christians to the ridicule or even malice of their "more realistic" enemies.[25]

That the hope Bonhoeffer described in these sermons entered into his personal life can be seen in two significant passages from the last years of his life. In his Christmas 1942 essay to his family and fellow conspirators, he urged them to remain resolute in their planning of the coup d'état. Given the powers lined up against them, pessimism may have its place, he wrote, but optimism is needed in their present danger because "it enables persons to hold their heads high when everything seems to be going wrong; it gives them strength to sustain reverses and yet to claim the future for themselves instead of abandoning it to their opponents."[26] Such optimism is not frivolous or naïve, especially in the chaos, disorders, and catastrophes of the war years and the dangers they still had to face. Neither resignation to these evils nor "pious escapism" would be any help in achieving a better future for the coming generations. Bonhoeffer urged the conspirators to exercise moral leadership, and never to lose their hope or cease devoting their energies to that better future even if they would not live to enjoy it.

Finally, when all their efforts to overthrow the Nazi government had failed, and just prior to his transfer to the Gestapo prison, he penned what became a farewell letter to his friend Eberhard Bethge. Here on a very personal level he told Eberhard that, despite the setbacks they had suffered in the resistance movement and his present imprisonment, he had never lost the certainty born of his trust in God's providential guidance. His letter is also a personal statement that sums up his confident attitude toward whatever fate might befall him; it reveals the depth of his hope:

> I am so sure of God's guiding hand that I hope I shall always be kept in that certainty. You must never doubt that I'm traveling with gratitude and cheerfulness along the road where I'm being led. My past life is brimful of God's goodness, and my sins are covered by the forgiving love of Christ crucified. I'm most thankful for the people I have met, and I only hope that they never have to grieve about me, but that they, too, will always be certain of, and thankful for, God's mercy and forgiveness.[27]

Words on Love

It would not be inaccurate to assert that love figures in one form or another in almost all of Bonhoeffer's sermons. However, the greatest concentration of his sermons on love, drawn directly from biblical texts that speak of the Christian mandate to love God above all and to love one's neighbor as oneself, came in his London pastorate.

Preaching in London, on October 14, 1934, the twentieth Sunday after the feast of the Holy Trinity, Bonhoeffer told his congregation that the German churches were entangled in a struggle where their faith and confession of Jesus Christ as their sole Lord and Savior were endangered in entirely new ways. Because Nazism was both powerful and clever, they needed to shake off their prideful self-righteousness and complacent dogmatism. This enemy could be overcome only by love. Such was, after all, the only way the early church was able to win over their pagan enemies. Bonhoeffer went on to detail what loving God above everything else demanded of them: rejoicing in God, not grieving God, loving others out of one's love for God, and "allowing God to question *us* about *our* love."[28] What he had God saying about our love reads like a description of the proper outlook on life of believing Christians:

> A life has meaning and value only in so far as love is in it. Furthermore, life is nothing, nothing at all, and has not meaning and value

if love is not in it. The worth of a life is measured by how much love
it has. Everything else is nothing, nothing at all, totally indifferent,
totally unimportant. All the bad things and all the good things
about life, all the large and small matters of life are unimportant. We
are only asked about one thing — whether we have love or not.[29]

The dynamic of love, Bonhoeffer went on to say, invests with meaning
one's understanding of and attitude toward happiness, wealth, poverty,
honor, disgrace, even death itself. Love cuts across civic morality and civic
order. Because of the mandate to love others as oneself, the world has to
be viewed differently than ever before. Those leaders who have striven
solely for power, domination, honors, pleasure, or material worth can be
toppled from their perches of distinction by the force of this word of God
spoken through Paul: "If I do not have love, I am nothing." Bonhoeffer
pointed out that this word of God is also severe.

In the presence of love, everything else becomes small. Whatever
seemed great is shattered and disintegrates; it is a picture of wretchedness and misery. What is a life full of pleasure, honor, fame, and
glamour compared to a life lived in love. But of course, the question
does not stop here. It has a tremendously aggressive force and
pushes on. What even is a life full of piety, morals, discipline, sacrifice, and self-denial if it is not a life lived in love?[30]

Even those endowed with political adulation, who seem in their majesty and grandeur beyond all criticism (is this Bonhoeffer's allusion to the
Führer of the German nation?) can be attacked and made to collapse by
the divine word that one who lacks love is nothing in the sight of God.
Bonhoeffer turns to the words, both sacred and profane, spoken by hierarchs and civic rulers, that can have an impressive grandiloquence to
them. Their words so admired and applauded are nothing more than
gonging nonsense compared to the hesitant but sincere speech of one
who speaks the truth in love (Eph. 4:15). This truth of the honest, compassionate Christian is in its own special eloquence "the clarity" endowed by
God and made possible by a loving heart. Effective moral leadership depends not on rhetorical eloquence alone, but on the eloquence inspirited
by love, honesty, and compassion.

Bonhoeffer likewise addresses the vaunted faith and heroic deeds of
avid churchgoers, which, like Paul, he counts as nothing if the practicing
Christians do not love God wholeheartedly and their brothers and sisters

as themselves. One can only speculate about the import of Bonhoeffer's words for a congregation separated from their homeland and left wondering about the direction their nation under Nazi rule was taking. The German Christians who hailed Hitler as their political messiah attended church, received communion, sang pious hymns, proclaimed allegiance to their faith, and worshipped Jesus as their Lord and Savior. Did they have love for those whom Hitler and his propaganda machine branded as worthy only of hatred and rejection? That is the underlying issue in Bonhoeffer's homiletic commentary on 1 Cor. 13:1-3, as the leader of his nation capitalized on the baser instincts and gullibility of ordinary citizens to advance his ideological agenda.

The following Sunday Bonhoeffer returned to the same theme with added emphasis on the power, passion, and meaning of Christian love. He cautions against the self-love that can become a misguided caricature of genuine Christian love. This is the kind of self-centered love that does not need others except for one's own self-satisfaction. The deceptions of this love Bonhoeffer would later expose in his book, *Life Together,* in his contrast of spiritual love with self-centered, self-gratifying love.[31] Bonhoeffer told his congregation that Paul exposed the clever pretensions of this selfish masquerade of love by painting a contrasting picture of the genuine love that God intends for the followers of Jesus Christ. True Christian love, he noted, "is patient and kind; love is not jealous or boastful; it is not arrogant or rude. Such love does not insist on its own way; it is not irritable or resentful; it does not rejoice at wrong, but rejoices in the right. Love bears all things, believes all things, hopes all things, endures all things. Love never ends" (1 Cor. 13:4-8). In the turbulent Nazi world, where vengeance-seeking and unjust judicial sanctions were applied indiscriminately, Bonhoeffer's words on true Christian love bring out the contrast between the uncritical patriotism trumpeted by Nazism and the love Jesus inspired among his followers. According to Bonhoeffer, Jesus' love

> is not resentful, it keeps no record of wrongs. Where justice seems to command us to keep a record of rights and wrongs, love is blind, knowingly blind. . . . It does not hold grudges. If we would only understand this one thing: love never holds grudges. Every day it faces the other with new love and a fresh start. It forgets what lies behind. By acting this way it makes itself the laughingstock of the people. It makes a fool of itself, but it is not deterred by such ridicule. Instead it continues to love.[32]

Where Nazism appeared to thrive on settling old scores, herding political dissenters into concentration camps, murdering enemies, and planning destructive vengeance on neighboring nations, Christian love demands forbearance and forgiveness. This contrast is brought out forcefully in Bonhoeffer's sermons.

While Christian love "keeps no record of wrongs," nonetheless, as Bonhoeffer went on to point out, this love is sensitive to right and wrong. Through it the Christian can face with courage the most terrifying aspects of human sin, foolish though this may seem to those who have learned the tricks of evasion, equivocation, and avoiding the concrete deeds of justice. Their Christian "foolishness" may even provoke the malice of unloving evildoers, but their love enables them to bear even the malicious persecution that may ensue. Asking who epitomizes this love, Bonhoeffer replies with a description of how this kind of love is found primarily in Jesus Christ, crucified despite his innocence, a courageous victim of systemic injustice. Jesus, Bonhoeffer insists, is the embodiment of the love of which Paul speaks. He is "the one who did not insist on his own way nor seek himself, the one who did not allow himself to become bitter, and who did not keep a record of the evil deeds perpetrated on him and thus was overwhelmed by evil. The one who even prayed on the cross for his enemies and in this act of love utterly overcame evil. Who is this love Paul spoke of in these verses if not Jesus Christ himself? Who is meant here if not Jesus?"[33] Bonhoeffer's words here elide with his strong statement in *Discipleship* that the passion of Jesus is in essence the overcoming of evil by the power of divine love. His followers, in communion with his cross, learn that "in the cross alone is it true and real that suffering love is the retribution for and the overcoming of evil."[34]

Bonhoeffer also dwelled on the extent of the love of Christ as it enters the hearts of Christians, moving them to undertake what seems the impossible task, the forgiveness of enemies. At the height of Hitler's campaign of revenge for the humiliation of World War I, Bonhoeffer asked his congregation to make the hard sacrifice of denying revenge to their hardened human nature and to forgive. He reminded them that in their faith they should see Jesus Christ standing beyond the enemy and entreating them not to get even. He adds these remarkable words, a paraphrase of Paul's advice to the Christians of Rome (Rom. 12:17-21) and a novel insight into Jesus' command to love our enemies:

Who indeed could be more worth our love, who could stand in greater need of our love than those who hate? Who is poorer than those, who is more in need of help, who is more in need of love than your enemy? Have you ever looked upon your enemies as those who, in effect, stand destitute before you. . . . All the threatening and showing of fist is really the result of this poverty: it is essentially a begging for God's love, for peace, for community. When you reject your enemy, you turn the poorest of the poor from your door.[35]

Bonhoeffer's words penetrate to what for many are the untapped depths of the love and compassion of Jesus Christ, who was able to forgive even his enemies and his executioners. In these days when American politicians, under the pretension of moral leadership, often vie among themselves to claim the "honor" of being toughest on crime, the strongest on using the nation's weaponry to insure national security, and the staunchest advocates of the death penalty, Bonhoeffer's sermon, delivered in a country where capital punishment was being meted out for the widest possible stretch of what could be considered breaking the law, has critical relevance. His binding Christian forbearance to the teachings and example of Jesus Christ could give pause to the political debate on capital punishment now raging in the United States.

In a later sermon in 1940 on the second day of Pentecost, Bonhoeffer alluded to the mission of the Holy Spirit to illuminate our minds with the light that is Jesus Christ. To speak about God's love for the world in this light can, Bonhoeffer admitted, present difficulties to Christians, used as they are to the repetition of set formulas. God comes across in these stylized phrases as the premier problem solver of the world. But Bonhoeffer objected: God's love for the world is most certainly *not* shown in bringing the war to an end, in taking away poverty, neediness, persecutions, all sorts of catastrophes — in a word, where we usually look for a showing of God's love in power and never find it. It baffles ordinary Christians that God's love can be so hidden. In the calamitous times in which Bonhoeffer preached, he told his people not to expect to find God in the powerful interventions associated with "deities" of old. Instead, he pointed out, "we need no longer seek God's love where it just is not to be found by us, but . . . this love leads us more clearly where alone it is to be found: in Jesus Christ."[36] It is because of God's love for the world in Jesus Christ, he said, that God can love the meanest enemy no less than Jesus' most avid followers. Jesus died for both. Bonhoeffer told his congregation that the love embodied in Jesus Christ is extended through Jesus' followers into every generation, even that of their own time bedeviled by the hatreds Hitler and the Nazi leadership had nurtured. No one, not even the enemy, is to be excluded from the Christians' outreach in love to the world in which Jesus Christ continues to dwell. Moral leaders who claim allegiance to Jesus Christ must also promote the inclusiveness that breaks down the barriers of hatred and vengeance-seeking; they are called to enter into Jesus' way, truth, and life.

Words on Truth and Freedom

Bonhoeffer's one sermon devoted entirely to God's gift of freedom was preached on the ninth Sunday after the feast of the Holy Trinity, July 24, 1932; it marked the end of the summer semester at the university. Bonhoeffer's text is important for judging the quality of moral leadership not only because of the unmistakable connection he makes between freedom and truth, but also in light of the historical events about to take place in Hitler's accession to power. Freedom and truth would be the first casualties in the Nazi takeover. Bonhoeffer's understanding of the truth that generates the freedom of which he speaks is far removed from the mastering of church-sanctioned truths in catechisms, creedal formulae, and dogmatic treatises. Bonhoeffer's "truth" is more in the Kierkegaardian sense of *the truth that one is,* not the true statements that one can recite. Truth and freedom are always correlative terms in Bonhoeffer's theology and preaching. It is not surprising, then, that the text he chose for his sermon at the conclusion of the university semester was taken from John 8:32, "the truth will make you free." Earlier in a sermon on truth given at the beginning of the summer semester at the Technical University of Charlottenburg, he included the preceding verse in his text: "If you continue in my word, you are truly my disciples; and you will know the truth and the truth will make you free" (John 8:31-32).

Bonhoeffer began his sermon by saying that John 8:32 is the most revolutionary statement in the New Testament, but it is understood by only a few revolutionaries. Too often freedom becomes a mere slogan for the masses in their desire for a better life. It can even blunt the revolutionary moments the sloganized battle cry of freedom is supposed to inspire. Bonhoeffer wondered aloud who are the genuine revolutionaries of whom the gospel speaks. For him they are those set free by Christ's truth and who live in the truth of Christ's teachings. He pointed out that at times even a child given to wonder can be freer than so-called mature adults caught in the throes of their own lies and anxieties. The truth of life can shine through in the good-humored innocence of the child who recognizes intuitively the truth about life that is avoided by more cautious, deception-bound adults, stuck in their lack of courage and spontaneity. The child can blurt out the truth that anxiety-ridden adults try to hide through their polite conversation aimed at giving no offense even when confrontation may be called for. Bonhoeffer's sermon at this juncture parallels the child of whom he speaks, who alone has the innocence to cry out that the emperor has no clothes. When one reads some of the German resistance literature, it is uncanny to note how so many opponents of the Nazi regime had to watch their words very carefully so as not to give offense to Nazi sympathizers. The ruthlessness and swiftness with which the Gestapo punished dissent enabled the Hitler government to enforce the denial of freedom of speech in Nazi Germany. People lived in that kind of anxiety.

At this juncture in his sermon Bonhoeffer offered another paradoxical example of the freedom that people should enjoy but that only the child-like innocents can express. In the halls of nobility the jester or fool, not the learned intelligentsia, has the freedom to speak the truth to power. He is not constrained by the rules of courtly manners and the pompous falsehoods of courtly life. Dressed as he is, treated as an outsider because he is not of the nobility, and considered undeserving of the reverence due to the more mannered courtiers, he is nonetheless an essential presence in every court. He alone is allowed to speak the truth, couched though it might be in his comic attitude toward the pomp and circumstances of court life. The fool was the only free person in the days when the customs of courtly life prevailed and nobility lived out their illusions. Do fools have the freedom to speak the truth that one's desires to conform to society's canons of proper behavior deny? Was it not an attractive quality of Jesus Christ that he could speak truth to power, though it cost him his life? These are the questions that Bonhoeffer used to probe the true exercise of freedom.

Bonhoeffer in fact only built his examples toward their climax in the divine incarnation of truth and freedom, the one who exalted the child and was taken for a fool, Jesus Christ. To Pilate's question, "what is truth?" Bonhoeffer remarked that Jesus could have answered, as he did in the gospel, "I am the truth." Jesus the truth was crucified; the truth was crucified in Jesus. Yet we can hear that truth in all its childlikeness and foolishness through the gospel. Bonhoeffer recognized at the same time that what has often been trumpeted publicly as the truth is often well phrased but vapid political, even pious piffle. These moral conundrums are remote from the truth that sets people free by opening their eyes and delivering them from their deceptions, insecurities, and anxieties.[37]

Bonhoeffer pointed out how ridiculously easy it was for people and their moral leaders so glibly and so easily to speak of freedom in those times. The word "freedom" had become commonplace. Their dreams of freedom had so often faded away into the reality of their less than happy lives. But to speak of freedom as the Bible does is difficult. Bonhoeffer concluded that everyone wants to be free and everyone strives to be free. But what does the sobering correlative, "truth," have to do with this freedom? He argued that in all honesty, people realize the "truth" may point to something less popular. There is so much that is less than the truth spouted in religion, politics and world views that the genuine "truth" by comparison can seem cold, disturbing, and even violent enough to arouse one's apprehension and worries. Bonhoeffer saw this coming down to our fear of what the truth may reveal to us about ourselves. "This anxiety," he said, "is basically our anxiety before God. God and no other is the truth. But we are frightened that God will suddenly shine the light of truth on us and expose our mendacity and lack of genuine freedom. Truth is a power that stands over us and at any moment can destroy us."[38] This truth is the living God and God's Word on which Christians must stake their lives. The clever ones of this world try to shield themselves from this truth by telling more refined lies and by polishing up their appearances. Soon enough, Bonhoeffer concluded, "they take their lies for the truth."[39] No one can deny that political lies, social lies, self-serving lies exercise a domineering power over people. Sooner or later, often too late, people realize the impact of the duplicity into which their lives have sunk.

Bonhoeffer tells his congregation that, despite the deceptions surrounding them and hemming them into corners of unhappiness, the truth happens not in the form of dazzling, unapproachable lordliness or with radiant, heart-stirring clarity, but in the crucified truth, Jesus Christ. Bonhoeffer has Christ ask, "who has crucified me, the truth?" To which he answers that all of us have crucified the truth with our fears, hatreds, and by putting ourselves in the place of God, looking only to ourselves for the source of truth that is found in God alone.[40] He goes on to denounce the truth-denying tactics so prevalent in the nation in which he and his congregation lived. His analysis of the procession from lies to the death-dealing force of the systemic mendacity into which Germany was plunged seems apropos the various decadent stages in which Hitler, by his clever manipulation of the masses, had led the German nation. According to Bonhoeffer, the seductions to which they were exposed had as their base self-hatred and hatred of others, as opposed to the truth of God's grace, which is love. Even more dangerous than the duplicities that people had embraced were those deeds of hatred for the truth.

Bonhoeffer saw hope in the midst of the deceitful policies of their rulers. Once persons are brought into the truth by God, they see that all their sham freedom was only servitude, and all their duplicitous "truth" a mere lie. Their prayer becomes, as Bonhoeffer voiced it: "Lord, free me from myself." In their longing to be freed from their imprisonment in lies and servitude they hear the Lord's answer: "The truth will make you free." Deliverance into true freedom, Bonhoeffer insisted at this point in his sermon, comes not from one's deeds, personal strength, and courage, but only in God's liberating us from ourselves. He then described the freedom that is the truth of Jesus Christ. "To be free does not mean to be great in the world, to be free against our brothers and sisters, to be free against God; but it means to be free from ourselves, from our untruth, in which it seems as if I alone were there, as if I were the center of the world; to be free from the hatred with which I destroy God's creation; to be free from myself in order to be free for others."[41] The love of which Bonhoeffer speaks here is God's own love, living in and from God's own truth.

This leads to Bonhoeffer's climactic statement: not the followers of Adolf Hitler, but "the people who love, because they are freed through the truth of God are the most revolutionary people on earth. They are the ones who upset all values; they are the explosives in human society. Such persons are the most dangerous. . . . The disturbance of peace, which comes to the world through these people, provokes the world's hatred."[42]

At a time, too, when the leading Nazis were depicting themselves as the Teutonic knights of old come to deliver Germany from its national shame and to lead the nation to new heights of military glory, Bonhoeffer reminded his congregation that the Knight of truth and love is not the national hero whom the people have honored because of his exploits and who is free of enemies, but the outcast, the one declared an outlaw, the one who, because he exemplifies God's truth, will be rejected and crucified. He closed his sermon on freedom with words that strike the reader as an uncanny prophecy of the fate to befall the people of Germany: "A people will remain in untruth and slavery until such time as they receive and continue to receive their truth and their freedom from God alone, until they know that truth and freedom lead to love; indeed, until they know that the way of love leads to the cross. If a people are really able to acknowledge this today, they then will be the only people who have the right to call themselves a free people, the only people that are not slaves to themselves, but who are the free servants of God's truth."[43] Freedom in

Bonhoeffer's sermon is ultimately the freedom that comes from being in communion with God's Word of truth, which is Jesus Christ. Living that freedom, which is a primary demand on every Christian, is to follow Christ and become the extension of Christ's compassion, peace, and love to those entrusted to one's care by the power of God's own truth.

Words on Peace

Bonhoeffer's efforts to bring about world peace and the reconciliation of peoples in a Germany seemingly hell-bent for war were at once his deepest passion and his greatest frustration. Bonhoeffer's views on peace, non-violence, forgiveness of enemies, and forbearance expressed in sermons, conferences, and in some of the most powerful sections of *Discipleship* mark him as not only a man of peace but as a strong advocate of pacifism in a nation where military prowess was honored and publicly celebrated. His biographer has noted the change that came over Bonhoeffer just before he began his teaching career at Berlin University. Something happened to him during his year at Union Theological Seminary in 1931; he appears to have undergone a transformation in his beliefs about patriotism and the duty to serve one's country in wartime. Scholars trace this to the influence of the French pacifist Jean Lasserre, a fellow student at Union Theological Seminary, who challenged him to pit the teachings of Jesus Christ against the evils condoned under the rubric of so-called just wars. Lasserre himself has testified that during their time together at Union Seminary he had noticed that Dietrich had gradually come to accept the way of peace as the only right decision for Christians, who are called to recognize the presence of Jesus Christ in one another.[44] Whatever the modifying labels put on his pacifism by later critics who cannot reconcile Bonhoeffer's pacifism with his having joined the conspiracy to assassinate Hitler, there can be little doubt that during the Hitler era he preached peace and worked arduously to achieve peace until there seemed no way to stop the war and the slaughter of millions short of efforts to overthrow the government through violent means. Before that change, however, what stands out is Bonhoeffer's development into such an advocate for peace that few sermons in support of peace movements, even in the contemporary world, can match the innovative fervor and intensity of his sermon entitled "The Church and the People of the World," delivered during the ecumenical conference in Fanø, Denmark, in September 1934.

Bonhoeffer preached this sermon to a formidable congregation of

Christian leaders and ecumenical delegates drawn from several nations representing an extremely diverse variety of Christian denominations. For Bonhoeffer, the typical focus of these ecumenical gatherings on reconciling dogmatic, liturgical differences, though admirable in itself, was not the most pressing need of the day. He had already perceived that under Hitler the German nation seemed to be heading for another round of violence in its quest to recapture the military glory lost in World War I. As he had in his earlier talk to the German Christian Student Movement in Berlin, Bonhoeffer came right to the point of God's no-compromise command. In Berlin, speaking on the need to be people of peace, he had said that refusing the divine command to love our enemy and ignoring God's unmistakable prohibition against the taking of human life only cheapened God's adverse judgments on human sin and demeaned God's grace of forgiveness.

Bonhoeffer's approach in 1934 to the issue of how these ecumenical delegates could help bring about peace was, first of all, to remind his distinguished congregation that the ecumenical churches' primary mission did not deal in politics as such. But even given this restriction, the churches had instead an unmistakable mandate from God at the advent of Jesus Christ: there shall be peace on earth. Unfortunately, hanging all over them as they received this command was the wily parsing of God's command to the effect that they were asked to believe God couldn't really have meant what was said so directly in the Scriptures. Surely God didn't actually mean peace. Didn't God also commission leaders to provide security, even if that meant tanks and poison gas? Or that most serious question that Bonhoeffer held up as their most devilish rhetorical deception: "Did God say you should not protect your own people? Did God say you should leave your own a prey to the enemy?" To which Bonhoeffer replied clearly and forcefully that "God did not say all that. What God has said is that there shall be peace among people — that we shall obey God without further question, that is what God means."[45]

Bonhoeffer went on to say there must be peace, because that is the mission of Christians and their churches. This church of Christ in its ecumenical dimensions "lives at one and the same time in all peoples, yet beyond all boundaries, whether national, political, social, or racial." The word of Christ thus transcends all the separations that are often invoked to legitimate enmities based on distinctions of blood, class, or language. Christ identifies with all. Therefore, Christians who wage war are, in effect, using their weapons against Jesus Christ himself.[46]

Bonhoeffer then went over the practical strategies nations bring into play to justify their own self-serving ways of "keeping the peace": political treaties, money and investments, building up strong armies and arsenals. The scene was 1934; it could also be today's world with the same rationalizations. None of these can succeed, he said, because they confuse peace with security while the belligerent nations never deal with the one attitude necessary for peace, mutual trust. In an earlier talk to the ecumenical delegates at Gland, Switzerland, in 1932, Bonhoeffer had denounced the political stratagem of turning national security into an idol to be worshipped at all costs, calling this idolatry the single most insidious rationale for the arms race, political extremism, and fanaticism. It was, he said, a shameful pretext for permitting hunger and destitution within a nation's borders and for inflicting shame on less powerful nations, victimized in the name of this idolatry. In that same conference Bonhoeffer proclaimed that the crucified Christ alone can exorcise the demons of war by proclaiming peace and denouncing the agents of hatred. "War in its present form," he told that audience, "annihilates the creation of God and obscures the sight of revelation. War as a means of struggle can as little be justified from the necessity of political problem-solving as torture as a legal means can be justified from the need for law."[47] Given the history of the twentieth century after the martyrdom of Bonhoeffer, it is amazing to note the contemporary relevance for fearless moral leadership of his observations in this segment of his sermon.

In 1934, given the nations' penchant for settling their grievances against each other by war, Bonhoeffer urged the delegates of the World Alliance to be courageous, even daring, in their efforts at peace making. "For peace," he said, "must be dared. It is the great venture."[48] Who would summon the nations to peace? Neither individual Christians whose witness was easily dismissed by the powers of the belligerent world, nor the few individual churches whose resistance was isolated and ineffective against the forces of internecine hatred. He concluded, therefore, that they as the Ecumenical Council of the holy church of Christ had the opportunity to speak out courageously and convincingly so that the nations would be forced to hear. It was in the church's power, he declared, to take the "weapons from their sons," to forbid war, and to proclaim "the peace of Christ against the raging world."[49]

One of Bonhoeffer's students, present at the sermon, remarked that Bonhoeffer had leapt so far ahead of everyone else in the cause of peace that none were able to follow him. But he left them with an uneasy conscience.[50] After the war, too late, his words would be taken seriously and incorporated into the official policies of the World Council of Churches, the successor of the ecumenical body to which Bonhoeffer belonged as representative of the young ministers of Germany.

It should have been no surprise that Bonhoeffer had goaded those placid ecumenical delegates to take a more courageous stand on preventing future wars. He himself had dared to preach against war on the Day of National Mourning in 1932. Facing a congregation filled with former soldiers bedecked in their medals of military valor, he used the occasion to call war a diabolical hypocrisy in which Christ's name is blasphemed to justify the violence done to Jesus Christ himself. Bonhoeffer repeated the rationalizations of those protagonists of war who claim they are engaged in *Realpolitik,* what it takes to survive in the *real* world, for whom the words of Christ have no political relevance. His reply to that politically self-serving reasoning was energetic and unabashed. He argued that to advocate war is akin to waging war against Jesus Christ himself: "The world bands together against the spirit of Christ, the demons are enraged: it is a revolt against Christ. And the great power of the rebellion is called — war! The others are called pestilence and expensive times. Thus war, sickness, and hunger are the powers who wish to take Christ's rule, and they are all incited by the archenemy of Christ."[51]

Against the powerful ideological ragings for vengeance even at the great cost of human life, and with firsthand knowledge of the murderous storms of violence that his people had endured, Bonhoeffer enjoined the church of Christ to be prophetic. He asked them not to be afraid to declare the judgment of God against wars waged by God's children against each other, to "stand with the Lord and preach his Word of peace, even if [the church] goes through abuse and persecution."[52] He was well aware of the fate of those who would dare preach peace in Nazi Germany. For Bonhoeffer, the real meaning of the Day of National Mourning was to mourn the dead, to be sure, but also to deliver Christ's message of peace and pray that the advent of Christ's kingdom would sensitize leaders to put an end to war for all peoples.

Bonhoeffer also preached on another day of national mourning, which in 1936 had been officially renamed the "Day for Commemorating the Nation's Heroes," obviously referring only to soldiers fallen in the First World War. After offering the consolation of the gospel to those honoring their dead and expressing their grief at their loss, Bonhoeffer led the congregation to ponder the meaning of wartime death for their faith. He mentioned that the change of name indicated also a change of attitude toward the great war. Sorrow had given way to pride in the achievements, sacrifice, and the heroic service of the solders for their country. Their sufferings for the people back home, he said, were embarrassing to those gathered to commemorate and mourn their loss. But, he asked, what did this mean for the people living in the mid 1930s who were still called to seek God above all? Bonhoeffer then pictured for his congregation a war photo showing the crucified Christ set in the middle of the barbed wire of a destroyed army trench. That symbol, he declared, is a graphic reminder that Christians, knowing the horrors of war, are called by Jesus Christ to repentance. Whether it be victory, or struggle, or defeat, the question is whether Christians have really listened to the preaching of Christ, whether they have moved from their sorrow and pride in wartime to repentance. He then shared his reasons why he believed repentance was called for: "our world is a forlorn world . . . since war is a sin against God's gospel of peace. . . . Christendom and the churches had become largely responsible for the war by blessing it and declaring it justified before God." Repentance was called for "because Christians were fighting against Christians, because the world war was a war among Christian peoples against one another." Then alluding to the photo of Christ crucified, he added, "Christ in the trenches — that means a judgment against a godless world."[53]

Bonhoeffer ended the sermon by proclaiming that in the face of war Christians should indeed pray for their leaders, but also offer daily prayers for peace. "Christianity," he said, "pleads and prays only for peace."[54] Given the military buildup then taking place in Germany, Bonhoeffer's words had the effect of turning the congregation's focus on the nation's military pride into a call to repentance for the suffering that war inflicts on Jesus Christ in the person of Christians ordered to kill one another and their innocent victims — what the United States military today might label unavoidable killing.

Bonhoeffer's words did not prevent Hitler's war of retribution and expansion from breaking out in 1939. But in the first year of that war, in a sermon on the first Sunday of Pentecost, Bonhoeffer returned again to the theme of peace. Drawing on Jesus' farewell discourse in which he bequeathed peace to his followers, Bonhoeffer reminded the congregation that Christ's legacy of peace is the peace of one who did not have a place to lay his head and who ended his life on the cross as an innocent victim of violence. War is not the path to peace, yet that was what the world seemed bent on doing. "What the world offers," he says, "can only be a dream fantasy from which we must awaken full of confusion and fear. But those who accept the peace of Jesus Christ need no longer let themselves be confused or frightened if the world is bereft of peace and plunged into turmoil. That is the kind of peace which Jesus gives his church community and which no one else can bestow."[55]

Later in that same year, still out of step with his compatriots in their support of the war, Bonhoeffer composed a sermon meditation for Christmas. The war was already progressing in Germany's favor, but he intruded on the feelings of satisfaction of a majority of Christians unaware of the future destruction in store for them. Bonhoeffer offered again his simple solution for peace on the troubled German earth as they awaited again the coming of Jesus, the "prince of peace," at Christmastime. "Is it any wonder," he asked, "that where Jesus has been genuinely acknowledged as Lord that peace also reigns? Is there a Christianity in which there is peace in that world? There can be no peace where Jesus does not rule, where human obstinacy, pride, hatred, and uncontrolled desires are permitted to run wild. Jesus will not bring about his kingdom of peace through acts of violence but only where people willingly subject themselves to him and permit him to rule over them. To them alone he grants his wonderful peace."[56]

From all the sermons cited here, we can detect both a consistency and a simplicity in Bonhoeffer's pleas to Christians and their churches to be active, even venturous, in seeking to restore peace on earth. He insisted that there can be no peace in the world which refuses to take seriously and obey Jesus' gospel teachings. The churches bear a large share of the responsibility for the loss of life in wars of the not-too-distant past. Too often they either blessed wars or failed to use their God-given responsibility to denounce war or wield their authority to forbid their sons and daughters to engage in murderous violence on the battlefields. But ultimately the dreadfulness of war, with all the loss of life and grief that wars inflict, is the legacy of those Christians and Christian nations who have either ignored or rejected the teachings of Jesus Christ. It is an intolerable hypocrisy that moral leaders can declare war justified, all the while proclaiming their fidelity to Jesus Christ who declared his own solidarity with all his brothers and sisters regardless of their race, class, or nationality, and who even mandated that Christians forgive their enemies. Bonhoeffer's hope for the future was expressed in the closing part of a sermon that he gave at Union Theological Seminary in 1930: "We know it is not enough only to talk and to feel the necessity of peace; we must work seriously. There is so much meanness, selfishness, slander, hatred, prejudice among the nations. But we must overcome it."[57] His words are all the more poignant in light of the war that would break out less than ten years later.

Words on Justice for the Poor

Bonhoeffer's compassion for the poor comes through strongly in several of his sermons. In the ecumenical conference in Gland, Switzerland, for example, he linked the frustration of the poor peoples of the world with the violence that turned national security into an idolatry. He spoke there of the fallout in nations that neglect their poor: "millions hungry, people with cruelly deferred and unfulfilled wishes, desperate people who have nothing to lose but their lives and will lose nothing in losing them."[58]

Bonhoeffer's defense of the poor appears most detailed and energetic in the one sermon that deals directly with their plight, using as its text the Lukan story of Lazarus and the rich man. The setting was Berlin, on the first Sunday after the feast of the Holy Trinity, May 29, 1932. Bonhoeffer told them at the outset of this sermon that this gospel must be understood and preached in such a way that people long for its fulfillment in their lives. The Lukan story is not intended to lull its listeners into smugness about their own virtue. Instead, Christians must ask ever anew how the gospel applies to their everyday living. All around him, however, he saw not eagerness to live the gospel, but deliberate attempts to avoid the possibility that Jesus' words could be insinuated into existence beyond their "feel-good" presence in church. And so he challenged his congregation to permit themselves to be confronted with the revolutionary words of Jesus in this gospel.

His congregation was familiar with the story of Lazarus and the rich man. Bonhoeffer had them imagine Jesus surrounded by the sick, poor, wretched Lazaruses, telling them of that destitute leprous Lazarus lying at the gates of the rich man's estate. At their deaths, of course, Jesus' impoverished listeners rejoice when he tells them of Lazarus being welcomed into heaven and the rich man being condemned to hell. Justice is finally done! This story, Bonhoeffer claimed, illustrates picturesquely Luke's earlier praise of the poor and his prophetic pronouncement of woes on the rich and self-satisfied.

On a more practical level, Bonhoeffer knew that the people to whom he was preaching were the same ones who had been exposed to the drumbeats of the Nazi promises of a new millennium, a new world order of prosperity and glory. Jesus' message is just the opposite, he reminded the people. Jesus proclaims not the promises of slick political leaders or the justification of violence done through hatred of the weak, the unproductive handicapped, and those considered of an inferior race, but the compassion that the rich person was unable to show to the leprous Lazarus.

"Blessed are you outcasts and despised," Bonhoeffer said, "you casualties of society, you men and women without work, you broken and ruined ones, you lonely and forsaken, you who endure violence and unjustly suffer, you who suffer in body and soul. Blessed are you since God's joy will come over you and will remain eternally with you. That is the gospel of the dawn of the new world, the new order, that is the world of God and the order of God. The deaf hear, the blind see, the lame walk, and the gospel is preached to the poor."[59] Bonhoeffer's words are a direct exposé of the seditious tactics of political leaders like Hitler who proclaim their ability to establish a "new world order," a utopian slogan far removed from Jesus' idea of how society should order itself.

But Bonhoeffer cautioned his congregation against those who pretend to know the gospel's meaning other than what Luke emphasizes. They spiritualize the stark, uncompromising words of Jesus. They sublimate, refine, embellish, and moralize the story, arguing that it is not the outwardly poor or rich who are blessed or condemned; it is, rather, how one handles poverty or wealth that is the basis for God's judgment. Inner attitude becomes then the sole basis for judging the poor and the rich. Bonhoeffer pointed out that while there is a half-truth lurking in this interpretation, it is dangerous, because it dismisses Jesus' emphasis as irrelevant and distorts his meaning. It is also too easy, giving Christians as it does a pretext to excuse themselves from the demands of Jesus that they show genuine compassion to the real needs of the poor. It also allows rich people who may have exploited the poor and made their poverty all the more unbearable grounds for boasting that in their hearts they are poor in spirit.

If the message is totally in the realm of the devotional or spiritualized piety, Bonhoeffer asked why Jesus did not speak of Lazarus's inner attitude. He must have been desperately poor to have lain at the rich man's gate unable to move away. Or, conversely, why doesn't Jesus speak of the condition of soul of the rich man? Jesus did not moralize; he simply described their material conditions. Bonhoeffer asked further why Jesus healed the sick and those in misery if he were not touched by their physical distress. Why then do we have the arrogance to spiritualize what moved Jesus so deeply? "We must put an end to this insolent and hypocritical spiritualizing of the gospel. Either take it for what it really is or hate it, but be honest about it."[60]

At this point in his sermon Bonhoeffer spoke frankly to the congregation, asking them truthfully to reflect on their attitudes toward the Lazaruses of German society in 1932. It would be honest to admit that "we really despise the multitude of Lazaruses among us and the gospel of the poor [because that gospel] stings our pride, pollutes our race, and weakens our power. We are rich but proud of it."[61] He went on to declare that it is too easy to scorn the multitudes of Lazaruses because they have no name. But can one really ignore the Lazarus who encounters us face to face in the many forms Jesus assumes and say that we deride this Jesus and his proclamation that the poor are indeed blessed and loved by God?

Bonhoeffer then told the congregation that he considered it a mockery to speak to the poor of heavenly comfort while denying them the earthly comfort they need.[62] His words here return in another form in his *Ethics*, where in even stronger language he declares that refusing food to the hungry is to blaspheme against God and one's neighbor. Attending to the actual physical needs of people, not offering them political bromides, is dearest to the heart of God, who cares for the needy through the compassionate outreach of people of faith.[63] The poor have little need for the cynicism behind the pious phrases they are dealt or the lies beyond the miserly handouts of politicians who are supposed to attend to their needs. Bonhoeffer then related care given to the poor, the paralyzed, the blind, the deaf, and the homeless to the part Christians contribute to the inbreaking of God's kingdom.

Who really is Lazarus? Bonhoeffer asked. He believed that deep down they knew the answer to that question. Lazaruses are those "who cannot cope with life, who are often foolish, impertinent, obtrusive, godless, but endlessly in need and, whether they know it or not, our brothers and sisters who suffer and who long for the crumbs that fall from our tables." If they feel sorry for themselves and see themselves as Lazarus, they may also ask if they are the rich man. Finally, he told them that Lazarus is "always the other person who encounters you in a thousand despised forms, the crucified Christ himself."[64] We are all Lazaruses, he concluded, and there is even salvation for the rich man, whose story of hope is that of the Good Samaritan. But the task of Christians is to see beyond Lazarus none other than God in Jesus Christ. If we are to see the poor Lazarus in all his frightful misery and wretchedness, Bonhoeffer said, we are also to see Christ, who invited this Lazarus to feast with him and proclaimed this Lazarus to be blessed.

Few sermons centered around the care of a nation's poor can match the passion with which Bonhoeffer so often called his congregation's attention to the plight of Germany's outcasts and destitute at a time when the nation had not yet recovered from the great depression and its citizens were being torn between conflicting ideologies preaching their own brand of envy, vindictiveness, and hatred of peoples. Bonhoeffer refused to be drawn into interpretations that tended to spiritualize and moralize the condition of the poor. Theirs was the immediate need for compassion and help. Just a month before his ordination, on the occasion of the Harvest Festival in 1931, he preached a sermon based on Psalm 63:3 ("your steadfast goodness is better than life"). His theme was the Christian responsibility to extend the material blessings of God to those needy people whose sustenance depends on the compassion that God inspires in true followers of Jesus Christ. Bonhoeffer very quickly drew a contrast between the words of the biblical world and the words of Bonhoeffer's own generation. The cry of Psalm 63 "is the exultant cry of the wretched and abandoned, of the weary and overburdened; the cry of longing uttered by the sick and the oppressed; the song of praise among the unemployed and the hungry in the great cities; the prayer of thanksgiving prayed by tax collectors and prostitutes, by sinners known and unknown."[65] Their prayers have been answered. But, he added, it was not the shout of joy in his Germany. It was a joyful acclamation only for the unreal world of the Bible.

Bonhoeffer took his congregation to the world of the psalmist to discover what he was really thinking. God had come into the psalmist's life. He could no longer escape the presence and demands of God. His life had become split. He was torn away from everything he had held onto; God was destroying every vestige of evil in him. There remained only his life; and God would take that too. The psalmist, like all creation, belonged to God. The Harvest Festival, Bonhoeffer said, was a good time to reflect seriously on what God's gracious generosity to human beings means. Nature produces food, indeed, but that year's harvest did not yield enough for the people's needs. The situation was bleak: "We must be prepared for the fact that this winter seven million people in Germany will find no work, which means hunger for fifteen to twenty million people next winter. . . . These are the cold statistics behind which stands a terrible reality. Should we overlook these millions of people when we celebrate our harvest festival in church? We dare not."[66]

But then he asked his people to imagine that, as they were sitting down to a full meal and thanking God for God's goodness, they could not avoid a certain uneasiness. Why should they be the ones who benefit from God's largesse and not their hungry brothers and sisters in town? At that moment comes a ring at the door; there is someone standing there who would also like to thank God for the gift of food and prosperity but has been denied. And that person is "starving with starving children and who will go to bed in bitterness." What can one conclude? That God blesses us and curses the other? Such thinking that God rewards us in this way for our virtue would be a curse. No, the point of the good food and prosperity we may enjoy is that this is the sign of an enormous responsibility that God lays on us. It is God's way of telling us to provide for our needy brothers and sisters. In Bonhoeffer's words: "If we want to understand God's goodness in God's gifts, then we must think of them as a responsibility we bear for our brothers and sisters. Let none say: God has blessed us with money and possessions, and then live as if they and their God were alone in the world. For the time will come when they realize that they have been worshipping the idols of their good fortune and selfishness. Possessions are not God's blessing and goodness, but the opportunities of service which God entrusts to us." Few sermons, either in Bonhoeffer's preaching days or in the present time, rise to the practical level of addressing rich Christians directly in the context of the biblical question: what can the rich do to be saved? Here Bonhoeffer threw the question onto the level of one's personal responsibility to use the prosperity that one enjoys for the benefits of the have-nots of today's world. Luke's curse on the rich is very well related to the example Bonhoeffer used, that of the unconcerned wealthy people who believe in their hearts that they have been rewarded for their virtue and in that conceit proceed to be indifferent to needy people, especially the weak and vulnerable around them. The task of moral leaders, if one can extrapolate from these sermons, is to pressure the strong to take care of their hurting brothers and sisters.

Social justice for the poor has everything to do with the protection believing Christians can offer to weak brothers and sisters in nearly every society on earth. That Christian duty became the point of Bonhoeffer's London sermon of 1934, based on Paul's exclamation in 2 Cor. 12:9, "My strength is made perfect in weakness." He began by stating that every philosophy has attempted to answer the question of what meaning weakness could have in this world. He admitted that everyone seems to have attitudes toward physical and emotional weakness, though people would rather ignore the problem of dealing with the presence of the weak among them lest it make them uncomfortable. But Paul's declaration opened the way for Bonhoeffer and his people to explore what Paul could have meant and, more important, what meaning dealing with human weakness could have for Christians in the 1930s.

Why does the existence of weak, handicapped, destitute people seem so important? Bonhoeffer's answer was a series of rhetorical questions: "Have you seen a greater mystery in this world than poor people, old people, insane people — people who cannot help themselves but who have just to rely on other people for help, for love, for care? Have you ever thought what outlook on life a cripple, a hopelessly sick man, a man exploited by society, a colored man in a white country, an untouchable [in India] may have?"[67] If they had ever thought of these very concrete examples of just what forms weakness might assume, he told them that, first of all, their own life was qualitatively different; and secondly, they were all inseparably bound to the weak.

Bonhoeffer insisted that Christianity was in its very origin a religion of and for the weak. Its identification with the miserable masses, the weak of this world, became at once its great attraction for Jesus' followers and a source of indignation and enmity for many others, including those who espoused a domineering philosophy of life in which strength, power, and violence were glorified. Bonhoeffer's comment on this was emphatic: "Christianity stands or falls with its revolutionary protest against violence, arbitrariness, and pride of power and with its plea for the weak."[68] But Christendom had too easily slipped into the worship of power, and Christians had failed to take the initiative in doing what was necessary to help the weak of this world. He called for bold initiatives from Christians courageous enough to follow the lead of Jesus Christ, saying, "Christians should give much more offence, shock the world far more, than they are now doing. Christians should take a stronger stand in favor of the weak rather than consider the possible moral right of the strong."[69] Christians and their moral leaders are, in other words, called to be countercultural, becoming persistent advocates on behalf of those who are powerless to escape their destitution.

Bonhoeffer wanted Christians to protest against those who minimize the crushing weight set by society upon the weaker citizens by exalting strength and heaping honors on the mighty of this world. Christians need to reverse their attitudes. There must be, he said, an overt preference given to those who are suffering and exploited; the strong should always look up to the weak. "Weakness is holy, therefore we devote ourselves to the weak. . . . The weak need not serve the strong, but the strong must serve the weak, and not with any feeling of benevolence but with reverence and love." He concluded that ultimately "Christianity turns our human scale of values upside down, and establishes a new order of values in the sight of Christ."[70] His words here are very close to the convictions he shared with his congregation in Barcelona, that "Christianity preaches the unending worth of the apparently worthless and the unending worthlessness of what is apparently so valuable."[71] They are reminiscent, too, of one of his earliest sermons, given during his internship in Barcelona. The theme was Advent. The message was that every day in their lives was an Advent of the Lord in which Christ stood at the door and knocked, asking "for help in the form of a beggar, in the form of a ruined human being in torn clothing."[72] In his sermons Bonhoeffer was unwavering in his insistence that Jesus comes to Christians in the form of those who, by reason of their poverty and weakness, have been given us by God to draw on our faith and energies by our concern for them and the care we give them.

Words on Suffering and Death

In a remarkable passage in his *Ethics,* Bonhoeffer confides in the reader that, when dealing with a bereavement, he often adopts the "penultimate attitude," and remains "silent as a sign that I share in the bereaved person's helplessness in the face of such a grievous event, and not speaking the biblical words of comfort which are, in fact, known to me and available to me."[73] As a preacher, however, Bonhoeffer was obliged to offer publicly the words that were available to him in dealing with the sorrows of his people. His sermons on those occasions are remarkably close to the letters he wrote during the war years offering words of consolation to the families of those who died during the war, or in letters to his seminarians when one of their brother seminarians was killed in action at the front.

He was able, for example, in announcing that their brother Theodor Maas was killed while serving in the army in Poland, to offer these words of comfort to his former Finkenwalde ordinands: "You will be as stunned by this news as I was. But I beg you, let us thank God in remembrance of him. He was a good brother, a quiet, faithful pastor of the Confessing Church, a man who lived from Word and Sacrament, whom God has also thought worthy to suffer for the gospel. I am sure that he was prepared to go. Where God tears great gaps we should not try to fill them with human words. . . . Our only comfort is the God of the resurrection, the Father of our Lord Jesus Christ, who also was and is his God."[74] At the height of the war and while he was actively involved in the resistance movement, he wrote again to his ordinands to announce the deaths of three of their brethren, Bruno Kerlin, Gerhard Vibrans, and Gerhard Lehne. "Now they sleep," he wrote, "with all the brothers who have gone before them, awaiting the great Easter Day of the resurrection. We see the cross, and we believe in the resurrection; we see death, and we believe in eternal life; we trace sorrow and separation, but we believe in an eternal joy and community."[75] He went on to single out the sterling qualities of these young men cut down in their prime. His words are a powerful affirmation of life in the face of death; they are reminiscent of his last recorded words before his own execution. His preaching on death at times of bereavement followed the same pattern of looking to God's scriptural Word for the meaning of death and attempting to console the grieving with the sharing of their common faith in God's promise of resurrection.

Preaching on "Death Sunday" in London, November 26, 1933, Bonhoeffer pondered with his congregation the questions raised by their grief: "Where are our dead? Where will we be after our own death?"[76] In reply he drew from the Wisdom of Solomon: "But they are in peace" (Wis. 3:3). The church, he said, also knows the answer to these impossible questions because it is the place where Jesus Christ nurtures the confident hope of Christians. The congregation knows that their loved ones who are being mourned have entered on that path from which no one ever returns to this earth. He insisted categorically that the church exists precisely to spread the comforting message that, though their loved ones do not speak, they remain silent only because they now rest in the bosom of their creator God. They have been taken from their families to live eternally in the peace of God. No human tricks and not even the church can make the dead talk — only God. God alone, Bonhoeffer said, can speak of the dead to those of faith. "Whoever knows about God, knows about the dead." God's message about the dead, entrusted to the church, is that the dead are at peace. Bonhoeffer shared with the congregation what that meant to him:

> God's peace means rest for those whom life has made tired; it means security for those who wandered through this life unsheltered and unguarded; a home for the homeless. It means quietness for the battle weary, relief for the tormented, comfort for the distressed and those who weep. God's peace is like a mother tenderly stroking her crying child's forehead. God has wiped away their tears. God has put an end to the ceaseless hustle and bustle of this life. They are in peace.[77]

Throughout the rest of his sermon Bonhoeffer repeated that phrase, "they are in peace," like a cadenced mantra. It is the Word of God that brings light into the gloom of a deathbed scene. The angels, he said, sing that reassurance over the caskets of young children and old people alike. Even while those left behind are sorrowing in seeming hopelessness and distress, God's Word comes through, telling them that their loved ones are in peace. Bonhoeffer went on to declare that the dead wake up in a new world, a paradise. The present life is but "the preliminary to a coming home with God." As for him, he told his congregation, "death is gentle, death is sweet, death is peaceful, death lures us with heavenly force if only we know that it is the gateway to home, to the tent of joy, to the eternal realm of peace." Without faith, he added, death can be hellish and frightening; with faith, "death turns into Christ himself." In a phrase that would be retrieved some sixty years later by Cardinal Bernardin, Bonhoeffer added that death comes as a friend if one has faith. It is then that one's eyes become like those of the unsuspecting, trusting child, the epitome of hope, thrilled at entering into a joyous time. Christians, he said, are called to be like innocent children become in death "children of the resurrection."[78]

Just a little over two years after preaching those words of comfort to his congregation in London remembering their dead, Bonhoeffer spoke at the funeral service of his grandmother, Julie Tafel Bonhoeffer. His tone was different. This was a beloved family member who was very close to him and to whom he could confide matters he kept even from his own parents. Here the sermon turned not on sorrow, but on gratitude for the gift of her life and all of the joy she had given her family during her ninety-three years of life. He expressed, too, his gratitude for the gifts she had received, not the least of which were the many years in which she could enjoy her children, grandchildren, and great-grandchildren. She gave her family time, patience, counsel, and the wisdom that came from her long experience.

This occasion, her funeral service, he told the family, was not to be one of sorrowing over her loss. Considering the times in which she lived, her death was a deliverance. The violence, repression, and vindictiveness in the nation were particularly vexing to her. Her freedom of speech, strength of character, integrity, and simplicity were her great gifts, but to her dismay, Germany had changed under Nazi rule. Their grandmother, he said, did not belong to this different world. It was a mercy, then, that she went to the Lord at such a time of national turmoil. "She couldn't bear to see these ideals disregarded, to see a person's rights violated. That is why her last years were clouded by the great sorrow that she bore on account of the fate of the Jews in our nation. She bore and suffered their fate with them. She came from a different time, from a different spiritual world — and this world does *not* sink with her into the grave."[79] He ended his sermon with a prayer that his grandmother "might behold God's eternal face in Jesus Christ," followed by an exhortation that the whole family be strengthened by the example of her life and her faith.

It is instructive to note the contrast between Bonhoeffer's words of consolation to a grieving congregation and his words to his family bespeaking gratitude over the many gifts his deceased grandmother had given the family. In each instance his words consoled, as he tried to turn their sorrow into peace of mind while looking back in gratitude for God's gift of life. Bonhoeffer did not deny the pain one suffers in the loss of a loved one. But his words are ultimately the sharing of his faith in the mystery of human suffering as a necessary core of one's faith and as the prelude to the peace that is Jesus' legacy to his followers.

In two sermons, the one on human weakness in 1934 and a sermon that he included in a circular sermon to his ordinands on March 14, 1938, when Hitler had annexed Austria, Bonhoeffer addressed the question of what meaning can be derived from suffering itself. Writing to his former seminarians in 1938 and basing his thoughts on Paul's statement in Romans 5 that "we rejoice in our sufferings," Bonhoeffer explained that God's gifts of peace, perseverance, character, and hope are based on the willingness to suffer while strengthened by the love that God "pour[s] into our hearts through the Holy Spirit." Repeating the Anselmian theory of atonement and satisfaction, Bonhoeffer depicted the innocent Christ struck down by God's wrath at human sin and in his sufferings setting an example of just how suffering for the sake of God can not only be redemptive but, as it was for Jesus Christ, also a gauge of spiritual strength. It was for this reason that Paul could claim that he rejoiced in his sufferings; he knew he was becoming like Christ. Hence Bonhoeffer told his people that the test of whether they truly had the peace of God came in how they handled the anguish that occurred in their lives. There are those, he said, who genuflect before the cross of Christ but reject every sacrifice they are called upon to make and every affliction that befalls them.

Bonhoeffer and his people knew that because of their criminal government they and their churches had suffered. He recited the tribulations to which, because of their faith, they had been subjected: "destruction of its order, the penetration of a false preaching, much hostility, evil words, and slander, imprisonment, and every kind of affliction, and no one knows what sufferings still await the church."[80] Such was the fate of those who would follow Jesus Christ against the Nazi government and its policies of repression. He asked to what extent they may have grumbled against and even hated their sufferings, even though it had been through their pain that God had refined their character and helped them to deepen their faith, acquire perseverance, and firm up their hope. Suffering was, he told them, the most tangible proof that God's love was poured out into their hearts. Suffering weans people away from their self-seeking, their refusal to be inconvenienced by others' needs, their lust for worldly goods. Suffering puts Christians to the test and forces them to be really honest about their declarations that they love God alone. It is an incomprehensible gift that can take place within them, "that they begin to love God for God's sake, not for the sake of worldly goods and gifts, not even for the sake of peace, but really for God's sake and God's sake alone."[81] These alone have truly encountered God's love in the cross of Jesus Christ, so that they can experience what it means to love Jesus Christ and to be able to say in all honesty and with joy that they have discovered the peace of God even in the midst of their sufferings.

In his sermon on human weakness Bonhoeffer took the experience of pain and suffering to a deeper level by declaring that suffering for the cause of Jesus Christ and social justice is holy. Why? "Because God suffers in the world through man and whenever he comes he has to suffer from man again." This is a daring statement, given a prominent theme in the theology of the time that emphasized God's inability to suffer because God is perfect in every way. He was certainly familiar with the prevailing Greek philosophical and theological categories, which taught that it was unthinkable for God's spirit to have something akin to human emotions. To say that God suffers with his human creatures and because of them, however, is to put an entirely new dimension on the problem of evil. But Bonhoeffer was adamant: In Jesus God suffered on the cross, and therefore all human suffering must be seen as sharing in God's own suffering and weakness. If we suffer, then God suffers much more intensely. "Our God is a suffering God," he declared in a now-famous quotation from his collected writings.[82] That line from his sermon would be echoed in his prison letters, where he wrote that "the Bible directs us to God's powerlessness and suffering; only the suffering God can help." In the next letter he wrote of sharing in God's sufferings in one's secular life.[83] In his 1934 sermon, he brought up the issue of God actually suffering in and through human suffering by telling the congregation that suffering transforms us into God's image and makes those struck down by physical, social, moral, or even religious weakness and suffering more like God because, in that unique way, and in common with Jesus Christ, they share God's own life. To the biblical affirmation that God is love, Bonhoeffer would add that, because of love, God is one who suffers.

Bonhoeffer's sermons not only reveal the inner depth of his spiritual life but they also show how he wanted moral leadership in his church and nation and the everyday lives of Christians to be exercised. Christians are called to live by faith, to love others, especially the weakest members of their society, to be advocates for freedom, peace, and social justice, and to be willing to suffer in the manner of the Christ whom they profess to follow. Moral leadership, extrapolated from these sermons, is itself a call to exemplify the compassion and concern for the least of Jesus' brothers and sisters that reflect God's own love for all God's children. Failing that, would-be moral leaders continue to inflict untold suffering on the God who identifies with those forced to endure hardships at the hands of the immoral leaders of their heartless governments.

CHAPTER TEN

Glimpses into the Soul of a Moral Leader

Bonhoeffer's Prayers and Poems

Daily, quiet attention to the Word of God which is meant for me, even if it is only for a few minutes, will become for me the focal point of everything which brings inward and outward order into my life. In the interruption and fragmentation of our previous ordered life . . . meditation gives our life something like constancy. It maintains the link with our previous life, from baptism to confirmation, to ordination. It keeps us in the saving community of our congregation, of our brothers and sisters, of our spiritual home.[1]

Come now, O supreme moment on the way to
    freedom eternal.
Death, lay down the burdensome chains,
break down the walls of our transient bodies,
    the barriers of our deluded souls,
that we might gaze at last on what here we are impeded
    from seeing.
Freedom, so long have we sought you in discipline,
    action, and suffering.
Dying, we now behold you indeed in the face of our God.[2]

T he first quotation above, from a circular letter to his former seminarians, brought back for them memories of Bonhoeffer's own lessons on prayer. Several recalled that he had taught them to pray as much by his

226

example as by any of his instructions. He, as their spiritual director, often took responsibility to lead them in the extemporized prayers at their community services. These prayers included thanks for their faith, for their community life, for the gifts of nature; intercession for the Confessing Church, for those in captivity, and even for enemies; and confession of the failings typical of those in ministry, along with prayers for their guidance and protection. Bonhoeffer prepared carefully for these extemporaneous prayers during their shared periods of meditation. His uncommon ability to concentrate while at prayer was to exercise a great influence on the seminarians in their later ministries. This led Bethge, his biographer and himself a seminarian at the time, to remark, "Such an indirect teacher of prayer we had never had before."[3]

Bonhoeffer's Life of and Lessons on Prayer: The Inspiration Behind Moral Leadership

Bonhoeffer, more noted as a man of action, is also revealed in his writings as a man of deep, personal prayer. His practice of quiet meditation on the Word of God helped him to become a unique advocate for truth and freedom as his own country was being overwhelmed with mendacious distortions of the truth by the Nazi government. The truth, as Bonhoeffer saw it, was that Jesus Christ was being crucified anew in the persecution of Jews and dissidents and later in those murdered in the death camps and on the battlefields of World War II. Many passages from his collected writings underline his conviction that the main task of Christians was not to stand on the sidelines in silence or to kneel in pious prayers for deliverance and safety while violence was being done. From his efforts in the church struggle and from his family connections in the resistance movement, Bonhoeffer was aware of the criminality of his government. His determination to resist Nazism was reinforced by his daily meditations on the biblical texts. It was in fact his dedication to prayer, as Bethge has observed, that kept Bonhoeffer's conspiratorial actions from degenerating into self-righteousness, that buoyed his spirits with unflinching perseverance, that kept his pursuit of justice in line with the gospel. No prayer seemed complete for him unless it was linked to prophetic action for justice.

This is why, in a revealing letter to Bethge, Bonhoeffer wrote of just how the practice of personal prayer had helped him integrate into a manageable whole the many conflicting directions his life was taking. At the time he was staying with the Kleist-Retzow family in Kieckow, Pomerania, and laboring over an initial draft of his *Ethics*. He wrote what could certainly constitute sage advice for Christian moral leaders of a resistance movement: "I enjoy the daily morning prayers here very much. These prayers compel me to ponder the meaning of the biblical text. Likewise, by reading the Bible, I am led to think a lot about you and your work. The regularly structured day for me means work and prayer. These make it easier for me in my relations with people and protect me from the emotional, physical, and spiritual troubles which ensue from a lack of discipline."[4] Bonhoeffer's adherence to the regimen of work and prayer, though springing from an entirely different context, is a counterpart of the action for justice and prayer that he advocated from prison in the hope that the church in postwar Germany could retrieve its allegiance to Jesus Christ.

To discover what Bonhoeffer's prayer life was like and, indirectly, what kind of prayer he was alluding to in his baptismal sermon from prison[5] is to explore how personal and community prayer always held a special place in his priorities. He once declared from the Monastery of Ettal, where he had been sequestered while awaiting orders from the German resistance movement, that for him, "a day without morning and evening prayers and personal intercessions was actually a day without meaning or importance."[6] So convinced was Bonhoeffer of the power of prayer to hold the various threads of one's otherwise scattered life together that he insisted on incorporating daily prayer and meditation into the training of the Confessing Church's seminarians at Finkenwalde. Although their communal life was structured into a balance of several activities that included coursework, study, leisure, and sport, the center of their spiritual formation was their beginning and ending the day in prayer and the practice of daily meditation on the Bible.

This daily meditative prayer, dubbed "Bonhoeffer's way," was an unexpected and at first misunderstood aspect of their seminary training. There were even jocose remarks about the strange monasticism that Bonhoeffer was attempting to impose on Protestant seminarians. When they complained about this after one of his protracted absences, he suggested that once a week they hold a communal service with public reflections on the scriptural texts. He himself took the lead, sharing his own meditative prayer with the seminarians. Gradually their opposition waned and they began to appreciate with him what the daily meditation was all about. They who were being prepared to be moral leaders of their respective communities would later consider themselves personally gifted by the Word of God in this form of prayer given to nourish their faith, strengthen them in their ministry, and empower them to preach the gospel with greater conviction. Bonhoeffer knew from his own personal experience that Christian ministers, and for that matter Christian moral leaders everywhere, had to "enter into a daily, personal communion with the crucified Jesus Christ" whose voice would come to them "directly from the cross . . . where Christ is so present to us that frankly he himself speaks our word; there alone can we banish the dreadful danger of pietistic chatter."[7]

As we have seen in Bonhoeffer's analysis of community life,[8] he introduced his seminarians to the practice of meditating on the brief daily texts drawn from the Scripture. Even in the war years that followed he used circular letters to call their attention to these "texts for the day," reminding them of the importance of meditation. In one such letter he urged them again not to abandon the practice of daily meditation, sharing with them his conviction that this prayer was "the focal point of everything which brings inward and outward order into [their] life," now fragmented by the war. The daily meditation preserved the unity of their lives and their community with one another.[9] He maintained these connections with their life together in Finkenwalde, during the period after it had been shut down by the Gestapo, and later when he himself had been imprisoned.[10]

Looking back on Bonhoeffer's ways of directing the seminary at Finkenwalde, one of his seminarians, Wilhelm Rott, recalled how Bonhoeffer's "love of Jesus, especially in the figure of the humiliated one, of the earthly Jesus in the Christ of faith, came through in Bonhoeffer's extemporized prayers. Here was the very heart and core of the existence of this highly intellectual Christian; we felt it in the improvised prayers of the morning and evening devotions; they sprang from the love of the Lord and of his brethren."[11] Both for himself and his seminarians Bonhoeffer stressed the need for moral leaders to allow the Word of God to speak to them daily. "Pastors," he insisted, "must pray more than others [because] . . . they have more to pray about." This statement comes from an essay he wrote to support the practice of daily meditation at the seminary. Under the title of "Why do I meditate?" Bonhoeffer replied that "prayer is the first worship of the day."[12] His words, sent as part of a circular letter in 1936, would return in *Life Together*, where he stipulated that their "life together under the Word begins at an early hour of the day with a worship service together. A community living together gathers for praise and thanks, Scripture reading, and prayer. The profound silence of morning is first broken by the prayer and song of the community of faith. After the silence of the night and early morning, hymns and the Word of God will be heard all the more clearly. Along these lines the Holy Scriptures tell us that the first thought and the first word of the day belong to God."[13]

Fittingly, the evening prayers were likewise the community's final word before the night's repose. Bonhoeffer and his seminarians closed the day as they began it, with praying the Psalms, a reading of Scripture, a hymn, and a concluding prayer. Among the various intentions that Bonhoeffer brought to the forefront of that prayer were those that pertained to their individual needs, their concern for those who were suffering from various illnesses, the poor, the outcast, and even their enemies. Bonhoeffer turned their attention to the need to forgive one another, particularly their sins of omission and any offences that hurt a fellow brother or sister. He made it the rule of his life and that of the community to seek healing for every division. No one, he said, should go to bed with feelings of enmity toward another. That reconciliation, he told them, was essential if the community was ever to be renewed in the love of Jesus Christ and of one another.[14] In these days when leadership is often exercised in stirring up animosities between opposition groups and in putting down dissent, Bonhoeffer's directives on prayer serve as a statement of the kind of moral leadership more congruent with the life and teachings of Jesus Christ on forbearance and forgiveness.

Bethge notes in his own recollections of those days that Bonhoeffer seemed to invest his very soul in their community worship. Bonhoeffer was convinced that to form a truly Christian community and to exercise their role as moral leaders of that community, they had to develop a prayerful relationship with God and a willingness to be led by God's Word. For this to happen, he believed that praying the Psalms, both in solitude and in common, was crucial. Why that was so can be seen in one of his citations from Luther to the effect that the Psalms made other prayers seem bloodless; in another revealing statement, he said that "those other easy, little prayers" lacked the "power, passion, and fire" that could be experienced in the Psalter.[15]

In several passages from the collected writings one can appreciate that, through the Psalms, Bonhoeffer seemed both to encounter the presence of God and to better make the connection between God's Word and everyday happenings. His biographer illustrates this through an examination of Bonhoeffer's jottings in the Bible he used for prayer and meditation. To show Bonhoeffer's prayerful sensitivity to the plight of the Jews, for example, Bethge calls attention to Bonhoeffer's marginal notes at Psalm 74:8. Bonhoeffer had written "9.11.38" (9 November 1938), the date of Crystal Night, in which synagogues were burned, Jewish shops were broken into, windows were smashed, and Jews were brutalized. The text reads, "They say to themselves. 'Let us plunder them.' They have set afire all the houses of God in the land." The following two verses are also marked with a stroke of his pen and an exclamation point: "Our signs we do not see; there is no longer a prophet to preach; there is nobody among us who knows how long. How long, O God, shall the foe blaspheme? Shall the enemy revile thy name forever?"[16] Against those who used the discredited theory that Crystal Night was God's vengeance on the Jews for the murder of Christ, Bonhoeffer retorted, "When today the synagogues are set afire, tomorrow the churches will burn."[17] Later Bonhoeffer incorporated his reactions to Crystal Night in a circular letter to his former seminarians now occupied with their own parish ministries. "During the past few days," he wrote, "I have been thinking a great deal about Psalm 74, Zechariah 2:12 ['he who touches you touches the apple of his eye!'], Romans 9:4f. ['Israel, to whom belongs the sonship, the glory, the covenant, the law, the service, the promises']; Romans 11:11-15. That takes us right into prayer."[18] This was a typical illustration of the way Bonhoeffer prayed the Psalms and meditated on them as God's Word for any given situation, especially unforeseen eruptions in ordinary life — in this case one of the most traumatic moments in Nazi Germany's vicious persecution of the Jews.

In 1942 Bonhoeffer published a lengthy commentary on the Psalms; it was to be his last published book. It earned him first a penalty fine from the "Reich Board for the Regulation of Literature," and then, after a repeal of the fine, a strengthened prohibition against any further publishing venture on his part because of the "dangerous dogmatic and spiritual connections" that conflicted with the prevailing Nazi ideology. In the context of the German church struggle, Bonhoeffer desired to retrieve the Psalms as the prayer book of Jesus Christ himself. Against the quasi-apocalyptic background of a Europe at war, a church divided, and a nation engaged in a malignant policy of genocide, Bonhoeffer's study of the Psalms takes on a new life. His book, coming from one who was representative of that small group of fellow Christians acting at great risk and seemingly in vain to restore true Christianity in Germany, stands in sobering contrast with the blind, flag-waving patriotism and nationalistic sloganeering that cheered on the violence against innocent peoples. It is not only "the prayer book of the Bible," as Bonhoeffer declared, but also a tapping into the strength of one's personal communion with Jesus Christ, the sustenance of the faith of Christians caught in a life-and-death struggle against evil.

From the very outset Bonhoeffer made it clear that the Christian use of the Psalms as a prayer book goes back to the plea of Christ's followers: "Lord, teach us to pray!" They, like the Christians of Bonhoeffer's day, were acknowledging their inability to pray on their own. They needed the help that only Jesus could provide. And Jesus, he points out, wants not only to teach his followers how to pray, but also to pray with them and to have them pray with him. The Psalms, he says, are like the child learning to speak the language of the parents. The Psalms are God's mode of enabling the followers of God's son Jesus to speak to and with Jesus. God hears those in the language of Jesus who, as God's Word, allows his followers to enter into his own prayer and thus to find their way with Jesus back to God.

Bonhoeffer argued that this prayer is God's gift to the followers of Jesus because it focuses them not on themselves but on Jesus, the biblical center, who leads them to pray as God wants. In this way they might even allow themselves to pray against the whims of their own hearts in order to pray as Christ believes they should. For Bonhoeffer, it is not just what they desire that is important, but what God wishes for them in Jesus' own prayerful communication with them. Hence, with Luther, Bonhoeffer considers the Psalter as of a piece with the Lord's Prayer. The Psalms penetrate the Lord's Prayer just as the Lord's Prayer inspirits the Psalter, thus creating an openness to God that reflects in turn God's many concerns for all God's people. In that perspective, the Psalms became for Bonhoeffer not only a written testimony to the prophetic foresight of David, their Jewish author, and of the people's hopes for Jesus, their messiah to come, but also the way in which both Jesus and his followers can pour out their hearts to God. Jesus, who knew human weakness and bore pain, suffering, guilt, and death, thus expresses himself in the name of all peoples. And the people in turn can make his prayer their own.[19]

This practical dimension of the Psalms helps explain why Bonhoeffer cherished them as his principal form of prayer. Above all, the Psalms enabled him to cope with his own shifting moods amid all the vicissitudes of his ministry, including his imprisonment. The Psalms taught him that God was near in all the sorrows and joys, successes, and disappointments that had marked his own days. Thus it came as no surprise to the seminarians who followed his lessons and shared his community life that he would insist on integrating the Psalms into their regular community prayer services. "The prayer of the Psalms," he told them, "teaches us to pray as a community."[20] Even during the most dismal days in Tegel Prison, he could send these comforting words to his parents: "I read the

Psalms every day, as I have done for years; I know them and love them more than any other book." In that same letter he told his parents that he derived spiritual solace from the Bible's answer to a prisoner's anguish over the apparent meaninglessness of his captivity. Psalm 31, in particular, helped him to concede that his life was still consigned to God: "My time is in your hands" (verse 15), he prayed, though Psalm 13 permitted him, nonetheless, to air his impatience and demand an answer to the agonizing question: "how long, O Lord?"[21] The Psalms were for him the prayer of Jesus Christ, who, as Bonhoeffer claimed, perhaps paraphrasing Augustine's *"Deus intimior intimo meo"* (God is more intimate to me than I am to myself), "knows us better than we know ourselves."[22]

It was predictable, therefore, that the prayers Bonhoeffer composed for his fellow prisoners were filled with the spirit of the Psalms. Their constant theme was trust in God's love and acceptance of whatever God has permitted in their regard. "Whatever this day may bring," he prayed, God's "name be praised." He commended into God's hands at close of day his loved ones and fellow prisoners, and even their wardens, as well as his own person. He asked for strength to bear what God might send and the courage to overcome their fears. In the all-pervasive distress of prison life, he would say to God, "I trust in your grace and commit my life wholly into your hands. Do with me according to your will and as is best for me. Whether I live or die, I am with you, and you, my God are with me."[23] These prayers, which were circulated illegally among the cells, manifest many of the insights that helped guide Bonhoeffer's own actions on behalf of peace and freedom and exude his concern for Christian community even in prison. In effect, Bonhoeffer was trying "to bring everyone in the sprawling prison of Tegel with whom he was able to make some kind of contact, by his own example into the field of force from which he drew his own strength."[24] A fellow conspirator and prisoner who survived the war has given this account of Bonhoeffer's solicitude for the spiritual well-being and morale of those around him. "To the very end," he wrote, "Bonhoeffer took advantage of [their] condition by arranging prayer services, consoling those who had lost all hope, and giving them fresh courage. A towering rock of faith, he became a shining example to his fellow prisoners."[25] Those words could very well describe the qualities one looks for in choosing a moral leader able to bring some order even out of the chaotic conditions of repression, imprisonment, and systemic injustice.

One student of Bonhoeffer's spirituality has remarked that a perusal of his prayers in prison made him begin "to realize with new appreciation the source of Bonhoeffer's spiritual stamina and vitality — his constant, daily, childlike relationship to God."[26] That "childlike relationship" also took on the form of a strong sense of solidarity with his family, friends, fellow ministers, co-conspirators, and especially the victims of Nazism. "The physical presence of other Christians," he wrote, in his lengthy description of Christian community, "is a source of incomparable joy and strength to the believer."[27] But whether they were physically present or close to him in prayers and meditative reflections, Bonhoeffer experienced intense comfort from the thought that they were all "in a community that sustains [them]." He specified that such community in Jesus Christ was the "firm ground" on which he had taken his stand.[28]

This was a solidarity that helps explain another important aspect of Bonhoeffer's faith in prayer: his belief in the power of intercession. His own refined sense of solidarity with family, friends, seminarians, and even co-conspirators fitted naturally into his appreciation of the need for intercessory prayers. They were united by ties of love, faith, compassion, and the dangers of their resistance to Nazism, to be sure. But however far apart physically, he believed they had been brought together by their communion in Jesus Christ and God's gift of a common faith, whether consciously or unconsciously, moving them to remember each other in their prayers and to intercede for one another with the Lord. Nowhere does Bonhoeffer assert the importance of intercession within a Christian community more than in his blunt assertion to the community of future ministers in Finkenwalde: "A Christian community either lives by the intercessory prayers of its members for one another or the community will be destroyed." Bonhoeffer valued their intercessory prayer as "the purifying bath into which the individual and the community must enter every day."[29] Bonhoeffer knew that to pray for others achieved what was often considered nearly impossible among people cast together by all the unpredictable directions one's life could take. In this prayer, enemies could be forgiven, burdens lightened, and sorrows alleviated.

Separated from his family and friends and denied the visible support of the Confessing Church while in prison, Bonhoeffer was strengthened by the thought of his being remembered in the prayers offered on his behalf. He was not ashamed to ask his friend, Bethge, to promise that they "remain faithful in interceding for each other. . . . And if it should be decided that we are not to meet again, let us remember each other to the end in thankfulness and forgiveness, and may God grant us that one day we may stand before [God] praying for each other and joining in praise and thankfulness."[30] Their union in prayer was more than mere empathy. If Bonhoeffer was able to persevere in his resistance to Nazi evil, this was due in large part to the continual inspiration he derived from Bethge's friendship and prayerful support. "Please don't ever get anxious or worried about me, but don't forget to pray for me," he pleaded in one of his final letters. He then added: "I'm sure you don't! I am so sure of God's guiding hand that I hope I shall always be kept in that certainty. You must never doubt that I'm traveling with gratitude and cheerfulness along the road where I'm being led. My past life is brim full of God's goodness, and my sins are covered by the forgiving love of Christ crucified."[31] In the intensity of such a friendship and mutual prayer, Bonhoeffer's concern for personal survival and the safety of his loved ones yielded to the quiet confidence in God's protection that made his eventual death an act of faith and resignation to what he perceived as his destiny under God's salvific will.

The attitude expressed here would be refined in the letter of February 21, 1944. There he tells Bethge that he must both confront and submit to this "fate," but all in its proper time. The problem for him was how to find God in the quiet neutral zone of what is judged to be one's destiny. He concludes that no one can define abstractly the boundary between resistance to evil and submission to the suffering that one endures for the sake of justice. Only his faith could give him enough flexibility of decision and action to "stand [his] ground in each situation."[32] After the failure of the assassination attempt on Hitler's life on July 20, 1944, his writings increasingly attest to the "submission" in faith to whatever God would permit, given that his efforts to deliver his nation and the victims of Nazism from their sufferings were now consigned to God's more powerful wisdom and God's ways of bringing good out of evil. His prayers in those circumstances led him more and more to faith in God's providential care despite the nagging realization that suffering, even death, was to be his fate. Just eight days after the failed assassination attempt, he wrote that "In suffering the deliverance consists in our being allowed to put the matter out of our own hands into God's hands."[33] His act of faith in that deliverance accords with his insistence in his book on Christian discipleship that to follow Christ was to give oneself over to the cross that is the destiny of those who brave persecution for the sake of justice. Such a death was in fact not the end of everything, but in faith the full blossoming of a Christian's communion with Jesus Christ.[34]

The note of being willing to suffer for the sake of justice is important if one is to understand the prayer life that was the inner force of Bonhoeffer's spirituality and moral leadership. As Bethge has pointed out, Bonhoeffer was equally convinced that, without being connected to concrete action for justice, prayers could deviate into pietistic self-righteousness and vapid otherworldliness. Bonhoeffer's moral leadership pivots on an undaunted following of Jesus Christ even to the cross as well as on the trustful prayers emanating from his Christian faith. Bonhoeffer's attitude toward prayer reveals an awareness that moral leaders who claim to be Christian must rely on the strength of their communion with Jesus Christ if their faith is to be genuine. Only when one's love of Jesus Christ transmutes into a ministry to foster peace and justice in a world of violence and injustice can Christianity regain its credibility in the postwar world. The prayer life of Bonhoeffer gives us a glimpse into his relationship with God in Jesus Christ. His vision of what is required of him in his allegiance to Jesus Christ is even more fully understood when one examines the poems that he composed in prison.

Glimpses into the Soul of a Moral Leader: Bonhoeffer's Poems

Until Dietrich Bonhoeffer spent part of 1943 and most of 1944 in prison, he had rarely if ever set his hand to writing poetry. One can scour his theological essays, his books and lectures, his sermons, the correspondence that streamed from his pen for a full fifteen years, 1928-1943, and not find a single poem. He did occasionally in his adolescent years experience the creative urge to poetize, but it was not until a year of life in Tegel Prison had elapsed that he was able hesitantly and creatively to express his emotions and deep-set convictions through the art form of poetry. It is noteworthy that the prison poems were among Bonhoeffer's first writings to appear in print after World War II.

The very first poem, "The Past," was prompted by a visit from Bonhoeffer's beloved Maria to Tegel Prison in Berlin. To his close friend and confidant, Eberhard Bethge, he confided in his letter of 5 June 1944, "I should be behaving like a shy boy if I concealed from you the fact that I am making some attempts here to write poetry. Up to now, I've been keeping it dark from everyone, even Maria, who would be most concerned with it — simply because it was somehow painful to me and because I didn't know whether it wouldn't frighten her more than please her."[35] Yet the poem itself is significant for the way it depicts Bonhoeffer's sense of loss at having to be separated from his loved ones. This is in many respects the cost of being a moral leader: the separations from a previous way of life, the loss of support when one has to go it alone, the sense of deprivation when the forces of evil can conspire to inflict suffering on those who would defend and protect the victims of injustice. The times past of familial nearness and loving encouragement dimmed in the hours of his imprisonment.

During the remainder of 1944, nine other poems were added to Bonhoeffer's written legacy, many of them accompanying the letters that were smuggled out of Tegel Prison. After being read, they were subsequently buried in the backyard next to the family residence in Berlin. When the war mercifully ended in the spring of 1945, the letters, together with the poems, were dug out of the ground and preserved for posterity.[36] Each shows in its own way how his Christian faith was beset by the complexities of his imprisonment and of his frustrated efforts to overthrow the Nazi government and end the killing.[37]

The tenth and final poem, "By the Powers for Good," was written in the Gestapo cellars of Prinz Albrecht Strasse in Berlin, where prisoner Bonhoeffer had been transferred from Tegel Prison a few weeks earlier. This poem is widely known in the Christian world because of its having been adapted into a hymn and translated into a variety of languages. It is included in church hymnals throughout the world.

The inherent worth of the prison poems as first-rate poetry may be debated and disputed interminably. They probably cannot be classified among the unforgettable, enduring gems of world literature, though they belong to an important epoch of Christian history. Bonhoeffer himself exhibited no illusions about their literary excellence. After crafting one of his poems, "Stations on the Way to Freedom," for example, he conveyed his diffident feelings in a letter to Eberhard Bethge: "I wrote these lines in a couple of hours this evening. They're rather rough; but they may perhaps give you some enjoyment and even serve as a kind of birthday present for you." His postscript, which was written the following morning, is revealing: "I see in this early morning hour that I'll have to completely revise these verses once more. Even so, I'm letting them go off to you in their rough form. I am certainly no poet!"[38]

Despite this disclaimer, Bonhoeffer's biographer saw their value as poetry because of the special circumstances in which they were composed and because the poetry was shared in such a personal way with him. In the extreme conditions of imprisonment and Gestapo interrogations, Bonhoeffer had bared his soul to Bethge as never before. In underscoring the significance of the poems for understanding Bonhoeffer's experiences as a prisoner, Bethge would write, "How are we to judge Bonhoeffer's attempts at poetry? They are efforts to overcome his isolation. In this situation he had begun to write poetry for the first time since his youth. The venture fascinated him for months on end. The thoughts in these pieces are important, but they are so densely packed that they burst the forms of poem, novel, and drama. Poems such as 'Sorrow and Joy,' 'Stations on the Way to Freedom' will probably live on because they convey the particular situation in an original statement and in an appropriate form."[39]

Though these poems are shockingly different from the prose of his prison letters, they serve as keys to interpret the moods and profound thoughts harbored by Bonhoeffer during the months of his forced confinement. In his own analysis of the prison poetry a British commentator has concluded that "the importance of the poems he wrote lies in the fact that they were the ultimate attempt to express his deepest feelings about himself, his friends, his church, the future of Germany, and his future."[40] One of Bonhoeffer's Berlin and Finkenwalde students, Winfried Maechler, sheds additional light on the significance of the prison poems. Back in Germany from the eastern front in late 1942, after serving in his country's army fighting the Russians, he wrote a poem, "King David," and showed it to Bonhoeffer, his mentor and friend. Upon reading it, Bonhoeffer began to laugh, commenting, "It is easy enough to write a poem. It is far more difficult to write prose." Years later, Maechler made mention of this and of his reaction: "Imagine my great surprise when after the war, Eberhard Bethge showed me the poems Bonhoeffer had written in prison! The poems were a way of reflecting his feelings and self-understanding."[41]

Precisely so! Bonhoeffer's poems represent a way of expressing his profound feelings, his faith, his love for his friends, his struggle for freedom, and the depths of his prison and life experiences. The poems serve veritably as windows into his own soul, carrying the freight of his loneliness, his anxiety, his longings, his faith, and his spirituality. Not only are they in large measure links to his autobiography; they also reflect his personal assessment of the cost of his moral leadership in the midst of Germany's Nazi nightmare.[42]

A consideration of just six of these prison poems effectively conveys the pathos and struggle within Dietrich Bonhoeffer's own soul, as he had to face realistically suffering and even his own death. They depict for us what assertive moral leadership might eventually mean.

Who Am I?
June 1944

Who am I? They often tell me I would step from my prison cell
poised, cheerful and sturdy,
like a nobleman from his country estate.
Who am I? They often tell me I would speak with my guards
freely, pleasantly and firmly,
as if I had the power to command.
Who am I? I have also been told that I suffer the days of misfortune
with serenity, smiles and pride,
as someone accustomed to victory.

Am I really what others say about me?
Or am I only what I know of myself?
Restless, yearning and sick, like a bird in its cage,
struggling for the breath of life,
as though someone were choking my throat;
hungering for colors, for flowers, for the songs of birds,
thirsting for kind words and human closeness,
shaking with anger at capricious tyranny and the pettiest slurs,
bedeviled by anxiety, awaiting great events that might never occur,
fearfully powerless and worried for friends far away,
weary and empty in prayer, in thinking, in doing,
weak, and ready to take leave of it all.

Who am I? This man or that other?
Am I then this man today and tomorrow another?
Am I both all at once? An impostor to others,
But to me little more than a whining, despicable weakling?
Does what is in me compare to a vanquished army,
that flees in disorder before a battle already won?

Who am I? They mock me, these lonely questions of mine.
Whoever I am, you know me, O God. You know I am yours.[43]

This self-searching poem is clearly one of the most autobiographical of
Bonhoeffer's poems. It points us toward the inner world of his own struggle, endeavoring to be fully honest with himself and at the same time to
be fully committed to Jesus Christ. The contradictions that he had to con-

front within himself had to be acknowledged, especially in his seeking to live according to the principles of the Sermon on the Mount. He had earlier described this commitment to Jesus as "a great liberation."[44] It was also, however, a liberation that carried the price of a lifelong wrestling with the demons of discouragement and pride. Bonhoeffer really knew his own weaknesses. In truth, was he that weakling or the person of strength on whom so many others had leaned for support? "Whoever I am," he concludes, "you know me, O God. You know I am yours."

"Who Am I?" invariably points beyond the personal experience of Dietrich Bonhoeffer to the stark reality of Christian moral leadership and spirituality in our contemporary times. All of us who seek to be faithful to Jesus and to the charter he gave us in the Sermon on the Mount are in various stages of a life of struggle. The assuring closing line of the poem is not only strikingly contemporary; it is also a confession of faith that should characterize every moral leader who proclaims himself or herself a follower of Jesus Christ.[45]

Christians and Pagans
July 1944

All people go to God in need,
For help and calm and food they plead.
That sickness, guilt and death may cease,
All, Christians and Pagans, pray for peace.

But some turn to God in God's need and dread,
A God poor, despised, without roof or bread.
By sin's harm weakened and by death distressed,
Christians stand steadfast by their God oppressed.

God goes to all in their need and dread,
Their souls' loving grace and their bodies' bread.
By the crucified Lord who for them was slain,
Both Christian and pagan God's pardon gain.[46]

This poem is in a unique way a summary of Bonhoeffer's understanding of the essence of a person's relationship with God. In the first verse the age-old traditional religious approach to life is asserted, namely, that God is primarily a supplier of our human needs and a satisfier of our human desires. This is an attitude that can hardly be described as distinct from paganism. In the second verse the Christian God is depicted as One who is wholly other from the "god" of religion. Embedded in these middle lines of the poem is the theology of the cross. It conveys the message that God suffers in and with God's people. Undergirding this message is the biblical portrayal of a God who calls on human beings to "stand by" God in God's suffering, even as God will "stand by" humans when they, in turn, are afflicted. The Christian God is a suffering God. The third verse affirms God's presence, caring for those who are in dire need, bringing nourishment to them in the Eucharist and in their daily bread. The poem's message leaps over the boundaries of religious propriety in affirming God in order to celebrate this fact of faith: For all, whether Christian or pagan, God needs our support even as God extends love in constant, ever-present forbearance and forgiveness of our sins.[47]

Stations on the Way to Freedom
July 21, 1944

DISCIPLINE

If you set out to seek freedom, then above all must you learn
So to discipline your senses and soul,
That by your lusts and your limbs you be not led hither and yon.
Chaste be your spirit and body, wholly subjected to your own control,
ready to strive for the goal that is set out before you.
For the secret of freedom no one discovers,
Without rigorous disciplining of self.

ACTION

Not what fancies the mind, but what is braved in the bold
    deeds of justice;
Not by lingering over dreams of the possible, but courageously
    grasping reality at hand,
Not through ideas soaring in flight, but only through action,
Is there ever freedom to be.
Step out of your anguished waverings and into the storm
    of events plunge ahead,
borne along solely by command of your God and your powerful faith.
Only then will that freedom exultant reach out to welcome
    your spirit's embrace.

SUFFERING

O wondrous transformation! Your hands, strong and active,
   are bound.
Powerless, alone, full clearly knowing your action has ended,
from your lips there yet comes the cry of relief,
that, calmly and trusting, you surrender your struggle
   to more powerful hands.
And contented in heart you rest now in peace.
For in one blessed moment the soul of freedom you touched,
to entrust it to God that God might fulfill it in glory.

DEATH

Come now, O supreme moment on the way to freedom eternal.
Death, lay down the burdensome chains,
break down the walls of our transient bodies, the barriers
   of our deluded souls,
that we might gaze at last on what here we are impeded from seeing.
Freedom, so long have we sought you in discipline, action,
   and suffering.
Dying, we now behold you indeed in the face of our God.[48]

An important key to an encounter with this poem is to note the date: 21 July 1944. This was the day after the failed attempt on the life of Adolf Hitler. There had been numerous previous attempts to do away with Hitler, but the July 20 episode came the closest to accomplishing the goal. From this point on Bonhoeffer knew that the chances for release were slight, while his chances for more intense interrogations and possible execution had increased. In the first verse one can discern the very issues that were raised earlier in *Discipleship*. Central here is the prime cost of the discipline that is needed to follow Christ. Moreover, the reader is reminded of the daring and courageous action needed to accomplish the deed that is altogether necessary to deliver the people from both their civil and spiritual servitude. Time has moved on to the point that one's trust must be utterly and wholly in God, followed by deliberate and determined action. This action that is framed in the second verse is motivated by a boldness and passion for justice in the land. It will inevitably issue in suffering, as the third verse intimates. No one can ever fully measure the suffering that was unleashed in Germany, in all the lands either occupied or controlled by Nazi imperialism, and in the world at large, the suffering of Christian moral leadership in the face of overwhelming and overpowering odds. For

Bonhoeffer, anticipation of death was now almost certain, but in his indomitable faith, this would ultimately transmute into the joy of beholding "the face of our God."[49] What is seen as a cruel death becomes in God's presence the experience of resurrection. This final line was to be echoed in Bonhoeffer's farewell message to his friend, Bishop George Bell of Chichester: "This is the end; for me, the beginning of life."[50]

The Death of Moses
September, 1944

Deuteronomy 34:1: "And the Lord Showed Him All the Land. . . ."

Upon the mountain peak where few have trod
stands the prophet Moses, man of God.

Absent is his gaze and tired his hand
as he surveys the sacred, promised land.

That he might for Moses' death provide,
the Lord appears now by his servant's side, . . .

spreads out at the tired wanderer's feet
his homeland, which he still may mutely greet,

offer it his blessing with dying breath,
and so, in peace, to go encounter death.

"You shall glimpse salvation from afar,
but your own feet shall tread that path no more!" . . .

"Thus, O Lord, you keep again your promise,
never has your Word departed from us.

Whether you sent grace or godly wrath —
Always they have kept us on our path.

You did ransom us from slavery's chains
and in your gentle arms, did soothe our pains;

through the desert and the threatening tide,
wondrously before us you did stride.

All the people's mumbling, whining, wailing
you did hear with patience never failing. . . .

Not with kindly hearts were they inclined
to let you lead them forth, faith's way to find.

They fell prey to greed, idolatry,
they saw not that the bread of grace is free. . . .

One thing of your people you would have:
that they trust in your own power to save. . . .

O Lord, your chastising I cannot flee,
and yet upon such heights death comes to me.

You who once were glimpsed on distant wind,
I became your chosen one, your friend,

Your mouth, the source of holiness so pure,
your eye to take in sorrows of the poor,

your ear to hear your people's sighs and woes,
your arm to break the might of all our foes. . . ."

"Behold the splendor of the land you see —
it is my promise that has set you free!"

Upon the mountain peak where few have trod
stands the prophet Moses, man of God.

Absent is his gaze and tired his hand
as he surveys the sacred, promised land.

"Your grace redeems and saves us from our pride,
your wrath is discipline that casts aside.

O faithful Lord, confess to you I must,
your servant knows that you are always just.

Fulfill it, then, your punishment decreed,
and sleep eternal to my soul concede.

Only faith untainted to this hour
can drink the nectar of the new land's flower.

To the doubter, give the bitter potion
and let his faith bring thanks and true devotion.

Wondrous deeds with me you have performed,
bitterness to sweetness here transformed.

You let me glimpse the promise through the veil,
you let my people go, their Lord to hail.

Sinking, O God, into Eternity
I see my people's stride is proud and free.

God, who punishes and then forgives,
this people I have truly loved now lives.

It is enough that I have borne its sorrow
and now have seen the land of its tomorrow.

Hold me fast! — for fallen is my stave,
O faithful God, make ready now my grave."[51]

Jonah
October 5, 1944

In face of death they scream and clutch the storm-drenched ropes,
Their hands stretch for the strands of fleeting, dying hopes.
Their horror stricken eyes see only torments of the night,
While raging waves and winds unleash their awesome, lethal might.

"O goodly eternal gods, but wrathful now," they shout,
"To us your help extend or that culprit single out,
Who unbeknown to us offends your lofty majesty,
With heinous murder, breach of oath, or scornful blasphemy.

"Who from us sins that soil our souls does hide,
To save the wretched remnants of his pride."
And tearful thus they pled til Jonah said, "Tis I!
I've sinned against my God and now deserve to die.

"Away from you, cast me you must. God's anger flies at me alone.
The sinless must not precious lives give up to sinner's deeds atone!"
They trembled ever more. But strengthened now their hands, their
  hearts with purpose filled,
The guilty one they seized and flung into the deep. The wind-
  churned seas were stilled.[52]

These two poems, "The Death of Moses" and "Jonah," were included in
letters sent to Eberhard Bethge after Dietrich Bonhoeffer had lived for
sixteen months in Tegel Prison. They represent Bonhoeffer's valiant endeavor amidst the Gestapo's closing in on the conspirators to glimpse
the future and to discern if any meaning at all might be found. He envi-
sions himself as Jonah of old, a sinner, being cast into the depths of the
sea in order to save the lives of the innocent crewmen who otherwise
would be dragged down by his sin against God. He is willing to give his
life for the sake of others. The work of the conspirators, who would per-
ish on Nazi scaffolds in their attempt to restore justice and morality in
their country, had something of the Jonah story about it. Bonhoeffer
also saw himself as a Moses on the threshold of the promised land. He
harbored hope in the midst of the massive destruction and ruin all
about him, hope that out of the ashes and shattered lives a new Germany, a new Europe, and a new world might eventually arise. His death
he now understood and accepted for the sake of his people. He would
not live to see their liberation but was content to know he had done all
he could to share in the sufferings of Christ at the hands of the godless
world of Nazism. As he sinks "into Eternity," it is enough to see his people marching free.[53] Very often moral leaders are called to sacrifice their
lives to bring about a better life for their people. Such was the fate of the
prophets who spoke out against injustice; such was the fate of
Bonhoeffer, who had so openly opposed Hitler and the cruelties of the
Nazi ideology.

By the Powers for Good
December 19, 1944

The forces for good in wonder surround us,
Through faith and peace they'll guard and guide.
And so these days with you I'll live,
With you, my friends, a new year abide.

The year just past still lingers in our hearts,
And evil times on us their burdens weigh,
O Lord, to shaken souls bestow your peace,
Your promised grace, your solace, this bleak day.

But should you tend your cup of sorrow,
To drink the bitter dregs at your command,
We accept with thanks and without trembling,
This offering from your gracious, loving hand.

But if joy be once again your gift bestowed,
To this our world with sunlit skies so fair,
May we always hearken to these days of old,
And commit our lives to your loving care.

May your waxen candles flaming spread their warmth,
As their glow flickers darkness into the light.
May your will be done to make us one again;
May your love's glimmering hope illumine our night.

When now the silence spreads around us,
O let us hear the sounds you raise,
Of world unseen in growth abounding,
And children chanting hymns of praise.

The forces for good surround us in wonder,
They firm up our courage for what comes our way,
God's with us from dawn to the slumber of evening,
The promise of love at the break of each day.[54]

This final poem from prison was composed by Bonhoeffer in the more severe surroundings of the Gestapo prison, where he was subjected to more intense interrogations in the wake of the July 20 assassination attempt. It is the one poem that German children learn early on because of its transposition into music and incorporation into several church hymnals. Bonhoeffer included the poem in a Christmas greeting to his fiancée, Maria, and through her to his family and friends. That letter speaks of his well-being because of the constant presence of his loved ones in prayers and kindly thoughts, the comfort of his Bible, the retrieval of their many conversations of long ago, the music he cherished in his memory, and the books that had nourished his spirit. In a word, these were, as he mentions in his poem, "the forces for good" that surrounded him even during the dire days of imprisonment.[55] Through his faith, these forces for good were his "guard and guide," enabling him still to live with his loved ones in spirit. The paradoxical peace he now experienced was, indeed, the "promised grace" and "solace" from the Lord in the bleakness of his harsh imprisonment.

Like many of his fellow prisoners, Bonhoeffer had hopes that a swift allied victory would liberate them before their execution by their Nazi captors for the crime of high treason. Nonetheless, should his lot be "to drink the bitter dregs" of Jesus' "cup of sorrow," Bonhoeffer would do so with courage and gratitude for being allowed to share in the cup now offered him by the Lord. Should he and his fellow prisoners be gifted with the joy of deliverance from their prison, they would once again commit their lives to God's "loving care." He prays for the light of Christ symbolized by the "waxen candles" whose "glow flickers darkness into the light." He prays: may God's "will be done to make us one again" as the glimmer of God's love illumines their night. The poem ends on a strong note of hope that in God's designs a new world is about to dawn with "growth abounding, and children chanting hymns of praise" as he and his fellow prisoners survive surrounded by the wondrous "forces for good." God's presence and promise of love no Gestapo, no Nazi weaponry, can take away. The never-ending presence of God is their abiding strength "at the break of each day."

This poem is in many ways reminiscent of Jesus' Gethsemane prayer of resignation to God's will, such that, through his continued trust in his Father God, Jesus was enabled to drink the cup of sorrow to the dregs and fearlessly face the agony of his passion and death. This poem offers unique insights into what can support Christian moral leaders, faced as they may be with frustration, opposition, rejection of their vision, and the shattering of their hopes. The sustaining forces for good are the same for Bonhoeffer as they can be for the Christian moral leader: faith in God's promised grace, solace from the risen Lord ever present in life's sorrows, and the breaking into each day of the divine love that overcomes hatred and the divine life that overcomes death itself.

The depths of the spirituality of Dietrich Bonhoeffer are disclosed in these poems, alongside the prayers that were born within the struggle to win freedom and to reach toward justice. The cost of his moral leadership during the darkest years of the twentieth century was ultimate; it cost him his freedom to continue his struggle against Nazism and his life. The tribute paid to him by his friend Bishop Bell, in writing the "Foreword" to the earliest translation of *Discipleship,* is perceptive in his analysis of Bonhoeffer's qualities as a moral leader: "He was one of the first as well as one of the bravest witnesses against idolatry. He understood what he chose, when he chose resistance. . . . He was crystal clear in his convictions; and young as he was, and humble-minded as he was, he saw the truth, and spoke it with a complete absence of fear. . . . Wherever he went, with whomever he was, with students, with those of his own age, or with his elders, he was undaunted, detached from himself, devoted to his friends, to his home, to his country as God meant it to be, to his church, to his Master."[56] Bishop Bell's words are a clear statement of why Bonhoeffer's spiritual strength made him so admired as a moral leader. They also support Dorothee Soelle's declaration that "Dietrich Bonhoeffer is the one German theologian who will lead us into the third millennium."[57]

Discussion Questions

Chapter One

1. Bonhoeffer's life story, described here as a "Chapter in the Modern Acts of the Apostles," has inspired countless Christians today. In a recent survey Bonhoeffer was listed among the top ten of the most influential Christian writers among general readers and scholars. How can his story and other stories of holy people be integrated into our personal spirituality?

2. Comment on Bonhoeffer's description of the church, "Christ existing as community," in terms of how church life influences one's personal spirituality. How can the churches of today enhance the spiritual life of their parishioners? How effective is your own church in nourishing your spiritual life?

3. Using Bonhoeffer's friendships at Union Theological Seminary as examples, reflect on and describe the impact of good friends in the development of your spiritual life. How have your own friendships been integrated into your spirituality?

4. How does Bonhoeffer's peace sermon at Fanø, Denmark, fit into the patterns of contemporary spirituality? Would Bonhoeffer's words be acceptable among politicians today? Among church leaders? Among typical American parishioners?

5. In his letter to Elizabeth Zinn, January 1, 1936, Bonhoeffer spoke of a "conversion" experience that took place earlier in which he discovered the Bible and became a Christian. Can you share stories of moments in which you personally discovered what it means at a deeper level to be a Christian?

6. Bonhoeffer's life and spirituality developed in the turbulent period of the ideologically motivated evil of Nazism. How is the spiritual life of Christians related to events in the everyday world of politics and international relations? Is it possible to have spirituality in isolation from that world? Explain.

7. Bonhoeffer never ceased to argue that genuine Christianity is expressed in solidarity with or outreach to oppressed peoples. Explain. How does parish life today express this solidarity?

8. Comment on Bonhoeffer's farewell letter to Reinhold Niebuhr in the light of a Christian spirituality that can embrace risk for the sake of Jesus Christ. Can you share stories of Christian "risk takers" for the sake of oppressed peoples?

9. In his letters from prison Bonhoeffer wrote that he never for a moment regretted returning to Germany in 1939 even though his decision would lead later to his imprisonment and execution. How have moments of personal decision in your past affected your spiritual life today?

10. How does martyrdom fit into the patterns of Christian spirituality today? Who, in your opinion, are the most inspiring of contemporary martyrs? Why?

Chapter Two

1. To what extent is our spiritual life today centered on the person of Jesus Christ? How would we describe our relationship with Jesus Christ in the light of Bonhoeffer's contention that Christ "asks us for help in the form of a beggar, in the form of a ruined human being in torn clothing"?

2. How can we answer Bonhoeffer's question: Who is this Jesus who con-

fronts the person of faith in his intrusions into our lives today? What did Bonhoeffer mean by the "incognito" of Jesus Christ?

3. Comment on Bonhoeffer's assertion that it is one thing to pray for deliverance and quite another to act with Christian courage and compassion to deliver people from their oppression.

4. How would you describe moral leadership lived with a conscious effort to follow the example and teachings of Jesus Christ? How does the example of Jesus help in resolving the moral dilemmas faced by Christians living in a secularized world?

5. Can we say that our recent history has been one of compassion and action for justice? How would we describe our own exercise of compassion? Our actions for justice?

6. How would you characterize the moral leadership of the church in the last few years if the gauge is identity with Jesus Christ in promoting the well-being of the least of Jesus' brothers and sisters?

7. Do you think Bonhoeffer's insistence on the "discipline of the secret" has any relevance in the spiritual life of the churches today?

8. Are there instances when, in your opinion, the churches were silent while evil was being done in our country or on the international scene? In our own spiritual life have we ever kept silent while evil was being done to the least of Jesus' brothers and sisters? How can the three steps Bonhoeffer advocated for church leaders in reaction to the Nazi persecution of the Jews be integrated into one's spirituality?

9. Can Bonhoeffer's critique be said of our churches today: they have "little personal faith in Christ" and "Jesus is disappearing from sight"? Can it be said of our own spiritual life?

10. How does the excerpt from Bonhoeffer's Christmas 1942 letter to his family and fellow conspirators ("Christians are called to compassion and action") apply to our own spiritual life, our exercise of moral leadership, and our parish life?

Chapter Three

1. How does the Holy Spirit's gift of prophecy affect individual Christians and their churches in the struggle against secular idolatries and systemic injustice? Give examples.

2. How in your opinion does the Holy Spirit express the anger of God in dealing with sins against the weakest of God's children? Give examples from history or from your own experience of what you would consider "prophetic outrage."

3. Do you agree with Bonhoeffer in his essay advocating a "pneumato-logical interpretation" of the Scriptures? Read the excerpt from Bonhoeffer's letter to his brother-in-law, Rüdiger Schleicher, telling him very personally how he read the Bible. What benefits can be derived from reading the Bible as a source of help and solace in this troubled world?

4. How is the Holy Spirit manifested in the creation of a Christian church community? Can you give examples of what you consider to be the work of the Holy Spirit acting on individuals in creating community?

5. Is it possible to draw a distinction between the presence and activity of Jesus Christ and the presence and activity of the Holy Spirit within the Christian church community? Explain.

6. Comment on Bonhoeffer's claim that the Holy Spirit acts on sinful, flawed Christians, gently helping them overcome their selfishness, estrangement, and brokenness in order to commit themselves to Jesus Christ and contribute through their own faith to the formation of a Christian community.

7. In what sense can we say that the Holy Spirit of God's love not only binds God's freedom to the freedom of God's people but also frees people to be, like God, living for and doing good to others?

8. In what ways has the Holy Spirit become a sustaining source of strength in the perennial struggle of Christians against the forces that erode faith, destroy community, and obstruct social justice? How is this strength related to personal prayer?

9. In the church struggle, Bonhoeffer declared that at times the Holy Spirit promoted dissension and division within communities for the sake of the truth of Jesus' teachings. This was why he never ceased his denunciation of those churches that had allied themselves with Nazi ideology. Are there contemporary examples where prophetic figures like Bonhoeffer have promoted discernment and division within their community and society for the sake of Jesus Christ and the truth of the gospel?

10. What does it mean today to be led by God's Holy Spirit in the following of Jesus Christ even along the way of the cross?

Chapter Four

1. What is meant by the phrase "solidarity with the oppressed"? How did Dietrich Bonhoeffer express that solidarity? How is this solidarity expressed today in parish life?

2. What are some of the political deceptions used by politicians to justify the existence of injustice in various segments of American society? How would you criticize these deceptions?

3. Liberation theology has often been labeled by its critics as nothing more than Marxism in Christian clothing. Is that true? If you disagree with that claim, how would you refute those who so criticize liberation theology?

4. What is your reaction to Bonhoeffer's criticism of "freedom" in the United States? Is his criticism accurate in any way? What are examples of a lack of freedom in the United States?

5. What did Bonhoeffer intend to say through his claim that God suffers? How does that theological assertion help in the struggle for liberation of oppressed peoples?

6. How does Bonhoeffer's theology of the cross support the task of liberation of peoples from the racism, poverty, exploitation, and violence from which they suffer? How does that theology relate to Bonhoeffer's question about the nature of Christian faith?

7. What is a non-religious, this-worldly Christianity? Are our churches like this? Should churches cross that line of separation between church and state? If so, how and under what circumstances?

8. How can Bonhoeffer's description of Jesus as the "man for others" impact on the nature and mission of the church in today's world?

9. What is the idolatry of national security that Bonhoeffer has criticized? Is the United States guilty of such an idolatry? If so, in what way and how would Christians attempt to remedy that?

10. What is a servant church? Does that phrase characterize the churches of today? Are churches part of the problem that liberation theologies address? Is Bonhoeffer justified in accusing the Christian churches of complicity in the crimes of Nazism?

Chapter Five

1. Bonhoeffer thought of Jesus' Sermon on the Mount as a mandate to promote peace in the world. Is such a perspective truly viable in the present world of conflict and violence?

2. Bonhoeffer lamented the fact that many Germans had made the dictates of Adolf Hitler their conscience. How does one form one's conscience according to the teachings of Jesus Christ? If, as Bonhoeffer counsels, Jesus Christ should become our conscience, how can Christians countenance war as a solution to political problems?

3. Is Bonhoeffer's urging of the ecumenical delegates in the name of Jesus Christ to take the weapons from the hands of their sons, and to forbid war, a realistic demand? Explain.

4. Do you agree with Bonhoeffer that in war the killing of others is a violence done to Jesus Christ himself? How does this apply to the loss of civilian life?

5. Jesus' commandment to love and forgive our enemies has never been withdrawn. How might such a mandate relate today to such contentious national and even international issues as capital punishment, war crimes,

or sanctions? To more personal issues such as family conflicts, interpersonal rifts, or divorce?

6. How does your congregation or denominational family see its role as "peacemakers" in this world where violence is so often exalted or taken for granted? Does this apply to recent wars against Iraq and Afghanistan?

7. How could the nonviolent, pacifist tactics of Mohandas Gandhi against war and violent oppression, in tandem with Jesus' Sermon on the Mount, be integrated into church life today?

8. Does your church have a peace and justice program? How does your parish care for families in strife, the handicapped, the sick, and the elderly?

9. In your opinion, does the United States allocate too much of its national budget to defense and national security spending to the detriment of education, health, and care of the poor and handicapped?

10. What oversight role can Christians and their churches play in promoting peace and reconciliation among nations and their citizens?

Chapter Six

1. Are we confronted today with Bonhoeffer's questions that open his study of *Discipleship:* What does Jesus want to say to us, what does Jesus want of us? How do we answer these questions? How can these questions and the statements in *Discipleship* be integrated into the qualities desired of a moral leader?

2. Are there parallels between the "cheap grace" that Bonhoeffer denounced and the way Christian churches today preach and teach the gospel? Can we say with Bonhoeffer that at times churches may be witting or unwitting accomplices in governmental evil?

3. How would you describe "costly grace" in Christian church life today? How is "costly grace" integrated into one's personal spirituality? How can "costly grace" be related to moral leadership?

4. Comment on the contemporary meaning of Bonhoeffer's statement that "whenever Christ calls us, his call leads us to death."

5. What does Bonhoeffer mean by his statement that Christians are truly free only in relationship to others? That we are bound to the self-sacrificing freedom of the God who in Christ became "weak" for our sakes?

6. What connection can we make between Bonhoeffer's insistence on the need to conjoin obedience to the gospel with faith and Kierkegaard's statement that faith is a leap into the unknown akin to the risk of love where the only certitude is trust in the beloved?

7. How can we apply the beatitudes of Jesus' Sermon on the Mount as described by Bonhoeffer to our society today? Do the values espoused in the beatitudes contradict the values held dear by Americans in today's society?

8. What are some of the ways in which Christians can enter into communion with the suffering Christ?

9. Are Bonhoeffer's strong statements about forgiveness of one's enemies and suffering without retaliation realistic, given the recent acts of terrorism against American citizens? In what sense are they applicable? How do the beatitudes apply if the victim is an abused child or a battered spouse?

10. Can you comment on how our baptismal consecration is related to the way Christ desires to take form in us so we may "live in the likeness of Jesus Christ"? How is such living "in the likeness of Jesus Christ" related to moral leadership?

Chapter Seven

1. Is Bonhoeffer's description of Christian community in *Life Together* realistic for today's parishes? Explain.

2. How effective against Nazism would Bonhoeffer's ideas on Christian community have been had such communities been more widespread throughout Germany?

3. Is it true, as Bonhoeffer claims, that often the church tries to be everywhere and ends up being nowhere? Explain.

4. Do you agree with Bonhoeffer's advice in his prison letters that if the church wished to regain its credibility it had to be like Christ, existing for others? Is his suggestion that the church make a good start by giving "all its property to those in need" realistic?

5. What difference does our faith in Jesus Christ and the claim that our church represents Jesus Christ make in our everyday parish life?

6. How is Christ's Sermon on the Mount, the guiding word in Bonhoeffer's *Life Together,* integrated into parish life today? If not, why not?

7. What is the role of Christians and their churches today in exposing the secular idolatries that Bonhoeffer inveighed against in the Nazi era? What are these secular idolatries? Have they infected the Christian churches in any way?

8. Using Bonhoeffer's analyses in *Life Together,* what are the forces that can shatter Christian community life in today's parishes? What are the dynamics that enhance the formation of genuine Christian community in our parishes?

9. How do the togetherness and the solitude that Bonhoeffer structured into his community complement each other in Christian life together today? What is the role of common prayer in all this?

10. How does service rendered to others in the community function to enhance Christian life together in the parishes of today? Tie this into the three forms of service that Bonhoeffer lists: listening, active helpfulness, and forbearance. Are the practices of confession and the celebration of the Lord's Supper helpful in creating a genuine Christian community in and through our parishes? Explain.

Chapter Eight

1. Is it proper to speak of God as being vulnerable and wounded?

2. In what sense is it accurate to declare that God does not answer the problem of evil, but that God suffers with us?

3. How does the story of Jesus Christ in the Gospels illustrate the paradoxical powerlessness and weakness of God in this world?

4. What does it mean for Christians to enter into solidarity with the oppressed of this world? How does that apply to the terminally ill? The prisoner on death row? The victims of ruthless dictators? The abused spouse, the abused child, the exploited poor of Latin America, the poverty-stricken citizens of the United States?

5. How should the Christian churches react toward those who are responsible for the oppressive poverty of the poor, or the oppressed in countries where the United States is perceived as an oppressor nation because it has looked out for and intervened only in order to protect the business interests of the multi-nationals?

6. Read that segment entitled "Who Stands Firm?" from his essay, "After Ten Years," sent to Bonhoeffer's fellow conspirators in 1942. What do you understand from his description of the free and responsible Christian not stuck on his own virtue? Who does stand firm in American society against systemic evil? Share stories of those whom you consider such people in our society today.

7. What lessons can we learn from the cross of Jesus Christ? Does the death of Jesus offer a possible answer to the problem of what appears to be senseless human suffering? In what sense are Christians called to be God's answer to the pleas for help from the most vulnerable of a nation's citizens?

8. Can you share your interpretation of and reaction to Bonhoeffer's statement: "Whenever Jesus calls us, his call leads us to death"? How would you interpret that in the context of Bonhoeffer's question of faith: "What do we really believe? I mean, believe in such a way that we stake our lives on it?"

9. What lessons can we learn for our faith and the everyday life of the Christian churches from the martyrdom of Bonhoeffer, Martin Luther King, and Archbishop Romero?

10. What can we personally do to alleviate the sufferings of God in those who call on our compassion and who may be those whom Bonhoeffer describes as having been sent by God to interrupt our plans for the next hour or the day? Have we experienced instances when we have interrupted our routine to help a person in need and, as a result, we have encountered Jesus Christ in the person of the least of his brothers and sisters? What spiritual satisfaction or comfort has come to us as a result of our outreach to the most vulnerable of people in our city?

Chapter Nine

1. How do Bonhoeffer's comments on the biblical story of Gideon apply to the moral leadership that should be exercised in both church and secular government? How does the faith demanded of Gideon correlate with the practical, complex task of administering the day-to-day affairs of an institution? In your opinion, does the United States rely too much on its weapons arsenal and too little on what God has mandated of leaders through the biblical Word?

2. What does Bonhoeffer mean by his assertion that "the church of success is far from being the church of faith"? Do we measure the worth of an institution or of persons by their "mighty deeds"? What is the measure of one's personal worth used by Jesus Christ in the Gospels?

3. What is the point of Bonhoeffer's criticism in his sermons of the slick way politicians and church leaders invoke God as a cover for their dubious policies? Does this occur today? Give examples.

4. Comment on the Advent sermon that Bonhoeffer preached in Barcelona in 1928 where he claims that Christ asks us "for help in the form of a beggar, in the form of a ruined human being in torn clothing. He confronts [us] in every person that [we] meet." How apropos are his observations today?

5. What is the problem Bonhoeffer exposes in his contrast of the grandiloquence of certain hierarchs and civic rulers with the words of a genuine moral leader whose words are inspirited by love, honesty, and compassion? Give examples of moral leaders whose words you have found to be

truly inspirational. What is there about these moral leaders that makes them so convincing?

6. Explain what Bonhoeffer means in his insistence with St. Paul that Christian love "keeps no record of wrongs." How is this related to Christ's mandate to Christians that they practice forbearance and forgiveness of enemies? Apply this to the current debate on war and capital punishment.

7. Do you agree with Bonhoeffer that John 8:32 is the most revolutionary statement in the New Testament? Comment on his claim: "The people who love, because they are freed through the truth of God, are the most revolutionary people on earth. They are the ones who upset all values; they are the explosives in human society."

8. Bonhoeffer spoke the words, "peace must be dared; it is the great venture," in his now famous sermon on world peace preached in Fanø, Denmark in 1934. How can moral leaders exert a Christian influence on a nation's policies on peace, national security, military power, and the arms race in today's world? Do you agree with Bonhoeffer that national security can become an idol and that "war is a sin against God's gospel of peace"?

9. Using Bonhoeffer's sermon on the Lukan story of Lazarus and the rich man, contrast the "world order" preached by Jesus with the "world order" preached by Adolf Hitler and political leaders of today. Why do people scorn the Lazaruses of our contemporary world?

10. Comment on Bonhoeffer's words of consolation to those suffering from bereavement. What does he mean by his declaration that "our God is a suffering God"? Can we share with one another how we cope with suffering and death of loved ones?

Chapter Ten

1. In your opinion how necessary is the practice of daily prayer for the individual person of faith, for the community, the moral leader?

2. Do you agree with Bonhoeffer that "a day without morning and evening prayer and personal intercessions [is] actually a day without mean-

ing or importance"? Explain. For what pressing issues connected to moral leadership and justice do you pray?

3. Share with one another the place of prayer in your lives. What is your favorite mode of daily prayer? in times of crisis? Have you discovered guidelines, such as the daily texts that Bonhoeffer strongly recommended, which provide inspiration and direction for your prayer life?

4. Bonhoeffer claims that meditation preserves the unity and meaning of our lives by bringing "inward and outward order" into what we are called to be and to do. How can daily meditation be practiced in our active, busy, and demanding lives, mired as we sometimes are in the endless details of our everyday activities? Would those who meditate on a regular basis share with others the benefits they derive from this practice?

5. Bonhoeffer sees the need for those in community to forgive one another both in prayer and in practice. He argues that no one should "go to bed with an unreconciled heart." How can we structure this forgiveness into our daily lives? How essential for moral leadership is the quality of forgiveness in prayer and action? How do prayers for forgiveness connect with our communities, parishes, or groups?

6. Discuss the practice and value of intercessory prayer. Bonhoeffer wrote that such prayer was sustaining during his imprisonment. What personal benefits have you derived from intercessory prayer? What has been your practice in interceding for the moral and political leaders of our nation? Of the nations of the world? Are you convinced that your prayers make a difference?

7. The Psalms, as the prayer book of the Bible and of the church, were Bonhoeffer's most supportive prayer. Do you pray the Psalms? How should one pray the Psalms? Why are the Psalms so important in church worship services?

8. Which of the poems in this chapter best illustrates Bonhoeffer's spirituality and moral leadership? Explain.

9. In poetizing on the "Way to Freedom" Bonhoeffer speaks in the stanzas of Discipline, Action, Suffering, and Death. How do these qualities apply

to moral leaders who have dedicated their lives to the achievement of freedom for their people? Give examples.

10. In what way can Bonhoeffer's poem, "By the Powers for Good," become both a Gethsemane prayer and a statement of hope in the midst of personal crises and suffering? What does this poem reveal about the depths of Bonhoeffer's spirituality?

Bibliography

Primary Sources

Dietrich Bonhoeffer Werke (DBW), edited by Eberhard Bethge et al. 17 vols. Munich: Chr. Kaiser Verlag, 1986-1999. See "Abbreviations" for the list of titles in individual volumes.

Dietrich Bonhoeffer Works English Edition (DBWE), edited by Wayne Whitson Floyd, Jr., et al. 16 vols. Minneapolis: Fortress Press, 1995-. See "Abbreviations" for the list of titles of individual volumes.

Other Editions and Translations of Bonhoeffer's Writings

Christ the Center. San Francisco: HarperSanFrancisco, 1978.

The Cost of Discipleship. New York: Macmillan, 1963.

Ethics. New York: Simon and Schuster, 1995.

Fiction from Prison. Edited by Renate and Eberhard Bethge with Clifford Green. Philadelphia: Fortress Press, 1981.

Letters and Papers from Prison. The Enlarged Edition. New York: Macmillan, 1971.

Love Letters from Cell 92: The Correspondence between Dietrich Bonhoeffer and Maria von Wedemeyer, 1943-45. Edited by Ruth-Alice von Bismarck and Ulrich Kabitz. Postscript by Eberhard Bethge. Nashville: Abingdon, 1994.

Meditating on the Word. Edited by David McI. Gracie. Cambridge, Mass.: Cowley Publications, 1986.

No Rusty Swords. Letters, Lectures and Notes, 1928-1936, from the Collected Works of Dietrich Bonhoeffer. Vol. 1. Edited by Edwin H. Robertson. New York: Harper and Row, 1965.

Preface to Bonhoeffer: The Man and Two of His Shorter Writings. Edited by John D. Godsey. Philadelphia: Fortress Press, 1965.

A Testament to Freedom: The Essential Writings of Dietrich Bonhoeffer. Edited by Geffrey B. Kelly and F. Burton Nelson. San Francisco: HarperSanFrancisco, 1995.

True Patriotism. Letters, Lectures and Notes, 1939-1945, from the Collected Works of Dietrich Bonhoeffer. Vol. 3. Edited by Edwin H. Robertson. New York: Harper and Row, 1973.

The Way to Freedom. Letters, Lectures and Notes, 1935-1939, from the Collected Works of Dietrich Bonhoeffer. Vol. 11. Edited by Edwin H. Robertson. New York: Harper and Row, 1967.

Secondary Literature (Selected)

Bethge, Eberhard. *Bonhoeffer: Exile and Martyr.* Ed. and with an essay by John De Gruchy. New York: Seabury Press, 1975.

————. *Dietrich Bonhoeffer. A Biography.* Translation revised by Victoria Barnett. Minneapolis: Fortress Press, 2000.

————. *Friendship and Resistance: Essays on Dietrich Bonhoeffer.* Grand Rapids: Eerdmans, 1995.

————. "Dietrich Bonhoeffer and the Jews." In *Ethical Responsibility: Bonhoeffer's Legacy to the Churches,* 43-96. See Godsey and Kelly, eds., 1981.

Bethge, Eberhard, Renate Bethge, and Christian Gremmels, eds. *Dietrich Bonhoeffer: A Life in Pictures.* Philadelphia: Fortress Press, 1986.

Bethge, Renate. "Bonhoeffer's Family and Its Significance for His Theology." In Larry Rasmussen, *Dietrich Bonhoeffer: His Significance for North Americans.* See Rasmussen.

Burtness, James H. *Consequences: Morality, Ethics, and the Future.* Minneapolis: Fortress Press, 1999.

————. *Shaping the Future: The Ethics of Dietrich Bonhoeffer.* Philadelphia: Fortress Press, 1985.

Clements, Keith. *A Patriotism for Today: Dialogue with Dietrich Bonhoeffer.* Bristol: Bristol Baptist College, 1984.

————. *What Freedom? The Persistent Challenge of Dietrich Bonhoeffer.* Bristol: Bristol Baptist College, 1990.

Coles, Robert. *Dietrich Bonhoeffer.* Modern Masters Series. Maryknoll, N.Y.: Orbis Books, 1998.

————. *Lives of Moral Leadership.* New York: Random House, 2000.

Day, Thomas I. *Dietrich Bonhoeffer on Christian Community and Common Sense.* Lewiston, N.Y.: Edwin Mellen Press, 1982.

De Gruchy, John W. *Bonhoeffer and South Africa: Theology in Dialogue.* Grand Rapids: Eerdmans, 1984.

De Gruchy, John W., ed. *Bonhoeffer for a New Day: Theology in a Time of Transition.* Grand Rapids: Eerdmans, 1997.

———, ed. *The Cambridge Companion to Dietrich Bonhoeffer.* Cambridge: Cambridge University Press, 1999.

De Lange, Frits. *Waiting for the Word: Dietrich Bonhoeffer on Speaking about God.* Grand Rapids: Eerdmans, 2000.

Dupré, Louis, and Don E. Saliers, in collaboration with John Meyendorff. *Christian Spirituality III: Post-Reformation and Modern.* New York: Crossroad, 1989.

Elder, Rozanne, with Introduction by Jean Leclercq. *The Spirituality of Western Christendom.* Kalamazoo: Cistercian Publications, 1976.

Feil, Ernst. *The Theology of Dietrich Bonhoeffer.* Philadelphia: Fortress Press, 1985.

Floyd, Wayne Whitson, Jr. *Theology and the Dialectics of Otherness: On Reading Bonhoeffer and Adorno.* Lanham, Md.: University Press of America, 1988.

———. *The Wisdom and Witness of Dietrich Bonhoeffer.* Minneapolis: Fortress Press, 2000.

Floyd, Wayne Whitson, Jr., and Charles R. Marsh, eds. *Theology and the Practice of Responsibility: Essays on Dietrich Bonhoeffer.* Philadelphia: Trinity Press International, 1994.

Fox, Matthew. *Western Spirituality: Historical Roots, Ecumenical Route.* Notre Dame: Fides/Claretian, 1979.

Glazener, Mary. *The Cup of Wrath: The Story of Dietrich Bonhoeffer's Resistance to Hitler.* Savannah: F. C. Beil, 1992.

Godsey, John D. *The Theology of Dietrich Bonhoeffer.* Philadelphia: Westminster, 1960.

Godsey, John D., and Geffrey B. Kelly, eds. *Ethical Responsibility: Bonhoeffer's Legacy to the Churches.* Lewiston, N.Y.: Edwin Mellen Press, 1981.

Green, Clifford J. *Bonhoeffer: A Theology of Sociality.* Grand Rapids: Eerdmans, 1999.

Gutiérrez, Gustavo. *The Power of the Poor in History.* Maryknoll, N.Y.: Orbis, 1983.

Holmes, Urban T. *A History of Christian Spirituality.* New York: Seabury, 1980.

Jones, Cheslyn, Geoffrey Wainwright, and Edward Jarnold, eds. *The Study of Spirituality.* New York: Oxford University Press, 1986.

Kelly, Geffrey B. *Liberating Faith: Bonhoeffer's Message for Today.* Minneapolis: Augsburg, 1984.

Kelly, Geffrey B., and F. Burton Nelson, eds. *A Testament to Freedom: The Essential Writings of Dietrich Bonhoeffer.* San Francisco: HarperSanFrancisco, 1995.

266

Kelly, Geffrey B., and C. John Weborg, eds. *Reflections on Bonhoeffer: Essays in Honor of F. Burton Nelson*. Chicago: Covenant Press, 1999.

Marty, Martin E. *The Place of Bonhoeffer: Problems and Possibilities in His Thought*. New York: Association Press, 1962.

Mursell, Gordon, ed. *The Story of Christian Spirituality: Two Thousand Years from East to West*. Oxford: Lion Publishing Co., 2001.

Marsh, Charles R. *Reclaiming Dietrich Bonhoeffer: The Promise of His Theology*. New York: Oxford University Press, 1994.

Pangritz, Andreas. *Karl Barth in the Theology of Dietrich Bonhoeffer*. Grand Rapids: Eerdmans, 2000.

Peck, William I., ed. *New Studies in Bonhoeffer's Ethics*. Lewiston, N.Y.: Edwin Mellen Press, 1987.

Pejsa, Jane. *Matriarch of Conspiracy: Ruth von Kleist 1867-1945*. Minneapolis: Kenwood Publishing Co., 1991.

Rasmussen, Larry, *Dietrich Bonhoeffer: Reality and Resistance*. Nashville: Abingdon, 1972.

Rasmussen, Larry, with Renate Bethge. *Dietrich Bonhoeffer: His Significance for North Americans*. Minneapolis: Fortress Press, 1990.

Ringma, Charles. *Seize the Day with Dietrich Bonhoeffer*. Colorado Springs: Piñon Press, 2000.

Senn, Frank C., ed. *Protestant Spiritual Traditions*. New York: Paulist Press, 1986.

Wind, Renate. *Dietrich Bonhoeffer: A Spoke in the Wheel*. Grand Rapids: Eerdmans, 1992.

Wüstenberg, Ralf K. *A Theology of Life: Dietrich Bonhoeffer's Religionless Christianity*. Grand Rapids: Eerdmans, 1998.

Young, Josiah Ulysses III. *No Difference in the Fare: Dietrich Bonhoeffer and the Problem of Racism*. Grand Rapids: Eerdmans, 1998.

Zimmerman, Wolf-Dieter, and Ronald Gregor Smith, eds. *I Knew Dietrich Bonhoeffer: Reminiscences by His Friends*. New York: Harper and Row, 1966.

Abbreviations

DBW	*Dietrich Bonhoeffer Werke.* The critical edition of Bonhoeffer's writings, published in Germany, 1986-1999.
DBW 1	*Sanctorum Communio*
DBW 2	*Akt und Sein*
DBW 3	*Schöpfung und Fall*
DBW 4	*Nachfolge*
DBW 5	*Gemeinsames Leben*
DBW 6	*Ethik*
DBW 7	*Fragmente aus Tegel*
DBW 8	*Widerstand und Ergebung*
DBW 9	*Jugend und Studium*
DBW 10	*Barcelona, Berlin, Amerika*
DBW 11	*Okeumene, Universität, Pfarramt 1931-1932*
DBW 12	*Berlin, 1932-1933*
DBW 13	*London, 1933-1945*
DBW 14	*Illegale Theologen-Ausbildung: Finkenwalde 1935-1937*
DBW 15	*Illegale Theologen-Ausbildung: Sammelvikariate 1937-1940*
DBW 16	*Konspiration und Haft*
DBW 17	*Register und Ergänzungen*
DBWE	*Dietrich Bonhoeffer Works.* The critical English-language edition of the collected writings of Bonhoeffer, 1996-.
SC (*DBWE* 1)	*Sanctorum Communio*
AB (*DBWE* 2)	*Act and Being*
CF (*DBWE* 3)	*Creation and Fall*
D (*DBWE* 4)	*Discipleship*

Abbreviations

LT (DBWE 5)	Life Together
PB (DBWE 5)	Prayerbook of the Bible
FT (DBWE 7)	Fiction from Tegel Prison
YB (DBWE 9)	The Young Bonhoeffer: 1918-1927

In Process

E (DBWE 6)	Ethics
LPP (DBWE 8)	Letters and Papers from Prison
DBWE 10	Barcelona, Berlin, New York: 1928-1931
DBWE 11	Ecumenical, Academic and Pastoral Work: 1931-1932
DBWE 12	Berlin: 1933
DBWE 13	London: 1933-1935
DBWE 14	Theological Education at Finkenwalde: 1935-1937
DBWE 15	Theological Education Underground: 1937-1940
DBWE 16	Conspiracy and Imprisonment: 1940-1945

GS 1-6	Gesammelte Schriften (Collected Writings). Edited by Eberhard Bethge. Munich: Kaiser Verlag, 1965-1974.
LPP	Letters and Papers from Prison
NRS	No Rusty Swords: Letters, Lectures and Notes, 1928-1936, from the Collected Works of Dietrich Bonhoeffer. Edited by Edwin H. Robertson. Vol. 1. New York: Harper and Row, 1967.
CC	Christ the Center. San Francisco: HarperSanFrancisco, 1978.
TF	A Testament to Freedom: The Essential Writings of Dietrich Bonhoeffer. Edited by Geffrey B. Kelly and F. Burton Nelson. San Francisco: HarperSanFrancisco, 1995.
TKC	Thy Kingdom Come, in John Godsey, ed., Preface to Bonhoeffer. Philadelphia: Fortress Press, 1965.
TP	True Patriotism: Letters, Lectures and Notes, 1939-1945, from the Collected Works of Dietrich Bonhoeffer. Edited by Edwin H. Robertson. Vol. 3. New York: Harper and Row, 1973.
WE	Widerstand und Ergebung: Briefe und Aufzeichnungen aus der Haft. Edited by Eberhard Bethge. Munich: Kaiser Verlag, 1970.
WF	The Way to Freedom: Letters, Lectures and Notes, 1935-1939, from the Collected Works of Dietrich Bonhoeffer. Edited by Edwin H. Robertson. Vol. 11. New York: Harper and Row, 1966.
WP	Worldly Preaching: Lectures on Homiletics. Edited by Clyde E. Fant. New York: Crossroad, 1991.

Secondary Literature

DB	*Dietrich Bonhoeffer: A Biography*
IKDB	*I Knew Dietrich Bonhoeffer*
LF	*Liberating Faith: Bonhoeffer's Message for Today*
USQR	*Union Seminary Quarterly Review*

Endnotes

Notes to Preface

1. See, for example, Geffrey B. Kelly, "Prayer and Action for Justice: Bonhoeffer's Spirituality," in John de Gruchy, ed., *The Cambridge Companion to Dietrich Bonhoeffer* (Cambridge: Cambridge University Press, 1999), 246-68; John D. Godsey, "Dietrich Bonhoeffer and Christian Spirituality," in Kelly and Weborg, eds., *Reflections on Bonhoeffer: Essays in Honor of F. Burton Nelson* (Chicago: Covenant Press, 1999), 77-86; F. Burton Nelson, "Bonhoeffer and the Spiritual Life: Some Reflections," *Journal of Theology for Southern Africa* 30 (March 1980): 34-38.

2. Godsey, "Dietrich Bonhoeffer and Christian Spirituality," 79.

3. *TF*, 514.

4. *D*, 87.

Notes to Chapter One

1. *LPP*, 369.

2. Reinhold Niebuhr, "The Death of a Martyr," *Christianity and Crisis*, June 25, 1945, 6.

3. Niebuhr, "The Death of a Martyr," 7.

4. See the introductions to *D* (*DBWE* 4) and *LT* (*DBWE* 5) in the new critical editions. See also Clifford Green, *Bonhoeffer: The Sociality of Christ and Humanity* (Grand Rapids: Eerdmans, 1999).

5. *DB*, 13. The most comprehensive study of the life of Bonhoeffer is still the classic biography by his closest friend and reliable interpreter, Eberhard Bethge. Indisputably, this account of Bonhoeffer's life and context reigns supreme among those that continue to be available.

6. In the Church of St. Michael in Schwäbisch-Hall, one can still see a prominent

plaque indicating Johann Friedrich Bonhoeffer as a pastor of the congregation (d. 1783).

7. A detailed account of Bonhoeffer's ancestral heritage can be found in *DB*, 3-13.

8. Sabine Leibholz-Bonhoeffer was the last of the surviving siblings. Over 93 years of age, she died at her home in Göttingen, Germany, in July 1999.

9. A detailed description of each member of the family, including the parents, can be found in Sabine Leibholz-Bonhoeffer, *The Bonhoeffers: Portrait of a Family*, ed. F. Burton Nelson (Chicago: Covenant Publications, 1994). The volume was originally published by Johannes Kiefel Verlag, Wuppertal-Barmen, Germany, 1968. The first English edition was published in 1971 by Sidgwick & Jackson, Ltd., London.

10. A description given by Dietrich Bonhoeffer's niece, Renate Bethge, "Bonhoeffer's Family and Its Significance for His Theology," in Larry Rasmussen, *Dietrich Bonhoeffer: His Significance for North Americans* (Minneapolis: Fortress Press, 1990), 16. Bethge uses the terms "empiricism, rationality, and liberalism" to depict the spirit of the parents' home, but especially relates them to the father.

11. *IKDB*, 21.

12. Renate Bethge, "Bonhoeffer and the Role of Women," in *Church and Society*, "Who Is Jesus Christ for Us Today? Dietrich Bonhoeffer After Fifty Years" (July/August 1995): 35.

13. *DB*, 17.

14. Bonhoeffer's sister, Sabine, offers an idyllic description of the enjoyable days at Friedrichsbrunn the children shared in *IKDB*, 25-27.

15. *LPP*, 40, 73, 88, 117, 206, 211.

16. *DB*, 28.

17. *DB*, 28.

18. *DB*, 36.

19. Renate Bethge, "Bonhoeffer and the Role of Women," 36.

20. Renate Bethge, "Bonhoeffer and the Role of Women," 36.

21. Ruth Zerner, "Dietrich Bonhoeffer's Prison Fiction: A Commentary," in Dietrich Bonhoeffer, *Fiction from Prison: Gathering Up the Past*, ed. Renate and Eberhard Bethge, with Clifford Green (Philadelphia: Fortress Press, 1981), 141.

22. Thomas Day, *Dietrich Bonhoeffer on Christian Community and Common Sense* (New York and Toronto: Edwin Mellen Press, 1982), 2.

23. See Eberhard Bethge, *Friendship and Resistance: Essays on Dietrich Bonhoeffer* (Geneva: WCC Publications; Grand Rapids: Eerdmans, 1995), 72-79. See also Bethge, "Marienburger Allee 43: The House, Its Family, and Guests," in *Bonhoeffer House: A Place of Memorial and Encounter* (Berlin: Board of the Bonhoeffer House, 1996), 9-10. This familial impact extended to his physicist brother, Karl-Friedrich, as can be seen in Bethge, "The Nonreligious Scientist and the Confessing Theologian: The Influence of Karl-Friedrich Bonhoeffer on His Younger Brother," in *Bonhoeffer for a New Day: Theology in a Time of Transition*, ed. John de Gruchy (Grand Rapids: Eerdmans, 1997), 39-56.

24. Renate Bethge, "Bonhoeffer's Family and Its Significance for His Theology," 1-30.

25. *DB*, 25.

26. *DB*, 47.

27. *DB*, 65.

28. "Italienisches Tagebuch," in *Jugend und Studium, 1918-1927* (*DBW* 9): 81-112.

29. Quoted in Eberhard Bethge, Renate Bethge, and Christian Gremmels, eds., *Dietrich Bonhoeffer: A Life in Pictures* (Philadelphia: Fortress Press, 1986), 55.

30. *TF,* 55.

31. *TF,* 9. See also Wayne Floyd's editorial introduction, which sets *Act and Being* (*DBWE* 2) in both historical and biographical context.

32. *TF,* 425 (*DBW* 14: 113 [*DB,* 205]). An excellent resource for considering this phase of Bonhoeffer's life story is Ruth Zerner's essay, "Dietrich Bonhoeffer's American Experiences: People, Letters and Papers from Union Seminary," *USQR* 3, no. 4 (Summer 1976): 261-82.

33. Dietrich Bonhoeffer, "Report on a Period of Study at the Union Theological Seminary in New York, 1930-31," *NRS,* 91 (*DBW* 10: 268 [*GS* 1: 90]).

34. Unfortunately, Niebuhr did not save most of the letters that had been written to him by Bonhoeffer in the 1930s. Personal conversation, Ursula Niebuhr and F. Burton Nelson, March 1983.

35. *DB,* 153.

36. For a more detailed account of this singular friendship, see F. Burton Nelson, "The Relationship of Jean Lasserre to Dietrich Bonhoeffer's Peace Concerns in the Struggle of Church and Culture," *USQR* 40, nos. 1-2 (1986): 71-84. See also Geffrey B. Kelly, "An Interview with Jean Lasserre," *USQR* 27, no. 3 (Spring 1972): 149-60.

37. *TF,* 11.

38. *DB,* 155.

39. *IKDB,* 64-65.

40. The chronologies of Bonhoeffer's teaching career, his various pastoral activities, his involvement in the ecumenical movement, and his role in the evolving church struggle all overlap. Readers are advised to keep this time factor in mind as the sections of Bonhoeffer's life are unfolded.

41. *IKDB,* 60.

42. *IKDB,* 62.

43. *DB,* 208; translation slightly altered.

44. *DB,* 208.

45. *TF,* 111.

46. *TF,* 380 (*DBW* 10: 90 [*GS* 1: 51]).

47. *DB,* 111.

48. Cited in *Dietrich Bonhoeffer: A Life in Pictures,* 69.

49. *DB,* 155.

50. See *Dietrich Bonhoeffer: A Life in Pictures,* 76.

51. *TF,* 384-85 (*DBW* 11: 49-51 [*GS* 1: 25]).

52. *DB,* 234. For an elaboration on Bonhoeffer's preaching and an analysis of some of his memorable sermons, see Chapter Nine.

53. *NRS,* 239 (*DBW* 13: 33 [*GS* 2: 137]).

54. Both of the church buildings were struck in bombing raids during the Luftwaffe's attack against London during the war. Eventually, a new church edifice, the Dietrich Bonhoeffer Kirche, was rebuilt on the same location in Forest Hill. The

congregation still meets for worship there, though only a few from both churches still personally remember the pastoral ministry of Bonhoeffer.

55. *DB*, 334.

56. For a more detailed account of this theme, see F. Burton Nelson, "Pastor Bonhoeffer," in *Christian History*, Issue 32, Vol. 10, No. 4 (1991): 38-39.

57. *DBW* 13: 112 (*GS* 1: 184).

58. The full text of Bishop Bell's appeal appears in the official minutes of the Fanø, Denmark, meeting, Universal Christian Council for Life and Work, Fanø, Denmark, 1934, 65-66.

59. For a more precise accounting of Bonhoeffer's role at the Fanø ecumenical conference, see F. Burton Nelson, "The Holocaust and the Oikoumene: An Episode for Remembrance," in *Faith and Freedom*, ed. Richard Libowitz (Oxford: The Pergamon Press, 1987), 71-81.

60. *TF*, 229 (*DBW* 13: 301 [*GS* 1: 449]).

61. *IKDB*, 85.

62. Correspondence from Jean Lasserre to F. Burton Nelson, 4 October 1976.

63. *TF*, 140.

64. For assessment of this impact, see the essay by W. A. Visser 't Hooft, "Dietrich Bonhoeffer and the Self-Understanding of the Ecumenical Movement," *The Ecumenical Review* 28 (1976): 198-203. See also Konrad Raiser, "Bonhoeffer and the Ecumenical Movement," in de Gruchy, ed., *Bonhoeffer for a New Day*, 319-39.

65. *TF*, 132 (*DBW* 12: 358 [*GS* 2: 53]).

66. Cited in Eberhard Bethge, "Dietrich Bonhoeffer and the Jews," in *Ethical Responsibility: Bonhoeffer's Legacy to the Churches*, ed. John D. Godsey and Geffrey B. Kelly (Lewiston, N.Y.: Edwin Mellen Press, 1981), 63.

67. Eberhard Bethge, "Dietrich Bonhoeffer and the Jews," 76.

68. *IKDB*, 38-39.

69. *Reichskirche*, the Reich Church, was the established church in Germany, dominated in the early Nazi era by the faction of "German Christians." Opposition to the "German Christians" led to the formation of the Confessing Church at Barmen in May 1934, which itself was an outgrowth of the Pastors' Emergency League. Bonhoeffer, together with Pastor Martin Niemöller, had been instrumental in forming the League, which by the end of 1933 numbered over 6,000 Protestant pastors.

70. *DB*, 412-13.

71. *TF*, 23; see also Chapter Five, 108-9.

72. *DBWE* 5 is a double volume containing *Life Together* and *Prayerbook of the Bible: An Introduction to the Psalms*. "The Editor's Introduction to the English Edition" by Geffrey B. Kelly provides a helpful contextual setting for both of these books, which are among the most widely read of Bonhoeffer's writings.

73. See "Editor's Introduction," *LT* (*DBWE* 5): 17-18. Two of the original group of six are still alive: Winfried Maechler and Albrecht Schönherr, each one embodying in a unique manner the legacy of Bonhoeffer, both living in Berlin.

74. *IKDB*, 133; see also *TF*, 26.

75. *D* (*DBWE* 4): 55.

76. This "Guertner Diary," kept over a five-year period by Hans von Dohnanyi, is

on microfilm in the Washington National Archives. The documents were used by the prosecution in the Nuremberg War Crimes Trials after World War II. See *DB*, 935-36.

77. *DB*, 592.

78. A recent booklet describes Bonhoeffer's life story from Finkenwalde eastward to Köslin and Schlawe, then southward to the landed estates of the von Kleists and the von Wedemeyers. See Jane Pejsa, *To Pomerania in Search of Dietrich Bonhoeffer* (Minneapolis: Kenwood Publishing, 1995). For another recent "snapshot" of the Finkenwalde community, see Ernest Gordon, *And I Will Walk at Liberty: An Eye-Witness Account of the Church Struggle in Germany* (Bungay, Suffolk: Morrow & Co., 1997). Ernest Gordon, Jewish in ancestry, visited Bonhoeffer in Finkenwalde, who committed him to the care of Bishop Bell in England. He served as a priest in the Church of England until his death in 1991.

79. The emotional and dramatic account of the Leibholz journey to freedom is told in detail in Leibholz-Bonhoeffer, *The Bonhoeffers*, 80-88.

80. *DB*, 596.

81. *TF*, 465 (*DBW* 15: 56-57 [*GS* 2: 314]).

82. *DB*, 655.

83. Leibholz-Bonhoeffer, *The Bonhoeffers*, 111.

84. Leibholz-Bonhoeffer, *The Bonhoeffers*, 112.

85. Title of Volume 3 of the letters, lectures, and notes of Bonhoeffer, 1939-45, edited by Edwin H. Robertson, and usually noted as *TP*. The subtitle of this anthology describes Bonhoeffer's persistent dilemma: "One man's struggle between individual conscience and loyalty to his country."

86. For a detailed account of Bonhoeffer's secret mission to meet Bishop Bell in Sweden, see F. Burton Nelson, "Bonhoeffer at Sigtuna, 1942: A Case Study in the Ecumenical Church Struggle," in Godsey and Kelly, eds., *Ethical Responsibility*, 131-42.

87. *TF*, 354.

88. Ruth-Alice von Bismarck and Ulrich Kabitz, eds., *Love Letters from Cell 92: The Correspondence between Dietrich Bonhoeffer and Maria von Wedemeyer, 1943-45* (Nashville: Abingdon Press, 1994), 246. The publication of this correspondence illumines the bond of love between Dietrich and Maria; in addition, as Eberhard Bethge phrases it, "We can now, step by step, trace the course of Dietrich's life in Tegel Prison far more completely and in much greater depth" (365).

89. *TF*, 424 (*DBW* 14: 273 [*GS* 3: 25]).

90. Title of a volume by Jane Pejsa (Minneapolis: Kenwood Publishing, 1991). The book is the most comprehensive coverage available of Ruth von Kleist, including details of the Dietrich-Maria connection.

91. *Love Letters from Cell 92*, 338.

92. *Love Letters from Cell 92*, 199-200.

93. *Love Letters from Cell 92*, 64; translation by Maria, from *LPP*, 415, and *TF*, 488.

94. *TF*, 40-42, 491-95.

95. Eberhard Bethge, "How the Prison Letters Survived," in Bethge, *Friendship and Resistance: Essays on Dietrich Bonhoeffer*, 38-57.

96. A few examples illustrate the breadth of this selection: Karl August von Hase, *Ideals and Errors*; Martin Heidegger, *Phenomenology of Time-Consciousness*; Adalbert

Stifter, *Thoughts and Reflections;* W. Dilthey, *Experience and Poetry;* N. Hartmann, *Systematic Philosophy;* Paul De Kruif, *The Microbe Hunters;* Delbrück, *World History;* R. Benz, *German Music;* Wolf Dietrich Rasch, *Lesebuch der Erzähler; Don Quixote;* Gotthelf, *Berner Geist;* W. H. Riehl, *Stories from Olden Times;* Karl Barth, *Doctrine of God.*

97. Sigismund Payne Best, *The Venlo Incident* (London: Hutchison, 1950), 200.

98. Best, *The Venlo Incident,* 200.

99. *TF,* 44.

100. *DB,* 927; and *IKDB,* 232.

101. *DB,* 928, and *IKDB,* 232.

102. Cited in Eberhard Bethge, *Bonhoeffer: Exile and Martyr* (New York: Seabury Press, 1975), 155.

103. "Memoir," in Dietrich Bonhoeffer, *The Cost of Discipleship* (New York: Macmillan, 1963), 35.

Notes to Chapter Two

1. *D (DBWE* 4): 284-85.

2. *LPP,* 279.

3. *LPP,* 382.

4. *TF,* 186 (*DBW* 10: 533 [*GS* 5: 477]).

5. *CC,* 107 (*DBW* 12: 343 [*GS* 3: 236]).

6. Already in February 1933, just two days after Hitler's accession to power, Bonhoeffer was on the radio in Berlin calling into question the leadership principle on which Nazi Germany seemed to pin its millennial hopes. See Chapter One, 16.

7. *LPP,* 14.

8. *E,* 114; translation from *TF,* 363.

9. "Stations on the Way to Freedom," *TF,* 516-17 (*DBW* 8: 570-72 [*WE,* 403-4/*LPP,* 372-73]); translation from *LPP* thoroughly revised.

10. *LPP,* 17.

11. See *E,* 236-38.

12. *TF,* 505 (*DBW* 8: 435 [*WE,* 328/*LPP,* 300]); translation from *LPP* altered.

13. *TF,* 505 (*DBW* 8: 435-36 [*WE,* 328/*LPP,* 300]); translation from *LPP* altered.

14. TF, 505 (*DBW* 8: 436 [*WE,* 328/*LPP,* 300]); translation from *LPP* slightly altered.

15. TF, 505 (*DBW* 8: 436 [*WE,* 328/*LPP,* 300]); translation from *LPP* slightly altered.

16. *LPP,* 281.

17. *LPP,* 286.

18. Larry Rasmussen, "Worship in a World-Come-of-Age," in *A Bonhoeffer Legacy: Essays in Understanding,* ed. A. J. Klassen (Grand Rapids: Eerdmans, 1981), 278.

19. *LPP,* 300; translation from *TF,* 505.

20. For a fuller discussion of these three steps, see below in Chapter Four, 89, 98-99.

21. *LPP,* 381.

22. *NRS,* 325 (*DBW* 14: 421 [*GS* 3: 323-24]); translation altered.

23. See *LF,* 23.

24. See *E,* 114-15, and below in Chapter Four, 98-99.

25. *LPP,* 14; translation from *TF,* 483-84; emphasis ours.

26. *TF,* 470.

27. *E,* 197; translation altered.

28. *E,* 197.

29. *TF,* 92 (*DBW* 12: 276); translation from *TKC,* 45, slightly altered.

30. *D* (*DBWE* 4): 87.

Notes to Chapter Three

1. *DBW* 15: 569 (*GS* 4: 495).

2. *TF,* 465 (*DBW* 15: 56-57 [*GS* 2: 314]).

3. *DBW* 9: 305-6.

4. *DBW* 9: 307.

5. *DBW* 9: 322 (emphasis ours).

6. *DBW* 9: 320.

7. See below, 77-79, for Bonhoeffer's remarks in his essay on "The Interpretation of the New Testament."

8. In the more abstract language that Bonhoeffer uses to describe this spiritual happening, we read his strong affirmation of this dynamic: "God or the Holy Spirit joins the concrete You; only through God's active working does the other become a You to me from whom my I arises. In other words, every human You is an image of the divine You." See *SC* (*DBWE* 1): 54-55.

9. *SC* (*DBWE* 1): 137.

10. *SC* (*DBWE* 1): 144.

11. *SC* (*DBWE* 1): 144; translation slightly altered. Bonhoeffer cites Irenaeus in support of his assertion: "Ubi enim ecclesia ibi et spiritus; et ubi spiritus dei illic ecclesia et omnis gratia" [For where the church is, there is the Spirit; and where the Spirit of God is, there is the church and every kind of grace].

12. *SC* (*DBWE* 1): 154.

13. *DBW* 11: 275 (*GS* 5: 252).

14. *SC* (*DBWE* 1): 160.

15. *SC* (*DBWE* 1): 161.

16. *SC* (*DBWE* 1): 165.

17. *SC* (*DBWE* 1): 175.

18. *SC* (*DBWE* 1): 178-79.

19. *SC* (*DBWE* 1): 202 (emphasis Bonhoeffer's).

20. *SC* (*DBWE* 1): 262.

21. *SC* (*DBWE* 1): 212-13.

22. *DBW* 11: 315 (*GS* 5: 494); emphasis ours.

23. *DBW* 14: 815 (*GS* 3: 363); emphasis ours.

24. See below, 63, where Bonhoeffer says explicitly in *Discipleship,* citing 2 Cor. 3:17-18, that "the Lord is the Spirit."

25. *SC* (*DBWE* 1): 138.

26. *NRS,* 147 (*DBW* 11: 235 [*GS* 3: 255]).

27. See Edmund Dobbin, "Towards a Theology of the Holy Spirit, I," *The Heythrop Journal* 16, no. 1 (January 1976). Dobbin cites Raymond Brown's essay "The Paraclete," from his *The Gospel According to John, XIII–XXI, The Anchor Bible* (New York: Doubleday, 1967), 113-32.

28. *AB* (*DBWE* 2): 92.

29. *AB* (*DBWE* 2): 128.

30. *Meditating on the Word,* translated and edited by David McI. Gracie (Cambridge, Mass.: Cowley Publications, 1986), 122-23 (*DBW* 15: 515-16 [*GS* 4: 522-23]).

31. *CF* (*DBWE* 3): 64.

32. *CF* (*DBWE* 3): 64; emphasis Bonhoeffer's.

33. *CF* (*DBWE* 3): 65.

34. *AB* (*DBWE* 2): 90-91.

35. *TF,* 516-17 (*DBW* 8: 570-72 [*WE,* 403/*LPP,* 370-71]); translation altered.

36. *DBW* 15: 567 (*GS* 4: 493).

37. *D* (*DBWE* 4): 180.

38. Sermon of November 24, 1935, *TF,* 265 (*DBW* 14: 913 [*GS* 5: 571]).

39. Sermon of November 24, 1935, *TF,* 267-68 (*DBW* 14: 917 [*GS* 5: 575]).

40. *D* (*DBWE* 4): 87.

41. *D* (*DBWE* 4): 194.

42. *D* (*DBWE* 4): 220.

43. *D* (*DBWE* 4): 221.

44. *D* (*DBWE* 4): 224.

45. *D* (*DBWE* 4): 228.

46. *D* (*DBWE* 4): 230.

47. *D* (*DBWE* 4): 232.

48. *D* (*DBWE* 4): 260.

49. *D* (*DBWE* 4): 260.

50. *D* (*DBWE* 4): 261.

51. *D* (*DBWE* 4): 267.

52. *D* (*DBWE* 4): 266.

53. *D* (*DBWE* 4): 267.

54. *DBW* 12: 307 (*GS* 2: 107).

55. Bonhoeffer's comments as recorded by Julius Rieger at the Pastors' Conference in Bradford, England, 27-30 November 1933, to discuss the Bethel Confession of Faith, in *DBW* 13: 40 (*GS* 2: 87).

56. *DB,* 289.

57. *DB,* 289.

58. *NRS,* 304-5 (*DBW* 14: 110-11 [*GS* 2: 214-15]); translation slightly altered; emphasis ours.

59. *NRS,* 306 (*DBW* 14: 111 [*GS* 2: 215]); emphasis ours.

60. *WF,* 110 (*DBW* 14: 696 [*GS* 2: 259-60]); translation altered; emphasis ours.

61. *WF,* 112-13 (*DBW* 14: 698 [*GS* 2: 262]); translation altered; emphasis ours.

62. *NRS,* 310-11 (*DBW* 14: 403-4 [*GS* 3: 306-7]); translation altered; emphasis Bonhoeffer's.

63. *NRS,* 311 (*DBW* 14: 404 [*GS* 3: 307]).
64. *NRS,* 311 (*DBW* 14: 404 [*GS* 3: 307]).
65. Letter of April 8, 1936, *TF,* 426 (*DBW* 14: 147 [*GS* 3: 29]).
66. *TF,* 505 (*DBW* 8: 435 [*WE,* 328/*LPP,* 300]); translation from *LPP* altered.
67. *DBW* 15: 569 (*GS* 4: 495).
68. *LPP,* 140.

Notes to Chapter Four

1. *TF,* 206 (*DBW* 11: 461-62 [*GS* 4: 79, 86-87]).
2. In his essay on Bonhoeffer's liberation theology, G. Clarke Chapman gives a brief survey of just how widespread Bonhoeffer's theology has been among liberation theologians. See his "Bonhoeffer, Liberation Theology, and the 1990s," in Geffrey B. Kelly and C. John Weborg, eds., *Reflections on Bonhoeffer: Essays in Honor of F. Burton Nelson* (Chicago: Covenant Press, 1999), 299-300.
3. Gustavo Gutiérrez, *The Power of the Poor in History* (Maryknoll, N.Y.: Orbis, 1983), 233. It should be made clear that Dietrich Bonhoeffer doesn't fit completely into the typically Latin American mode of liberation theology. Bonhoeffer was unable to theologize from firsthand experience of the plight of Nazi Germany's underclass. He had little knowledge of the evil living conditions that colonialism and raw capitalism had inflicted on the native peoples of Latin America and Africa. Finally, Bonhoeffer was hardly enthusiastic about socialism's solutions for curing a nation's ills, such as was advocated in the early years of liberation theology.
4. Jon Sobrino, *Christology at the Crossroads* (Maryknoll, N.Y.: Orbis, 1980), 197; see also 221-22.
5. *TF,* 470-71 (*DBW* 15: 225-27 [*GS* 1: 300-302]).
6. *TF,* 476 (*DBW* 15: 237-38 [*GS* 1: 312-13]).
7. *TF,* 524 (*DBW* 15: 443-45 [*GS* 1: 337-38]).
8. *DBW* 10: 275 (*GS* 1: 98).
9. *IKDB,* 64-65.
10. See *TF,* 15-18, 132-40 (*DBW* 12: 349-58 [*GS* 2: 49-52]).
11. *TF,* 52 (*DBW* 10: 318 [*GS* 5: 152]).
12. Bethge, "Dietrich Bonhoeffer and the Jews," in *Ethical Responsibility: Bonhoeffer's Legacy to the Churches,* ed. John D. Godsey and Geffrey B. Kelly (Lewiston, N.Y.: Edwin Mellen Press, 1981), 71.
13. *TKC,* 44-45 (*DBW* 12: 271 [*GS* 3: 283]); translation slightly altered from *TF,* 92.
14. *CC,* 107 (*DBW* 12: 343 [*GS* 3: 236]). See also *TF,* 122.
15. *LPP,* 17 (*DBW* 8: 38).
16. *TKC,* 45 (*DBW* 12: 276 [*GS* 2: 441]); translation slightly altered from *TF,* 92.
17. *TF,* 186 (*DBW* 10: 532 [*GS* 5: 477]).
18. Bethge, "Dietrich Bonhoeffer and the Jews," 71-73.
19. *D* (*DBWE* 4): 285.
20. *D* (*DBWE* 4): 106-7; we have substituted the word "compassionate" in place of "merciful" as our translation of *Barmherzigkeit.*

21. *LPP*, 5.

22. *E*, 136.

23. See Geffrey B. Kelly, "Bonhoeffer and Romero: Prophets of Justice for the Oppressed," in *Theology and the Practice of Responsibility: Essays on Dietrich Bonhoeffer*, ed. Wayne Floyd and Charles Marsh (Valley Forge, Pa.: Trinity Press International, 1994), 92-95.

24. *LPP*, 362.

25. *LPP*, 369.

26. Letter of August 12, 1943, in *TF*, 488. This translation, done by Maria herself, is used here in lieu of the translation of the same letter in Ruth-Alice von Bismarck and Ulrich Kabitz, eds., *Love Letters from Cell 92: The Correspondence between Dietrich Bonhoeffer and Maria von Wedemeyer, 1943-45* (Nashville: Abingdon Press, 1994), 63-64.

27. *LPP*, 300.

28. *LPP*, 382.

29. *LPP*, 381.

30. These quotations are all taken from Bonhoeffer's "Outline for a Book," *LPP*, 380-83.

31. See Robert McAfee Brown, *Gustavo Gutiérrez: An Introduction to Liberation Theology* (Maryknoll, N.Y.: Orbis, 1990), 2-7.

32. *LPP*, 378.

33. *LPP*, 279.

34. Kelly, "Bonhoeffer and Romero," 96.

35. "The Church and the Jewish Question," in *TF*, 132 (*DBW* 12: 354 [*GS* 2: 48]).

36. *TF*, 16-17.

37. *E*, 114.

38. *LPP*, 371; translation from *TF*, 516.

Notes to Chapter Five

1. *TF*, 228 (*DBW* 13: 299-300 [*GS* 1: 217-18]).

2. F. Burton Nelson, "The Relationship of Jean Lasserre to Dietrich Bonhoeffer's Peace Concerns in the Struggle of Church and Culture," *Union Seminary Quarterly Review* 40, nos. 1-2 (1985): 74.

3. Nelson, "The Relationship of Jean Lasserre to Dietrich Bonhoeffer's Peace Concerns," 74.

4. *DB*, 203.

5. *TF*, 424-25 (*DBW* 14: 113 [*GS* 6: 367-68]).

6. *TF*, 426 (*DBW* 14: 146 [*GS* 3: 28]).

7. *TF*, 424 (*DBW* 13: 272-73 [*GS* 3: 25]).

8. *TF*, 94 (*DBW* 17: 117 [*GS* 5: 360]). The version of this essay in *DBW* 17: 116-20 is expanded over the previous version found in *DBW* 12: 232-35.

9. *TF*, 94-95 (*DBW* 17: 117-18 [*GS* 5: 361]).

10. *TF*, 202 (*DBW* 11: 404 [*GS* 4: 39]).

11. See his "Das Recht auf Selbstbehauptung," *DBW* 11: 215-26 (*GS* 3: 261-69). See

also Larry Rasmussen, *Dietrich Bonhoeffer: Reality and Resistance* (Nashville: Abingdon Press, 1972), 101-2.

12. *NRS*, 187-88 (*DBW* 11: 355 [*GS* 1: 168]); translation altered.

13. *NRS*, 188 (*DBW* 11: 355 [*GS* 1: 168]); translation altered.

14. *NRS*, 170 (*DBW* 11: 341 [*GS* 1: 155]); translation altered.

15. *NRS*, 172 (*DBW* 11: 341-42 [*GS* 1: 156-57]).

16. *NRS*, 169 (*DBW* 11: 339 [*GS* 1: 153]).

17. R. Rouse and S. C. Neill, *A History of the Ecumenical Movement, 1517-1948* (London: SPCK, 1954), 583.

18. *TF*, 228-29 (*DBW* 13: 300-301 [*GS* 1: 218-19]).

19. See also Chapter Nine for a further analysis of this and another peace sermon by Bonhoeffer.

20. *DB*, 389.

21. Willem A. Visser 't Hooft, "Dietrich Bonhoeffer and the Self-Understanding of the Ecumenical Movement," *The Ecumenical Review* 28, no. 2 (April 1976): 201, 203.

22. *TF*, 228 (*DBW* 13: 303 [*GS* 1: 218]); translation altered.

23. Larry Rasmussen, "Bonhoeffer, Gandhi, and Resistance," in Geffrey B. Kelly and C. John Weborg, eds., *Reflections on Bonhoeffer: Essays in Honor of F. Burton Nelson* (Chicago: Covenant Press, 1999), 54.

24. *TF*, 229 (*DBW* 13: 301 [*GS* 1: 219]). We have used the more benign expression "non-Christian" to translate *Heiden*, which means, literally, "heathen."

25. *DB*, 407.

26. *D* (*DBWE* 4): 108.

27. *D* (*DBWE* 4): 139.

28. *TF*, 287-88 (*DBW* 15: 469 [*GS* 4: 433]).

29. *E*, 243-44.

30. *E*, 243-44.

31. *E*, 240-41.

32. *E*, 237; translation altered.

33. *E*, 159.

34. *E*, 162.

35. *E*, 244; translation slightly altered.

36. *E*, 245.

37. *E*, 245.

38. Jean Bethke Elshtain, "Seeking Justice," *The Christian Century*, November 14, 2001, 26.

39. An additional reason for the ethical sanction of the United States' military response against the Taliban rulers of Afghanistan and the terrorist networks they had sheltered can be related to the deliverance from evil of the women who were among the prime victims of the terrorism sponsored by the religious police of the Taliban. Their plight was not at all unlike that of the victims of Nazism languishing and perishing in the concentration camps of the Hitler era. One has only to read the documented reports of the sufferings inflicted on the women of Afghanistan to see an additional justification for the United States' war of retribution: that of liberating women from a dehumanizing oppression. It is difficult to imagine the immeasurable

harm done to these women who, under the guise of a spurious interpretation of the Quran, were forbidden to be educated, to hold jobs outside the home, or to leave home without a male escort, even though prior to the Taliban takeover 70 percent of the teachers and 40 percent of the doctors were women. Women were forced to wear the stifling burka that covered them from head to toe, with only a small netlike opening through which they could see. The religious police brutally beat with whips those who were caught not wearing the burka. The same religious police would pull out the fingernails of women who displayed fingernail polish in public. Cosmetics of any kind were forbidden. Photography was banned. Adultery was punished by summary execution. (Reported by Peter Norman, *People*, Nov. 14, 2001, 26.)

40. *LPP*, 14.

41. *E*, 94.

42. Nowhere has the dilemma posed by a just war to Christian morality been expressed so forcefully than by one of Bonhoeffer's greatest influences, Karl Barth. Writing from his native Switzerland against the militarism and destructiveness of Nazi Germany's glorying in its victories, Barth, not a pacifist himself, asked: "Does not war demand that almost everything that God has forbidden be done on a broad front? To kill effectively . . . must not those who wage war steal, rob, commit arson, lie, deceive, slander . . . not to speak of the almost inevitable repression of all the finer and weightier forms of obedience? And how can they pray when at the climax of the world of dubious action it is a brutal matter of killing? . . . It is certainly not true that most people become better in war." John Phelan, President and Dean of North Park Theological Seminary, comments on this Barthian statement with a series of questions of his own: "How do we return to truth-telling, once we have gotten used to lies? How do we return to respect for property, once we have gotten used to wanton destruction? How do we return to peace, once we have gotten used to explosive violence?" He concludes, "It is not disloyal to suggest that particular actions within war are wrong or excessive. It would, in fact, be disloyal *not* to — disloyal especially to Christ." John Phelan, "Markings," *The Covenant Companion*, November 2001, 5.

43. *TF*, 228 (*DBW* 13: 300 [*GS* 1: 218]).

44. *LPP*, 279.

45. "Throw Out the Pollsters: An Interview with Paul Simon," *The Christian Century*, October 18, 1995, 958.

46. *TF*, 104 (*DBW* 11: 353-59 [*GS* 1: 166-67]); translation slightly changed.

47. Geffrey Kelly, "Bonhoeffer and Romero," in *Theology and the Practice of Responsibility: Essays on Dietrich Bonhoeffer*, ed. Wayne Floyd and Charles Marsh (Valley Forge, Pa.: Trinity Press International, 1994), 94.

48. Maguire, *The Moral Core of Judaism and Christianity: Reclaiming the Revolution* (Minneapolis: Fortress Press, 1993), 10.

49. Barbara Bennett Woodhouse, "Remember Our Own War-zone Children," *The Philadelphia Inquirer*, Wednesday, December 27, 1995.

50. See *LPP*, 378-79, 382-83 et passim.

51. Maguire, *Moral Core of Judaism and Christianity*, 10. Maguire was not alone in his opposition to the Persian Gulf War. In addition to pleas from the pope to both President Bush and Saddam Hussein to halt the march toward war and statements from

the United States Bishops and the Canberra Resolution by the World Council of Churches against the war, the strongest possible denunciation of the war was issued in a joint declaration from the Catholic Theological Society of America and the College Theology Society. See "Statement of the Morality of the War in the Persian Gulf by American Catholic Theologians and Professors of Religious Studies," *Horizons* 20, no. 1 (Spring 1993): 118-26.

52. The quotations here are taken from Patrick O'Neill, "Theologian's Feisty Faith Challenges Status Quo," *National Catholic Reporter* 38, no. 32 (June 21, 2002): 3-4.

53. "After Ten Years," *LPP,* 4.

54. See Geffrey B. Kelly, "Who Stands Firm?" *Weavings: A Journal of the Christian Spiritual Life* 15, no. 6 (November/December 2000): 5-6.

55. Based on *LPP,* 391, with the translation altered.

Notes to Chapter Six

1. *D (DBWE* 4): 53.

2. *D (DBWE* 4): 37.

3. It is intriguing to note in connection with the title of this book that the spiritual classic *The Imitation of Christ* by Thomas à Kempis is entitled in German *"Nachfolge Christi."* Bonhoeffer frequently refers to the Latin original of this text which was among the books in his library that survived the destruction of Berlin. Bonhoeffer's personal copy was among his possessions when he was executed in 1945. It can still be seen under glass at the Dietrich Bonhoeffer Kirche in South London, Forest Hills. It was presented to the congregation by Bonhoeffer's close friend, Bishop Bell of Chichester.

4. The complete text of Barmen's declarations, resolutions, and motions can be found in Arthur Cochrane, *The Church's Confession Under Hitler* (Pittsburgh: Pickwick Press, 1976), 237-47.

5. *DB,* 450.

6. *D (DBWE* 4): 43.

7. *D (DBWE* 4): 44.

8. *D (DBWE* 4): 45.

9. *D (DBWE* 4): 58-59.

10. *D (DBWE* 4): 53.

11. *D (DBWE* 4): 54.

12. *D (DBWE* 4): 55.

13. *CF (DBWE* 3): 63-64.

14. *LF,* 62.

15. *D (DBWE* 4): 63.

16. *TF,* 95 *(DBW* 17: 118 [*GS* 5: 361]).

17. Eberhard Bethge, "Freedom and Obedience in Dietrich Bonhoeffer," in *Prayer and Righteous Action in the Life of Dietrich Bonhoeffer* (Ottawa: Christian Journals Ltd., 1979), 54.

18. *D (DBWE* 4): 59-61.

19. *D* (*DBWE* 4): 63.

20. Louis Dupré, *Kierkegaard As Theologian: The Dialectic of Christian Existence* (New York: Sheed and Ward, 1963), 128-29. Dupré draws this conclusion from Kierkegaard's Journals, 10, A.

21. *D* (*DBWE* 4): 73-76.

22. *D* (*DBWE* 4): 59.

23. *D* (*DBWE* 4): 87.

24. *D* (*DBWE* 4): 89.

25. *D* (*DBWE* 4): 104.

26. *D* (*DBWE* 4): 103-4.

27. *LPP,* 336-37.

28. *LF,* 31.

29. *D* (*DBWE* 4): 106.

30. *D* (*DBWE* 4): 108.

31. *D* (*DBWE* 4): 108.

32. *D* (*DBWE* 4): 109-10.

33. *D* (*DBWE* 4): 113.

34. *D* (*DBWE* 4): 139.

35. *D* (*DBWE* 4): 144.

36. *D* (*DBWE* 4): 152.

37. *D* (*DBWE* 4): 168; translation slightly altered.

38. *D* (*DBWE* 4): 197.

39. *D* (*DBWE* 4): 221.

40. *D* (*DBWE* 4): 222.

41. *D* (*DBWE* 4): 233.

42. *D* (*DBWE* 4): 247.

43. *D* (*DBWE* 4): 251.

44. *D* (*DBWE* 4): 279.

45. *D* (*DBWE* 4): 285.

46. *D* (*DBWE* 4): 285.

47. *E,* 91.

48. *D* (*DBWE* 4): 287.

Notes to Chapter Seven

1. *SC* (*DBWE* 1): 179-80.

2. *LT* (*DBWE* 5): 25.

3. *DB,* 207-34. See also "Editor's Introduction," *LT* (*DBWE* 5): 9-11.

4. *TF,* 86-87 (*DBW* 11: 298-99 [*GS* 5: 270]); translation altered.

5. *LPP,* 382.

6. *SC* (*DBWE* 1): 272. We have used the expression "poor working class" in place of the term "proletariat."

7. See *TF,* 54-55. The material in this section is drawn from our essay on "Sanctorum Communio," in *TF,* 54-56.

8. See *SC* (*DBWE* 1): 140-41, 190, and passim.

9. *SC* (*DBWE* 1): 179-80.

10. *TF*, 385-86 (*DBW* 11: 64 [*GS* 1: 27-28]).

11. *IKDB*, 57.

12. *DB*, 134.

13. *DB*, 408.

14. *DB*, 409.

15. *TF*, 412 (*DBW* 13: 204 [*GS* 1: 42]).

16. *DB*, 413.

17. See *TF*, 457 (*DBW* 16: 241 [*GS* 2: 584-85]).

18. Letter of March 1, 1942, *TF*, 457 (*DBW* 16: 241 [*GS* 2: 584-85]); translation altered.

19. Personal conversation between Winfried Maechler and Burton Nelson, 1983.

20. *DBW* 14: 175 (*GS* 6:376).

21. "Editor's Introduction," *LT* (*DBWE* 5): 20.

22. See the "Editor's Introduction" and the bibliography for the history of and more data on this text, *LT* (*DBWE* 5): 20-23; 185-200.

23. *LT* (*DBWE* 5): 47.

24. *LT* (*DBWE* 5): 29.

25. *LT* (*DBWE* 5): 31.

26. *LT* (*DBWE* 5): 36-37.

27. *LT* (*DBWE* 5): 37.

28. *LT* (*DBWE* 5): 44.

29. *LT* (*DBWE* 5): 44.

30. *LT* (*DBWE* 5): 49.

31. *LT* (*DBWE* 5): 51.

32. *LT* (*DBWE* 5): 52.

33. See Chapter Ten for a fuller development of Bonhoeffer's prayers and poetry, including his analysis of the Psalms.

34. *LT* (*DBWE* 5): 62.

35. *LT* (*DBWE* 5): 69.

36. *LT* (*DBWE* 5): 71.

37. *LT* (*DBWE* 5): 79.

38. *LT* (*DBWE* 5): 83.

39. *LT* (*DBWE* 5): 83.

40. John Selby, *Solitude*, cited by Kostya Kennedy in *Attaché*, February 2001, 50.

41. *LT* (*DBWE* 5): 85.

42. *LT* (*DBWE* 5): 87.

43. *LT* (*DBWE* 5): 89.

44. *LT* (*DBWE* 5): 90.

45. *LT* (*DBWE* 5): 90.

46. *LT* (*DBWE* 5): 93.

47. *LT* (*DBWE* 5): 96.

48. *LT* (*DBWE* 5): 98.

49. *LT* (*DBWE* 5): 99.

50. *LT* (*DBWE* 5): 100-102.

51. *LT* (*DBWE* 5): 105-6.

52. *LT* (*DBWE* 5): 109.

53. *LT* (*DBWE* 5): 109.

54. *LT* (*DBWE* 5): 111-13.

55. *LT* (*DBWE* 5): 113.

56. *LT* (*DBWE* 5): 118.

57. *LT* (*DBWE* 5): 118.

Notes to Chapter Eight

1. From a London sermon in St. Paul's Church, *DBW* 13: 412 (*GS* 4: 182).

2. *LPP*, 382.

3. *LPP*, 391.

4. There were multiple attempts on Hitler's life, the most renowned, of course, being that of 20 July 1944. See Joachim Fest, *Plotting Hitler's Death: The Story of the German Resistance* (New York: Henry Holt and Company, 1994), and Peter Hoffmann, *German Resistance to Hitler* (Cambridge: Harvard University Press, 1988).

5. *LPP*, 391-92.

6. *LPP*, 337.

7. *LPP*, 348-49; translation from *TF*, 515.

8. For a detailed analysis of this poem, see chapter 10, 240-41.

9. *TF*, 52 (*DBW* 10: 316-17 [*GS* 5: 149-50]).

10. *D* (*DBWE* 4): 106-7.

11. *TF*, 53 (*DBW* 10: 316-17 [*GS* 5: 150]).

12. *LT* (*DBWE* 5): 99-100.

13. *NRS*, 363-64 (*DBW* 10: 437-38 [*GS* 3: 113-14]).

14. *D* (*DBWE* 4): 89.

15. *TF*, 53 (*DBW* 10: 321 [*GS* 5: 154]).

16. John D. Godsey, "Dietrich Bonhoeffer on Suffering," *The Living Pulpit* 4, no. 2 (April-June 1995): 4.

17. Josiah Young, "Nobody Knows But Jesus," *The Living Pulpit* 4, no. 2 (April-June 1995): 13.

18. *LPP*, 4-5; translation altered.

19. Anthony Harvey, "Historical Note," in "A Celebration of the Martyrs of the Church in the Twentieth Century," Program for the Liturgy, Westminster Abbey, July 9, 1998.

20. The other martyrs singled out for this honor were Maximilian Kolbe of Poland, Janani Luwum of Uganda, Grand Duchess Elizabeth of Russia, Manche Masemola of South Africa, Lucian Tapiedi of Papua, New Guinea, Esther John of Pakistan, and Wang Zhiming of China. For a complete description of the significance of each martyr chosen for these niches, along with their biographical sketches, see Andrew Chandler, ed., *The Terrible Alternative: Christian Martyrdom in the Twentieth Century* (London: Cassel, 1998).

21. Martin Luther King, Jr., *I Have a Dream: Writings and Speeches that Changed the World*, ed. James M. Washington (San Francisco: HarperCollins, 1992), 90-91.

22. *TF*, 132 (*DBW* 12: 353 [*GS* 2: 48]).

23. King, *I Have a Dream*, 94.

24. King, *I Have a Dream*, 96.

25. King, *I Have a Dream*, 97.

26. There are amazing parallels between the life of Bonhoeffer and the life of King. Both were cut down by murderers in the prime of life at the age of 39. Both were killed in April, Bonhoeffer in 1945, King in 1968. Both have been more celebrated after their deaths than while they lived.

27. Archbishop Oscar Romero, *Voice of the Voiceless: The Four Pastoral Letters and Other Statements* (Maryknoll: Orbis, 1985), 138.

28. Geffrey B. Kelly, "Bonhoeffer and Romero: Prophets of Justice for the Oppressed," in Floyd and Marsh, eds., *Theology and the Practice of Responsibility: Essays on Dietrich Bonhoeffer* (Valley Forge: Trinity Press International, 1994), 86.

29. *LPP*, 17.

30. Romero, *Voice of the Voiceless*, 182.

31. *LPP*, 360-61.

32. *LPP*, 14.

Notes to Chapter Nine

1. "The Proclaimed Word," *DBW* 14: 506-7 (*GS* 4: 243-44); translation from *WP*, 104.

2. *DB*, 234; translation slightly altered.

3. F. Burton Nelson, "Pastor Bonhoeffer," *Christian History*, Issue 32, Vol. 10, No. 4 (1991): 39.

4. *DB*, 284.

5. *DB*, 285.

6. "The Pastor and the Bible," *DBW* 14: 512 (*GS* 4: 257); translation from *WP*, 118.

7. "The Proclaimed Word," *DBW* 14: 506-7 (*GS* 4: 240-44); translation from *WP*, 101-4.

8. "Gideon," *DBW* 12: 454 (*GS* 4: 116); translation by Clyde E. Fant, Jr., and Werner Tobler, in Clyde E. Fant, Jr., and William M. Pinson, Jr., eds., *20 Centuries of Great Preaching: An Encyclopedia of Preaching*, Vol. 12 (Waco: Word Books, 1971), 131 (hereafter *GP*).

9. *LT* (*DBWE* 5): 99.

10. "Gideon," *DBW* 12: 453 (*GS* 4: 114); translation from *GP*, 131.

11. *TF*, 250 (*DBW* 13: 400 [*GS* 5: 556]); emphasis Bonhoeffer's.

12. *TF*, 252 (*DBW* 13: 403-4 [*GS* 5: 560]).

13. *LPP*, 382.

14. *TF*, 424 (*DBW* 13: 273 [*GS* 3: 25]).

15. *TF*, 295 (*DBW* 15: 478 [*GS* 4: 443]).

16. *TF*, 296 (*DBW* 15: 480 [*GS* 4: 445]).

17. *DBW* 11: 416-17 (*GS* 1: 133]); translation from *GP*, 117.

18. *DBW* 11: 420 (*GS* 1: 136]); translation from *GP*, 119.

19. *DBW* 11: 422-23 (*GS* 1: 139]); translation from *GP*, 121.

20. *TF*, 225 (*DBW* 13: 336 [*GS* 4: 169]).

21. *TF*, 186 (*DBW* 10: 533 [*GS* 5: 477]).

22. *TF*, 250 (*DBW* 13: 400-401 [*GS* 5: 556-57]).

23. *TF*, 250 (*DBW* 13: 401 [*GS* 5: 557]).

24. *TF*, 252 (*DBW* 13: 404 [*GS* 5: 560]).

25. *TF*, 247 (*DBW* 13: 392 [*GS* 5: 548]).

26. *LPP*, 15.

27. Letter of August 23, 1944, *LPP*, 393.

28. *TF*, 240 (*DBW* 13: 380 [*GS* 5: 536]); emphasis Bonhoeffer's.

29. *TF*, 241 (*DBW* 13: 381 [*GS* 5: 536]).

30. *TF*, 242 (*DBW* 13: 380-81 [*GS* 5: 538]).

31. See *LT* (*DBWE* 5): 38-46.

32. *TF*, 246-47 (*DBW* 13: 390 [*GS* 5: 546]).

33. *TF*, 248 (*DBW* 13: 392-93 [*GS* 5: 548-49]).

34. *D* (*DBWE* 4): 136-37.

35. *TF*, 288 (*DBW* 15: 469 [*GS* 4: 433]).

36. *DBW* 15: 572 (*GS* 4: 499).

37. *DBW* 11: 455-56 (*GS* 4: 80-81).

38. *DBW* 11: 458 (*GS* 4: 82-83).

39. *DBW* 11: 458 (*GS* 4: 83).

40. *DBW* 11: 459-60 (*GS* 4: 84).

41. *TF*, 206 (*DBW* 11: 461 [*GS* 4: 86]).

42. *TF*, 206 (*DBW* 11: 462 [*GS* 4: 86]).

43. *TF*, 207 (*DBW* 11: 462 [*GS* 4: 87]).

44. See Kelly, "An Interview with Jean Lasserre," and Nelson, "The Relationship of Jean Lasserre to Dietrich Bonhoeffer's Peace Concerns in the Struggle of Church and Culture." See also *DB*, 153-54.

45. *TF*, 227 (*DBW* 13: 298-99 [*GS* 1: 216-17]).

46. *TF*, 228 (*DBW* 13: 299-300 [*GS* 1: 217]).

47. *TF*, 104 (*DBW* 11: 356 [*GS* 1: 168]).

48. *TF*, 228 (*DBW* 13: 300 [*GS* 1: 218]).

49. *TF*, 228-29 (*DBW* 13: 301 [*GS* 1: 219]).

50. *IKDB*, 90.

51. *TF*, 202 (*DBW* 11: 404 [*GS* 4: 39]).

52. *TF*, 204 (*DBW* 11: 407 [*GS* 4: 42]).

53. *DBW* 14: 766-67 (*GS* 4: 198-99).

54. *DBW* 14: 767 (*GS* 4: 199).

55. *DBW* 15: 570 (*GS* 4: 496).

56. *DBW* 16: 638 (*GS* 4: 576).

57. *TF*, 192 (*DBW* 10: 390 [*GS* 1: 74]).

58. *TF*, 104 (*DBW* 11: 354 [*GS* 1: 167]).

59. *TF*, 205 (*DBW* 11: 428 [*GS* 4: 52-53]).

60. *DBW* 11: 430 (*GS* 4: 55).

61. *DBW* 11: 431 (*GS* 4: 55).

62. *DBW* 11: 431-32 (*GS* 4: 55-56).

63. *E*, 136.

64. *DBW* 11: 434 (*GS* 4: 58).

65. *TF*, 195 (*DBW* 11: 377 [*GS* 4: 17-18]).

66. *TF*, 196 (*DBW* 11: 380-81 [*GS* 4: 20-21]).

67. *DBW* 13: 409-10 (*GS* 4: 179-80).

68. *DBW* 13: 411 (*GS* 4: 180).

69. *DBW* 13: 411 (*GS* 4: 181).

70. *DBW* 13: 411-12 (*GS* 4: 181).

71. *TF*, 52 (*DBW* 10: 317 [*GS* 5: 150]).

72. *TF*, 186 (*DBW* 10: 533 [*GS* 5: 477]).

73. *E*, 126.

74. *TF*, 445 (*DBW* 15: 267 [*GS* 2: 553]).

75. *TF*, 456 (*DBW* 16: 240 [*GS* 2: 583]).

76. *TF*, 219 (*DBW* 13: 325 [*GS* 4: 160]).

77. *TF*, 220 (*DBW* 13: 328 [*GS* 4: 162].

78. *TF*, 221-22 (*DBW* 13: 330-31 [*GS* 4: 164-65]). On Cardinal Bernardin's attitude toward death as a "friend," see his chapter, "Befriending Death," in *The Gift of Peace* (New York: Doubleday Image Books, 1997), 127.

79. *TF*, 270 (*DBW* 14: 924 [*GS* 4: 459]); emphasis Bonhoeffer's.

80. *TF*, 291 (*DBW* 15: 473 [*GS* 4: 437]).

81. *TF*, 293 (*DBW* 15: 476 [*GS* 4: 441]).

82. *DBW* 13: 412 (*GS* 4: 182).

83. *LPP*, 361.

Notes to Chapter Ten

1. *TF*, 457 (*DBW* 16: 241 [*GS* 2: 584-85]); translation slightly altered.

2. "Stations on the Way to Freedom," *TF*, 516-17 (*DBW* 8: 571 [*WE*, 403/*LPP*, 370-71]); translation from *LPP* thoroughly revised. See note 42.

3. Eberhard Bethge, *Bekennen und Widerstehen: Aufsätze-Reden-Gespräche* [To Confess and to Resist: Essays-Talks-Discussions] (Munich: Kaiser, 1984), 163.

4. *DBW* 16: 65 (*GS* 2: 376).

5. *LPP*, 300 (*DBW* 8: 428-36 [*WE*, 321-28]); excerpted with translation revised in *TF*, 504-5.

6. *DBW* 16: 128 (*GS* 2, 398).

7. *DBW* 16: 25 (*GS* 3: 43).

8. See above, 156-72.

9. *TF*, 457 (*DBW* 16: 241 [*GS* 2: 584-85]).

10. *LPP*, 176. On Bonhoeffer's use of the "Daily texts," see especially F. B. Nelson, "Bonhoeffer and the Spiritual Life: Some Reflections," *Journal of Theology for Southern Africa* 30 (March 1980): 34-38.

11. *IKDB*, 134.

12. *DBW* 14: 946 (*GS* 2: 479).

13. *LT* (*DBWE* 5): 51.

14. *LT* (*DBWE* 5): 78-79.

15. "Editor's Introduction," *PB* (*DBWE* 5): 147.

16. Eberhard Bethge, "Bonhoeffer and the Jews," in John D. Godsey and Geffrey B. Kelly, eds., *Ethical Responsibility: Bonhoeffer's Legacy to the Churches* (Lewiston, N.Y.: Edwin Mellen Press, 1981), 74-75.

17. Bethge, "Bonhoeffer and the Jews," 74.

18. *TF*, 444 (*DBW* 15: 83-84 [*GS* 2: 544]).

19. Geffrey B. Kelly, "The Prayerbook of the Bible: Dietrich Bonhoeffer's Introduction to the Psalms," *Weavings* 6, no. 5 (September/October 1991): 36-39. See also "Editor's Introduction," and Bonhoeffer's entire text in *PB* (*DBWE* 5): 143-77.

20. *LT* (*DBWE* 5): 57.

21. *LPP*, 39-40.

22. *PB* (*DBWE* 5): 160.

23. *LPP*, 139-43.

24. J. C. Hampe, *Prayers from Prison* (Philadelphia: Fortress Press, 1979), 45.

25. Fabian von Schlabrendorff, *The Secret War Against Hitler* (London: Hodder & Stoughton, 1966), 324.

26. Nelson, "Bonhoeffer and the Spiritual Life," 36.

27. *LT* (*DBWE* 5): 29.

28. *LPP*, 391.

29. *LT* (*DBWE* 5): 90.

30. *LPP*, 131.

31. *LPP*, 393.

32. *LPP*, 217-18.

33. *LPP*, 375.

34. *D* (*DBWE* 4): 106-7.

35. *LPP*, 319.

36. To read the dramatic description of the process by which the poems and letters were preserved, see Eberhard Bethge, "How the Prison Letters Survived," in *Friendship and Resistance: Essays on Dietrich Bonhoeffer* (Grand Rapids: Eerdmans, 1995), 38-57.

37. These ten poems, in the order in which they were composed, are as follows: "The Past," "Sorrow and Joy," "Who Am I?" "Night Voices in Tegel," "Christians and Pagans," "Stations on the Way to Freedom," "The Friend," "The Death of Moses," "Jonah," and "By the Powers for Good."

38. *LPP*, 372; translation from *TF*, 517.

39. *DB*, 841-42.

40. Edwin T. Robertson, *The Prison Poems of Dietrich Bonhoeffer: A New Translation with Commentary* (Surrey: Inter-Publishing Service, 1998).

41. Correspondence from Winfried Maechler to F. Burton Nelson, February 17, 1987. At the age of 90, now retired, Maechler still lives in Berlin.

42. F. Burton Nelson, "A Martyr's Poetry," *Christianity and the Arts* 3, no. 2 (Spring 1996): 4-6.

43. *TF*, 514 (*DBW* 8: 513-14 [*WE*, 381-82/*LPP*, 347]); translation slightly altered. The

English translations of all the poems included in this chapter, with the exception of "The Death of Moses," translated by Nancy Lukens, are taken from the translations of Geffrey B. Kelly that appeared in *TF*.

44. *TF*, 495.

45. F. Burton Nelson, "A Martyr's Poetry."

46. *TF*, 515 (*DBW* 8: 515 [*WE*, 382/*LPP*, 348-49]).

47. *TF*, 495.

48. *TF*, 516-17 (*DBW* 8: 570-72 [*WE*, 403/*LPP*, 370-71]).

49. *TF*, 517.

50. *TF*, 44.

51. *TF*, 518-20 (*DBW* 8: 590-98 [*GS* 4: 613-20]). We have included here only excerpts of this long poem, "The Death of Moses," translated by Nancy Lukens; an English translation of the full text can be found in Robertson, *Prison Poems of Dietrich Bonhoeffer*, 81-89. This poem is not included in *LPP*.

52. *TF*, 521 (*DBW* 8: 606 [*WE*, 434/*LPP*, 398-99]).

53. *TF*, 520.

54. *TF*, 522 (*DBW* 8: 606-7 [*WE*, 435-36/*LPP*, 400-401]).

55. Letter of December 19, 1944, in *Love Letters from Cell 92*, 268-69.

56. Bishop G. K. A. Bell, "Foreword," in Dietrich Bonhoeffer, *The Cost of Discipleship* (New York: Simon and Schuster, 1995), 11.

57. Dorothee Soelle, statement on the jacket of the *Dietrich Bonhoeffer Works English Edition (DBWE)*.

Index of Names

Index of Names

Weborg, C. John, xvi, 269, 278
Wedemeyer, Maria von, 24, 30-31, 95,
  236, 247, 264, 274, 279
Wedemeyer, Max von, 31
Wedemeyer, Hans von, 31
Werner, Friedrich, 26
Wilhelm II, Kaiser, 3
Wind, Renate, 267
Wise, Stephen, xvi
Wolf, Hugo, 7

Woodhouse, Barbara Bennett, 124
Wüstenberg, Ralf K., 267

Young, Josiah, 179, 267, 285

Zerner, Ruth, 6, 272
Zimmermann, Helga, 13
Zimmermann, Wolf-Dieter, 12, 13,
  267
Zinn, Elizabeth, 30, 251

Index of Subjects

Index of Scriptural References